MW01629907

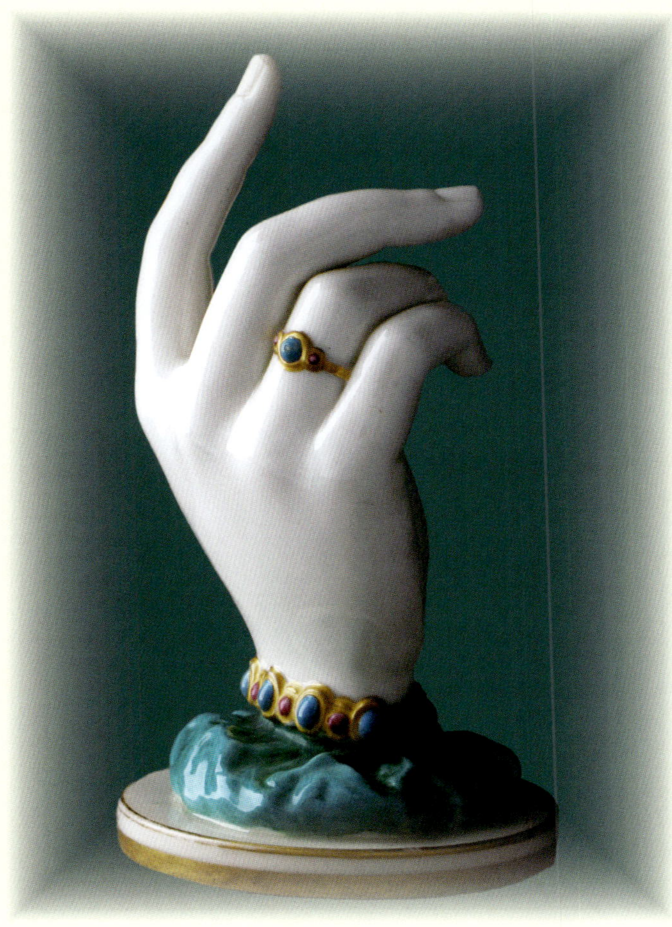

Royal Worcester porcelain ring tree.
The design was registered in April 1865.

RINGS
1800 - 1910

A STUDY OF
ENGLISH AND RELATED DESIGNS

by VERLAINE DAVIES

Published by

Write Designs, LTD
Ruidoso, NM

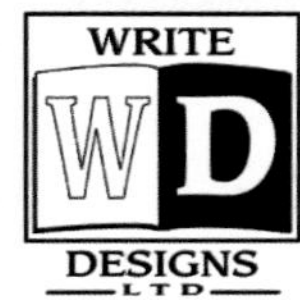

TABLE OF CONTENTS

DEDICATION

In Memory of

Geoffrey and Narée Craik

and

Charles and Mildred Davies

ACKNOWLEDGEMENTS

My heartfelt thanks to Marilyn L. Smith for all the support she has given me since I met her in Bond Street, London in 1977. Without her encouragement, her contacts in the field of antique jewellery, her expert advice and her constructive criticism, this book may never have seen the light of day.

My thanks to Michael D. Marcus of Reginald Davis (Oxford) Ltd, England, and to Keith Austin, Las Cruces, New Mexico, USA who allowed me to photograph many nineteenth-century rings in their possession.

I was fortunate to find two photographers who took a great deal of time and interest to produce the majority of the photographs for this work: Hanna Tuominen and Michael O'Neill. My thanks also go to Debbie Rindge who stepped in at the last minute with some additional photography.

The following individuals have given advice, support, specific information, or edited the manuscript over a span of twenty years, in particular, Evan Davies who encouraged me to write the book. I have given the name of the museum or establishment where individuals worked at the time I was in contact with them:

John Bannerman (Richard Ogden, Burlington Arcade, London), Patricia Beckman, Michael Blicq (Cameo Corner in Liberty's of London), M.W. Bell (S.J. Phillips, London), Shirley Bury (Victoria & Albert Museum, London), Majorie Clampitt, Richard Digby, Ted Donohoe, Nicolas du Quesne Bird, Joy Fell, Diana Foley, Nicholas Golby, Peter Goodban (The Antiquary, Oxford), Nancy Hamilton, Amanda Herries (Museum of London), Brian and Lynn Holmes, Roy G. Hughes (Derby Museum), Anthea M. James, Constance Kallman, K.S. Love (Cameo Corner, London), Colin Manton (Museum of London), Judy McMillie, Pat Novissimo, Charles Oman, Madeleine Popper, Payne & Sons (Oxford), Judy Rudoe (British Museum), Gertrude Seidmann, M. Seligmann, Gerald Taylor (Ashmolean Museum, Oxford), Mark and Heather Whiting.

INTRODUCTION

A finger ring was the most cherished item in the entire sphere of jewellery, and no other piece of jewellery has been used to convey such a variety of sentiments. In addition to betrothals and weddings, rings celebrated other special occasions, such as the birth of a child. They even commemorated public celebrations such as the fiftieth (1887) and sixtieth (1897) jubilees of Queen Victoria. Rings were given and worn to express friendship, particularly in the latter part of the century. Commemorative rings were also worn to mourn the death of a relative, a friend, royalty or national figures such as Lord Nelson or the Duke of Wellington. Mourning rings form an important part of the overall production of nineteenth-century rings and were often examples of the highest quality of craftsmanship. The primary function of the ring, however, was to decorate the hand.

Men, as well as women, wore finger rings - signet, wedding, mourning, decorative and other types - but it is in ladies' rings that the greater variety of style and fashion is evident, therefore the illustrations and text deal principally with these.

Ring styles reflected the changes in fashion and mood throughout the century. From about 1800 to 1820, gowns and rings alike embraced the simple, uncluttered lines of classicism; from about 1820 to 1860, jewellery and costumes were romantic, feminine and colourful, following the trend started by the flamboyant George IV and continued by a young, vivacious Queen Victoria upon her accession to the throne in 1837. The high Victorian era, *circa* 1860 to 1885, exhibited a bolder, somewhat exaggerated style of dress, while the late Victorian and Edwardian period, *circa* 1885 onward was typified by slender silhouettes and delicate colours. The work of many jewellers reflected and complemented these trends.

At the beginning of the nineteenth century, rings were fashionably worn on many fingers of both hands. Gradually it became customary to wear several rings on the same finger, hence the popularity of the half-hoop ring with its narrow bezel. As the century progressed, some women, including Queen Victoria, continued the custom of wearing numerous rings, while others reduced the number they wore to two or three. During the first half of the century, rings were sometimes worn over gloves by both men and women; this accounts for the large size of some rings.

In 1800 rings were made almost entirely by hand. With the discovery of new gold sources in the 1840s came the incentive to invent machines for the production of jewellery. It must be stressed that jewellery in general was expensive in the nineteenth century despite the advent of machinery. However, the change in the law which allowed the use of lower qualities of gold, together with the development of mass-production techniques, did help to reduce the cost so that the less affluent could afford jewellery. Generally speaking, handmade rings were the forerunners of the commercial designs; it was not until a style became popular that it was viable for manufacturers to set up machinery to produce a new style in quantity.

The Victorian jeweller was able to produce good work even when operating under financial constraints. The large variety of rings which have survived from the nineteenth century is a testimony to the quality of the production, particularly since rings are vulnerable to damage. Fortunately for the historian and the collector, the less expensive rings were not worth dismantling for their gems, thus many of these have survived the female urge to be completely in fashion. Large numbers of important rings of the period, set with fine gems, have been lost as their stones were removed and reset in a 'modern' style.

Jewellers frequently looked to the designs of previous eras for inspiration. Earlier styles were adapted to suit nineteenth-century taste. Gothic and Renaissance styles occur at intervals from about 1830 onward, while from about 1840 to 1885, many items were fashioned as exact copies of archeological jewellery.

Egyptian excavations during the early years of the century, the discovery of Etruscan tombs in Italy in 1836, 1842 and 1850, and excavations in Assyria at the end of the 1840s unearthed jewellery which caught the imagination of the public. Jewellers were soon producing copies to satisfy the new demand.

In the latter part of the century, the advent of mass-produced jewellery mounts and progress in lapidary techniques resulted in attention being focused on the gemstones rather than the design and workmanship of the metal. In many instances, the ring mount was merely a means of showing off the gems held within it.

During the last quarter of the century, individual craftsmen rebelled against mass production and a lack of imaginative design. In Britain the Arts and Crafts movement promoted high quality individual workmanship and innovative styles; many of the designs were too extreme, however, to attract a wide appreciation and consequently could not be produced economically. At the same time, the Art Nouveau movement in Europe became popular in England too, and some designs were produced commercially on a widespread scale.

By the end of the century, the possession of rings and other jewellery was no longer the prerogative of the wealthy. Fortunately many Victorians cherished their rings and passed them on to succeeding generations, and knowing the provenance of a ring adds to the enjoyment of owning it.

References are made to rings from America, France, India and Italy, owing to the considerable interchange of ideas and travel between various countries. England looked to France as the arbiter of fashion, and America followed both English and French fashions, so that certain similarities appear in some styles. As foreign travel increased more souvenir rings were brought home to England. Archeological rings from Italy were especially popular, and a number of Italian jewellers set up workshops in England during the second half of the century. The expatriate community in India followed the fashions from home, albeit with an Indian influence. In due course some of this work was brought back to England.

For descriptive purposes the ring has been divided into four parts: the bezel - the central ornament of the ring; the shoulders, flanking the bezel; the gallery, that raises the stones above the finger; and the shank or hoop, which encircles the finger. To simplify the description of diamonds, generally the terms rose-cut and brilliant-cut have been used.

Precise dating of rings can be difficult, and the author is aware that readers may disagree with dates given for specific styles. There are few distinct breaks in style; styles overlapped and a number of designs trickled on through several decades, despite a general change in taste, but that in itself is of interest. How much more enduring was the style of a ring than that of a new gown!

Unfortunately, there is a dearth of advertisements or pattern books from the early part of the century which could verify dates of ring styles; however, later in the century, manufacturing jewellers advertised in trade journals, and a number of these advertisements, with dates and prices, are still in existence.

The author hopes the reader will appreciate the charm of nineteenth-century and early twentieth-century rings and be more broadly aware of the scope of the work of the early designers and craftsmen of this period.

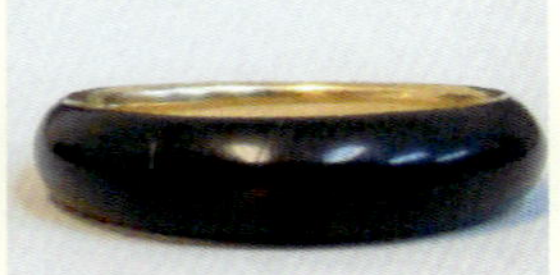

Fig. 1. Tortoiseshell hoop ring lined with gold, probably Scottish. Rose gold. *Circa* 1800-1815. Hoop diameter 20mm, front of hoop 5mm.

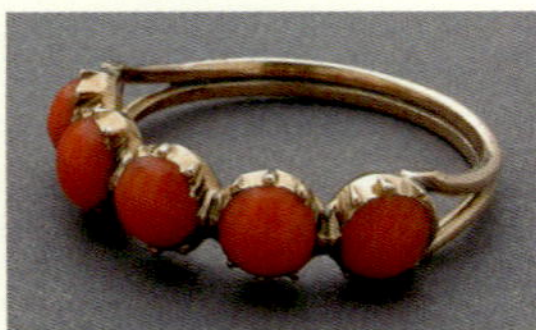

Fig. 2. Neo-classical half-hoop set with five corals in closed, cut-down collets, plain double wire shank separates at the shoulders. Pale rose gold. *Circa* 1800-1815. Shank diameter 17mm.

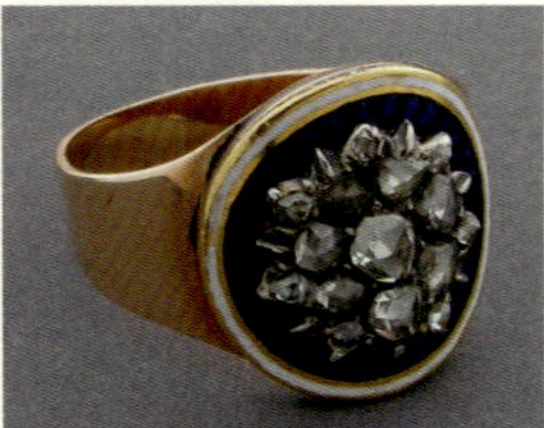

Fig. 3. Gentleman's ring. Curved, round bezel decorated with a cluster of small rose-cut diamonds set in silver, surrounded with royal blue enamel edged with white enamel. Plain, wide, flat shoulders taper to the shank. Rose gold. *Circa* 1800-1810. Bezel 13x13mm, shank diameter 16mm.

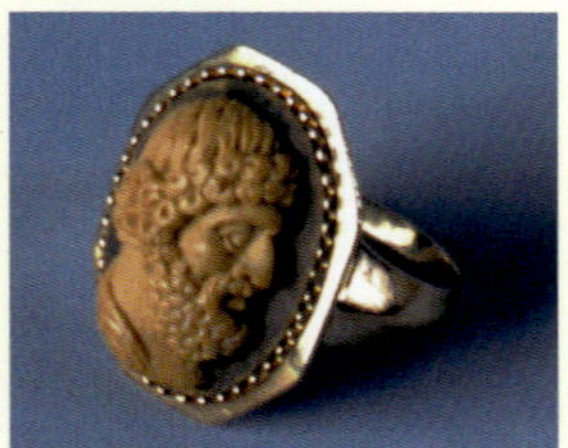

Fig. 4. Gentleman's ring. Softstone cameo secured in a substantial saw-tooth setting in an hexagonal border. Plain shoulders, triangular in section, and a plain, flat shank. Yellow gold. *Circa* 1820. Bezel 25x18mm, shank diameter 16x20mm.

DECORATIVE RINGS

1800-1820

London was the centre of the jewellery trade at the beginning of the nineteenth century, and there the finest pieces were undoubtedly made. Jewellery was also being made in other parts of England and Scotland; however, few decorative rings were hallmarked early in the century, and it is impossible to be sure where most rings originated. (Fig. 1).

Between 1800 and 1815, rings reflected the prevailing taste of the day: neo-classicism. (Fig. 2). Its predominant characteristic was well-proportioned simplicity. The neo-classical style in rings combined simple, elegant designs with occasional filigree work. The extravagant taste of the Prince Regent greatly influenced the transition from the neo-classical to the more ornate 'romantic' style, which gained acceptance after 1815.

Gentlemen's rings of this period were suitable accessories to the flamboyant costume worn by men. In the first decade large rings with a rectangular or oval bezel of royal blue or red enamel with diamonds were still fashionable, a style that began in the latter years of the previous century. (Fig. 3) Gentlemen also wore rings set with intaglios, cameos (Fig. 4) and gems in addition to mourning rings and rings produced for members of various professional bodies. The designs followed ladies' rings, the size of the hoop often being the only indication that the ring was made for a gentleman. By today's standards the rings worn by men appear very feminine. (Fig. 5a, b).

In the following excerpts from the ladies' magazine, *La Belle Assemblée*, young women are urged, in vain, to wear rings sparingly. In the issue for March 1806, the author of the article entitled, 'The Ladies' Toilette, or Encyclopedia of Beauty' wrote:

But to return to the hand of a pretty woman...a hand loaded with jewels is no longer a hand. Let young females, in particular, shun this useless luxury. Rings are chains, and these they ought not yet to wear. (p.80)

It appears the advice was ignored according to this excerpt from the November 1807 issue of *La Belle Assemblée,* in 'Letter on dress, introductory and descriptive, from Eliza to Julia. Portman Square',

> I must not forget to tell you that rings are invariably, and abundantly displayed by us fashionables; three or four are worn on the little finger. They consist of the simple gold hoop, with a small stone in the centre of each, of the diamond, ruby, emerald, and amethyst. (p.284) (Fig. 6)

The most popular styles of this period were the hoop ring, the half-hoop and the cluster ring. Hoop rings were usually set with a single type of gem such as diamond, garnet (Fig. 7), onyx (Fig. 8) or pearl. The inside of the ring was often convex, a shape which feels very comfortable on the finger. A few hoop rings were set with different gems, as described in the following excerpt from *La Belle Assemblée,* July 1806, p.335, 'A Letter On Dress, From a Young Lady resident in London, to her Friend in the Country':

> ...but the Eutopian [sic] ring, given her by the Dowager, her mother-in-law, is the most splendid ornament of the kind I ever saw, and is now anxiously sought for by all our women of fashion; it consists of one row of precious stones set separately, in the form of a hoop; each stone the size of a small pea. Lady Louisa's is formed of the diamond, ruby, emerald, amethyst, topaz, sapphire, and cornelian, and has a most attractive and brilliant effect.

Today, multi-gem rings are called 'harlequin' rings. (Fig. 9) (Fig. 10 a, b)

Decorative gold hoop rings were also fashionable at this time according to *La Belle Assemblée,* February 1807, p.106, 'General observations on the prevailing fashions carefully selected':

> [T]he broad gold hoop-ring, with Egyptian or Old English characters engraved as a motto, are a trinket or ornament entirely new in the fashionable world.

Half-hoop rings were made with single, double or triple rows set with the same gem or with a mixture of gems

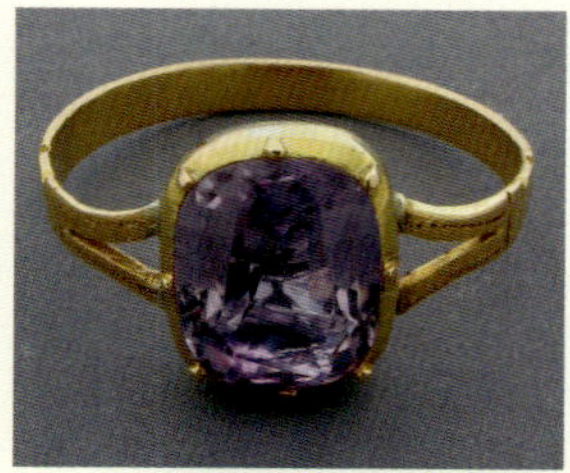

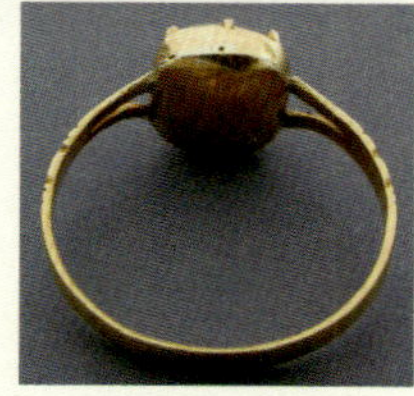

Fig. 5 a, b. Gentleman's ring set with a light amethyst in a closed, foiled cut-down collet setting. The back of the setting is convex. Lightly chased, bifurcated shoulders above ribbing, cross hatching on hoop. The shoulders and hoop are very worn. *Circa* 1810-1820. Bezel 11x9mm, hoop 18x20mm.

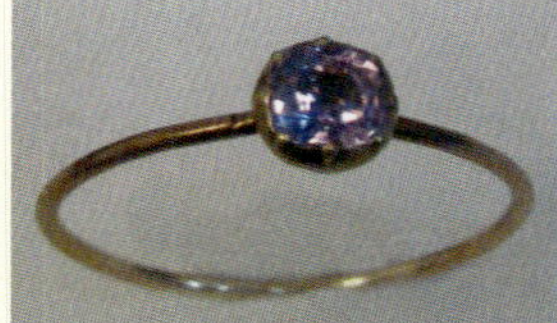

Fig. 6. Mauve-blue star-cut cushion-shaped sapphire set in a convex-backed, foiled, cut-down collet, the upper section of the collet is made from yellow gold, the lower part and the single wire shank are fashioned from rose gold. *Circa* 1805. Bezel 5x5mm, shank diameter 17mm.

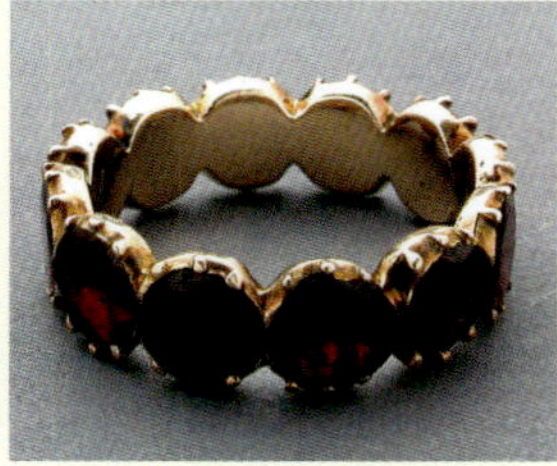

Fig. 7. Hoop ring set with twelve foiled, flat-cut, garnets in closed cut-down collets. Pale rose gold. *Circa* 1800-1810. Band width 5mm, hoop diameter 16mm. *Reginald Davis (Oxford) Ltd.*

[1800 - 1820]

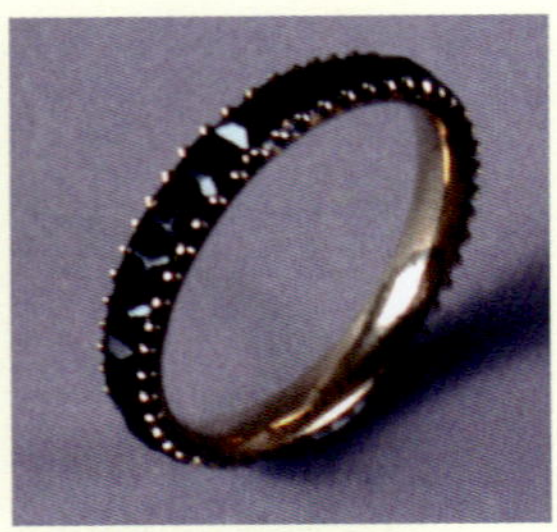

Fig. 8. Hoop ring, convex on the inside, is set in its entirety with square, faceted onyx. Rose gold. *Circa* 1800-1815. Band width 3mm, hoop diameter 17mm.

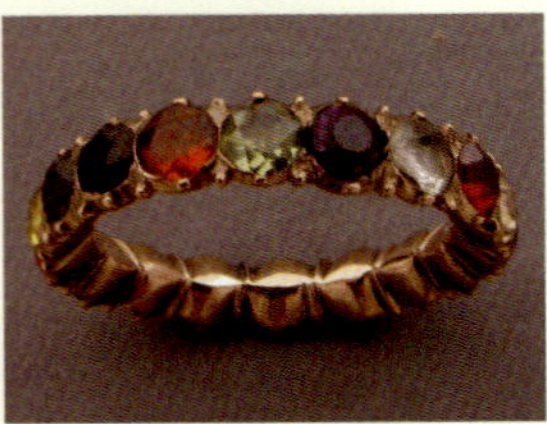

Fig. 9. 'Harlequin' hoop ring set in its entirety with fifteen star-cut gems, one brilliant-cut gem (a replacement), one cabochon and one rose-cut stone in cut-down collets the backs of which are triangular. The following stones are set in the ring: onyx, green tourmaline, citrine, fire opal, garnet, cat's eye, haematite, rose-cut diamond, amethyst, chrysoberyl. Pale rose gold. *Circa* 1800-1810. Hoop diameter 16mm, width 4mm.

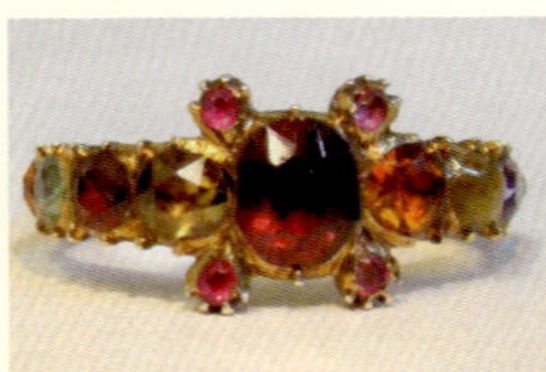

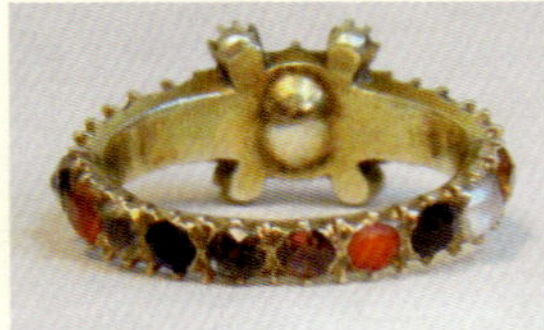

Fig. 10 a, b. Harlequin ring with a garnet bezel and variety of graduated gems in cut-down collets that form the hoop. Pale yellow gold. *Circa* 1800-1810. Bezel 9x10mm, hoop diameter 19mm width 5mm.

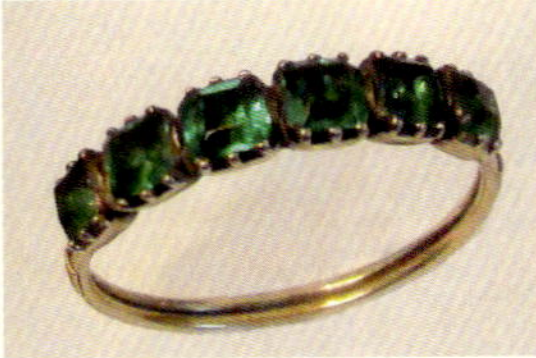

Fig. 11. Half-hoop set with six green pastes in closed-back cut-down collets, double wire shank ends with four transverse ribs supporting bifurcated shoulders. Rose gold. *Circa* 1800-1815. Bezel width 4mm, shank diameter 18mm.

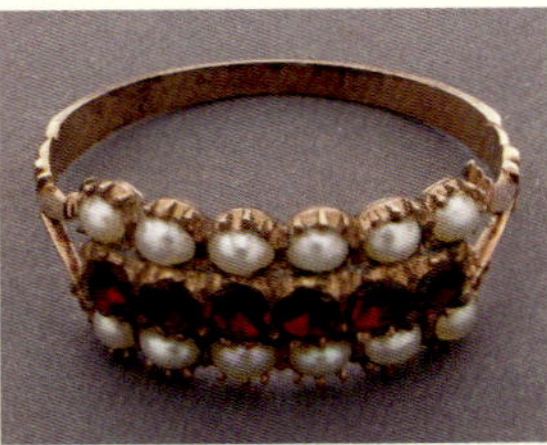

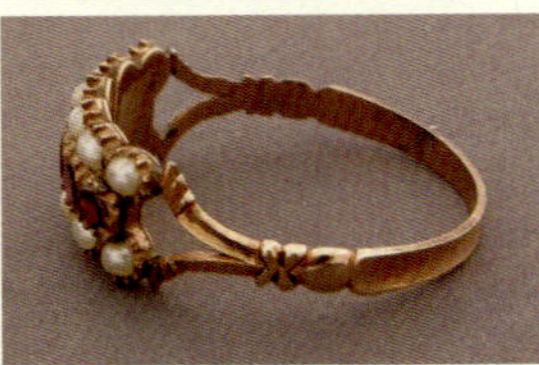

Fig. 12 a, b. Georgian half-hoop comprising two rows of half pearls and a row of flat-cut almandine garnets in closed cut-down collets. Bifurcated shoulders emanate from a concave hoop. Rose gold. *Circa* 1800-1815. Bezel 17x7mm, hoop diameter 19mm.

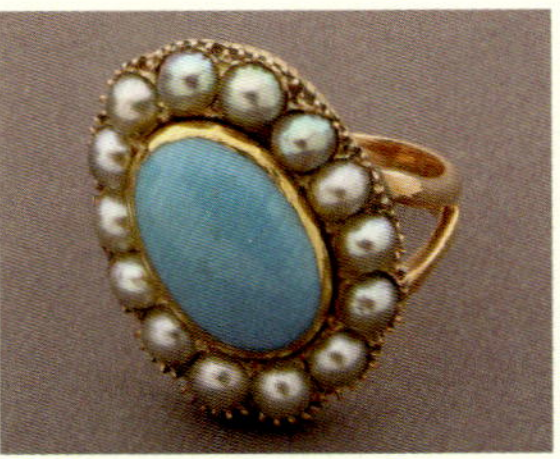

Fig. 13. Diagonal bezel set with a large turquoise in a yellow gold rub-over setting, surrounded by half pearls in a 'communal' cut-down collet setting of rose gold. The plain shank, also of rose gold, has a single, narrow groove in the centre ending at the bifurcated shoulders. *Circa* 1800-1810. Bezel 18x13mm, shank diameter 17mm.

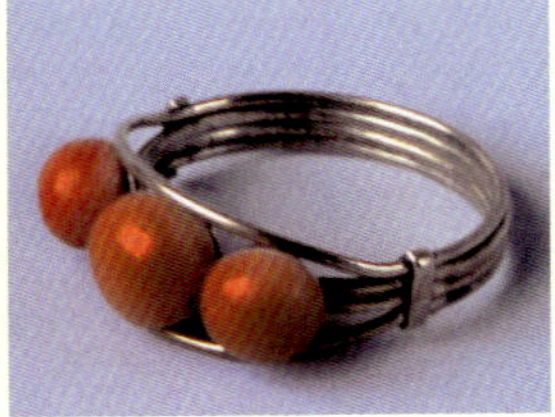

Fig. 14. Neo-classical coral ring. The two outer corals are secured by dowels to the shank, and the centre coral is set in a 'saucer' of gold. Quadruple wire shank separates at the shoulders and the two outer wires continue as a border to the coral, a transverse rib decorates each shoulder. Rose gold. *Circa* 1800-1810. Bezel depth 8mm, shank diameter 18mm, width 3.5mm.

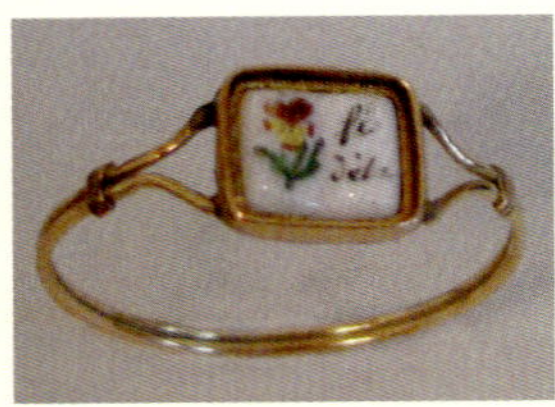

Fig. 15. Porcelain bezel formed as an open book, surrounded by hatched gold-work in a closed-back collet, decorated with a pansy and 'fidele', meaning 'faithful thoughts'. The double wire hoop separates at the shoulders that are decorated with transverse ribs. Rose gold. *Circa* 1810. Bezel 7x6mm, hoop diameter 18mm.

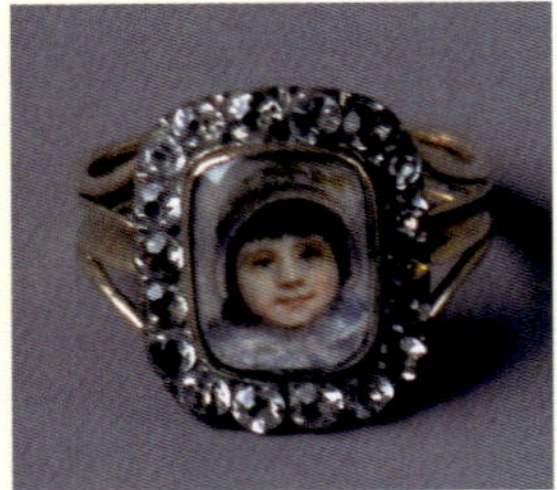

Fig. 16. Miniature of a young girl in a bonnet, under glass, surrounded by single cut white pastes set in silver. The shank separates at the shoulders, outer wires flank a central concave leaf. Pale yellow gold. *Circa* 1800-1810. Bezel 18x15mm, shank diameter 20mm, width 3.5mm.

in cut-down collets. (Fig. 11) (Fig.12 a, b) Cluster bezels were round, rectangular, square, rounded oblong, oval or oblique oval. (Fig. 13) Wide-set gems were secured in individual cut-down collets, or a centre stone was bordered by seed pearls or rose-cut diamonds. Sometimes there was a thin strip of hatched gold between the main gem and the border of gems surrounding it.

A number of other styles were also popular during this period. Coral rings were much sought after (Fig. 14), and cameos were fashionable; some cameos were antique, set in a nineteenth-century mount; others were carved at this time from sardonyx and occasionally shell and lava. Filigree rings were made but few have survived owing to their fragility. Similarly rare today are rings decorated with a single gem set in a closed-back, cut-down collet attached to a thin wire hoop, see Fig. 6, and rings set with painted porcelain decorated with a sentimental motif. (Fig. 15) Portrait miniatures were occasionally set into rings at this time. (Fig. 16)

Following the fashion of the 'harlequin' ring, 'acrostic' rings became popular in about 1810. The first letter of each gem formed a word or a name such as Dearest or Regard. (Fig. 17 a, b)(Fig. 18 a, b)

Notable curiosities from this period include rings set with baby teeth (Fig. 19), either alone or with other gems in a half-hoop; and a bezel comprising an eye painted on ivory or porcelain, a fashion that continued into the next period, see Fig. 40.

After the French Revolution in 1789, diamonds went out of fashion in France; it was considered neither patriotic nor safe to parade oneself in diamonds. However, by 1805, when Napoleon became Emperor of France, diamonds had regained their popularity. In England diamonds had been worn continuously during this period; such sacrifices had not been demanded of the English. France, however, dictated changes in fashion. Less costly gems, such as the amethyst, aquamarine, chrysoberyl (including cat's eyes), topaz and turquoise, had been worn in lieu of diamonds on the Continent; consequently they also became fashionable in England. Other stones and materials in common use in neo-classical rings were rubies, emeralds, pearls (Fig. 20), garnets, coral, cornelian, onyx and jet (Fig. 21 a, b). Paste was used frequently, the settings being quite as fine as those for gemstones. (Fig. 22 a, b) A few rings

17

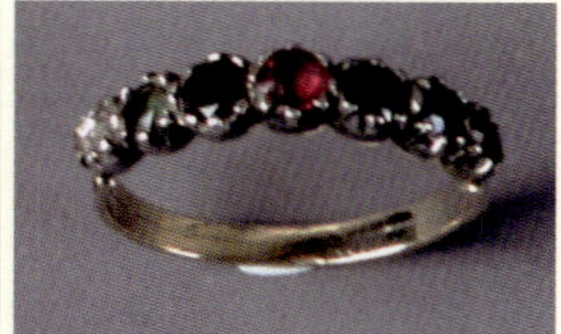

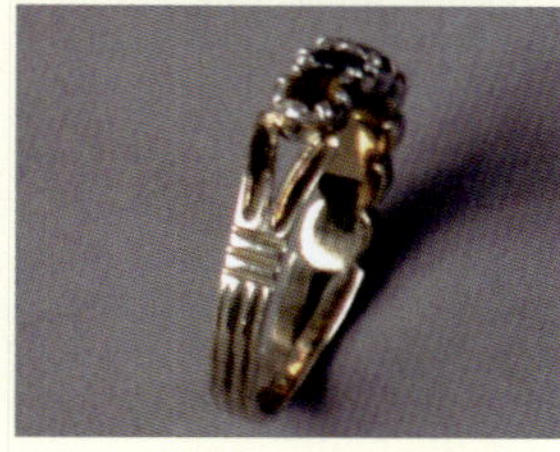

Fig. 17 a, b. 'Dearest' half-hoop ring. A diamond, emerald, amethyst, ruby, emerald, sapphire and a topaz are set in silver cut-down collets backed with gold; channelled shoulders above transverse ribs, lightly channelled hoop. Pale yellow gold. *Circa* 1810-1815. Hoop diameter 16mm.

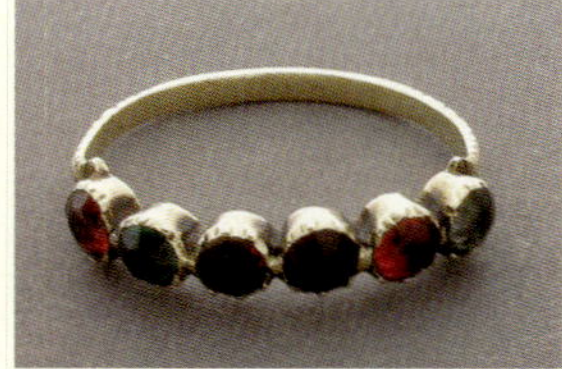

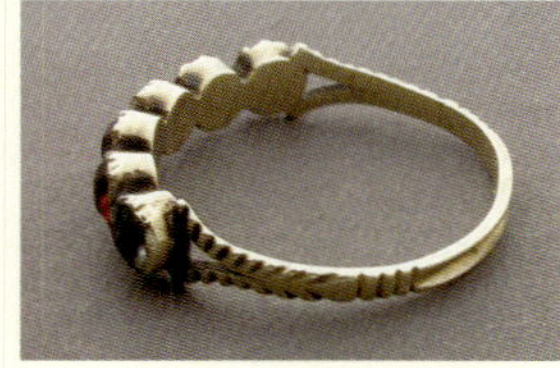

Fig. 18 a, b. Regard ring set with paste in closed-back cut-down collets. Bifurcated shoulders on a channelled hoop. Pale yellow gold. *Circa* 1810-1815. Hoop diameter 16mm.

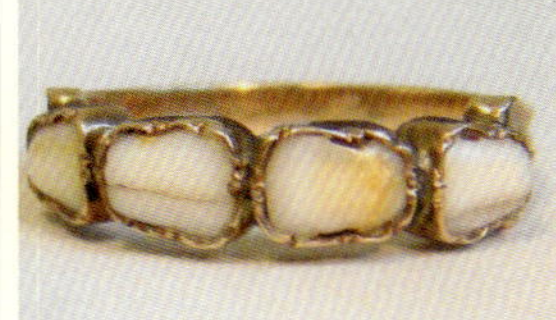

Fig. 19. Half-hoop set with four baby teeth in closed, crimped collets, channelled hoop separates at the shoulders. Pale rose gold. *Circa* 1805-1815. Bezel 4x18mm, hoop diameter 17mm, width 2.5mm.

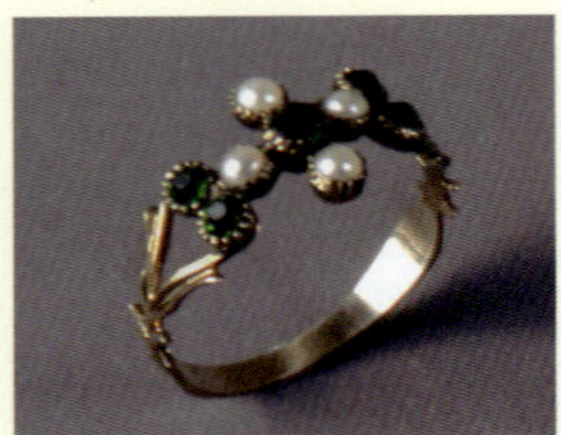

Fig. 20. Green paste and pearls set in closed cut-down collets, bifurcated carved shoulders, channelled hoop. Pale yellow gold. *Circa* 1810. Bezel 4x18mm, hoop diameter 17mm, width 2.5mm.

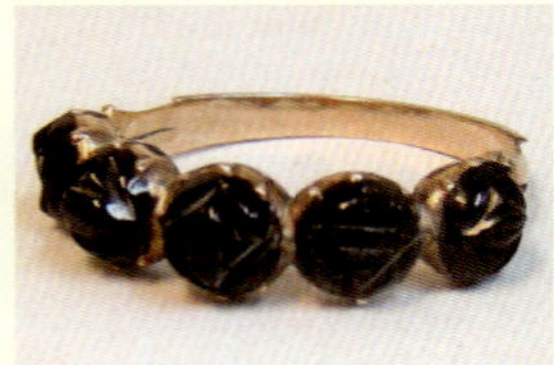

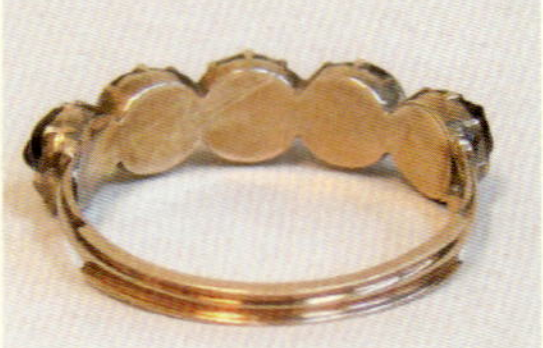

Fig. 21 a, b. Half-hoop of five carved jet beads in cut-down collets, plain bifurcated shoulders, shank with crisp flanged edges. Pale rose gold. *Circa* 1805-15. Diameter of jet beads 4mm, shank diameter 17mm, width 2mm.

were made from tortoiseshell piqué (Fig. 23), horn (Fig. 24) and cut-steel, see the illustration under CUT-STEEL in the Glossary.

Although rose-cut diamonds were used extensively, brilliant-cut diamonds were used more frequently during the early part of the nineteenth century than has sometimes been suggested. (Fig. 25) There are numerous references to brilliants in contemporary works of the day, as well as many examples in early rings. According to John Mawe in *A Treatise on Diamonds and Precious Stones* (London 1813):

> Brilliant cut diamonds are so infinitely superior to the others that of late many rose-cut stones from Holland have been recut into Brilliants, notwithstanding the additional expense and the loss of size necessarily attendant on this operation.' (p.60)

In the revised edition for 1823, Mawe says:

> ...shallow brilliants, that have a great surface, are for this reason always in request and generally set close[d] - fine brilliants are always set open.... Six carats for rings sell for £230 - £250 per stone. (p.5)

Gems were usually set in a cut-down collet, a cup-like device of silver (backed with gold to prevent discolouration of the skin), silver-gilt or gold, which was cut down from the top leaving small buttress-like claws at regular intervals around the setting, see Fig. 9. In other styles the stones were not set in individual collets but side by side, with each stone touching the next, secured by the setting at the outer edges. (Fig. 26) Flush or Roman settings, in which the gold was worked against the girdle of the stone, were employed for intaglio and cameo rings. The rub-over or glass setting was used for hair compartments or cabochon gems. (Fig. 27 a, b) Occasionally one finds a ring with the gems set in closed-back collets; sometimes the edge of the collet was decorated with millegrain.

The custom of foiling and mounting stones in a closed setting was the most common method of setting all but the finest diamonds and coloured stones. Foil was used to give fire and uniformity of colour to gems in closed settings. See Fig. 5.

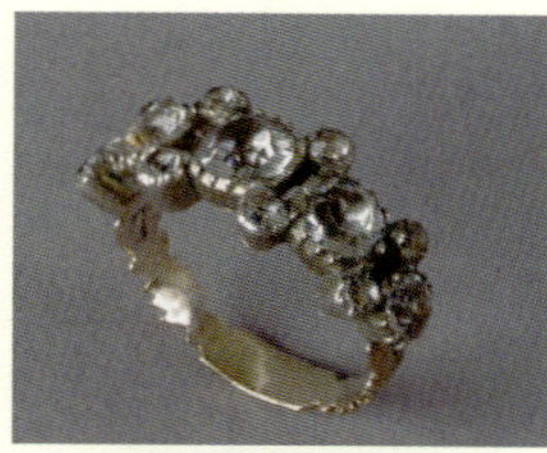

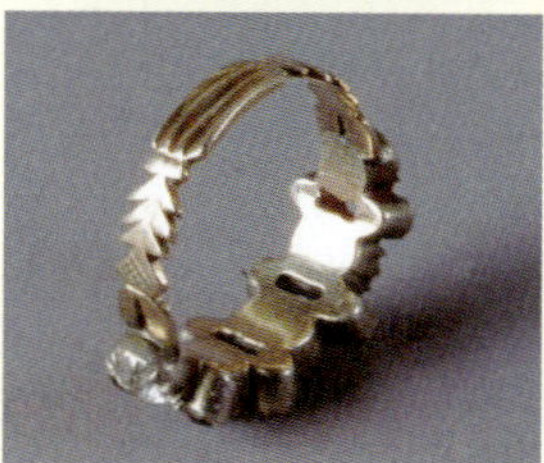

Fig. 22 a, b. Half-hoop comprising sixteen star-cut white pastes set in silver cut-down collets backed with rose gold. The shoulders have a short divided section above an engraved pineapple motif and foliate design, ribbed shank. The gold work is as fine as any found in a diamond ring. *Circa* 1815. Depth of bezel 8mm, shank diameter 15.5mm, width 3mm.

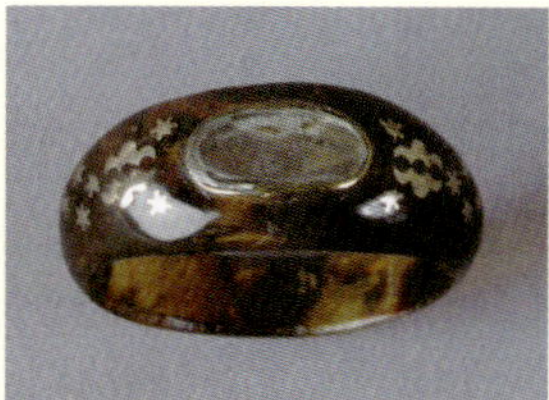

Fig. 23. Tortoiseshell ring decorated with gold piqué work around a hair compartment. *Circa* 1800-1810. Depth of bezel 10mm, hoop diameter 19mm.

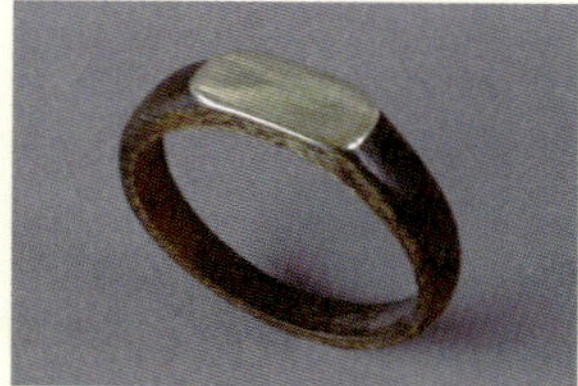

Fig. 24. Horn ring set with an oblong pale yellow gold plaque. *Circa* 1820. Bezel 9x4mm, hoop diameter 16mm.

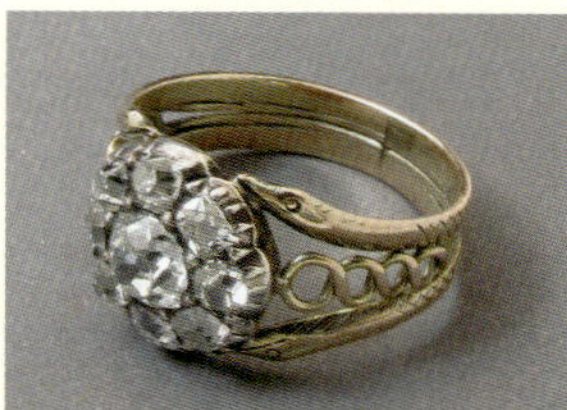

Fig. 25. Cluster bezel comprising nine brilliants secured in cut-down collets and silver grains then lined with gold, two serpents decorated with cross-hatching form the shank and shoulders; double wires between the serpents form into a looped design on the shoulders. Rose gold. Inscribed on reverse of bezel: 'Maxwell Garthshore M.D. Died 1 Mar 1813'. He was an eminent urologist.

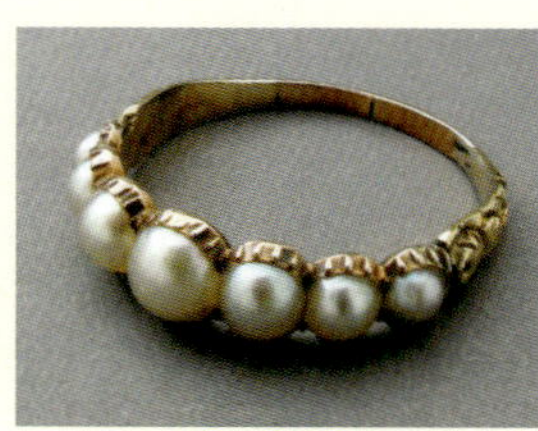

Fig. 26. Half-hoop comprising seven graduated half pearls in closed cut-down collets, deeply chased shoulders, plain shank. Pale yellow gold. *Circa* 1815-1825. Shank diameter 16mm.

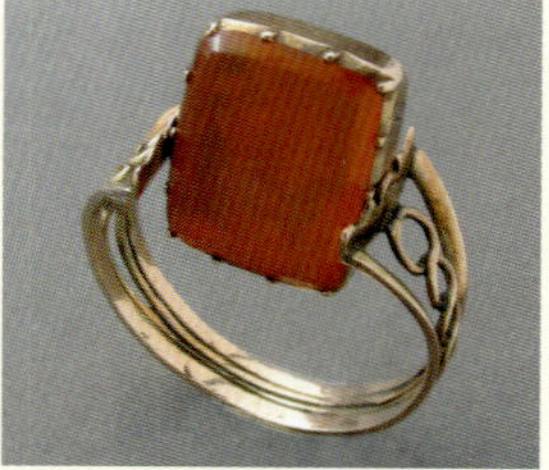

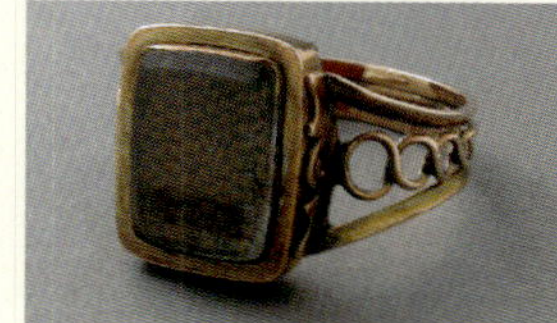

Fig. 27 a, b. Swivel bezel set with a sard in a cut-down collet, the reverse contains woven chestnut hair under glass in a rub-over setting. Bevelled shank separates to flank a looped wire design in the shoulders. Rose gold. *Circa* 1805-1815. Bezel 15x12mm, shank diameter 21.5mm, width 4mm.

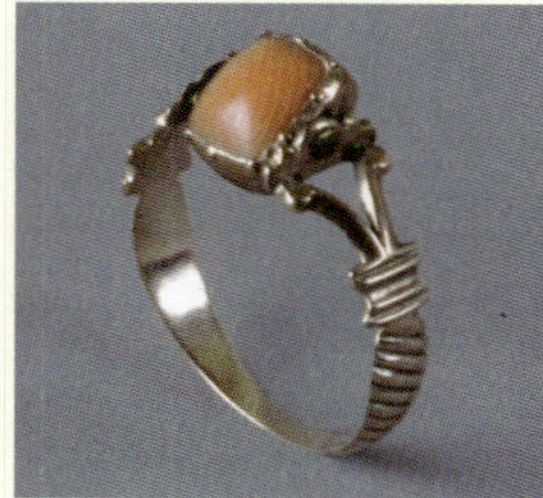

Fig. 28. A swivel bezel set with plain coral in a cut-down collet on one side, the other contains a hair compartment. The shank is partially decorated with diagonal hatch marks above which two transverse ribs support forked shoulders. Pale rose gold. *Circa* 1805-1815. Bezel 7x6mm, shank diameter 16.5mm.

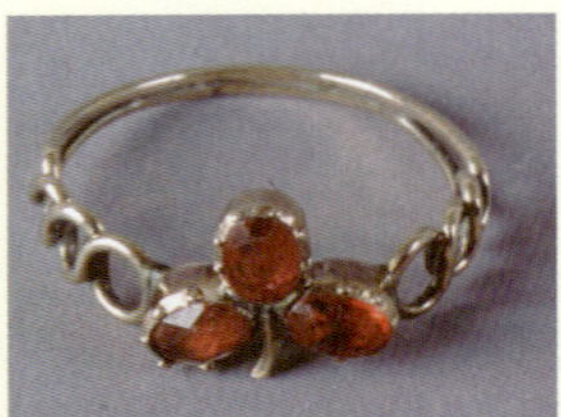

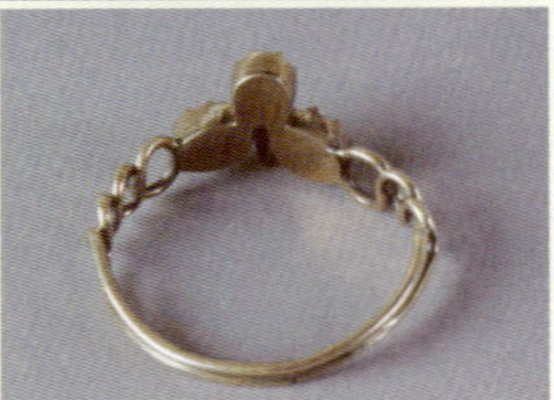

Fig. 29 a, b. Trefoil bezel set with orange-red faceted paste in closed cut-down collets, double wire shank separates into a looped design on the shoulders. Rose gold. *Circa* 1810. Bezel 9.5x11mm, shank diameter 19mm.

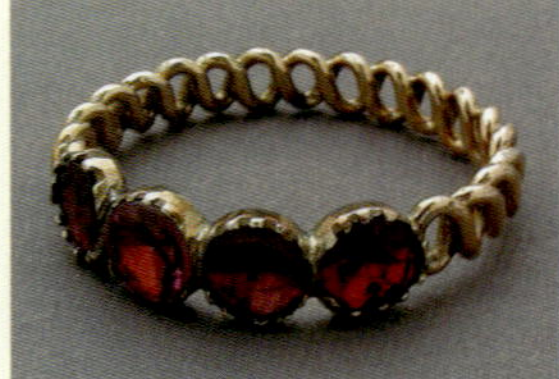

Fig. 30. Half-hoop set with four foiled almandine garnets in cut-down collets, wirework shank. Pale rose gold. *Circa* 1800-1815. Diameter of garnets 4mm, shank diameter 18mm, width 3mm.

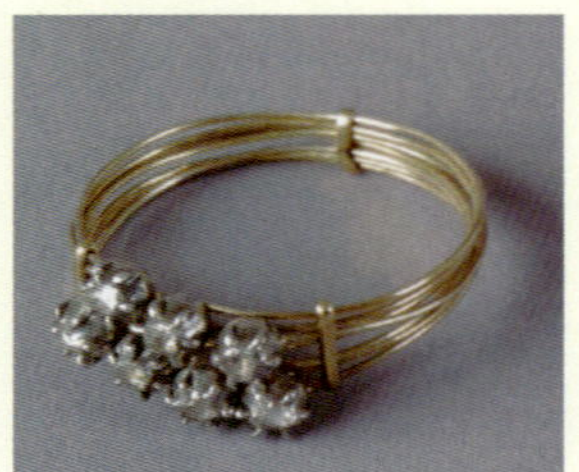

Fig. 31. Seven wire hoops, each set with an applied, silver, cut-down collet holding a rose-cut diamond. Each hoop is attached beneath the bezel. Three slides hold the hoops in place. Rose gold. Barely discernible mark on the outside of each hoop, probably French. *Circa* 1810. Hoop diameter 18mm.

Rings from this period were generally made from an alloy of gold and copper; the colour was pale with a pinkish tint, known as 'rose gold'. Usually the gold was burnished, sometimes enamelled or decorated with hatch marks; (Fig. 28) it was seldom chased before 1815. In contrast, a few rings were made from yellow gold. The change from rose to a predominance of yellow gold occurred about 1815. In 1806 and 1807 reference was made in *La Belle Assemblée* to 'dead' gold, possibly meaning 'coloured' gold, because most gold thus treated was left with a matt or 'dead' appearance.

'Colouring' is a technical term given to a chemical process which leaves a pure gold surface on the alloyed gold. It is possible to tell whether a ring has been 'coloured' if it has been damaged or even well worn, because the original pink alloy shows through the pure yellow gold surface. The technical terms 'colouring' of gold, or 'coloured' gold should not be confused with the tinting of gold, which refers to the actual colour of the alloy.

Gold wirework was a common feature of neo-classical rings. (Fig. 29 a, b) Some designs employed two, three or four wires soldered together to form the shank, with the wires then radiating outwards to create the shoulders. Sometimes the two central wires of the shoulders were fashioned as intertwining circles. Another design had a convex or grooved leaf set between the two outer wires of the shoulders. Similar shoulders and shanks had bevelled gold flanking wirework or convex strips of metal. Other shanks were formed entirely of intertwined wires to make an openwork looped design. (Fig. 30) Single wire shanks were plain or decorated with hatching (from about 1815). Occasionally rings were made with shanks comprised of several strands of wire held together by gold slides. (Fig. 31)

In complete contrast to the various wire designs were those with flat gold shoulders tapering to a narrow shank. The shoulders of this style were plain, enamelled or hatched. From about 1810 some shanks were channelled, and this decoration extended into divided shoulders. Occasionally the shank was reeded. Some shoulders were formed into two or more radiating panels of flat gold, at times with flat transverse ribs at the base of the shoulders. From about 1815 many more rings were fashioned with chasing on the shoulders and shank, a fashion which continued into the 1820s.

1820 – 1840

The restoration of the French monarchy in 1815 inspired a rapid change in fashion. During the next five years, the simple lines of Napoleonic classicism gave way to the highly decorative styles of the Romantic period. (Fig. 32) (Fig. 33) London still looked to Paris as the arbiter of fashion; it was considered imperative by the Prince Regent (an avid collector of French works of art and a great admirer of French taste) and by the fashionable world that they should be up-to-date with Paris.

Towards the end of this period, in 1837, came the accession of the eighteen-year-old Princess Victoria to the throne. For the first time since Queen Anne, Britain had a queen on the throne, and a young one at that. Confined and cut off from society as a child, Victoria now had the opportunity to indulge herself, which she did, and the rest of society followed her example.

On 18 May 1836, Princess Victoria received a visit from Prince Albert, who gave her an enamelled ring set with a diamond; on 15 October 1839 their betrothal was commemorated with a ring in the form of a serpent set with diamonds and emeralds. Later in their lives together Prince Albert took an interest in the Queen's jewellery and even designed items for her himself.

Production of jewellery in Birmingham gathered momentum during this period, particularly after 1824, when the right to assay and mark wrought gold was conferred upon the Birmingham Assay office. By 1836 the Birmingham workshops were producing large enough quantities of jewellery to be considered a major competitor in the national market.

Decorative ring styles varied from delicate filigree to finely chased work to sturdy enamelled rings reflecting the Gothic revival of the 1830s. Most rings hugged the contour of the finger, but occasionally rings were fashioned with openwork galleries that raised the gem from the finger.

Many cluster and wide-bezel rings contained a hair compartment covered with glass in the reverse of the bezel. The hidden hair compartment was used for

21

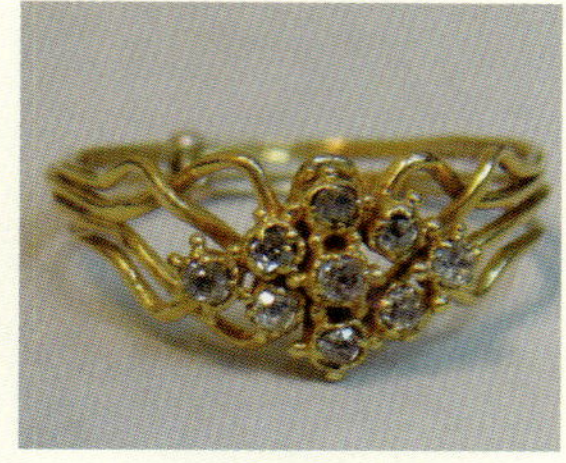

Fig. 32. Puzzle ring comprising four wire hoops that support a bezel of nine brilliant-cut diamonds in closed cut-down collets decorated with beads. A small slide holds the hoops together. Yellow gold. *Circa* 1830-1840. Hoop diameter 19mm.

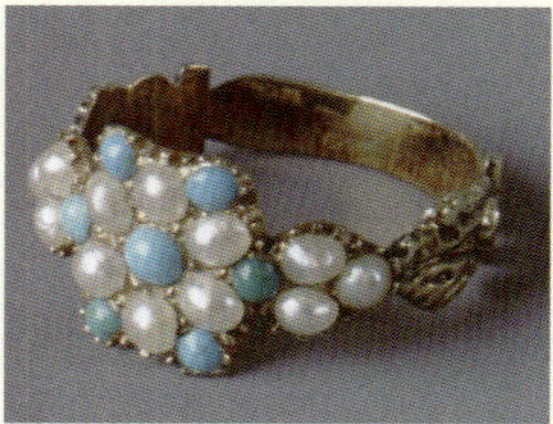

Fig. 33. Flat bezel set with turquoise and pearl, with three pearls on the shoulders, all in cut-down collets. Bold chasing decorates the lower shoulders and part of the shank, the remainder being plain. Pale yellow gold. *Circa* 1820-1830. Bezel 10x10mm, shank diameter 17mm.

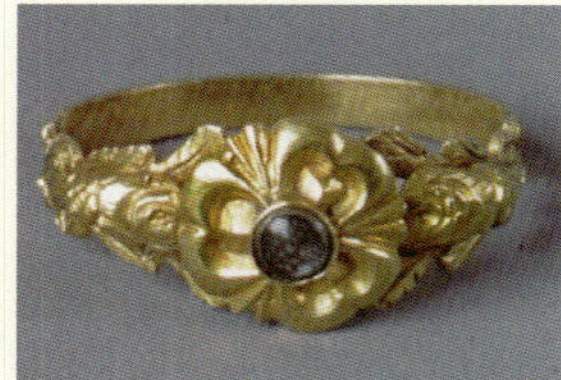

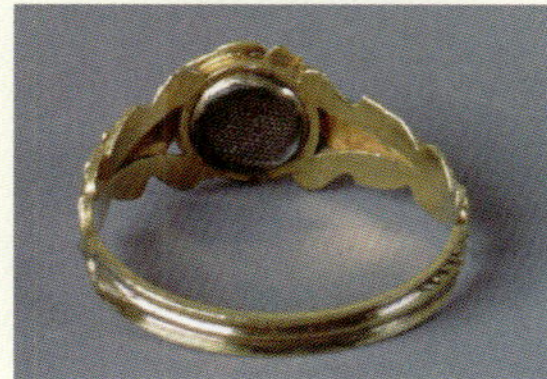

Fig. 34 a, b. Unusual Gothic trefoil bezel containing hair visible from both sides of the bezel. Chased shoulders, channelled shank. Rich yellow gold. *Circa* 1835. Bezel diameter 8mm, shank diameter 16mm, width 2mm.

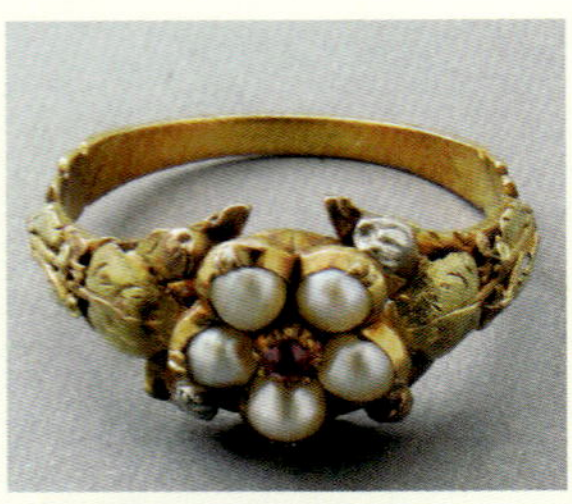

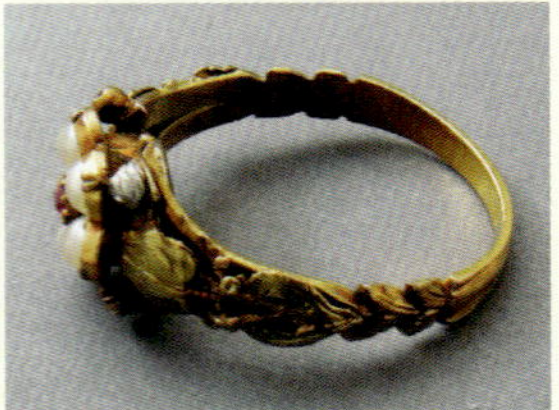

Fig. 35 a, b. Cluster ring with an applied bezel comprising pearls set in conical cut-down collets, a ruby in a cut-down collet and a single bead of white or rose gold decorating each corner of the bezel. A foliate design of green gold, above four leaves, is applied to the shoulders, channelled shank, hair compartment in reverse of bezel. Yellow gold. *Circa* 1825-1835. Shank diameter 16mm.

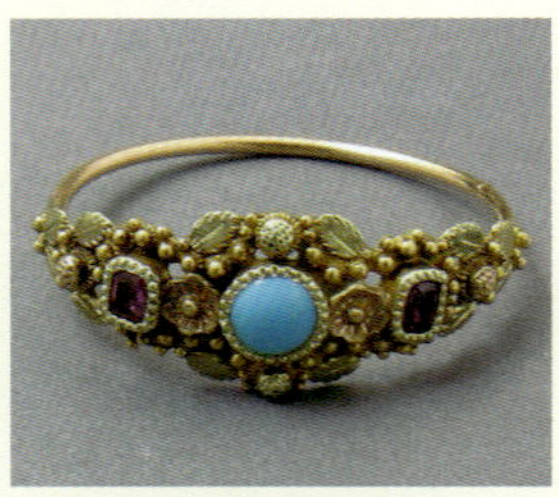

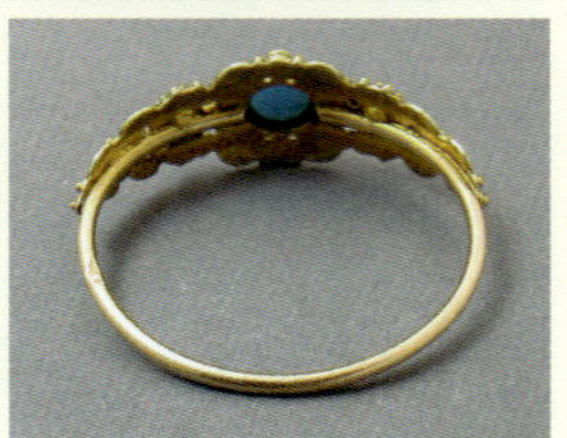

Fig. 36 a, b. Intricate design of flowers, leaves and beading in yellow and rose gold with rubies and a turquoise in beaded collets. Wire hoop. French, *circa* 1825-1835. Bezel depth 7mm, hoop diameter 18mm.

sentimental reasons rather than for mourning; in mourning rings of this period, the hair was still set in the face of the bezel. The use of a hair compartment in decorative rings ceased towards the end of the 1870s. (Fig. 34 a, b)

By the 1820s, yellow gold predominated in the making of jewellery, though some rings were fashioned from different shades of gold in a single ring. The colour variations of the gold were achieved by alloying pure gold with different metals such as copper, zinc or silver. The goldsmith used rose, yellow (in varying degrees of intensity), white, green and red gold to decorate his work. (Fig. 35 a, b) (Fig. 36 a, b)

Many rings of the period were set with striking combinations of gems. (Fig. 37 a, b) A notable fashion in the 1820s was the mixture of amethyst or pink topaz with turquoise. (Fig. 38) Pearls, emeralds, and rubies or garnets were often set together. The setting of ruby with turquoise symbolized exalted love and protection from danger. (Fig. 39) Combinations of pearl, turquoise and green chrysoberyl or pink topaz with green chrysoberyl were also very popular. Coral was no longer as widely used in rings as it had been before 1815.

A rounded oblong bezel with a gem surrounded by pearls or diamonds was one of the characteristic designs of these years. Until about 1830 this style of ring occasionally held a painted miniature of an eye. (Fig. 40) An oval bezel surrounded by gems was also fashionable. Single or multiple cluster rings frequently were set with pearls or turquoises surrounding a tiny ruby, emerald or diamond spark. (Fig. 41 a, b)

Ornate, wide-bezel, half-pearl rings remained very fashionable until about 1835. See Fig. 33. Another wide-bezel design was set with a row of gems on a matted ground surrounded by a flanged border. (Fig. 42 a, b)

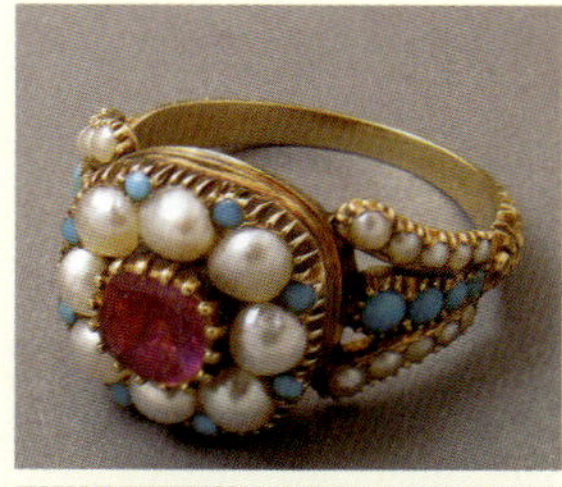

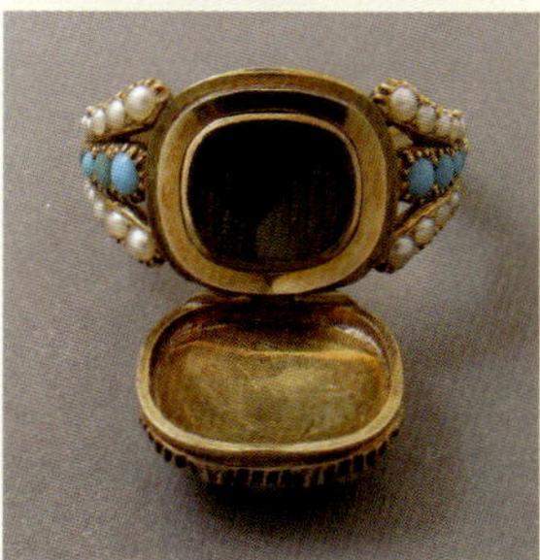

Fig. 37 a, b. Hinged bezel, concealing hair compartment, is set with a ruby surrounded by half pearls and turquoises, all collet set. Three radiating panels form the shoulders, set with tiny pearls and turquoises, deeply chased shank except for a small area at the back. Yellow gold. *Circa* 1820-1830.

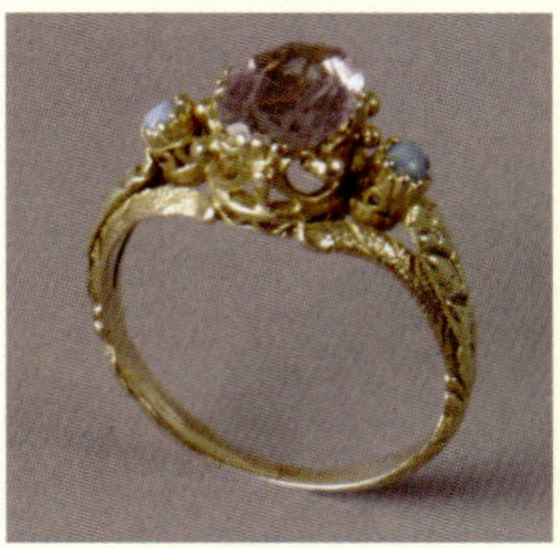

Fig. 38. Openwork gallery supports a claw-set amethyst flanked by turquoises in open-back, cut-down collets set on a gallery of tiny rings. Bifurcated, chased shoulders are overlaid with a chased leaf of green gold, partially chased shank. Yellow gold. *Circa* 1825-1840. Bezel 11x8mm, depth of gallery 5.5mm, shank diameter 18mm.

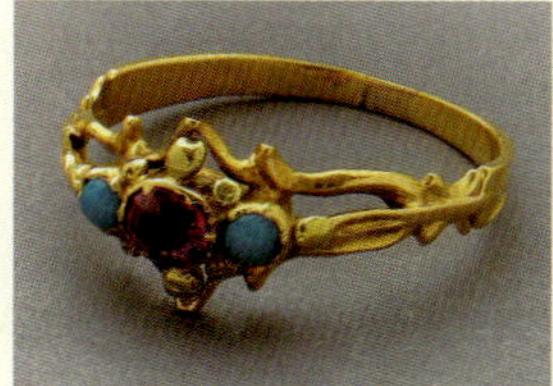

Fig. 39. Ruby flanked by turquoise coloured glass in closed cramp settings, green gold beads decorate the bezel and openwork shoulders, double channelled shank. Warm yellow gold. *Circa* 1830-1840. Bezel 8x11mm, shank diameter 18mm.

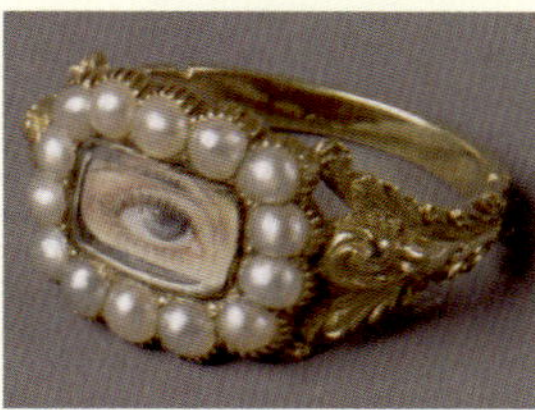

Fig. 40. A single eye, painted on ivory and under glass, is surrounded by half pearls in a 'communal' cut-down collet, supported by finely chased foliate and shell shoulders on a channelled shank. Yellow gold. *Circa* 1825. Bezel 12x14mm, shank diameter 18mm.

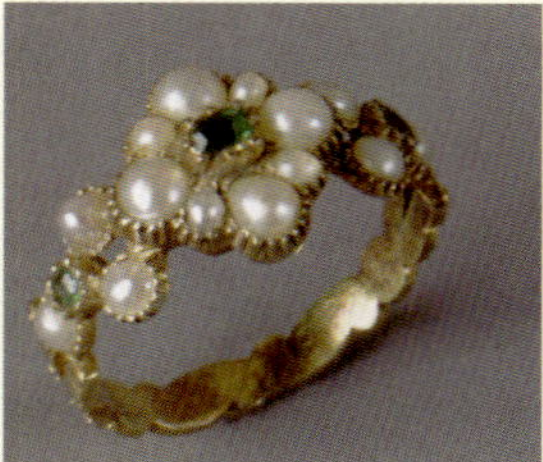

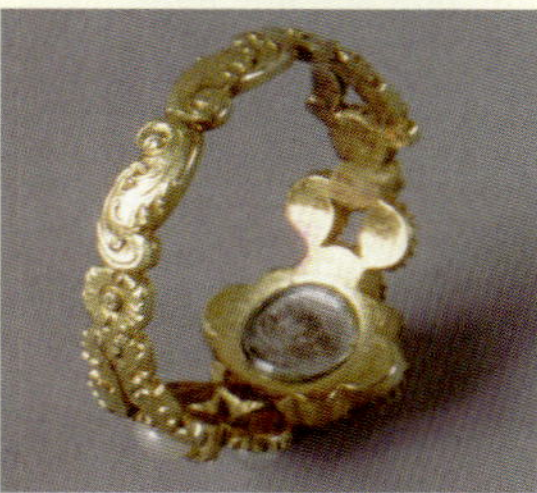

Fig. 41 a, b. Cluster bezel set with pearls and an emerald. Three pearls and an emerald decorate each finely chased bifurcated shoulder. The scrolled shank is also finely chased. All the gems are set in cut-down collets. Hair compartment set in reverse of bezel. 'Coloured' yellow gold. *Circa* 1825-1835. Bezel 10x10mm, shank diameter 16mm.

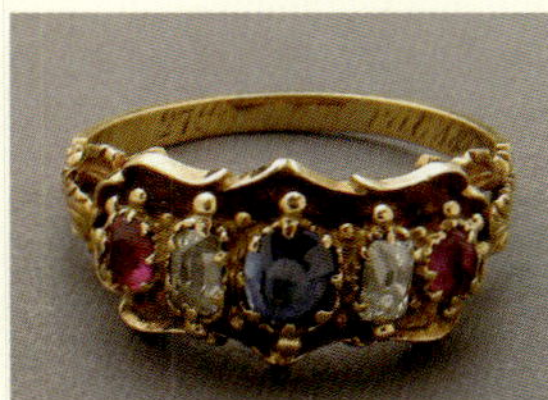

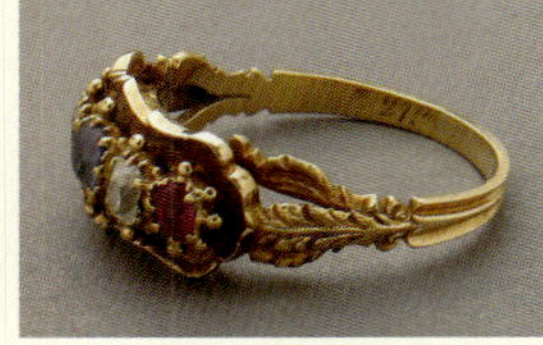

Fig. 42 a, b. Sapphire, two rubies, two diamonds in cramp settings are surrounded by a serpentine flanged border, with hair compartment in reverse of bezel. Lightly chased foliate design decorates the shoulders, channelled shank inscribed inside: '27 April 1840'. Yellow gold. Bezel 8x21mm, shank diameter 17mm, width 2mm.

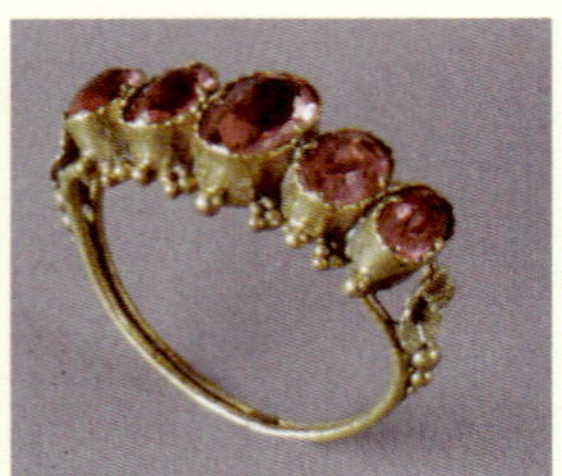

Fig. 43. Five oval pink pastes in closed-back cramp settings are decorated with small beads, the shoulders are decorated with a flower above three graduated beads, double wires with hatch marks form the shank. Matt yellow gold. *Circa* 1820-1835. Bezel depth 9mm, shank diameter 17mm.

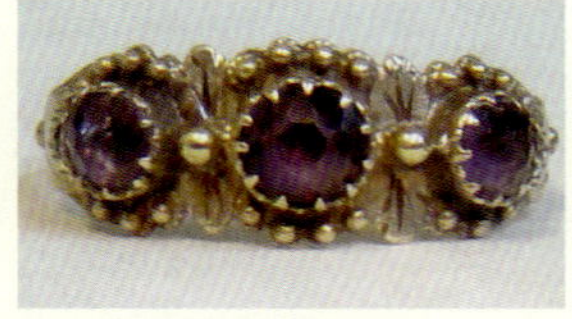

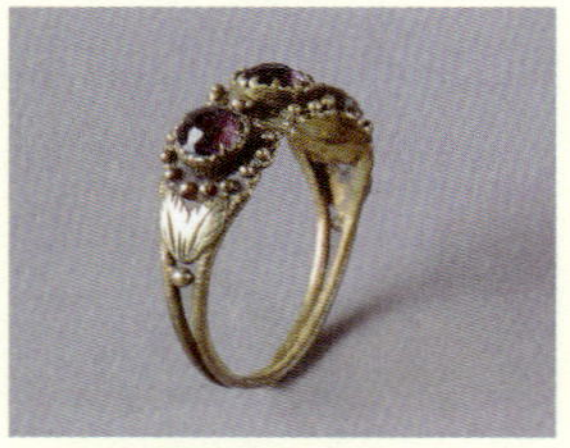

Fig. 44 a, b. Wide beaded bezel comprises three amethysts in closed-back saw-tooth settings, an engraved foliate design and single bead between the gems. Double wire shank of hatched gold separates at the shoulders to accommodate a single bead and two leaves in green gold. The ring is made from yellow gold which tarnishes quickly, indicating low carat gold. *Circa* 1825-1835. Bezel depth 7mm, shank diameter 17mm.

Half-hoop rings were composed of one or two rows of uniform or graduated gems or paste, usually in closed, cut-down collet or cramp settings. (Fig. 43) Some rings were quite plain; others were decorated with gold beads around the gems. (Fig. 44 a, b)

A single gem, or a gem surrounded with a border of pearls, with a group of three pearls on each shoulder was fashionable from about 1820 to 1830. (Fig. 45 a, b)

The pansy design was common in the 1820s and 1830s. (Fig. 46) Gem-set rings contained either dark amethysts or a variety of gems such as amethyst and chrysoberyl, or turquoise and pearl. Alternatively, the pansy might be enamelled in naturalistic colours.

Occasionally a ring was made with a hinged bezel which concealed a compartment beneath the jewelled 'lid', see Fig. 37. The cavity was usually filled with woven hair and covered with glass. Another style which sometimes contained a hidden compartment was a fairly wide hoop ring chased on the outside. A small dowel on the outside or edge of the hoop released the hinged flap inside the ring, and a tiny hair relic could be placed within the small cavity.

Filigree rings formed entirely of wire, often milled along the edge, were fashionable between 1820 and 1840. (Fig. 47) A particular style of filigree called cannetille was popular at the same time. Its characteristics were tight spirals built up from fine wire, gold beads in the peascod motif, sometimes interspersed with leaves, shells and flowers. (Fig. 48 a, b) Green chrysoberyl, emerald, garnet, pearl, ruby and pink or gold topaz, were commonly set in cannetille and filigree work. The gems were mounted in open or closed-back cramp or saw-tooth settings. By the end of the 1830s the popularity of filigree was declining to be superseded by plump-looking embossed work.

'Acrostic' rings were very popular during this period. Gemstones, the initial letter of which, spelt out the word R-E-G-A-R-D [Ruby, Emerald, Garnet, Amethyst, Ruby, Diamond], were set in half-hoop, filigree or cluster designs. (Fig. 49 a, b) Gem-set 'regard' rings continued to be popular until about 1875. There is an attractive example of the 'regard' arrangement in the British Museum; the ring is composed of seven hoops of hatched gold, each set with a single gem, held together with a slide. Opinions vary as to the significance of the 'regard'

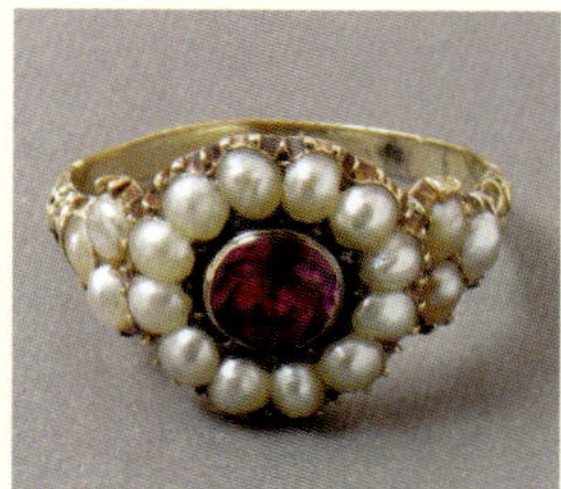

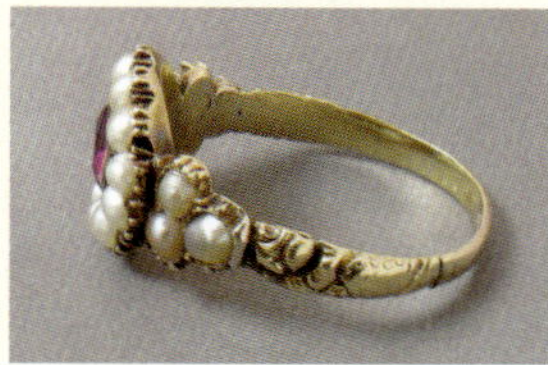

Fig. 45 a, b. Foiled almandine garnet surrounded by pearls, all in cut-down collets. Chased shoulders terminating with three pearls, plain shank. Yellow gold. *Circa* 1820. Bezel 11x11mm, shank diameter 18mm.

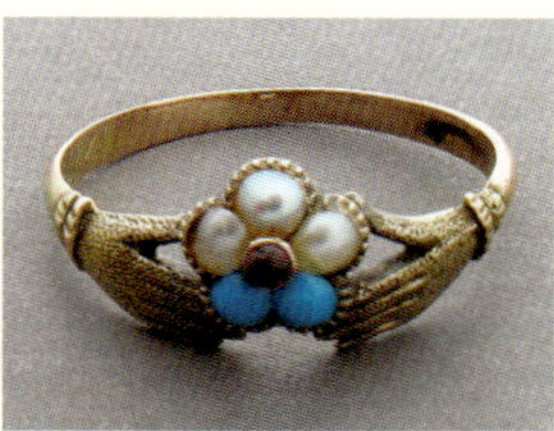

Fig. 46. Pansy bezel set with pearls, turquoises and a cabochon garnet held by tooled hands. Hair compartment in reverse of bezel. Plain hoop. Pale yellow gold. *Circa* 1830. Depth of cluster 6mm, hoop diameter 16mm.

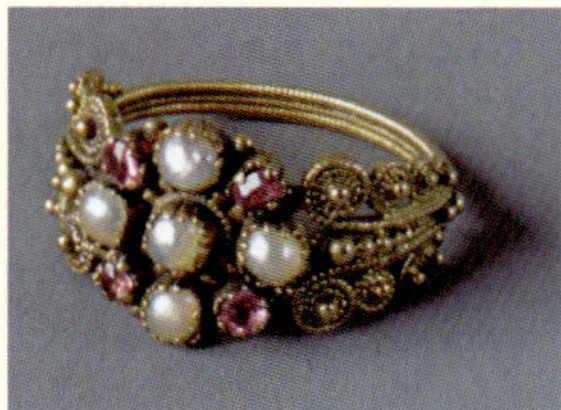

Fig. 47. Filigree ring decorated with pale rubies and half pearls in closed cramp settings, shoulders formed from graduated gold beads flanked by milled-edged wirework; hatched, triple wire shank. Matt yellow gold. *Circa* 1825. Bezel 11x12.5mm, shank diameter 17mm.

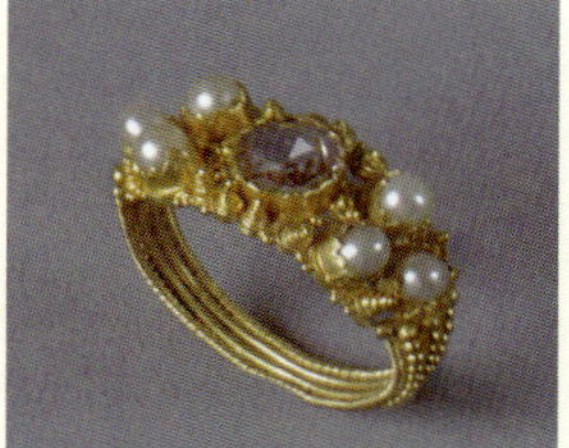

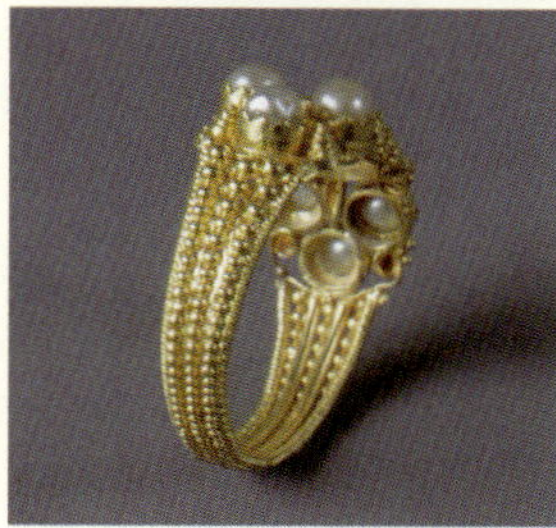

Fig. 48 a, b. Filigree ring set with six whole pearls and a pale pink topaz in openback sawtooth settings. The shank is formed from three strands of wire decorated on the outer edge with small beads. Bright, rich yellow gold. Possibly made by the firm of Hamilton & Co., Calcutta, India, following the English styles fashionable between 1820 and 1835. This ring has many features of English rings but there are significant differences: whole pearls are used rather than half pearls, the stones are set open rather than closed, and the gold is much brighter than most English rings of the period, many of which were made from lower quality gold. Bezel 10x28mm, shank diameter 18mm, width 3mm.

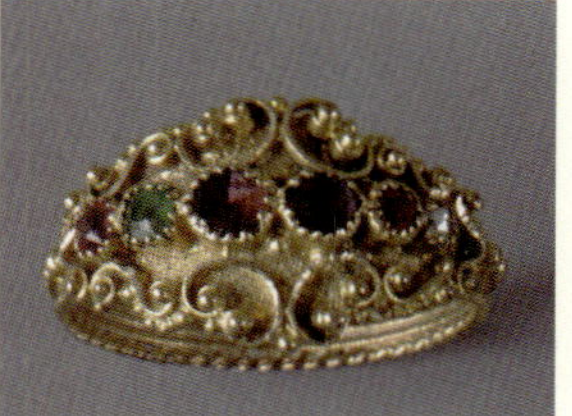

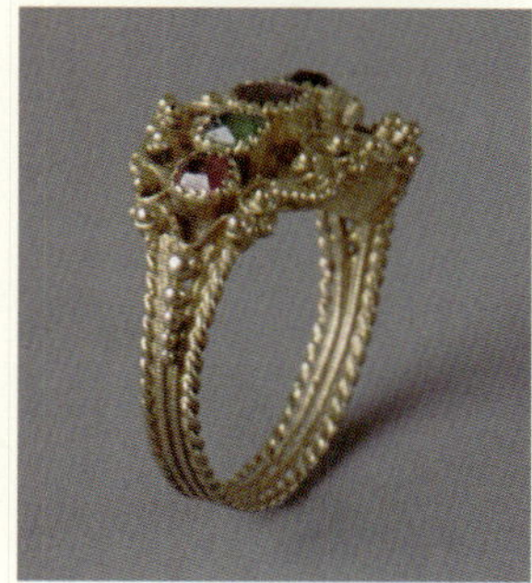

Fig. 49 a, b. 'Regard' ring. The gems, in saw-tooth settings, are applied to a tooled ground, bordered with applied filigree. The shoulders, decorated with five tiny gold beads, are an extension of the shank comprising two hatched wires and outer purled wires. Rich yellow gold. *Circa* 1830-1840. Bezel 12x22mm, shank diameter 18mm, width 2.5mm.

[1820 - 1840]

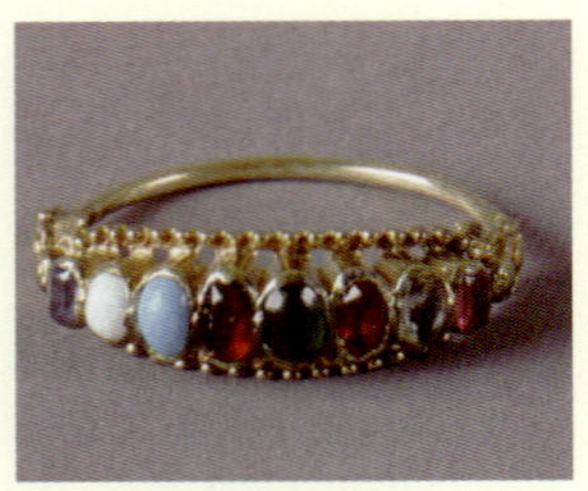

Fig. 50. Multi-gem half-hoop. All the gems are set in closed collets bordered by a strip of very worn beading. Two leaves, a single flower and a bead in green and red gold decorate each shoulder, single wire hoop (a replacement) continues in a full circle beneath the bezel. Possibly a French 'souvenir' ring, since the turquoise is a replacement stone. *Circa* 1825-1835. Depth of bezel 6mm, hoop diameter 18mm.

ring: it may have been used as an engagement ring, as a token of friendship, or to celebrate the birth of a child. It was also used as a mourning ring.

Other gemset 'acrostic' rings conveyed messages such as 'dearest', 'repeal' (a reflection of the political agitations in Ireland for the repeal of the English Corn Laws c.1838-1846), or spelled out names such as 'Sophia' or 'Rose'. In France 'souvenir' rings were fashionable (Fig. 50), as were the 'la semaine' rings which contained gems representing the days of the week.

Serpent rings were worn at this time, some set entirely with gems such as diamond and turquoise, others chased on the body and set with gems in the head.

Gothic-style jewellery enjoyed a revival in the 1830s. The designs were based on architectural motifs such as quatrefoils, trefoils and single roses. Some Gothic jewellery was enamelled, and the style recurred throughout the remainder of the century.

The signet ring also reappeared in this period, having been eclipsed by the fob seal in the middle of the eighteenth century. The ring was usually of plain gold, set with a round, oval or shield-shaped bloodstone or with a red or white cornelian. Occasionally signet rings in the 1830s were richly chased.

In addition to signet rings, gentlemen decorated themselves with a fair amount of other jewellery and accessories, as is recorded by Charles Dickens in *Pickwick Papers*, (set in 1827) Vol.II, Ch.VII:

> The friend was a charming young man of not much more than fifty, dressed in a very bright blue coat with resplendent buttons, black trousers, and the thinnest possible pair of highly-polished boots. A gold eye-glass was suspended from his neck by a short broad black ribbon; a gold snuff-box lightly clasped in his left hand; gold rings innumerable, glittered on his fingers; and a large diamond pin set in gold glistened in his shirt-frill.... (p.103)

Some gentlemen of this period dressed as dandies and Benjamin Disraeli (1804-1881) was among them. In 1837 he entered Parliament and for his maiden speech he wore a black velvet coat over a scarlet waistcoat, purple trousers, with gold braid along the outside seam, and diamond rings over white gloves. In the latter half of the century the custom of wearing rings over gloves declined though Disraeli, himself, still followed the custom.

A number of rings made between 1820 and 1835 were decorated on the convex shoulders with deep, crisp chasing, usually of flowers, shells and scrolling foliage. Other rings had bifurcated shoulders set with tiny gems or additional embossed and chased work. Towards the end of the 1830s, chased work took on a feathery and matted appearance. Graduated gold beads, leaves, flowers or milled wirework, sometimes in contrasting shades of red or green gold, were used to embellish ring shoulders. Some shoulders were carved, and occasionally delicate hands supported the bezel. (Fig. 51 a, b, c)

Ring shanks were formed from lightweight gold with one or two shallow channels, others were entirely chased. Some were made from two or more wires which were plain, hatched or purled. Occasionally, on filigree rings, beading and openwork were combined with wirework to form the shank. Grooved shanks, comprising a D-shaped shank with a fine groove along each edge, were used at this time, and occasionally, reeded shanks and shanks that were triangular in section.

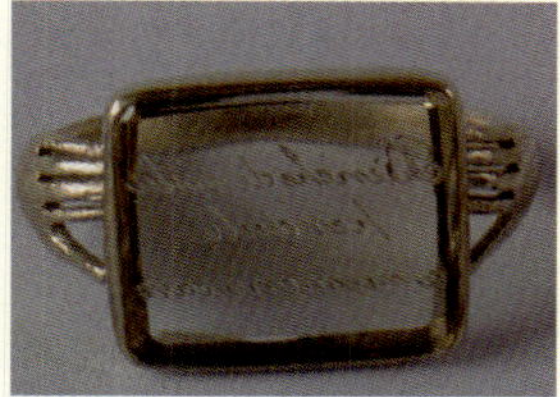

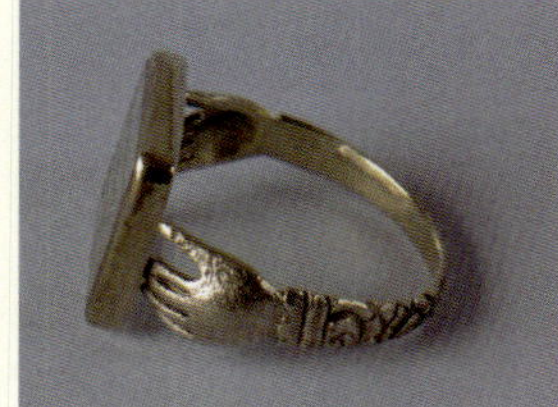

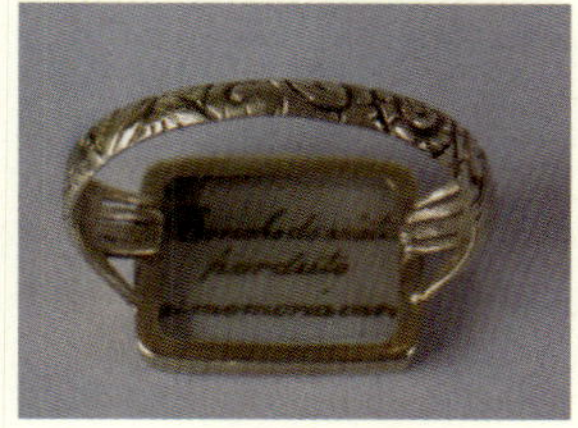

Fig. 51 a, b, c. Gentleman's seal ring set with a citrine engraved in Italian: 'Benche de vista perduto a memoria caro', meaning 'Although lost to sight to memory dear'. Chased floral shank terminates in hands which hold the bezel. Pale yellow gold. *Circa* 1825. Bezel 13x15mm, shank diameter 19mm.

[1820 - 1840]

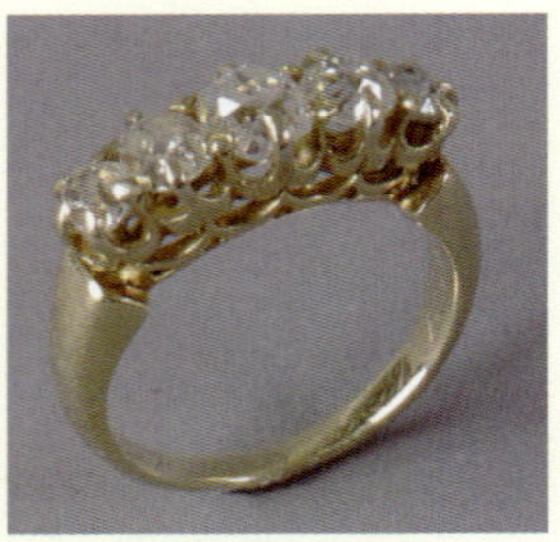

Fig. 52. Half-hoop of five chunky brilliants in open claw settings which are attached to a gallery of shallow scallops; bevelled, spatula-shaped shoulders, plain D-shaped shank inscribed inside: 'R I H to A F B 1859'. Yellow gold. This ring is an early example of the half-hoop designs that were so fashionable later in the century. Depth of gallery 5mm, shank diameter 15mm.

1840-1860

The Victorian era was one of contrast: sentiment and vigour. The sentimental side of the British character gathered momentum during the reign of Queen Victoria and continued until the years of the First World War. This characteristic was displayed in popular art, literature and music as well as in designs for rings and other types of jewellery. Victorian vigour was demonstrated by the enthusiastic reception and aggressive pursuit of new ideas and inventions, including the widespread use of machinery for mass-production to satisfy the requirements of the growing middle class.

The change from handmade rings to machine-made component parts for rings was accelerated by the discovery of gold in California in 1848 and in Australia in 1851. Gold was also discovered later in the century in the South African Transvaal (1886) and in the Klondike River in Canada (1896). Prior to 1848, most gold had come from Brazil and Russia and was comparatively rare and expensive. This resulted in the practice of melting down old pieces jewellery for use in contemporary styles.

On 22nd December 1854, the law was changed to allow a reduction in the standard of gold used in jewellery (22ct. and 18ct.) to include 15ct., 12ct. and 9ct. The widespread use of lower gold standards in America had resulted in British manufacturers of watch cases having difficulty selling their wares. The lowering of the gold standard enabled Birmingham workshops to compete profitably against foreign manufacturers and a boom in British trade resulted.

From 1784 only mourning rings had to be hallmarked, but a change in the law in 1855 required that wedding rings also be hallmarked: gem-set rings were still exempt. Regardless of this law, Birmingham goldsmiths voluntarily submitted gem-set rings to the assay office for hallmarking because of the demand by the general public for proof of the quality of the gold. The legacy of this policy is that a large proportion of nineteenth-century rings available today are hallmarked, which helps to determine the lifespan of many styles. One should remember when trying to date the beginnings of a new style that the finer rings initiated each new trend, which was later copied in quantity when public demand encouraged it. (Fig. 52)

The manufacturing jewellers of Birmingham who supplied London retailers with rings and other articles were reluctant to exhibit their goods at the 1851 and 1862 International Exhibitions held in England for fear of competing with their London trade customers and thereby losing established wholesale markets for their products. Still, the rivalry between London and Birmingham was intense. Birmingham manufacturers tried to prove their goods equal to those produced in London, and the London jewellers tried to brush aside the Birmingham trade as unworthy of notice. It should be noted that some fine work was produced by Birmingham goldsmiths in addition to mass-produced work, and that many Birmingham firms had premises in London. Contemporary writers took great pains to inform the public that the jewellery they purchased in London, as London made, was in fact made in Birmingham. Cornish's *Stranger's Guide Through Birmingham for 1853* noted that:

> For jewellery, Birmingham at one time had no
> very high reputation. Much of that Character it
> has now, however, lost; and the greater portion of
> jewellery disposed of in the Kingdom comes from
> Birmingham workshops .... Some idea may be
> formed of the extent of the business done in some
> of these branches, when we state that instances
> have been known of nearly 30,000 wedding rings
> alone having passed through the [Birmingham]
> assay office in the course of a single year. (p.97).

Regardless of its reputation, Birmingham supplied stock for jewellery retailers nationwide and abroad, while London continued to capture high-grade individual orders. (Fig. 53 a, b)

The use of decorative gold alloys, such as rose, yellow, green, and white, was still very fashionable in the early 1840s but was necessarily confined to handmade rings. As more rings were made using machinery, this fashion declined, although it does appear occasionally in the latter years of the century, usually on decorative hoop rings. See Fig. 196.

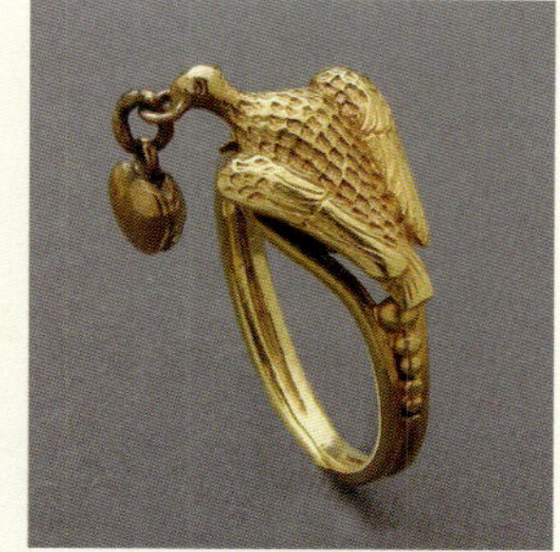

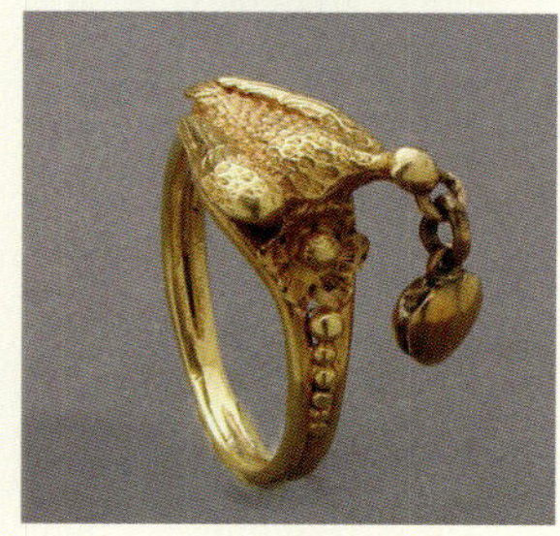

Fig. 53 a, b. A resting dove, a flower at its breast, holds a pendant heart in its beak. Hair compartment inside the dove. A double wire shank separates slightly at the shoulders to accommodate six tiny graduated beads. Rich yellow gold, exquisitely tooled. *Circa* 1840. Length of dove 14mm, shank diameter 15mm.

[1840 - 1860]

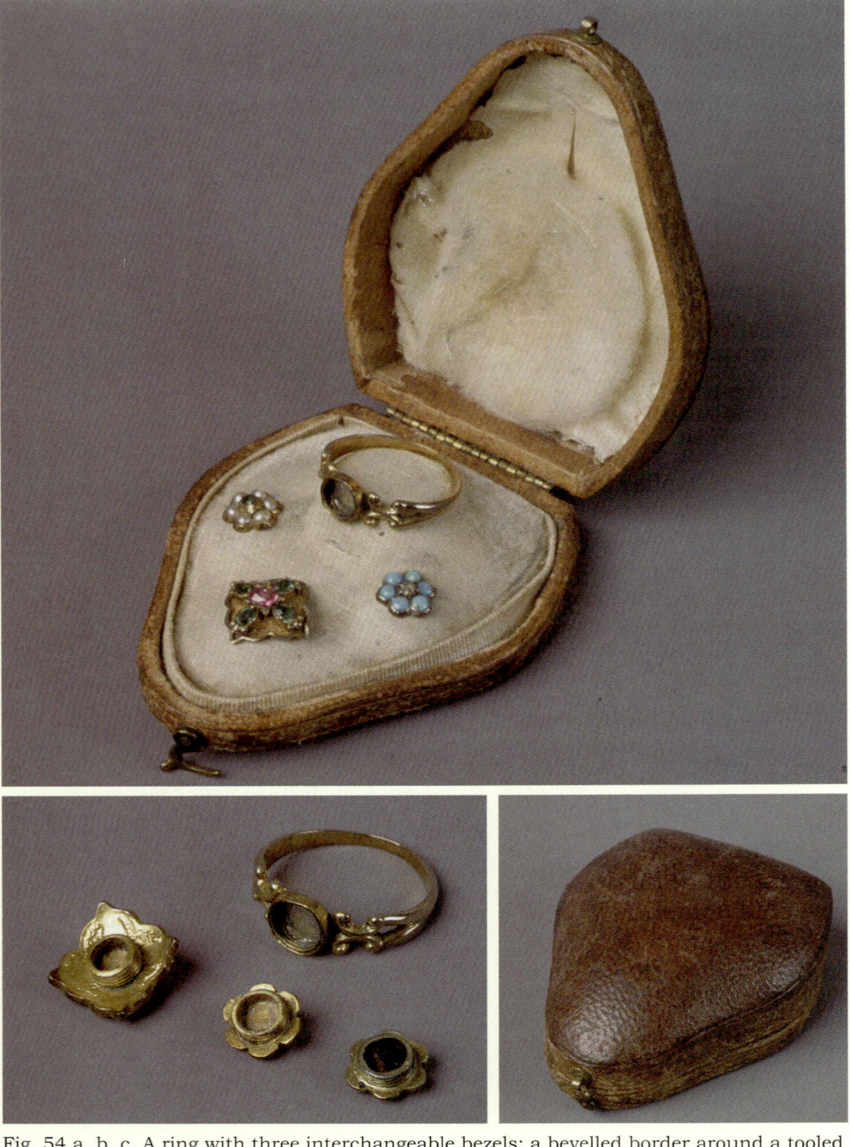

Fig. 54 a, b, c. A ring with three interchangeable bezels: a bevelled border around a tooled ground set with emeralds and a ruby in cramp settings; the second comprises a pearl cluster with an emerald spark; the third a turquoise cluster with a diamond spark. The pearls and the turquoises are set in cut-down collets. Divided shoulders are attached to a plain shank, D-shaped in section. Very pale yellow gold. *Circa* 1840-1850. Original box.

Victorian craftsmen employed numerous techniques
in the treatment of gold: it was chased, embossed,
engraved, stamped, and 'coloured'. The technique of
'colouring' was used principally on 15ct. and 12ct.
gold, sometimes on 18ct. gold. The surface was usually
left frosted (or bloomed) though occasionally it was
burnished.

From about 1860 onward, jewellers in England, inspired
by designs found in archeological projects such as
the Etruscan excavations between 1830 and 1850,
experimented with the finished appearance of gold.
Members of the Castellani family were the greatest
proponents of the Etruscan style and came closer than
anyone else to solving the mystery of granulation, but
even they did not perfect the technique. Occasionally,
one finds a ring decorated with granulation, but it is a
rare find.

A vast range of ring styles was made during this period.
Many completely new designs appeared as well as the
perennial favourites, such as half-hoops and clusters.
(Fig. 54 a, b, c) Ladies' rings usually hugged the finger,
and the gems were tiny to medium in size rather than
massive. (Fig. 55) Vinaigrette rings were made in this
period; a typical example had a hinged bezel which
opened to reveal a pierced grille, beneath which a
perfumed sponge would have been placed. (Fig. 56 a, b)

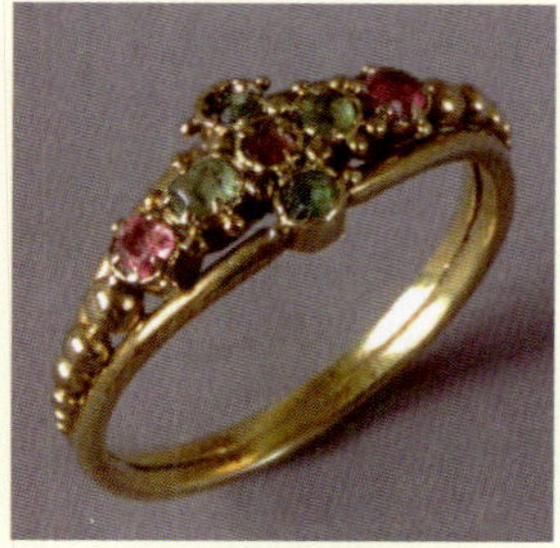

Fig. 55. Bezel comprising
pale emeralds and rubies in
closed cramp settings and
individual beads decorating
the settings. Double wire
shank separates at shoulders
to accommodate seven
graduated gold beads. Yellow
gold. *Circa* 1840-1850. Bezel
7.5x15mm, shank diameter
17mm.

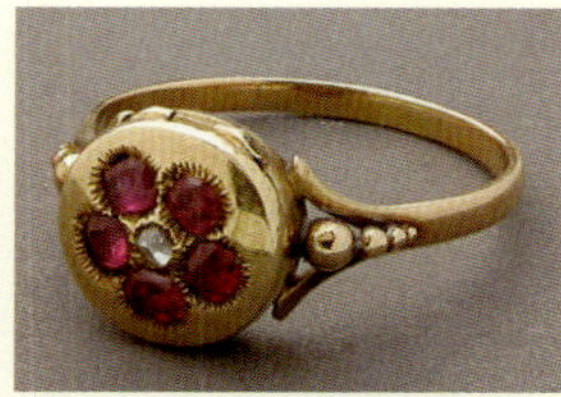

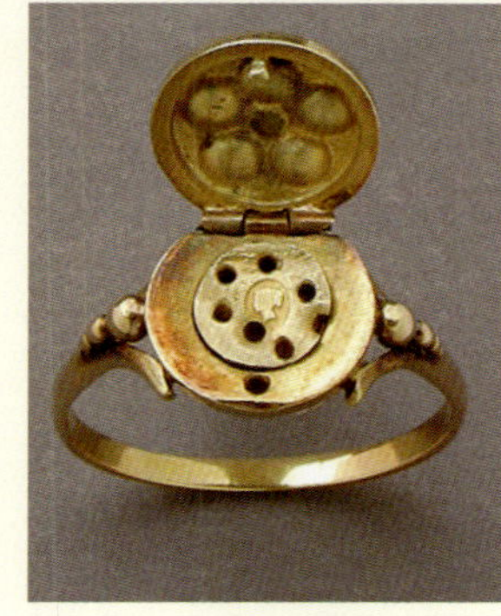

Fig. 56 a, b. Vinaigrette ring
set with a cluster of rubies
around a rose-cut diamond
with delicate tooled work
radiating from the stones.
The ring opens to reveal
a tiny grille with six holes
around an impression of
the young head of Queen
Victoria. Narrow, plain
shank separates at the
shoulders to accommodate
four graduated gold beads.
Pale yellow gold. 1850s.
Diameter of bezel 9mm,
shank diameter 16.5mm.

[1840 - 1860]

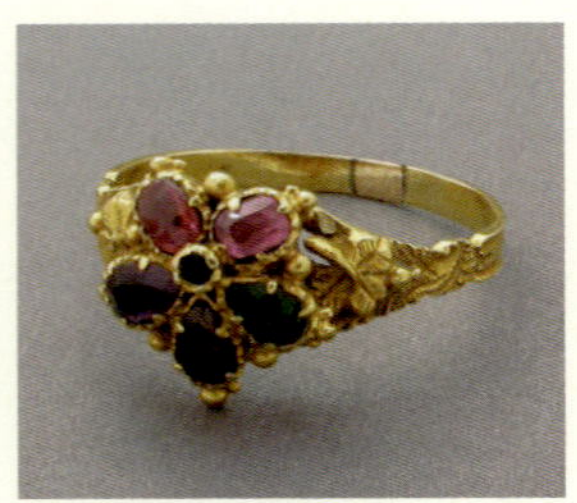

Fig. 57. 'Regard' ring set as a cluster with a ruby, emerald, garnet, amethyst, ruby and centre diamond in closed cramp settings, embellished with gold beads, and a hair compartment inside the bezel. Lightly chased shoulders are decorated with a three-leaf clover, thin channelled shank. Rich yellow gold. *Circa* 1835-1850. Shank diameter 17mm, width 2mm.

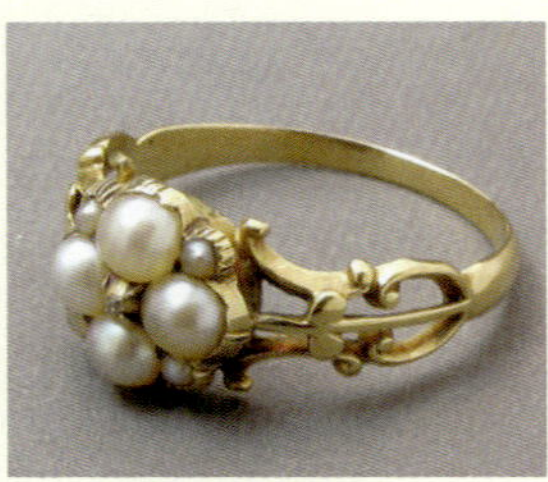

Fig. 58. Pearls set around a diamond spark in conical cut-down collets, hair compartment inside bezel. Symmetrical openwork shoulder, plain hoop. Yellow gold. *Circa* 1850. Cluster 9mm in diameter, hoop diameter 16.5mm.

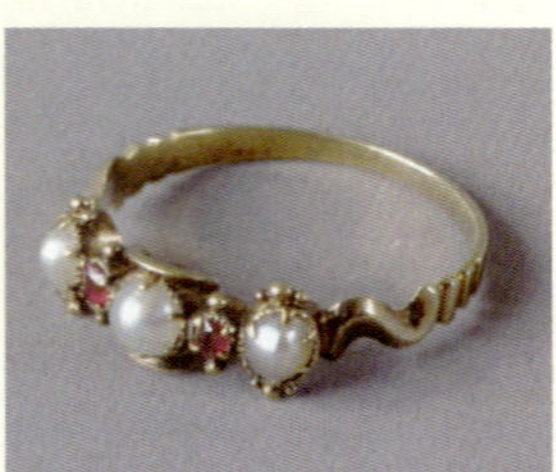

Fig. 59. Half hoop comprising pearls and rubies in closed-back cramp settings decorated with beads, and wirework on either side of the middle pearl. S-shaped shoulders supported by transverse ribbing, plain, flat shank. Yellow gold. *Circa* 1845-1855. Depth of bezel 6mm, shank diameter 17mm.

[1840 - 1860]

Information on ladies' and gentlemen's rings appears in a catalogue produced by A.B. Savory & Sons of Cornhill, London, in 1851. The following rings are advertised (p.62) as 'THE BEST JEWELLERY, London made':

LADIES' GEM RINGS

	Neat	*Elegant*	*Rich*
Fine gold Rings, set with garnets and opals; turquoise and pearl; pearl and rubies; or pearl and emeralds...each	14s	18s	21s
Fine gold Regard Rings, set with real gems.......................	30s	45s	63s
Fine gold Rings, set with real Oriental pearls, in cluster with ruby, emerald, or brilliant centres.....	25s	45s	75s
Fine gold Rings, set with emeralds and brilliants; or opal and brilliants...	75s	125s	210s
Fine gold half-hoop Brilliant Rings, set with five stones, each of the finest water.......................	105s	140s	210s

(Fig. 57, Fig. 58, Fig. 59)

GENTLEMEN'S RINGS

	Neat	*Elegant*	*Rich*
Fine gold Signet Rings, set with bloodstone, white cornelian, carbuncle, or onyx......	30s	45s	63s
Fine gold Rings, set with a fine single-stone brilliant.........	65s	105s	148s
Fine gold Rings, set with a fine single-stone brilliant, (larger).	£ 10	£ 14	£ 30

32

Contemporary literature also attests to the wearing of rings by gentlemen:

Wilkie Collins, *The Woman in White*, 1860, Part 1, chapter V11, p.31. The story was set in 1850.

> He was dressed in a dark frock-coat, of some substance much thinner than cloth, and in waistcoat and trousers of spotless white. His feet were effeminately small, and were clad in buff-coloured silk stockings, and little womanish bronze-leather slippers. Two rings adorned his white delicate hands, the value of which even my inexperienced observation detected to be all but priceless.

During the 1840s and 1850s, rings were decorated with delicate chasing (1840s), beading, wirework, engraving (1850s), enamel, embossed work, strapwork and saw-piercing, and there was an avid interest in naturalistic designs. During the 1850s many designs were asymmetrical. Enamel was brightly coloured, with combinations such as green and orange, red and green, and royal blue or turquoise blue contrasted with gold ribs or intricate, engraved gold designs. Pearls and diamonds afforded a pleasing contrast with turquoise blue or royal blue enamel. Popular gems of the 1840s and 1850s included amethyst, chrysoberyl, chrysoprase, rose and brilliant-cut diamond, emerald, garnet, opal, pearl, ruby, pink topaz and turquoise. Rings were colourful and pretty, to match the mood of the young Queen and the gowns of the period. (Fig. 60) (Fig. 61) (Fig. 62 a, b) (Fig. 63) (Fig. 64) (Fig. 65)

Cluster rings, in addition to the 'regard' and 'dearest' configuration, were set with a single variety of gem (Fig. 66) or with different coloured gems with no specific meaning attached to them. The pansy design was still fashionable, set with a combination of pearl, turquoise and garnet or amethyst, chrysoberyl and garnet. The traditional cluster style of small gems surrounding a larger gem was still being worn in this period.

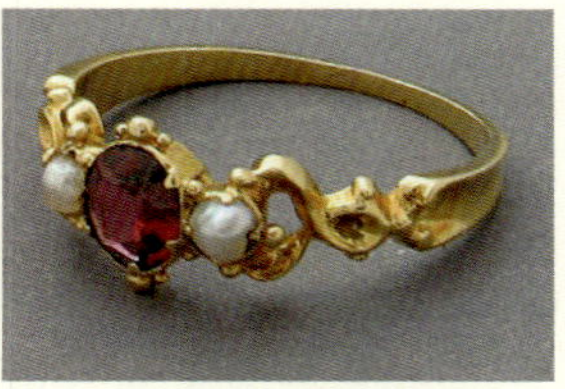

Fig. 60. Almandine garnet in open-back cramp setting, flanked by pearls in closed-backed cramp settings, all embellish with small beads. Symmetrical openwork shoulders, single channel shank, rich yellow gold. 1840s. Bezel centre 7mm deep, shank diameter 16mm.

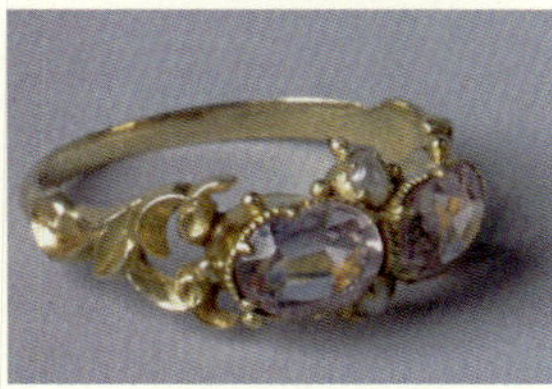

Fig. 61. Bezel comprises pale pink topaz and pearls in open-back cramp settings decorated at intervals with individual beads. Asymmetric saw-pierced shoulders, plain D-shaped shank. Bright yellow gold. *Circa* 1845-1855. Bezel 8x17mm, shank diameter 16mm.

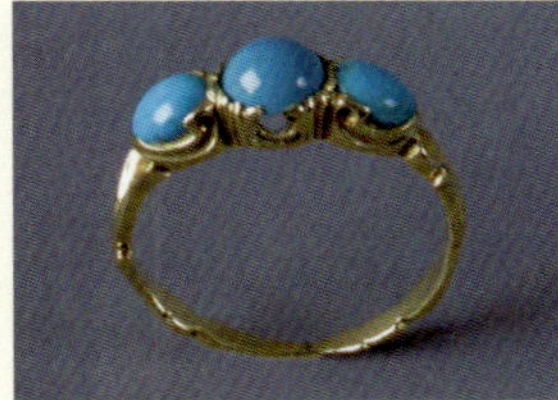

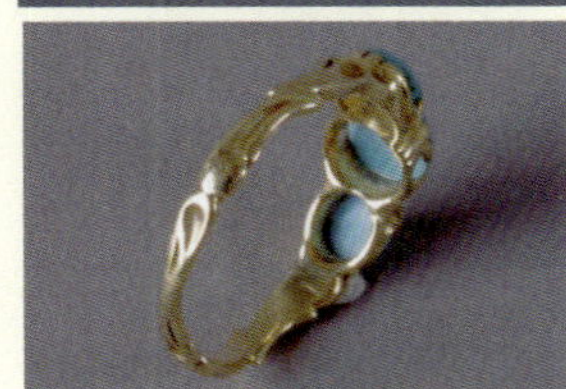

Fig. 62 a, b. Three-stone ring set with open-back turquoises (middle stone is a replacement), the extension of the asymmetric carved gallery is an example of the transition from cramp to claw setting. Shank and shoulders are composed of asymmetric, concave sections. Yellow gold. 1850s. Gallery 2mm deep, shank diameter 16mm.

[1840 - 1860]

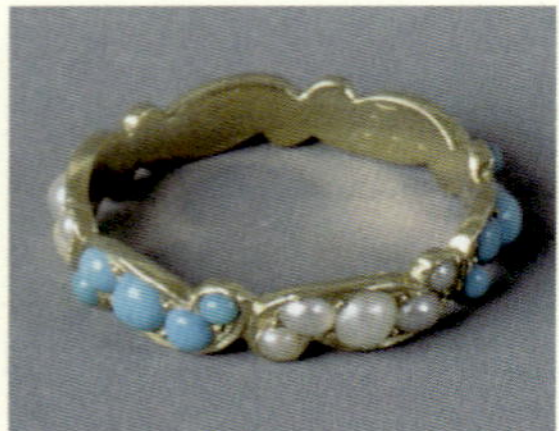

Fig. 63. Hoop ring formed with alternating scrolls of turquoise and pearls. Yellow gold. *Circa* 1845-1855. Hoop diameter 15mm.

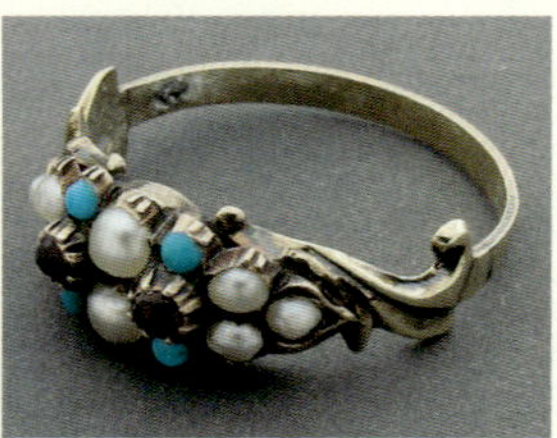

Fig. 64. Cluster of pearls, Persian turquoise and rose-cut pyrope garnets in closed-back cut-down collets, with hair compartment in the back of the bezel. Asymmetric carved shoulders, plain flat hoop. Very pale yellow gold. *Circa* 1840-1850. Bezel 6x17mm, hoop diameter 16.5mm.

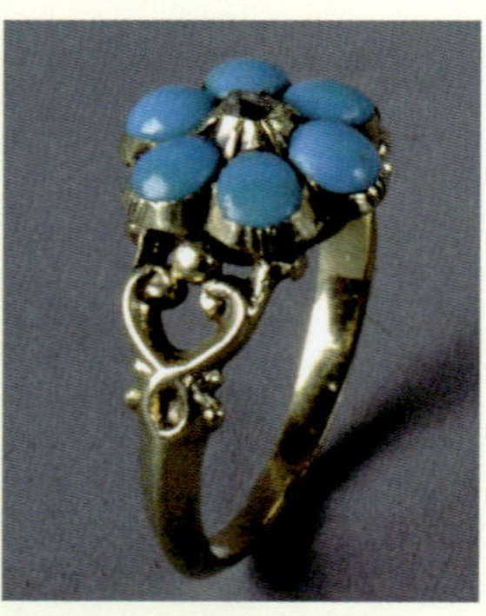

Fig. 65. Applied cluster bezel set with turquoises and a diamond spark in conical cut-down collets, hair compartment in reverse of bezel. Symmetrical openwork shoulders, shank - triangular in section. Yellow gold. *Circa* 1845-1860. Cluster 9mm diameter, shank diameter 15mm.

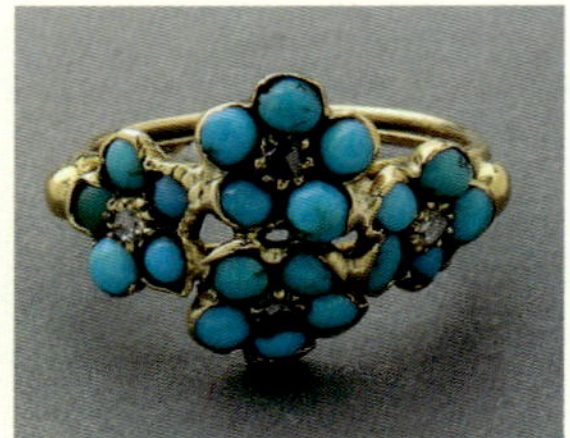

Fig. 66. Turquoise forget-me-nots in closed collets with centre rose-cut diamond sparks. Double wire shank separates at the shoulders and continues beneath the bezel. Two beads decorate each shoulder. Yellow gold. *Circa* 1835-1850. Bezel 11x20mm, shank diameter 16mm.

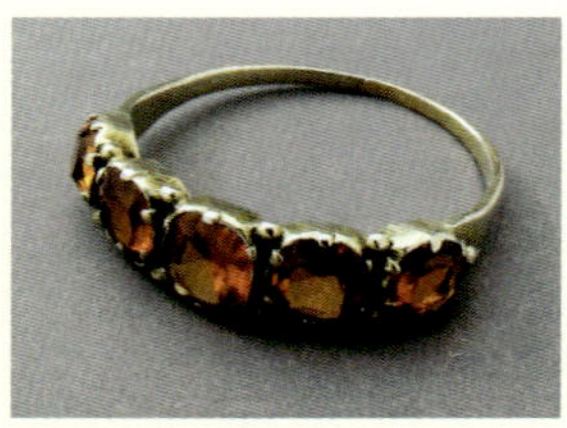

Fig. 67. Half-hoop of five hessonite garnets open-set in green gold, decorated with beads between each gem; narrow, plain shank expands slightly at shoulders. *Circa* 1860. Bezel depth 5mm, shank diameter 16.5mm.

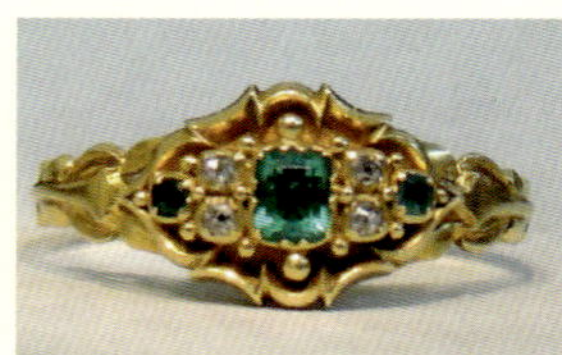

Fig. 68. Emeralds and diamonds in cramp settings set on a matted ground bordered by a serpentine flanged edge. Burnished foliated shoulders, channelled hoop. Oval hair compartment in reverse of bezel. Rich yellow gold. *Circa* 1845. Bezel 8.5x16mm, hoop diameter 18mm, width 2mm. *Reginald Davis (Oxford) Ltd.*

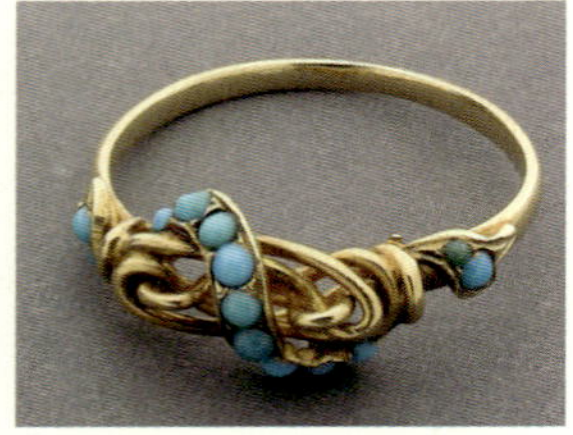

Fig. 69. Knot ring comprising turquoise studded strap-work set diagonally across the knot, plain shank. Yellow gold. *Circa* 1840-1850. Shank diameter 16mm.

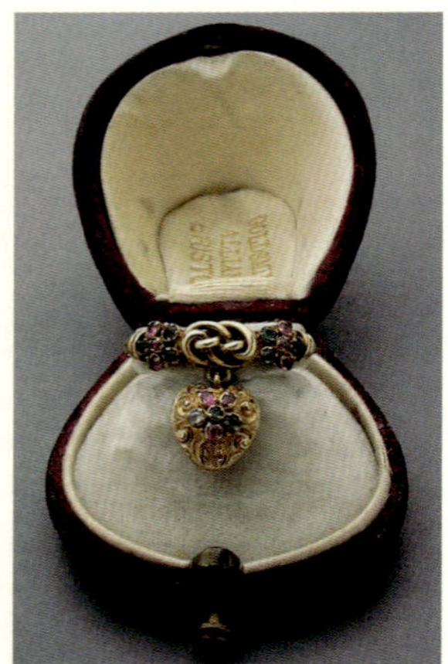

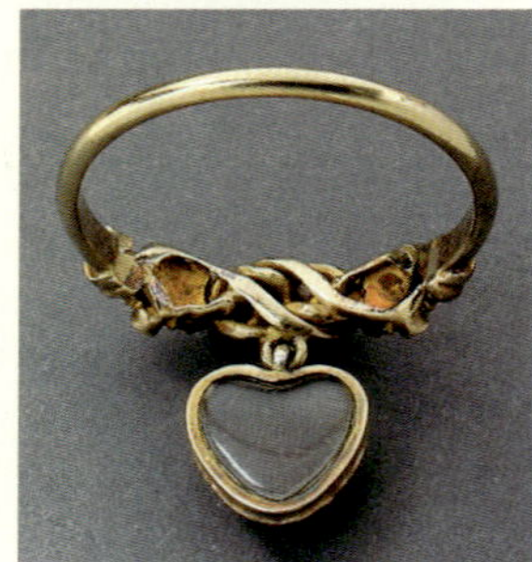

Fig. 70 a, b. Knot ring with pendant heart in its original box. A cluster of pale rubies and emeralds flank the knot and decorate the chased heart which holds a hair compartment. Two transverse ribs separate the plain D-shaped shank from the bezel. Matt, yellow gold. *Circa* 1840. Heart 8mm long, shank diameter 16mm.

Half-hoop rings were as popular as ever, set with a single variety or with a combination of gems. (Fig. 67) Some settings were embellished with beading or wirework. Wide-bezel rings set with a row of gems surrounded by a flanged border often had a hair compartment in the reverse of the bezel. (Fig. 68)

During the 1840s, knot rings in a variety of styles became very fashionable (Fig.69), particularly a knot ring with a pendant heart containing a hair compartment. The latter were usually set with tiny gems such as diamonds, emeralds, rubies or turquoises on either side of the knot and on the heart. (Fig. 70 a, b) Today many knot rings have lost the pendant heart and are sold without it, or a small gold drop is attached in lieu of the original heart.

One new and distinctive style comprised a single gem in a cramp setting with wirework decorating the gallery, and embossed shoulders, which might be set with a single pearl. The silhouette of this design is reminiscent of Renaissance-style rings. (Fig. 71, a, b) Three-stone rings were popular in the 1850s (Fig. 72), and a ring with a 'turban' style bezel made its appearance at this time. (Fig. 73)

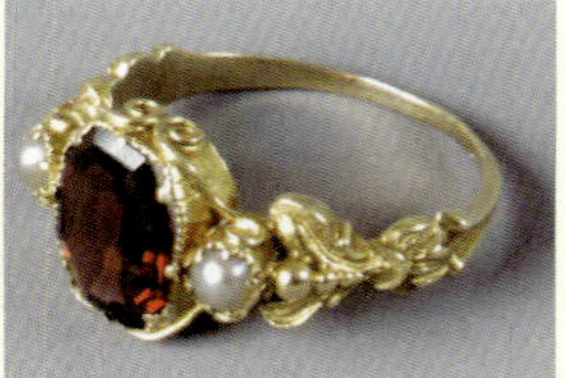

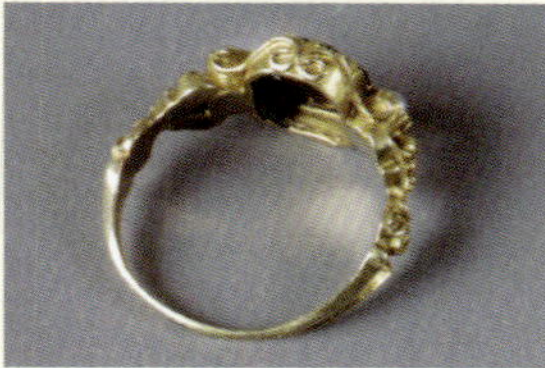

Fig. 71 a, b. Garnet in an open-back cramp setting flanked by pearls in closed-back cramp settings, the gallery decorated with applied wire, embossed shoulders rise from a very narrow channelled shank. Rich yellow bloomed gold. 1850s. Garnet 10x7mm, gallery 3mm deep, shank diameter 18mm.

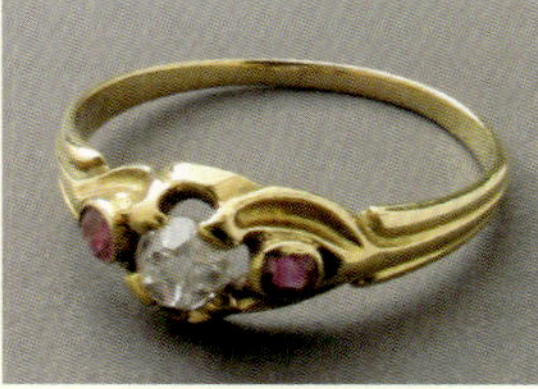

Fig. 72. Chunky, cushion-shaped brilliant-cut diamond flanked by two rubies in open-back collet settings, gallery carved with a scroll pattern ending in claws holding the diamond, a transition from cramp to claw setting. Two grooves decorate the shoulders, plain shank D-shaped in section, pale yellow gold. 1850s. Bezel centre 7mm deep, shank diameter 17mm.

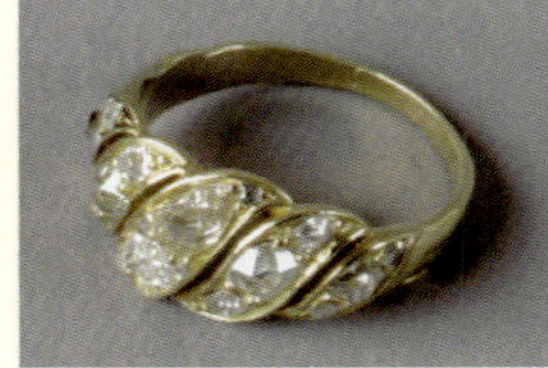

Fig. 73. Turban-style ring comprising 5 separate sections set with 8 tiny rose-cut diamonds and 10 brilliant-cut diamonds, set open at the back. Asymmetric shoulders (worn). Yellow gold. *Circa* 1855. Bezel 9mm deep tapering to 5mm, hoop diameter 17mm.

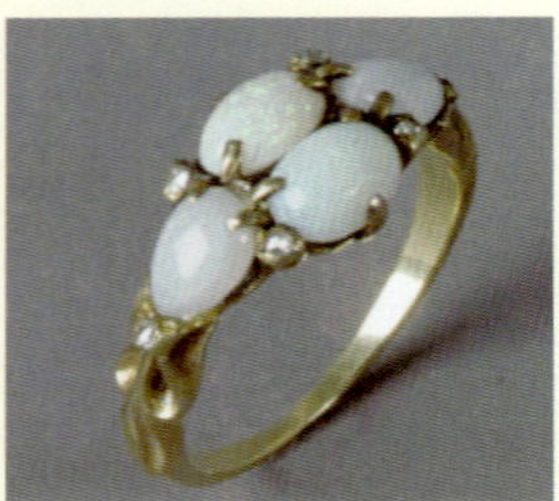

Fig. 74. Four opals in open-back claw settings are interspersed with six tiny rose-cut diamonds in closed collet settings that also secure the opals. A carved foliate design decorates the shoulders that are set on a plain, squared hoop. Pale yellow gold. *Circa* 1855-1870. Bezel 8x20mm, hoop diameter 17mm.

During the 1850s another distinctive design emerged in which a bezel was set with a group of three or four principal gems in the form of a triangle or a lozenge. The main gems were interspersed with tiny stones or gold beads. (Fig. 74)

An important ring type which became widely produced at this time was the buckle. The buckle motif had been used occasionally in the past and became a standard design for the remainder of the century. Charles Edwards in *The History and Poetry of Finger-Rings*, 1855, relates:

> Rings of gold are common in England at the present day, made to form a strap with buckles, precisely, in shape, a common belt or collar. It lies flat like an ordinary leather strap, and is formed of small pieces of gold which are kept so delicately together that the lines of meeting are scarcely perceptible. This is accomplished by having many minute and unseen hinges, which make the whole pliable and allow it to be buckled (as a ring) upon the finger. (p.37)

A similar ring, though from a slightly later date, is shown in Fig. 75 a, b, c.

Other buckle rings were made in plain gold, or could be decorated with enamel, gems or engraving.

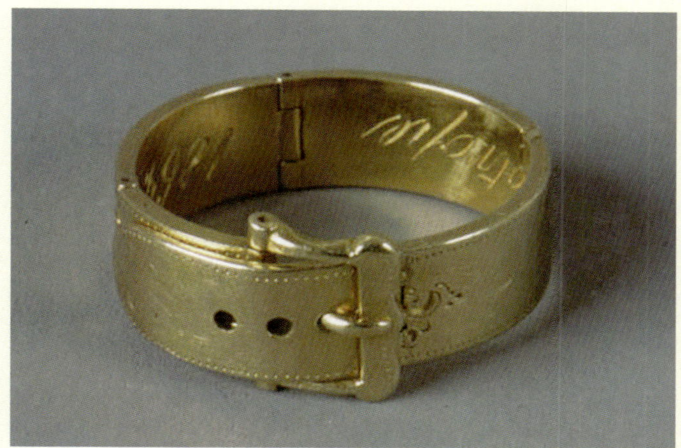

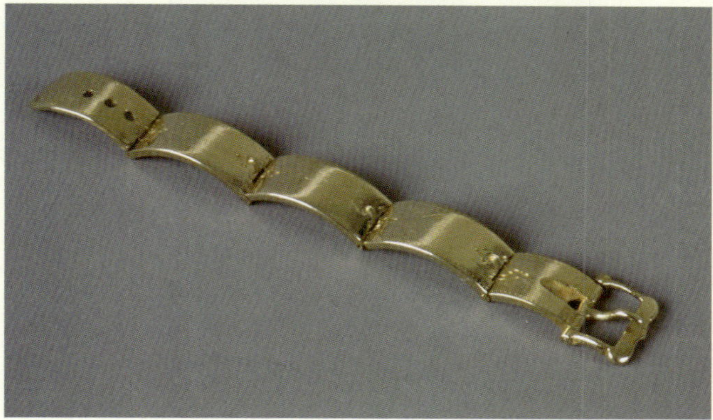

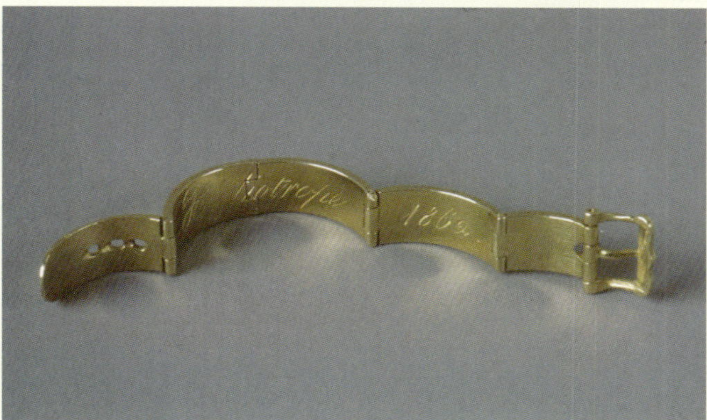

Fig. 75 a, b, c. Flexible buckle ring with four hinges decorated with light tooled work, inscribed inside hoop: 'He'liotrope 1862'. Heliotrope represents 'devotion' in Victorian flower language. Yellow gold. Length 68mm, width 6.5mm.

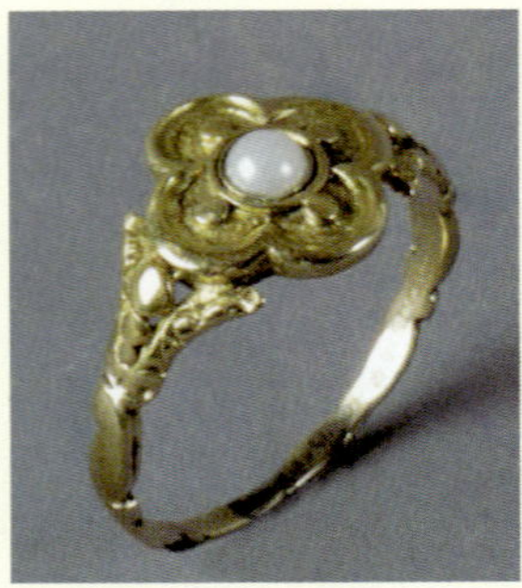

Fig. 76. Gothic-style quatrefoil bezel decorated with a half pearl and four beads on a tooled ground, forked shoulders chased and decorated with three graduated gold beads, serpentine sections of gold form the shank (very worn). Yellow gold. *Circa* 1845. Bezel 11x11mm, shank diameter 18mm.

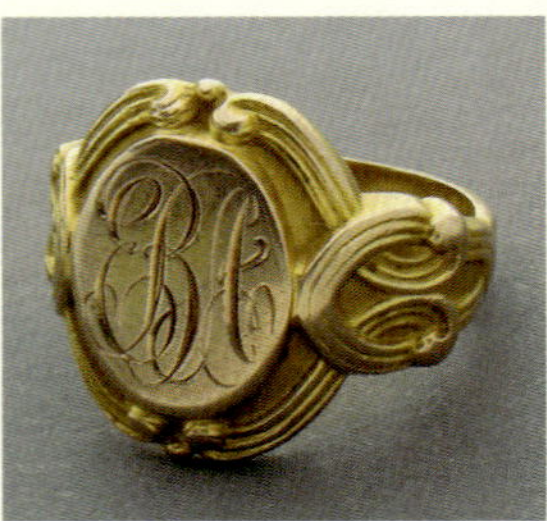

Fig. 77. Gentleman's signet ring in 'coloured' gold decorated with scroll work on the bezel and shoulders. American, *circa* 1865-1880. *Keith Austin Collection.*

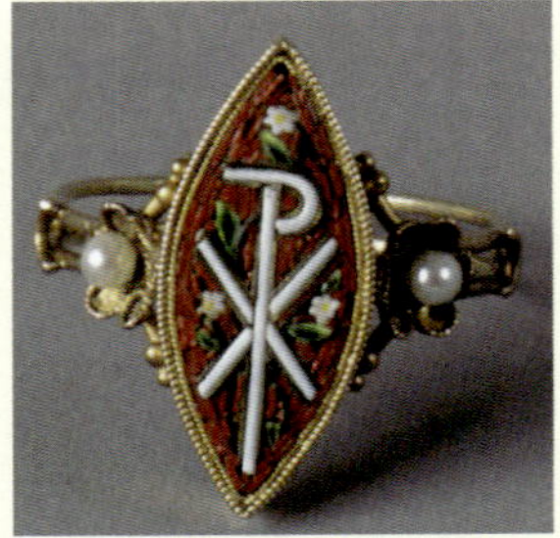

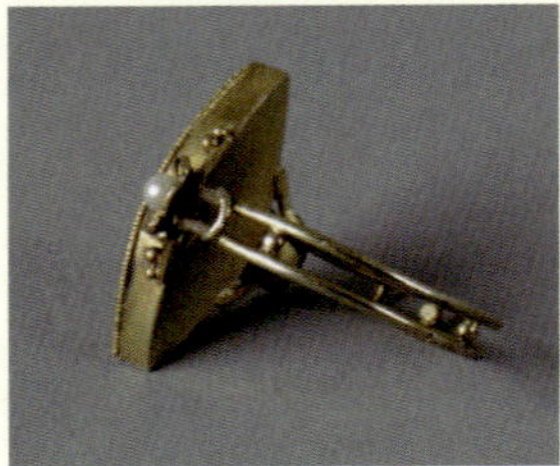

Fig. 78 a, b. Marquise bezel comprising Roman mosaic in the form of a Chi Rho decorated with flowers and leaves. The setting is decorated with a row of purled work. The shoulders are decorated with an applied filigree flower set with a pearl, double wire shank has three connecting gold beads. There is a small, but illegible, stamp on the outside of the shank at the back. 'Coloured' gold. Italian, *circa* 1865. Bezel 18x8mm, shank diameter 16mm.

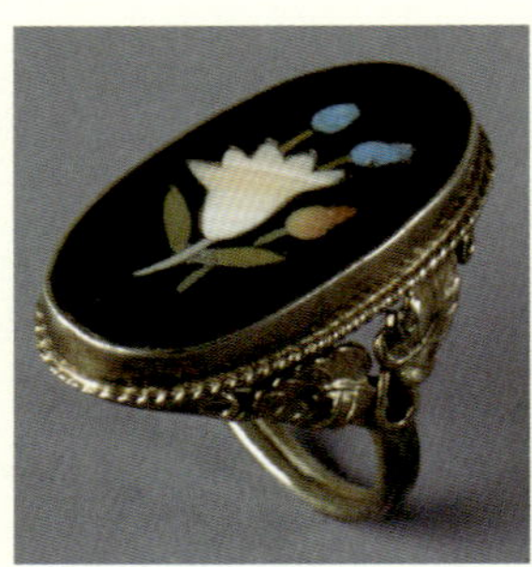

Fig. 79. Oval bezel of pietra dura, *circa* 1860, in a floral design with purled work applied to the base of the rub-over setting. The shoulders are decorated with vine leaves and tendrils, double wires are soldered together to form the shank. Yellow gold setting. *Circa* 1890. Bezel 26x15mm, shank diameter 18mm.

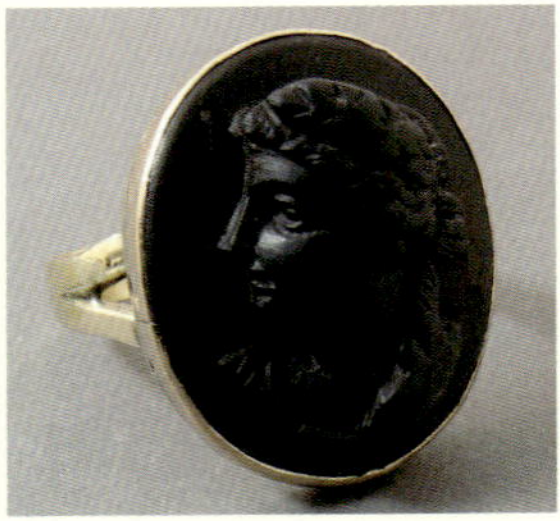

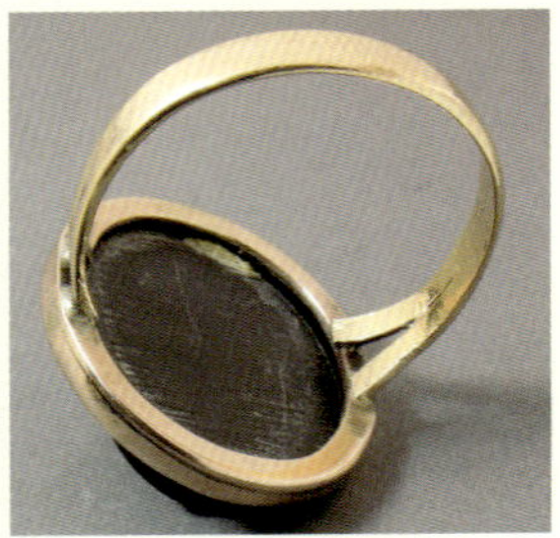

Fig. 80 a, b. Black lava bezel, *circa* 1855, attached to modern hoop. The lava bezel came from another piece of jewellery such as a bracelet or a necklace. If the ring were original, the bezel would be curved to fit the finger, and the join of the shoulders to the bezel would be smoother. Bezel 22x19mm, hoop diameter 20mm.

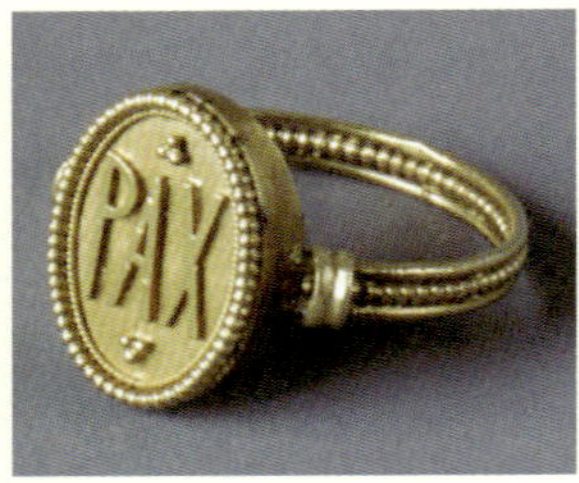

Fig. 81. PAX in raised letters is set inside a border of knurled work and an inner row of purled work. Transverse ribs cross the triple wire shank (the middle section is beaded) at the shoulders. An illegible mark is stamped into the outer edge of the shank, at the back. 'Coloured' gold. Italian, mid-nineteenth century. Bezel 12.5x9mm, shank diameter 16mm, width 2mm.

A number of Gothic-style rings were produced in this period. It is easy to recognize these rings with their geometric designs, Tudor roses, fleurs-de-lis and trefoils. (Fig. 76)

Renaissance-style jewellery became popular in the 1850s and continued to be so until the end of the century. The distinctive elements incorporated into nineteenth-century Renaissance work included colourful enamelling, strapwork, scroll-work and even a reclining figure on each shoulder. (Fig. 77)

Mosaic work in all forms of jewellery, including rings, was brought back to Britain from Italy. Roman mosaic, which was formed from tiny pieces of tesserae, was particularly popular from about 1840 to 1865. The bezel was often oval or a short, plump marquise shape which allowed ample room for the representations of architectural scenes, religious symbols, insects or birds so frequently depicted in these colourful rings. (Fig. 78 a, b) Florentine mosaic of inlaid hardstone, known as pietra dura, was also popular at the same time. Pietra dura usually employed floral motifs in a ground of black onyx. The mounts of these Italian mosaic rings were sometimes unadorned or decorated with beading and wirework. (Fig. 79)

Travellers also returned to England with lava jewellery from Italy. Lava came in shades of grey or brown, occasionally pale pink and yellow, and it was usually carved as a cameo. Many rings found today were converted from another piece of jewellery, such as a section from a linked bracelet or necklace, and set into a modern ring mount. (Fig. 80 a, b)

Rings with religious symbolism were also purchased in Italy by travellers. A great show of religious feeling was demonstrated in the Victorian period, so such rings were popular. (Fig. 81) (Fig. 82 a, b)

Serpent rings were worn during this period, but fewer were made than in the later years of the century. Some were embellished with diamonds, garnets, pearls or turquoises in the head of the snake; others were pavé-set in their entirety, while a rare design was made in flexible form; this might be enamelled, in royal blue or turquoise blue, and set with diamonds and garnets. A few cluster rings had tiny snakes wriggling along the shoulders, and occasionally a serpent surrounded the bezel.

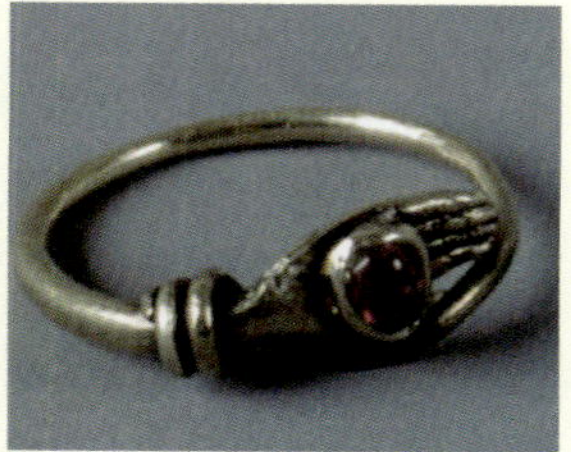
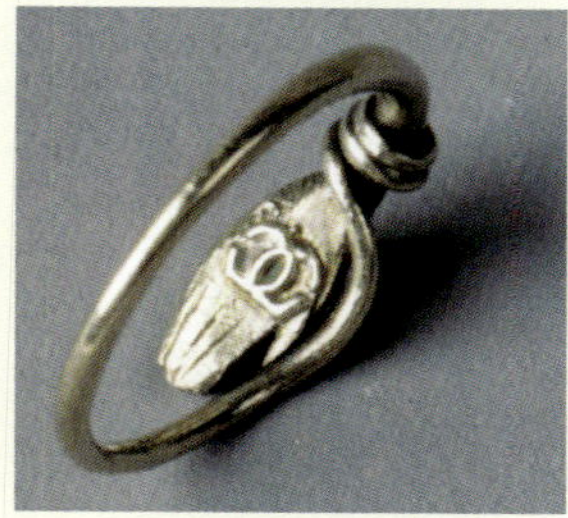

Fig. 82 a, b. The palm of a hand set with a cabochon ruby in a rub-over setting. The end of the round wire shank circles the wrist to form a cuff. The Castellani mark (overlapping back-to-back Cs) is applied to the back of the hand. Pale yellow gold. Mid-nineteenth century. Hand to cuff is 12mm, shank diameter 16mm.

[1840 - 1860]

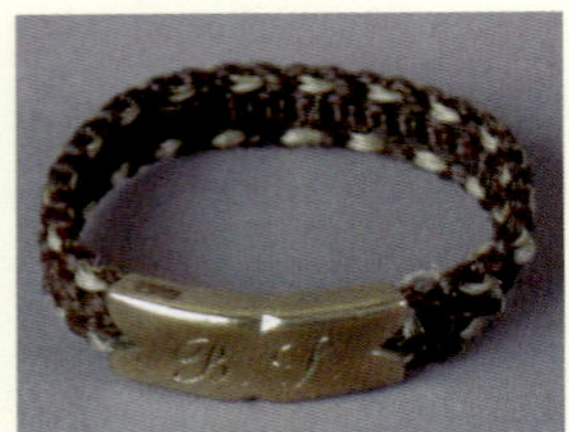

Fig. 83. Brown hair edged with blond hair is secured with a pale gold slide, engraved with the initials B.I. *Circa* 1850. Bezel 5x9mm, hoop diameter 20mm, 4.5mm wide.

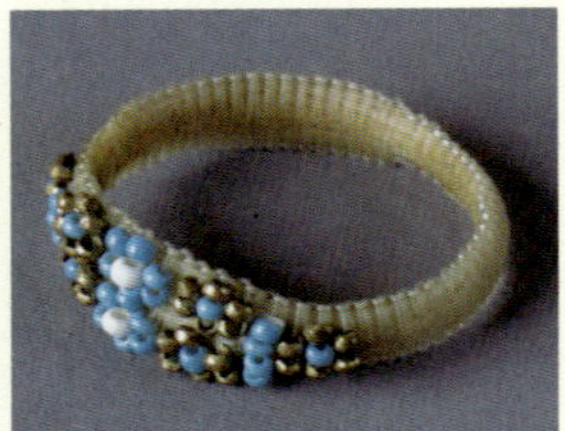

Fig. 84. Cat gut ring decorated with white, copper and turquoise glass bead flowers. *Circa* 1840. Bezel depth 7mm, hoop diameter 18mm, width 4mm.

Human hair, from the head of a loved one, was frequently incorporated into rings. Some were formed almost entirely from plaited hair; the ends were secured by a hollowed rectangular section of gold, engraved with the initials of the loved one. (Fig. 83) The tighter the hair was plaited the firmer the ring: a loosely plaited ring could be stretched to fit different-sized fingers. These rings are surprisingly resilient but would not survive the rigours of daily wear today. Other rings contained hair enclosed in a gem-set bezel.

Occasionally hair was displayed in place of gems, as the following passage from *The Woman in White* by Wilkie Collins, set in 1850, illustrates:

> "Dear Laura" was to receive his present - a shabby ring, with her affectionate uncle's hair for an ornament, instead of a precious stone, and with a heartless French inscription inside, about congenial sentiments and eternal friendship - "dear Laura" was to receive this tender tribute from my hands immediately, so that she might have plenty of time to recover from the agitation produced by the gift before she appeared in Mr. Fairlie's presence. (p.170)

Natural or dyed horsehair was also used in hair jewellery. This type of jewellery became so popular that plaited hair could be obtained from specialist firms producing it in a variety of designs. In a similar vein, the occasional ring was made from cat gut. (Fig. 84)

Signet rings of this period were set with bloodstone, white cornelian, banded onyx, or nicolo; they could also be fashioned entirely of gold, with a coat-of-arms or monogram carved into a shield-shaped bezel. The shoulders of signet rings were decorated with one of a variety of moulded patterns, with engraving and enamelling (1850s and 1860s), or were plain. See Fig. 77.

Decorative ring shoulders of the 1840s and 1850s were sometimes fashioned from pierced asymmetrical or symmetrical work. Others chased (1840s) or plain, were divided, then decorated between the fork with a variety of designs such as a flower, an engraved leaf, a three-leaf clover, a single gem, a row of graduated gold beads or gems. The solid, spatula-shaped or asymmetrical outline was in fashion during this period, and in the mid-1850s was often decorated with finely engraved scrolls and flowers. Embossed work (Fig. 85) and carved designs were popular, as was wirework that twisted around the divided shoulders of Italian souvenir rings. Engraved decoration was used from the early 1840s, but it was in the mid-1850s that it became particularly prevalent.

Ring shanks were channelled, reeded, engraved, asymmetrical, occasionally decorated with diamond-shaped facets which caught the light, or were plain and D-shaped in section. Substantial single or double wire shanks were still popular in the 1840s, but by the late 1850s the fashion had declined.

Wire decoration was often applied to the galleries of rings and was the forerunner of the rather fussy work produced in the 1860s and 1870s. Rows of tiny beading (individual beads if handmade or in a strip if machine-made) were applied halfway down the depth of the gallery in upward or downward curves, (Fig. 86) and some designs had widely spaced beads attached to cramp settings, see Fig. 61. Stamped asymmetrical galleries were a feature of the 1850s, see Fig. 62.

The most common settings for gems were the cramp (either open or closed at the back), the conical cut-down collet and the crimped collet. The rub-over or glass setting was used for cameos and for cluster rings containing a large gemstone. In the 1850s the transition was made from the cramp to the claw setting. Open or closed settings were used with equal frequency; some rings employed both forms.

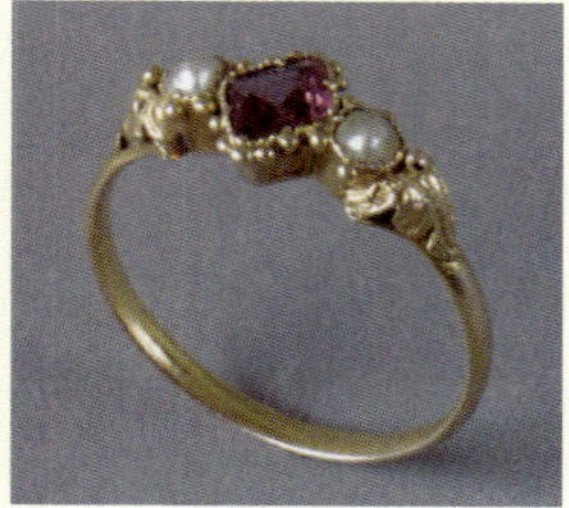

Fig. 85. Diamond-shaped, open-set almandine garnet flanked by two closed-backed pearls in cramp settings embellished with tiny beads. An embossed, foliate design forms the shoulders, plain, D-shaped shank. Yellow gold. A girl's ring, judging by its small proportions. *Circa* 1850-1860. Centre setting 8x5mm, shank diameter 17mm.

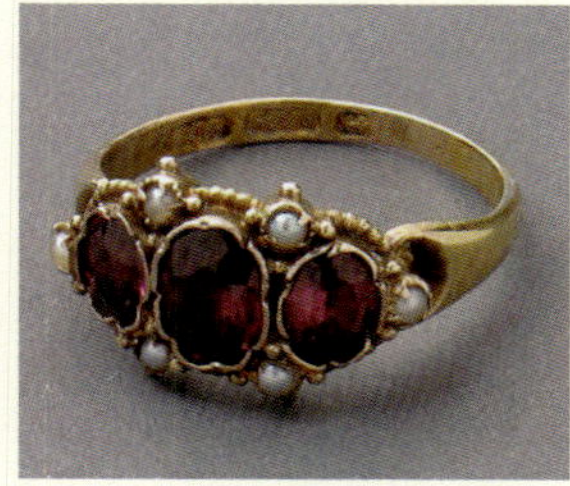

Fig. 86. Almandine garnets in closed-back crimped collet settings, pearls in cramp settings are bordered by a strip of beading. Plain D-shaped shank expands slightly ending in a single scallop at the shoulders. Originally the gold was 'coloured' but resizing removed the finish. Birmingham, 15(.625)ct. yellow gold. Damaged date and maker's marks. *Circa* 1860. Bezel 9.5x18mm, shank diameter 17mm.

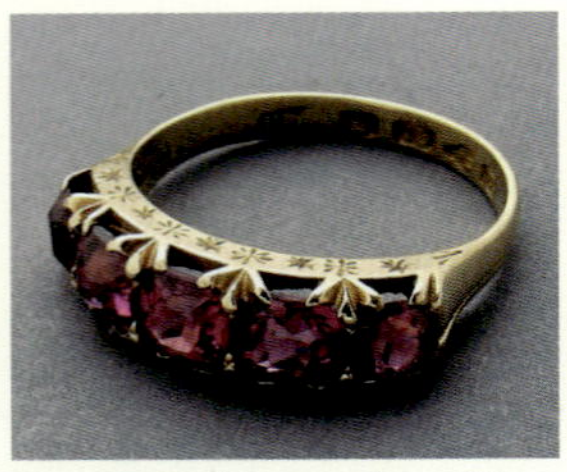

Fig. 87. Half-hoop ring of five claw-set, cushion-shaped almandine garnets. Flowers and stars decorate the gallery, a deep groove extends the length of the shoulders, plain shank. Hallmarked: 1883, Chester, 18ct. yellow gold. Bezel depth 5mm, gallery depth 3mm, shank diameter 17mm.
Reginald Davis (Oxford) Ltd.

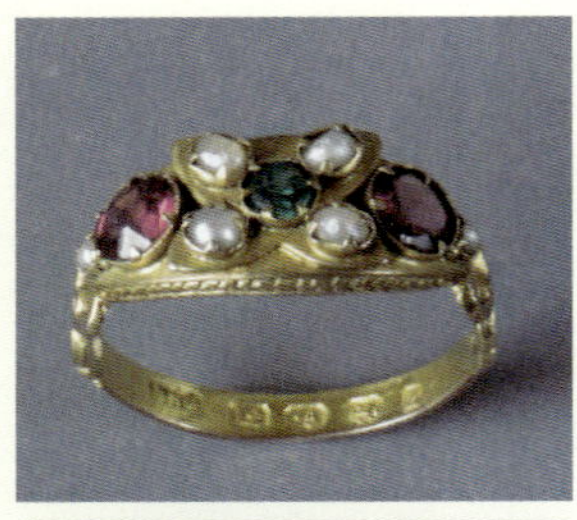

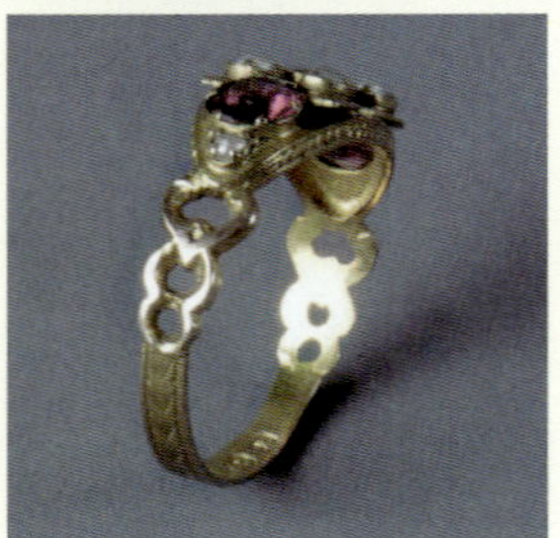

Fig. 88 a, b. Gothic-style ring. Boat-shaped bezel has an applied quatrefoil design decorated with a green stone in an open-back cramp setting, and four half pearls, flanked by almandine garnets and pearls. Openwork shoulders, engraved shank. Hallmarked:1874, Birmingham, 12(.5) ct. 'coloured' gold, maker's mark L.H.J. Bezel 8x22mm, shank diameter 17mm, width 2mm.

1860-1885

During this period mass-production of jewellery in general reached its height; however, rings continued to receive a certain amount of finishing by hand. (Fig. 87) Large quantities of almost identical styles were produced, such as the serpent, gypsy, buckle, cluster and half-hoop. The emphasis was transferred gradually from ornate settings to simpler metal work and to the best means of displaying gemstones. The availability of diamonds increased when the South African diamond mines opened in 1867, and diamond cutting improved greatly, with the advent of power operated tools in the 1870s. Eventually round brilliants superseded the cushion-cut. Curiously, one finds a few rings set with large rose-cut diamonds during the 1870s and 1880s. Small rose-cut diamonds were used in quite a number of rings for decorative effect until the end of the century. Rings became somewhat more substantial in appearance, and their silhouettes more streamlined to match the fashions of the period.

At the start of mechanization, there was tremendous enthusiasm for the new method of making jewellery that could cut the cost of an item by half. The following excerpt from *The Queen*, 30 November 1867, states:

Novelties
Machine-made Jewellery

We have just paid a visit to the establishment of Mr. E.W. Streeter of 37, Conduit-street, Bond-street, and have had submitted to us numerous specimens of gold ornaments produced by the aid of machinery. By the application of the appliances used by Mr. Streeter, the tedious process of hand punching and setting up in detail is in great measure done away with . . . and the despatch [sic] with which this is done, are so great, that a saving of over 50 per cent. is, we are assured, effected by the purchaser. (p.427)

The demand for jewellery in large quantities soon
led to a decline in the quality of both design and
manufacture. Mass-production of poor designs and
light, flimsy settings became commonplace. (Fig.
88 a, b) (Fig. 89) (Fig. 90) Machinery curtailed the
jeweller's inventiveness; he had to confine himself to
the capabilities of the machine, whereas a skilled hand-
craftsman had no such restrictions. Dissatisfaction with
these shortcomings was expressed in the following letter
to the editor of a new trade magazine, *The Goldsmith*,
which was published in the edition for 1 May 1869:

Norwich, April 30th 1869

Dear Sir, - I write to wish you every success. If
you can induce the manufacturers to improve
their designs, to make them more artistic,
you will be doing a great service. I often name
the question put to me - why cannot you sell
us jewellery such as we buy in Rome? The
truth is the manufacturers, both jewellers and
silversmiths, think only of how much they can
get out of an article; they will not even take the
trouble of getting an elegant design. It takes
no more silver or gold to make a good thing
than it does to make a bad one. One of your
correspondents says we don't want to know
about Cellini; I say we want to know more of
him. Again wishing you every success, I am, sir,
yours truly,

THEODORE ROSSI

Claims were made that some of the fine, artistic
jewellery sold in London was made in Birmingham. A
contributor to *The Resources, Products and Industrial
History of Birmingham*, in 1866 observed:

It is only necessary to walk from the Bank to
Hyde Park to enable any person to form an
idea of the ingenuity, skill and taste of the
Birmingham artisans. The shopkeeper will
not voluntarily admit that his articles are
Birmingham manufacture, yet we believe we
speak within bounds if we say at least 1/2 of
all the gold and silver work seen in the shops of
London jewellers is the production of this town.
(p.453)

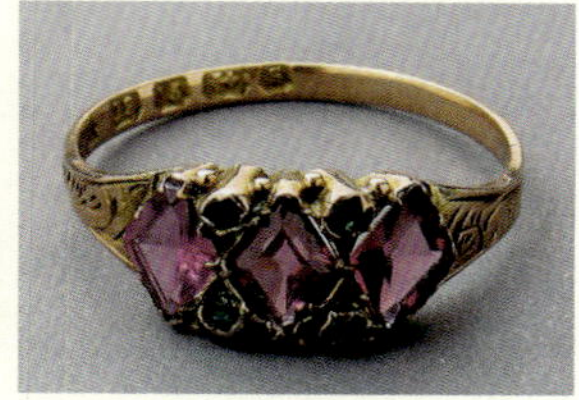

Fig. 89. Bezel comprising
three almandine garnets and
four emerald sparks in open-
back cramp settings, flat
spatula-shaped shoulders
taper to the shank, both
engraved. Hallmarked:
Birmingham, 12(.5)ct. rose
gold, maker's mark D.G,
1867. Bezel 7x13mm, shank
diameter 17mm.

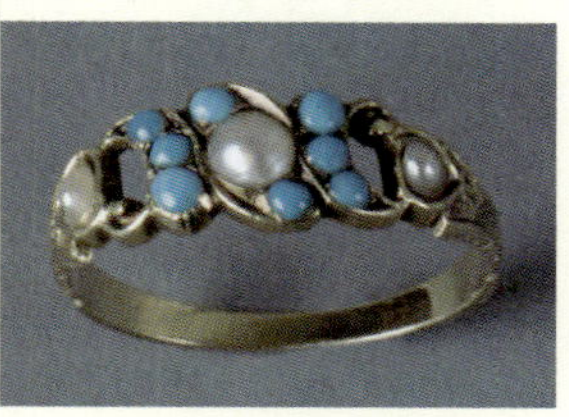

Fig. 90. Asymmetric bezel set
with pearls and turquoises,
with a single pearl at the top
of each engraved shoulder.
Shank is engraved in its
entirety. Yellow gold. *Circa*
1860-1870. Bezel depth
7mm, shank diameter 17mm.

[1860 - 1885]

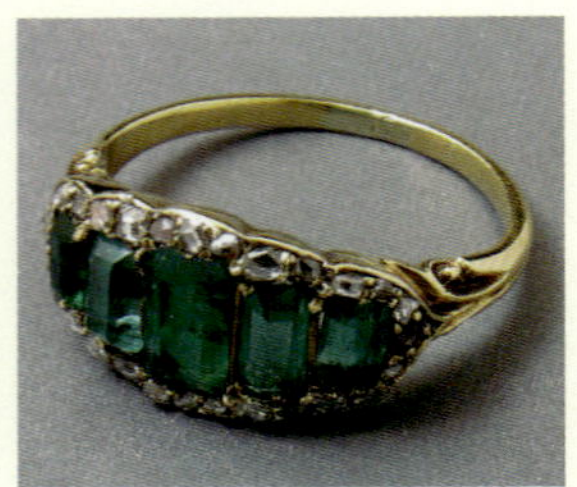

Fig. 91. Five open-set emeralds bordered by 28 closed-set rose-cut diamonds. Carved, scrolled shoulders, single groove in hoop. Yellow gold. *Circa* 1870.

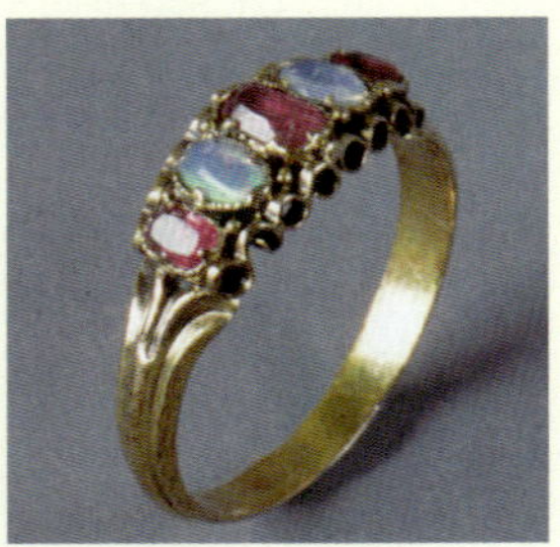

Fig. 92. Half-hoop comprising rubies (set closed) and water opals (set open) in cramp settings, figure-of-eight wirework decorates the gallery, grooved D-shaped shank divides at the shoulders. Yellow gold. *Circa* 1865-1880. Bezel 6x15.5mm, shank diameter 16mm, width 2mm.

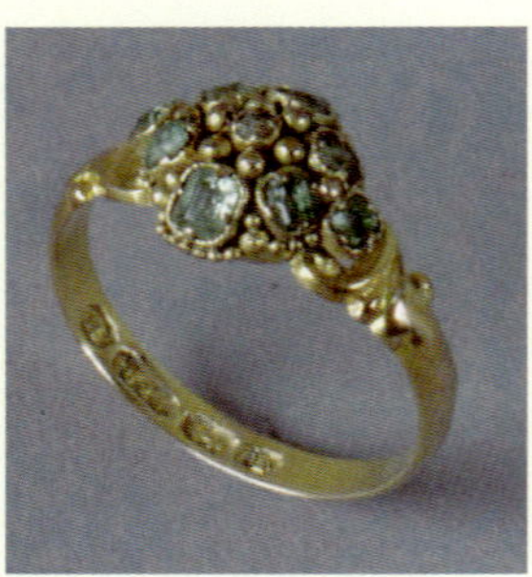

Fig. 93 Boss-shaped bezel set with a diamond spark surrounded by six beads and pale emeralds, with strip beading decorating the outer edge of the bezel. Carved asymmetric design decorates the shoulders, plain shank D-shaped in section. Empty hair compartment. Hallmarked: Birmingham, 15(.625) ct. yellow gold, 1868. No maker's mark. Bezel 9x12mm, shank diameter 16mm.

Cassell's *Guide to the International Exhibition,* 1872, in the article 'Jewellery', gives an interesting description of four styles of rings:

> Among the articles exhibited are the ladies' fancy gem and diamond rings, set with diamonds, rubies, emeralds, pearls, and turquoises, and fancy cluster rings. Among many beautiful articles especially deserving attention, we may select a few specimens of the jeweller's art, a lady's gipsy ring set with four brilliants, and roses on a new ornamental thread setting, the delicate carving on which was done after the stones were set in the solid gold; an exquisitely finished half-hoop ring, with ruby centre and emerald ends, round which are set thirty-eight rose diamonds; a fancy cluster ring, set with opals, diamonds and rubies, with a star in the centre and richly carved setting; and a ring containing fifteen pearls, interlaced with a continuous thread. Of these articles Messrs. T. Willis and Co. are conspicuous exhibitors.(p.35) (Fig. 91)

One easily recognizable group of rings, widely produced from about 1860-1885, was the dainty half-hoop, wide-bezel or cluster ring set with a single variety of gem or a colourful combination, usually in cramp settings. Amethyst, chrysoberyl, diamond, emerald, garnet, opal, pearl, ruby, turquoise and paste were used most often in these rings. The galleries were usually decorated with a figure-of-eight or an ornate wirework design. By the 1870s the use of beading on the gallery or as a border around the bezel had declined. The shoulders and shank could be completely engraved, or the shoulders could be made of pierced work supported by a plain or engraved shank; alternatively the shoulders might be carved and set on a plain or grooved shank. Gem-set 'regard' and 'dearest' rings often fall into this group, and were made until about 1875. (Fig. 92, Fig. 93, Fig. 94, Fig. 95 a, b)

During the 1860s and 1870s, three-stone rings were fashioned with a plain hoop supporting finely carved galleries and shoulders. (Fig. 96 a, b) Many of these rings held fine-quality gems, often two diamonds flanking a coloured gem, held secure by claws or by tiny collets containing rose-cut diamonds. Half-hoop rings with stones set in a variety of claw settings were now becoming fashionable. (Fig. 97)

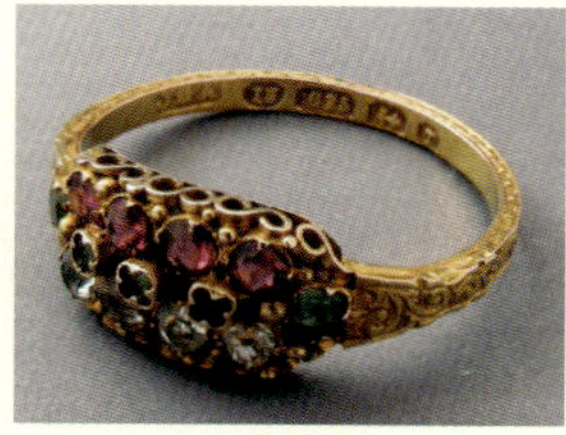

Fig. 94. The bezel comprises three rows of gems in cramp settings: almandine garnets set open, emeralds set closed, white quartz set open, reverse of bezel is engraved 'M. Wishart'. Figure-of-eight wirework applied to gallery, shank engraved on edges and outer surface. Hallmarked: Birmingham, 15(.625) ct. 'coloured' gold, maker's mark J*A (seven pointed star between the letters), 1868. Bezel 8x15mm, shank diameter 18mm, width 1.5mm.

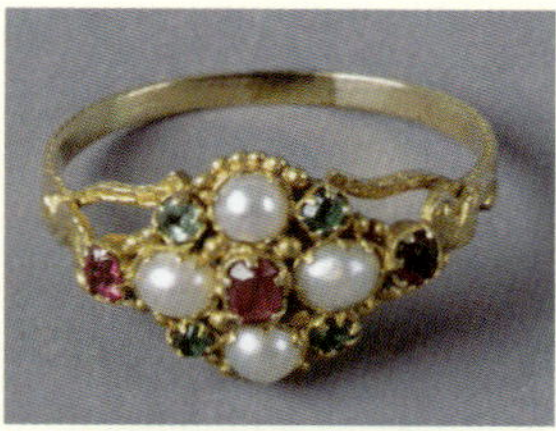

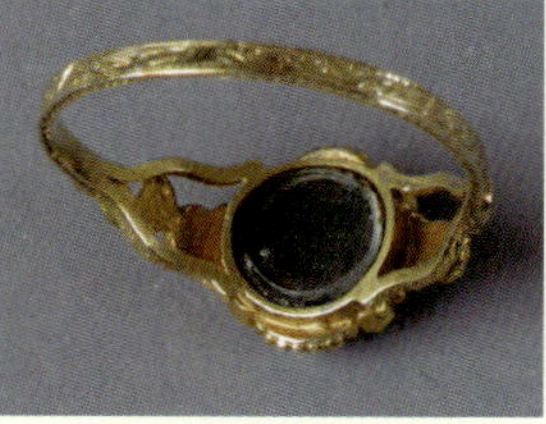

Fig. 95 a, b. Cluster bezel edged with beading and set with pearls, emeralds and rubies in cramp settings, and a hair compartment set in the back of the bezel. Split, engraved shoulders set on an engraved hoop. Yellow gold. *Circa* 1865. Bezel 12x16mm, locket diameter 8mm, hoop diameter 19mm, width 1.5mm.

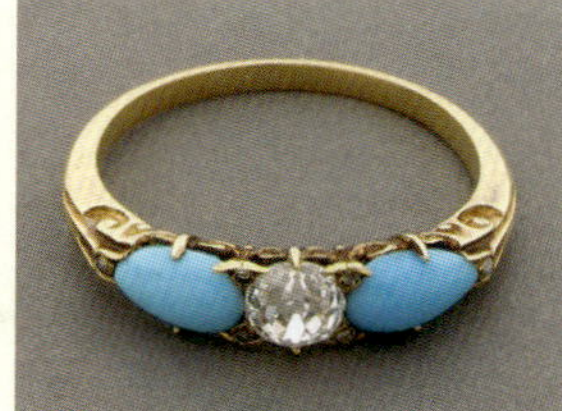

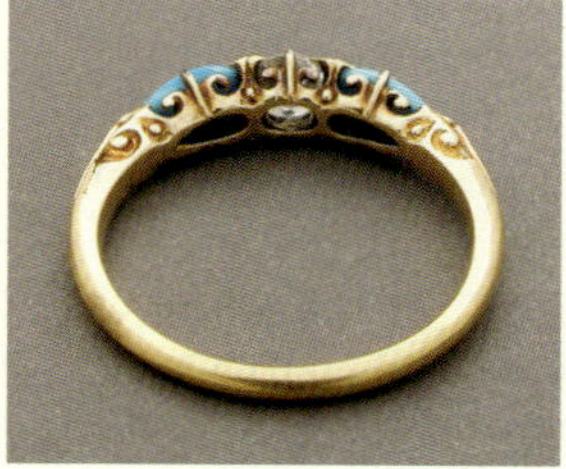

Fig. 96 a, b. A chunky brilliant-cut diamond secured by tiny rose-cut diamonds in triangular settings flanked by tear-drop shaped Persian turquoise. A small diamond is set at the top of each carved shoulder. Openwork scrolls and claws form the gallery. Plain shank. Yellow gold. *Circa* 1870. Gallery 3mm deep, shank diameter 16mm.

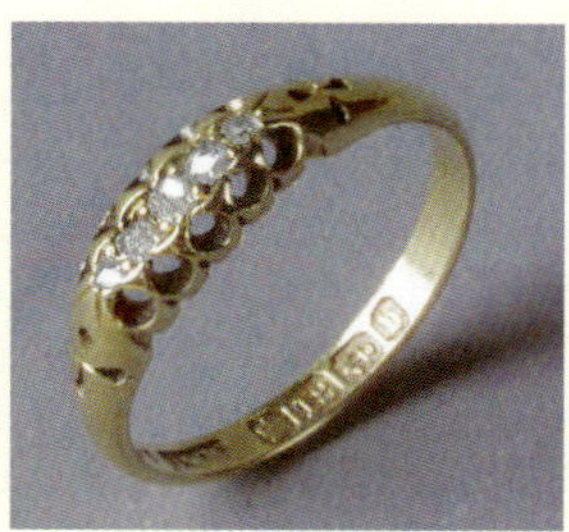

Fig. 97. Half-hoop of five claw-set rose-cut diamonds, hollow petal-shaped decoration embellish the narrow shoulders, plain D-shaped shank. Hallmarked: Birmingham, 18ct. pale yellow gold, maker's mark G.W.W., 1875. In addition, 753 is stamped inside the shank. Shank diameter 17.5mm.

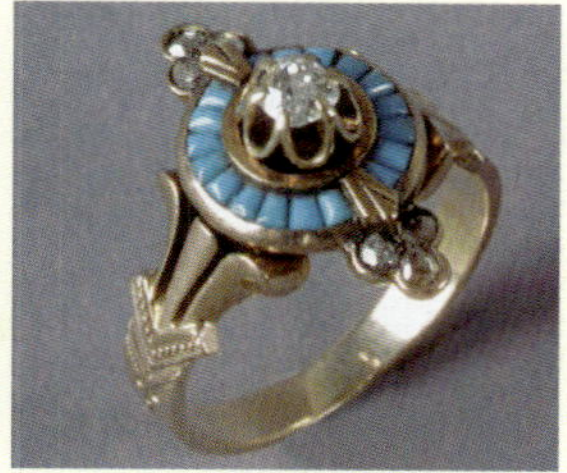

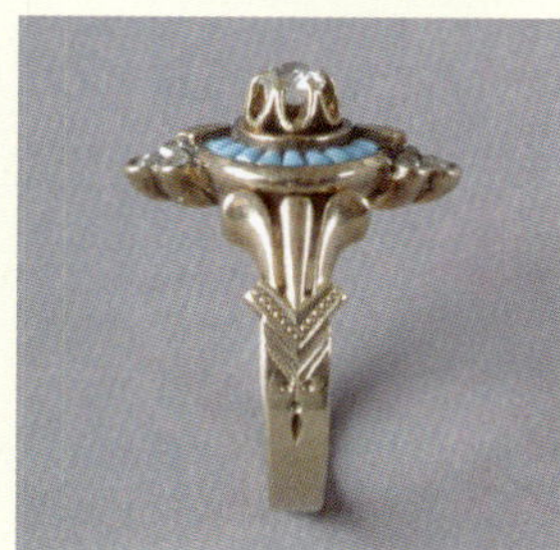

Fig. 98 a, b. Egyptian-style ring comprising a cushion-shaped brilliant in a claw setting surrounded by calibré-cut turquoises and trefoil terminals holding rose-cut diamonds in glass settings. Three radiating panels above V-shaped beading form the shoulders, plain, flat shank. Rose gold. *Circa* 1870. Bezel 18x10mm, shank diameter 16mm, width 2.5mm.

[1860 - 1885]

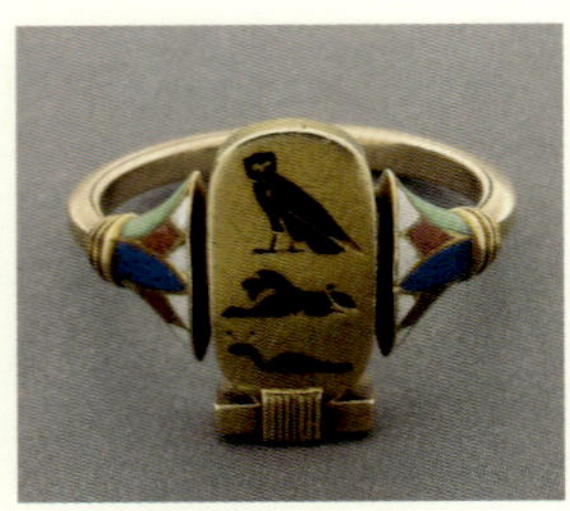

Fig. 99. Egyptian-style ring comprises a cartouche decorated with enamelled hieroglyphic characters. Shoulders are decorated with a lotus flower, enamelled in pale green, white, red and blue, set on transverse ribs. Plain shank, squared in section, has been reduced in size by adding a thin inner hoop. Yellow gold. *Circa* 1870. Cartouche 13.5x6.5mm, shank diameter 17mm.

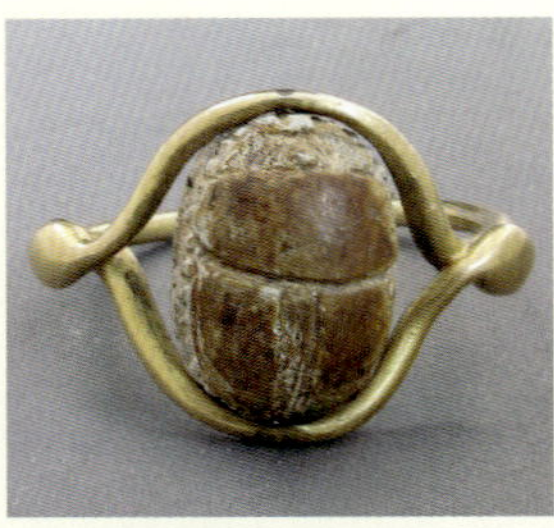

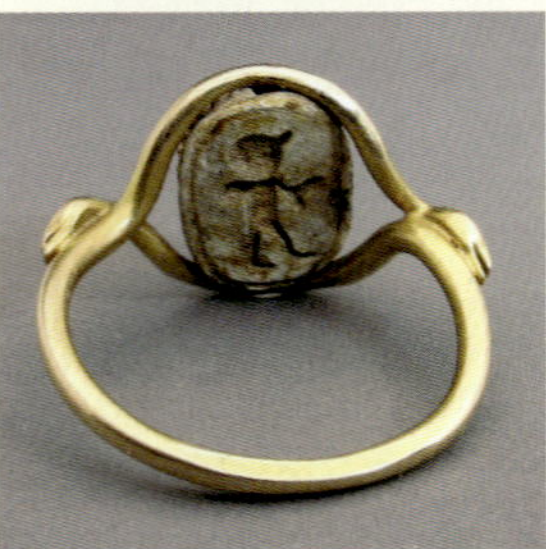

Fig. 100 a, b. Antique scarab, from the second Intermediate period Dynasties XIII - XVII B.C., possibly from the 17th Dynasty B.C., set in a yellow gold mount comprising a round hoop which surrounds the scarab, ending as a serpent's head on each shoulder. *Circa* 1870. Scarab 12.5x8mm, hoop diameter 18mm.

With the opening of the Suez Canal in 1869, renewed public interest in the Egyptian style was reflected in the jewellery of the 1870s and 1880s. The style was well represented at the South Kensington international exhibitions that took place each year from 1871 to 1874. Rings were decorated with Egyptian motifs such as the lotus plant, hieroglyph and scarab - the latter made from glass, ceramic or carved stone. Enamel, mosaic, carved gems and calibré-cut turquoise were often used to decorate Egyptian-style rings. (Fig. 98 a, b) (Fig. 99) (Fig. 100 a, b)

The gypsy ring became fashionable in the late 1860s; its popularity with both men and women grew as the nineteenth century progressed. (Fig.101) The Oxford English Dictionary sheds some light on the subject:

> 1880 BREWER *Reader's Handbk.* 1885 385/1 Gipsey Ring, a flat gold ring, with stones let into it, at given distances. So called because the stones were originally Egyptian pebbles-that is, agate and jasper.

The gypsy ring was a simple hoop which expanded at the front to accommodate gems which were deeply set into the gold; the girdle of the stone was level with the surface of the metal, and the crown of the gem appeared only slightly above it. Some of these rings were domed at the front, while others were thick but flat. Men's rings were much heavier than the ladies' styles. Some gypsy rings were carved with star-like rays that appeared to emanate from the stone. The gem was secured by tiny grains of gold at the base of each ray. Other gypsy rings were carved on the shoulders or around the gems. The most frequently used gems were diamond, ruby, sapphire, garnet, pearl, turquoise or coral.

Other ring designs of the period had a simple form similar to the gypsy ring, but wider at the bezel and much daintier in their dimensions. (Fig. 102) (Fig. 103) (Fig. 104) Another particular style, used either as a decorative or a mourning ring, had vertical or diagonal alternating bands of gems and enamel; the enamel was usually royal blue, black or turquoise, and the gems were pearls or diamonds. (Fig. 105) Yet another distinctive ring had a boat-shaped recess holding five gems secured with grains of gold.(Fig. 106)

A notable fashion, worn by both men and women, lasting from about 1860 to 1880, was the applied diamond-set

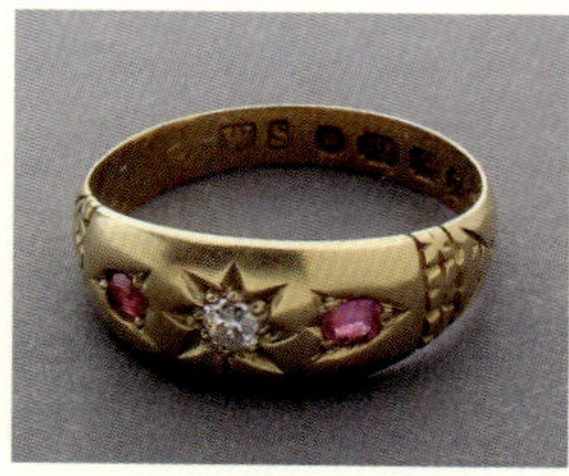

Fig. 101. Gypsy ring set with a brilliant-cut diamond in a star setting, two rubies in shield-shaped settings, geometric designs on shoulders. Hallmarked: Birmingham, 22ct. 'coloured' yellow gold, maker's mark W S, 1868. There is an additional mark of 18 and a crown near the back of the bezel. Bezel depth 7mm, hoop diameter 17mm.

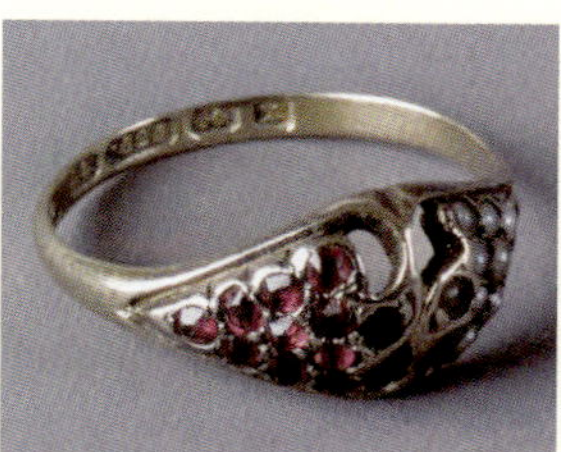

Fig. 102. Bezel comprises a bunch of red (garnet) and a bunch of white (pearl) grapes on a narrow plain shank. Hallmarked: Birmingham, 15(.625) ct. yellow gold, 1872. One bunch of grapes measures 8x10mm, shank diameter 17.5mm.

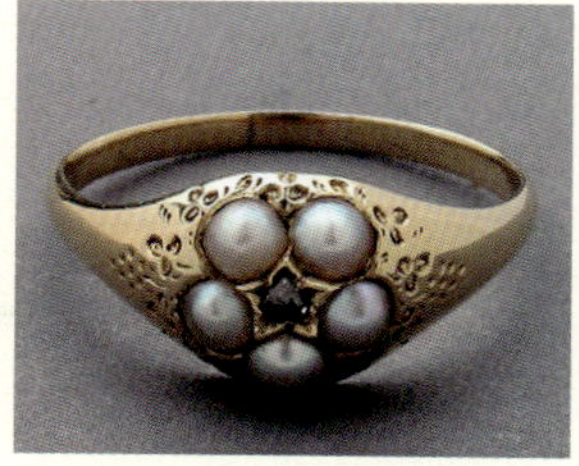

Fig. 103. Plain gold shank expands to accommodate a cluster of five gypsy-set pearls around a diamond spark set in a gold star. A lightly tooled design of grapes and leaves surrounds the pearls. A hair compartment is set in the reverse of the bezel. Pale yellow gold. *Circa* 1860-1870. Cluster 7mm in diameter, shank diameter 17mm.

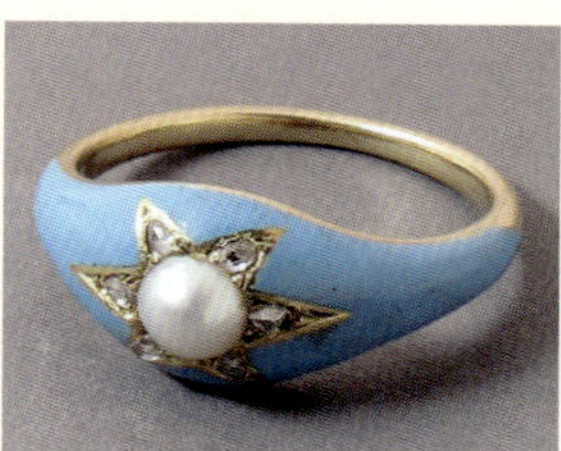

Fig. 104. Turquoise enamel surrounds a six-pointed star set with a half pearl and rose-cut diamonds. Oval hair compartment inside the bezel. Plain shank. Yellow gold. *Circa* 1860. Shank diameter 16mm.

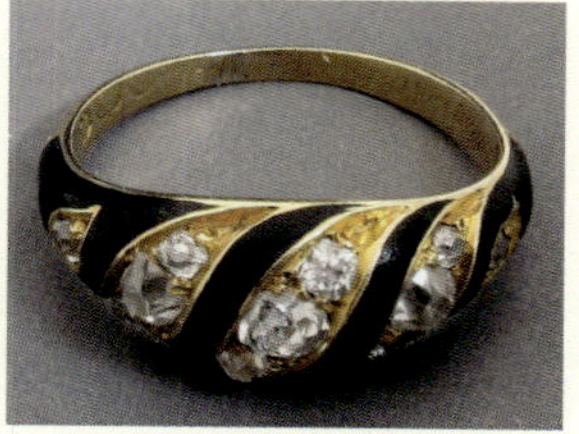

Fig. 105. Turban bezel is decorated with diagonal bands of brilliant-cut diamonds and black enamel that extends onto the shoulders. Plain shank inscribed inside: 'Maria Elizabeth Pippett Obt. 4th May 18— —'. (Date partly erased). Hallmarked: London, 18ct. rich yellow gold, no date mark. *Circa* 1870.

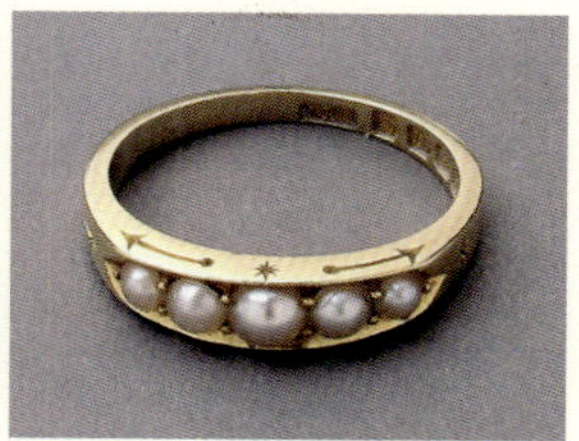

Fig. 106. Half pearls recessed into a boat-shaped bezel, secured with gold grains. Gallery is engraved with a star flanked by an arrow pointing towards the shoulders which are decorated with a single star. Plain shank, rectangular in section. Hallmarked: Birmingham, 18ct. yellow gold, maker's mark J.E.C., 1882. Bezel 4x17mm, shank diameter 16mm.

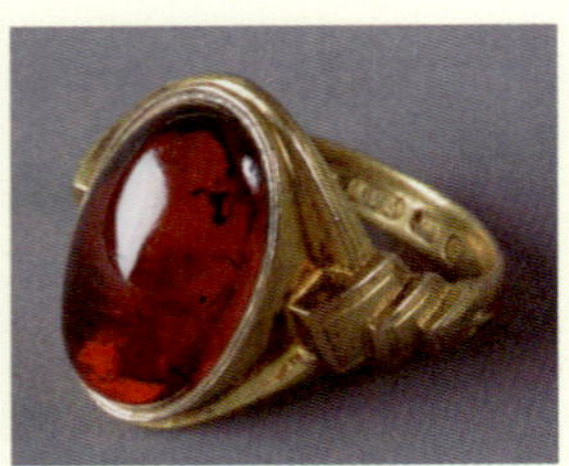

Fig. 107. Gentleman's ring set with a carbuncle in a closed-back Roman setting. The shoulders are designed with triple geometric shapes superimposed one upon the other, and engraving along the edges. Plain shank, D-shaped in section. Hallmarked: Birmingham, 15(.625) ct. 'coloured' gold, maker's mark H & U, 1874. Gemstone 17x10mm, shank diameter 19mm, width 3.5mm.

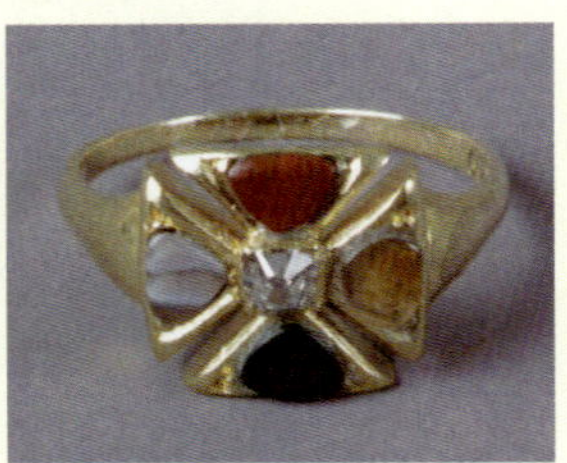

Fig. 108. Gentleman's Scottish pebble ring. The formée cross is set with different coloured agates around a rock crystal. Belcher shoulders, plain hoop. 18ct. yellow gold, maker's mark SW. *Circa* 1865. Bezel diameter 13mm, hoop diameter 20mm.

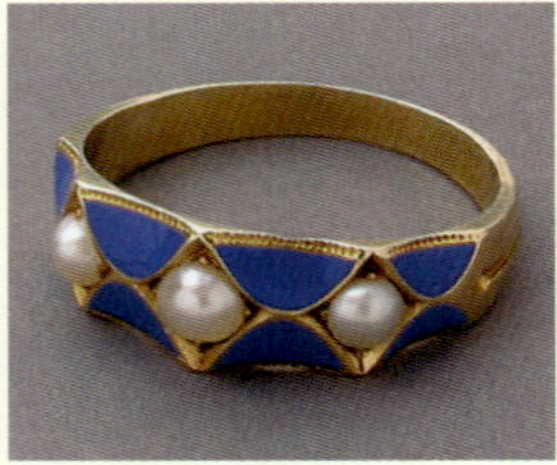

Fig. 109. Half-hoop decorated with three pearls and blue enamel in a scalloped design. A single groove decorates the middle of the shank. Marked: 18ct., maker's mark BG. Yellow gold. *Circa* 1860-1870. Bezel depth 7mm, shank diameter 18mm.

or pearl-set star or flower onto a cabochon amethyst or garnet. The cabochon was in a rub-over setting decorated with purled wire. Surviving examples are rare. Rings made with cabochon-cut dark blue glass were usually Continental. Carbuncle rings were also favoured by gentlemen at this time. (Fig. 107)

After the death of her husband, Prince Albert, in 1861, Queen Victoria was so distraught that she retreated to Balmoral in Scotland for long periods. A fashion for Scottish pebble jewellery lasted until about 1880, though very few rings were made. (Fig. 108)

Enamelling was still used to decorate rings in the 1860s and 1870s. (Fig. 109)

The single or double horseshoe ring became popular in the early 1880s (Fig. 110, Fig. 111).

A number of handsome neo-Renaissance rings were made in the 1870s and 1880s, but they were not common and were probably made to order.

In the 1870s there was a revival of single and double heart rings (Fig. 112) and marquise rings (Fig. 113, Fig 114); both had been fashionable during the eighteenth century. It is easy to distinguish the Victorian rings from earlier examples; they are much more substantial than the delicate eighteenth-century rings.

Many serpent rings from the 1870s onwards were fashioned without gems into single or multiple coils, and some were made from brass rather than gold, see Fig. 341 in the Glossary. Other serpents had gem-set eyes or gem-set heads. Generally the gold was plain, resulting in a rather uninteresting yet robust ring, suitable for daily wear by ladies and gentlemen. (Fig. 115) (Fig. 116)

Stone cameo rings regained favour in the 1860s. Cameos made from shell were sufficiently fragile that few rings set with it have survived, whereas stone and coral cameos set in rings can still be found with relative ease. (Fig. 117) (Fig. 118)

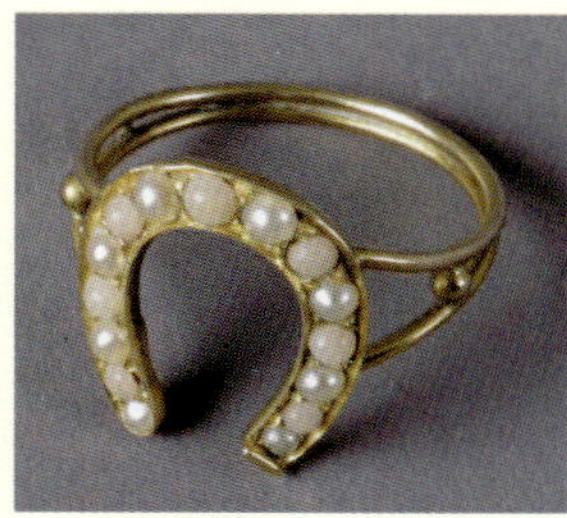

Fig. 110. Horseshoe bezel set with alternating pale pink corals and pearls, secured by tiny grains of gold, double wire shank separates at the shoulders above by a single bead. 'Coloured' gold. 1880s. Bezel 15x14mm, shank diameter 18mm.

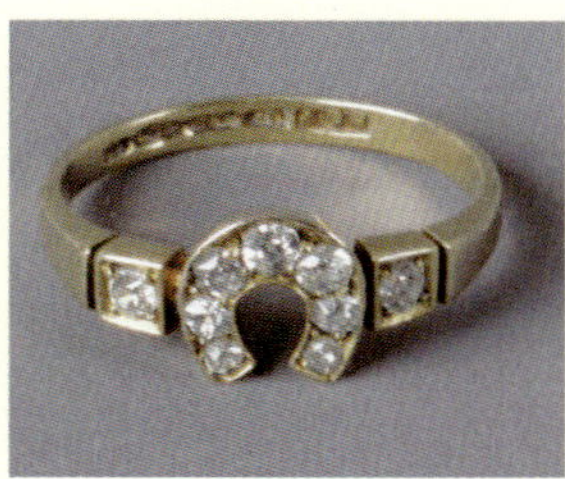

Fig. 111. Horseshoe bezel set with brilliant-cut diamonds, square shoulders also set with brilliants. Plain squared shank. Hallmarked: Chester 18ct. yellow gold, 1885. Bezel 8x7mm, shank diameter 18mm.

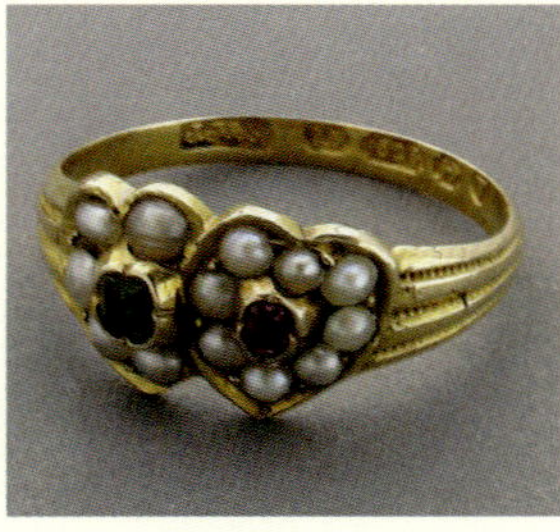

Fig. 112. Double heart bezel set with an emerald and a ruby surrounded by half pearls. Reeded shoulders, plain hoop. Hallmarked: Birmingham 15(.625) ct. 'coloured' gold, 1870. One heart 8x7mm, hoop diameter 18mm.

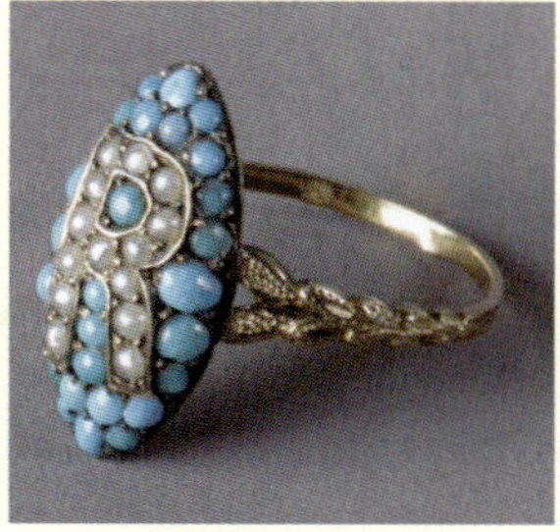

Fig. 113. A marquise bezel pavé-set with turquoises in silver, and pearls thread-set in gold in the letter R. A tooled, foliate design decorates the shoulders, narrow channelled shank with two French punches. *Circa* 1870. Bezel 18x10mm, shank diameter 16.5mm.

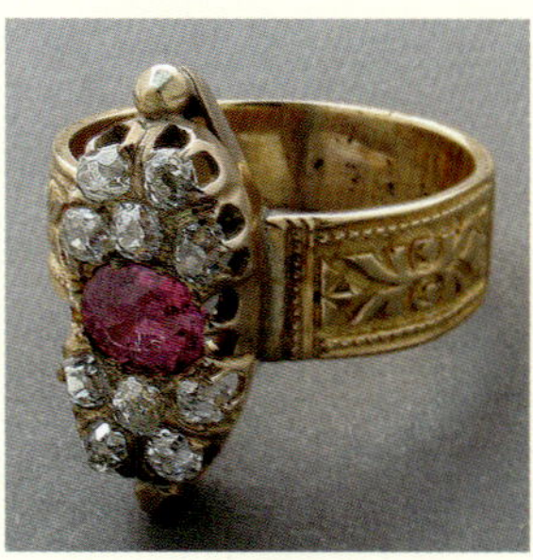

Fig. 114. Marquise bezel set with a ruby and old mine-cut diamonds in a crown claw setting. Wide, flat engraved shoulders. Wide, plain flat hoop. Yellow gold. American, *circa* 1870-1885.
Keith Austin Collection.

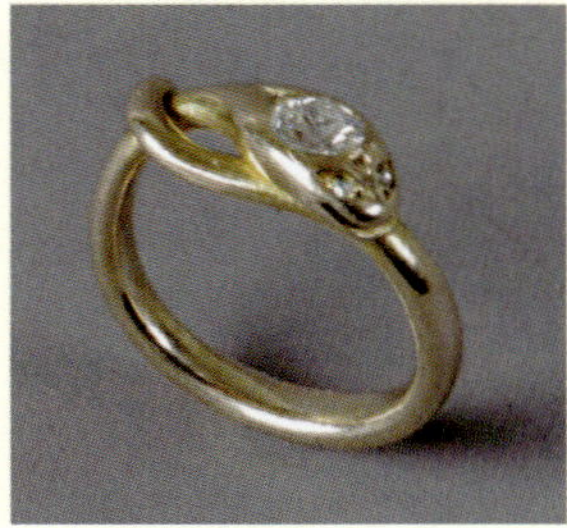

Fig. 115. Gentleman's rounded, single coil serpent ring set with a brilliant-cut diamond and pale emerald sparks in the head. The gold 'colouring' has worn away except beneath the head and tail; the gold now has a pink cast to it. The ring has been re-sized to fit a woman's finger. *Circa* 1870. Hoop diameter 17mm, width 3mm.

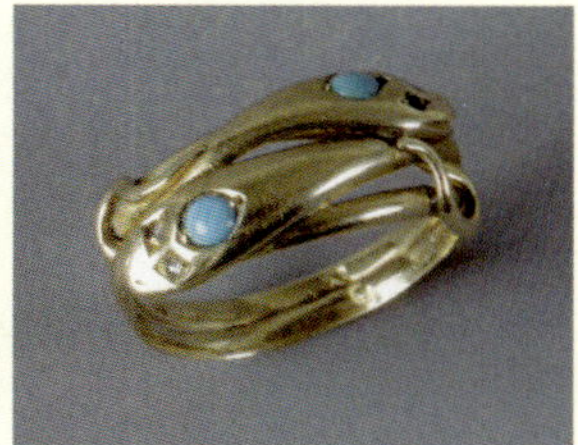

Fig. 116. Double snake ring, both heads set with a single turquoise, one head has rose-cut diamond eyes, the other has pale emerald eyes. Each hoop is hallmarked: Birmingham, 18ct. yellow gold, 1872. Hoop diameter 18.5mm, width 4mm.

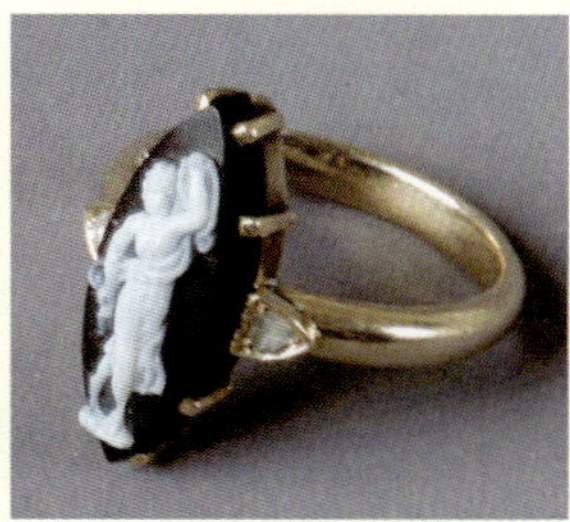

Fig. 117. Onyx cameo secured with eight claws. Rose-cut diamonds in a triangular frame decorate the shoulders. Plain D-shaped shank. Pale yellow gold. *Circa* 1875-1885. Bezel 18x7mm, shank diameter 16mm.

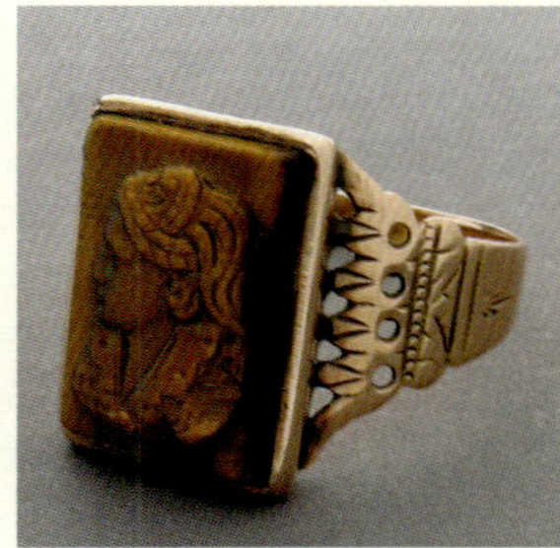

Fig. 118. Tiger's eye carved with a female bust in a glass setting. Ornate shoulders, tapering flat hoop. Inscribed inside the bezel: 1884, and a name that is now illegible. Rose gold. American.
Keith Austin Collection.

Cluster rings, some with a sizeable claw-set gem surrounded by smaller pearls or diamonds, were fashionable in the 1870s (Fig. 119 a, b) (Fig. 120) as were double cluster rings. (Fig. 121)

A single gem in a claw setting continued to be popular (Fig. 122), as was the buckle ring fashioned in 'coloured' gold and set with a few gems, the heavier examples being worn by gentlemen. Some buckle rings were flat, others were rounded, some had a hinged bezel (Fig. 123 a, b), and an occasional example was hinged in sections so that the ring could be removed from the finger by unbuckling it, see Fig. 75. Occasionally buckle rings were engraved and set with tiny gems.

Simple hoop rings made from silver, with mottos such as 'Regard' (Fig. 124), 'Forget Me Not' (Fig. 125 a, b, c) or 'Who Shall Separate Us' (Fig. 126 a, b, c), were fashionable during the early 1880s, but the widespread use of silver did not last long.

Rings with a narrow rectangular bezel or a long oval bezel were fashionable about 1880, and continued into the next period. Some of these rings were set with cameos or miniatures painted on porcelain, bordered with small pearls; others had openwork gem-set bezels; yet other rings were set with pearls and turquoise. (Fig. 127 a, b) (Fig. 128) (Fig. 129)

Shoulder designs used during this period were varied and included the following: asymmetrical (until about 1875) or symmetrical open-work (Fig. 130) (Fig. 131); engraved, sometimes enamelled during the 1870s; carved designs; flat or bevelled spatula-shaped with a straight wide end joined to the bezel by a narrow neck; hands supporting a cluster or heart bezel (to about 1875), not common; shoulders terminating in a triangular point; graduated gold beads, but not used with the frequency of earlier years; single or multiple square-set gems in the shoulders from 1880.

Shanks with decorative engraving were still widely produced until about 1875, but it is during this period that the transition to plain shanks occurred. Some were D-shaped in section, sometimes with a thin groove cut close to each edge; others were triangular or rectangular in section.

Mass-produced openwork galleries, in a variety of designs, were widely used from about 1870. The gallery raised the gems from the finger, allowing the light to pass beneath, thereby enhancing their appearance.

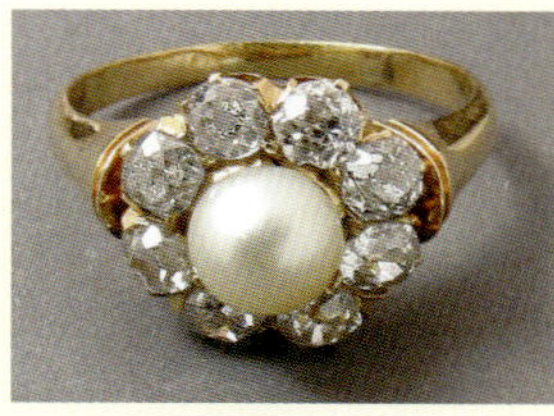

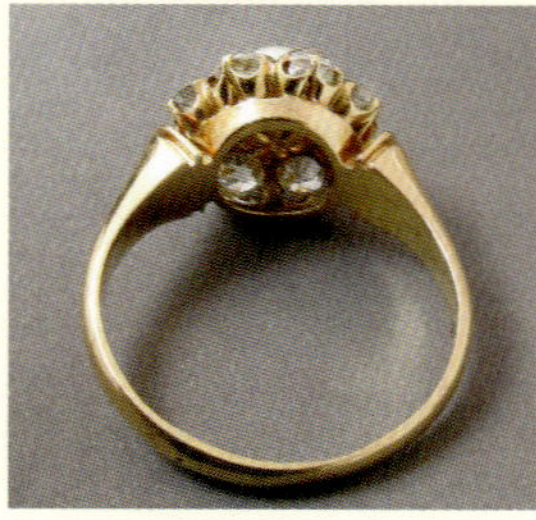

Fig. 119 a, b. A whole pearl surrounded by brilliant-cut diamonds in claw settings. Belcher shoulders, plain shank. Yellow gold. *Circa* 1870. Bezel diameter 11mm, gallery depth 3.5mm, shank 16.5 diameter.

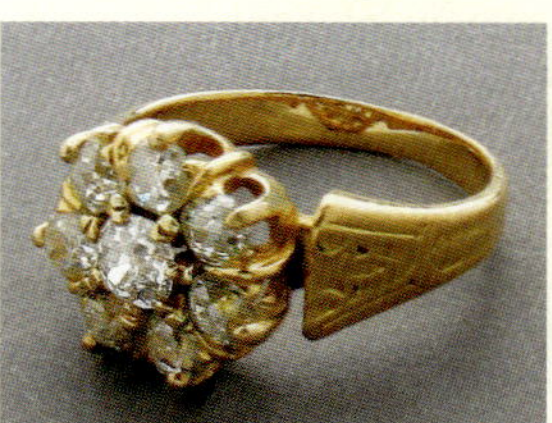

Fig. 120. Cluster of diamonds in a crown claw setting. Engraved spatula-shaped shoulders. Yellow gold. *Circa* 1880. *Keith Austin Collection.*

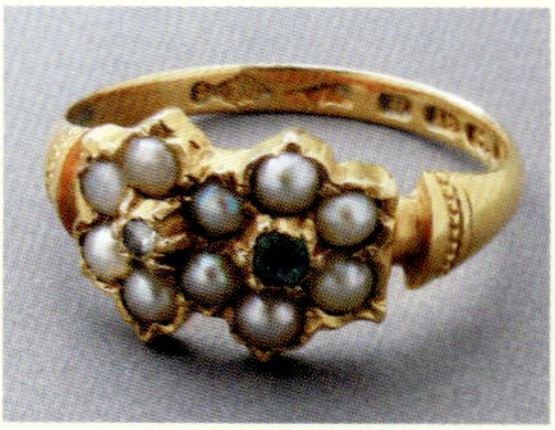

Fig. 121. Double cluster ring comprising half pearls, set in closed, crimped collets, around an emerald and a diamond spark each set in a cut-down collet. Horizontal beading decorates the convex spatula-shaped shoulders, joined to the bezel by a short neck. Plain shank, D-shaped in section. Hallmark: Birmingham, 18ct. 'coloured' gold, maker's mark A.A., 1872 and a registration mark for 1870. Bezel 9x12mm, shank 18mm in diameter.

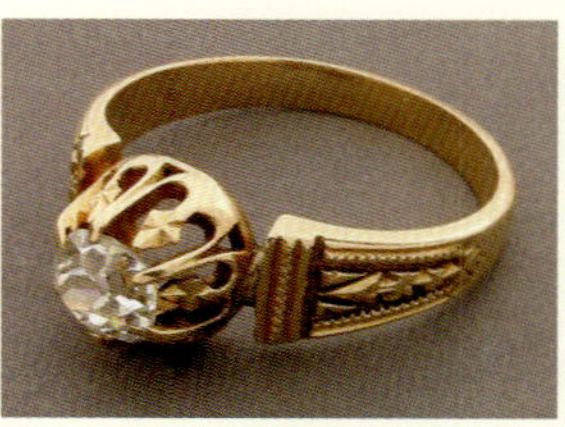

Fig. 122. Cushion-shaped brilliant-cut diamond set in six long claws, with a spear-shaped motif between each claw. Spatula-shaped shoulders are decorated with tiny beading and a carved geometric pattern, plain shank rectangular in section. Yellow gold. 1870s. Gallery depth 5mm, top of shoulder 5.5mm wide, shank diameter 17.5mm. *Reginald Davis (Oxford) Ltd.*

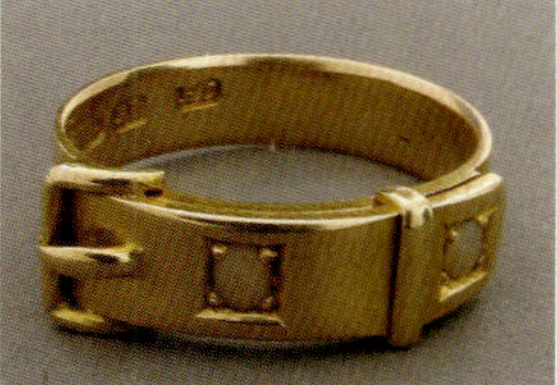

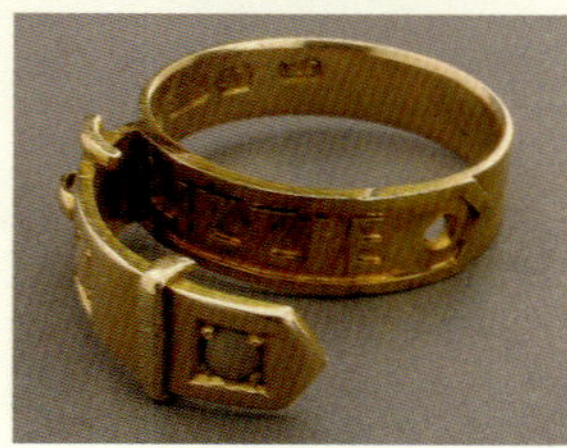

Fig. 123 a, b. Buckle ring set with pale coral in square settings. Beneath the hinged buckle LIZZIE is displayed in relief. Hallmarked: Birmingham, 15(.625) ct. gold, maker's mark JH, 1879. Gold 'colouring' has worn away from years of use. The ring belonged to the author's great-grandmother. Hinged bezel 6x22mm, hoop diameter 16mm, width 4.5mm.

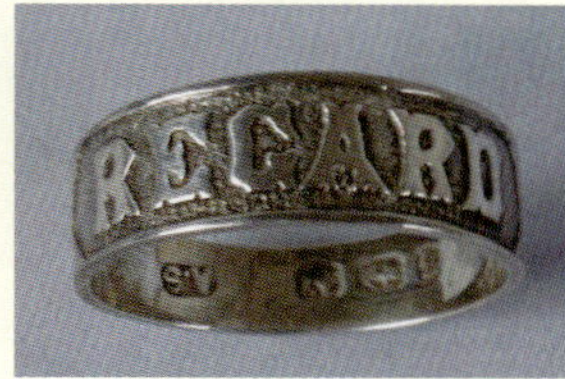

Fig. 124. Flat, silver, hoop ring decorated with REGARD on a tooled ground. Hallmarked: Birmingham, maker's mark A.S, 1881. Hoop width 6.5mm tapering to 4mm.

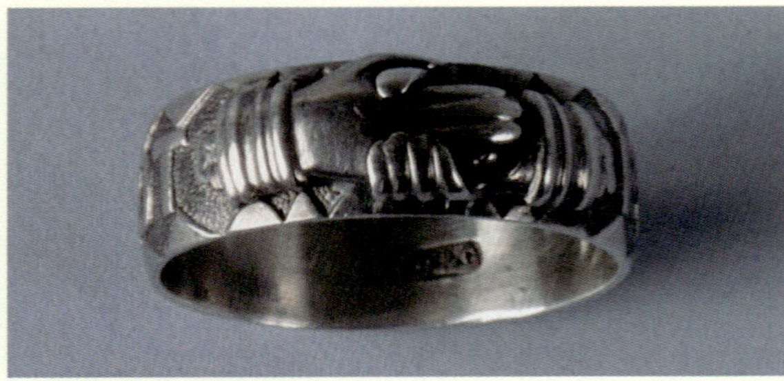
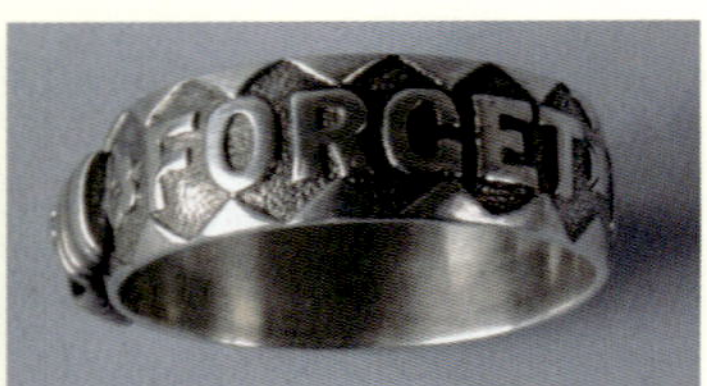
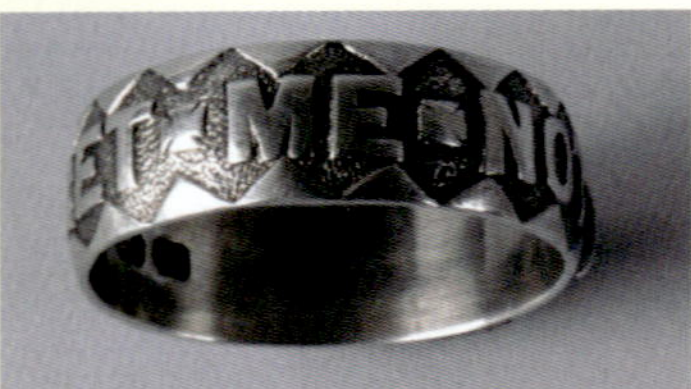

Fig. 125 a, b, c. Fede and forget-me-not silver hoop ring.
Hallmarked: 1881, Birmingham, maker's mark S&G. Hoop
diameter 19.5mm, width 7mm.

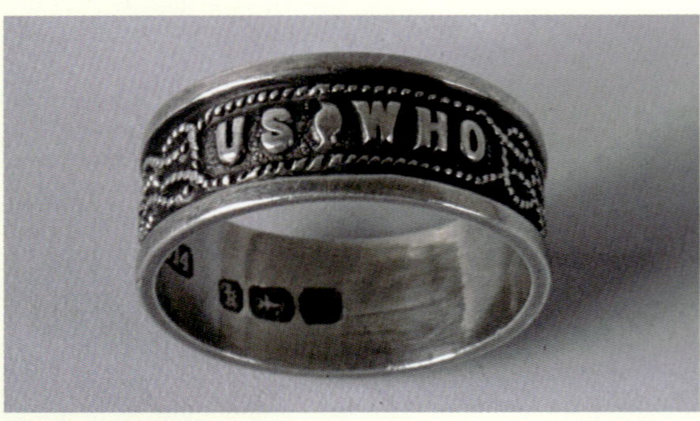
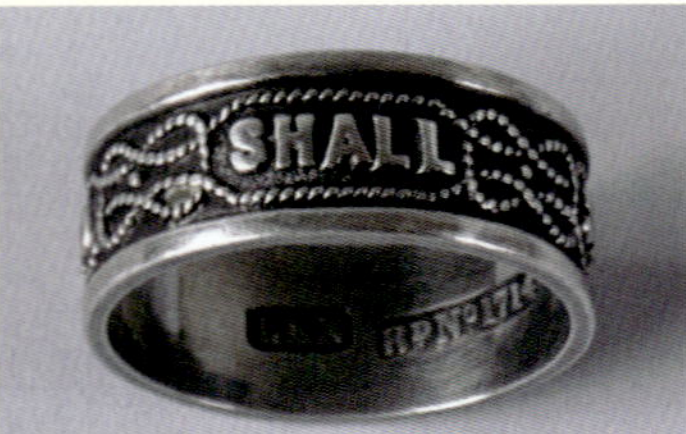
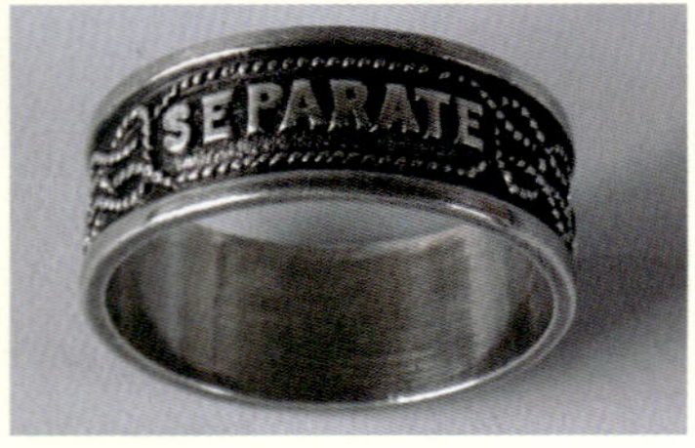

Fig. 126 a, b, c. Silver hoop ring decorated with lovers'
knots and the message WHO SHALL SEPARATE US.
Hallmarked: 1884, Birmingham, maker's mark LEN,
registered design no. 1714 (for 1884). Hoop diameter
16.5mm, width 7mm.

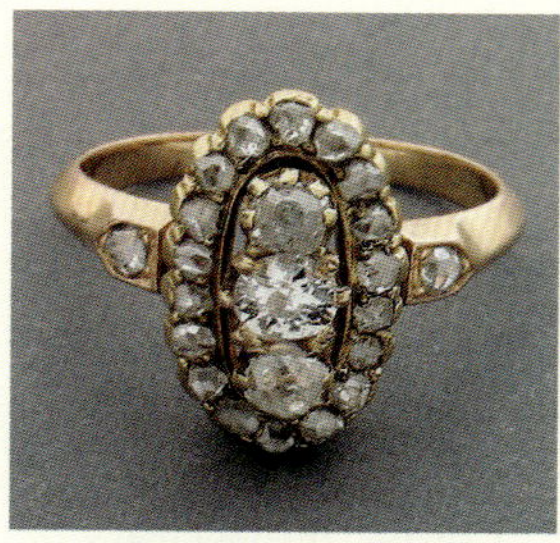

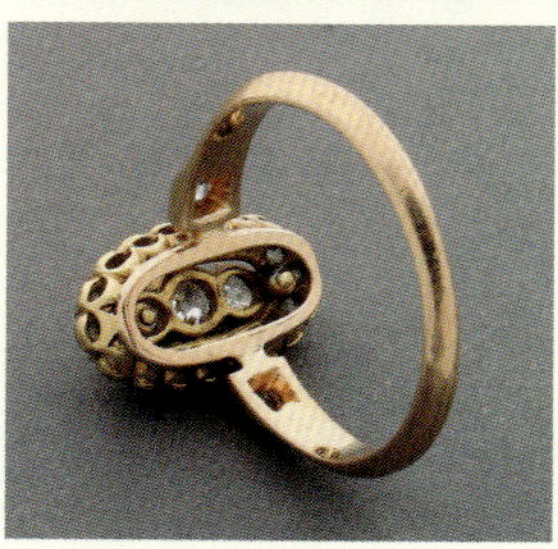

Fig. 127 a, b. Oval bezel comprising two double-cut diamonds and the middle diamond of a later cut (a replacement) set in claws, surrounded by a border of diamonds secured on the outside in a cut-down setting and on the inside of the border with gold grains. A shield-shape setting holds a diamond at the top of each triangular-shaped shoulder. Triangular shank. Rose gold. *Circa* 1870. Bezel 13x8mm, gallery depth 3mm, shank diameter 15mm.

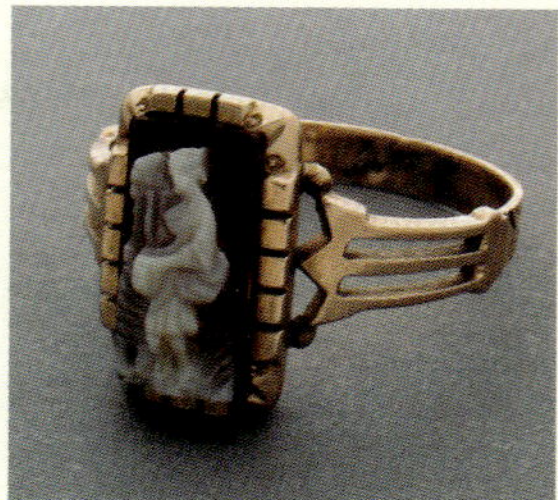

Fig. 128. Cameo in a rectangular bezel secured with small squares of gold on all four sides. Beads and engraving decorate the shoulders, flat hoop. Rose gold. American, *circa* 1880. *Keith Austin Collection.*

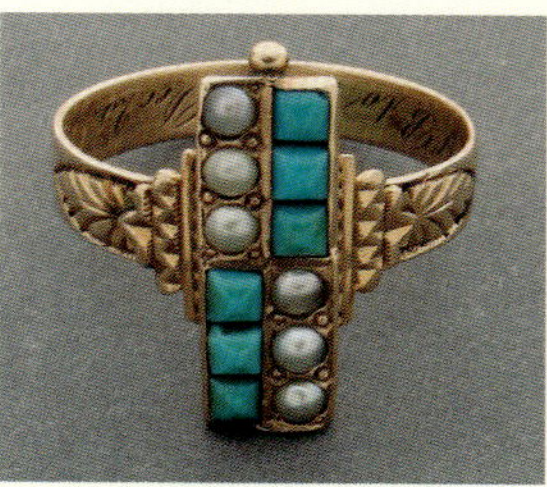

Fig. 129. Oblong bezel comprising pearls and turquoises in a thread setting. Carved shoulders extend into a plain, flat shank that is inscribed: V . J. B to M. J. Dec 25th 1880. Bead missing from one end of bezel. Rich yellow gold. American. Bezel 14x4.5mm, shank diameter 16mm, width 3mm.

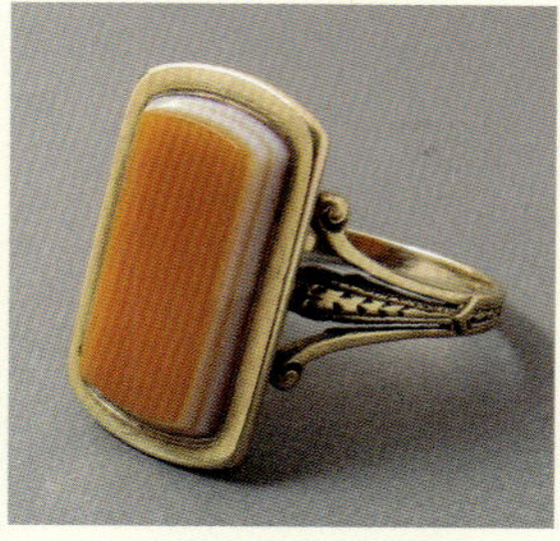

Fig. 130. Gentleman's ring. Sardonyx in a flush setting. Bifurcated shoulders with a chased inset. Plain, squared hoop. Yellow gold. American, *circa* 1880. Bezel 20x12mm, hoop diameter 18mm.

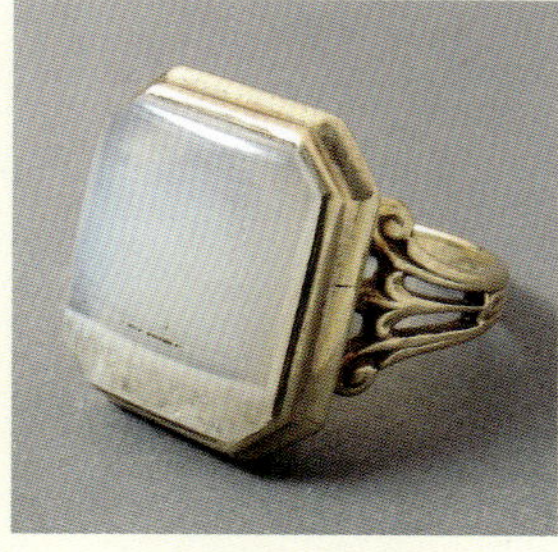

Fig. 131. Gentleman's ring. Moss agate in a flush setting. Bifurcated shoulders with fleur-de-lis inset. Reeded hoop, sized down. Yellow gold. American, *circa* 1870. Bezel 16.5x14mm.

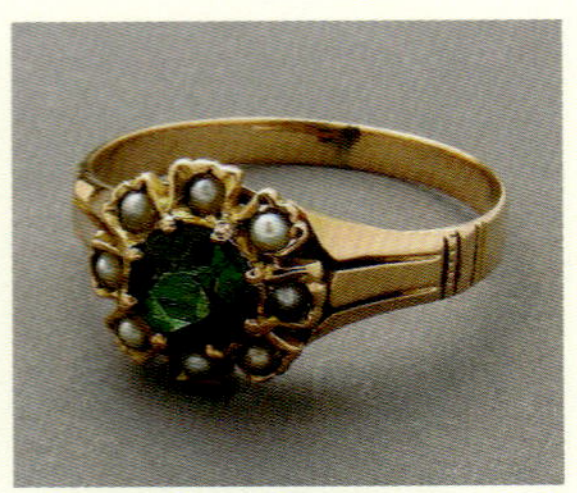

Fig. 132. A cluster bezel comprising an open-back, claw set, dark green tourmaline surrounded by seed pearls in square settings. Three simulated radiating panels form the shoulders, plain, flat shank. Rose gold. *Circa* 1880. Bezel 9x9mm, shank diameter 17mm.

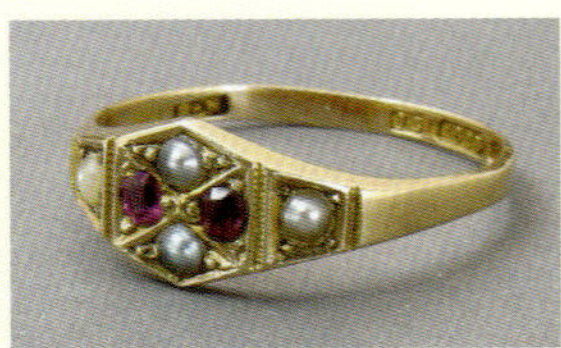

Fig. 133. Geometric bezel with pearls (worn) and tourmaline in thread settings. Hallmarked: Birmingham, 15(.625) ct. yellow gold, maker's mark R.N, 1872. Bezel 7x15mm, hoop diameter 18mm.

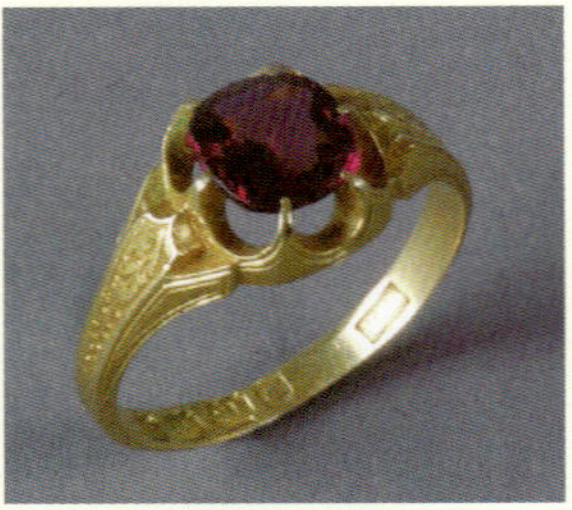

Fig. 134. Gothic-style ring. Cushion-cut almandine garnet secured in a claw setting with engraved edges, engraved bevelled shoulders, plain, squared shank. Hallmarked: Birmingham, 18ct. 'coloured gold', maker's mark, W.R, 1869. Bezel 10x8mm, shank diameter 19mm.

The new square setting was used in rings dating from the early 1860s. The stone was placed in a square frame with grains of gold in each corner to secure the gem. (Fig. 132) Variations of this geometric setting were triangular, diamond-shaped or shield-shaped frames. (Fig. 133)

During the 1860s and 1870s gold was frequently 'coloured' (Fig. 134), but in the mid-1870s the transition from 'coloured' gold to plain burnished gold occurred, particularly for costly half-hoop claw rings. Many mass-produced rings made from 15ct. and 12ct. gold continued to be 'coloured' for the remainder of this period.

1885-1910

During the last fifteen years of the nineteenth century and at the beginning of the twentieth century, marked changes in social attitudes were reflected in the changing fashions of dress and jewellery. A reaction to mass-production manifested itself in a revival of hand crafts. The Art Workers' Guild was founded in 1884, the Arts and Crafts Exhibition Society in 1887, and the Guild of Handicraft in 1888. These societies were followed by similar groups. Their aims were to restore individuality and originality in design and to improve craftsmanship in all areas. As is so often the case, such an endeavour was not supported by the majority of the population but by an enthusiastic minority. Even though these movements were rarely a commercial success, they did help to revive creativity in jewellery and encourage craftsmen to make a total break from the much-repeated styles of the 1870s and 1880s. The influence can be seen in the jewellery of the Art Nouveau period, followed by the Art Deco of the twentieth century.

There was a noticeable decline in the use of daytime jewellery during the late 1880s. By 1890 the jewellery trade was crying out for help from the leaders of society, even from Princess Alexandra, because of a serious slump in sales.

The Ladies' Treasury, 1 December 1893, stated:

> Jewellery is less and less worn, especially in the daytime. A little while ago it was indulged in to excess, and consequently a reaction against it has set in, and it is either banished altogether, or is of the lightest and brightest description. Diamonds for evening wear are never out of place or favour, and small gold heart shapes, set with these or other gems, are a good deal worn. (p.754) (Fig. 135)

Ring makers fared somewhat better than makers of other forms of jewellery; rings were always required for engagements, weddings and sentimental occasions.

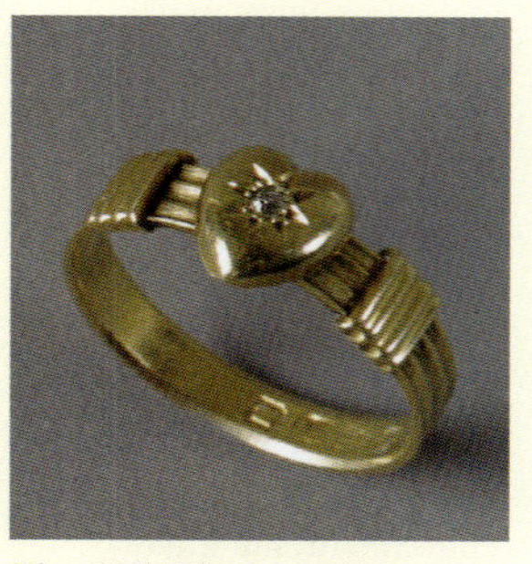

Fig. 135. Plump gold heart embellished with a star-set brilliant-cut diamond is applied to a channelled shank with a strip of the same design forming the shoulders. Chester, 18ct. yellow gold, 1895. Heart 7x7mm, shank diameter 16mm, width 3.5mm.

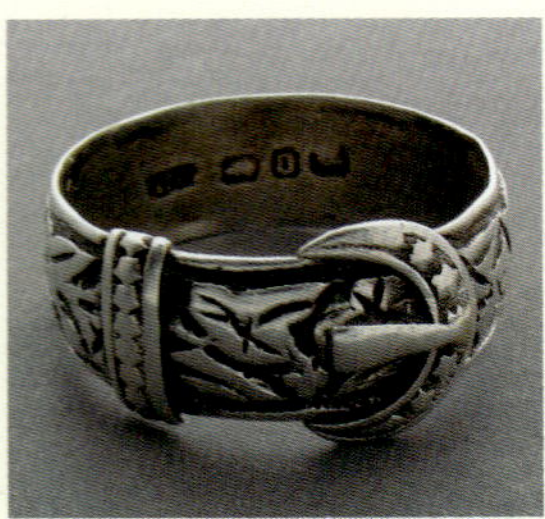

Fig. 136. Silver buckle ring chased with ivy leaves. Hallmarked: Birmingham, maker's mark T.H, 1888. Hoop diameter 18.5mm, width 7mm.

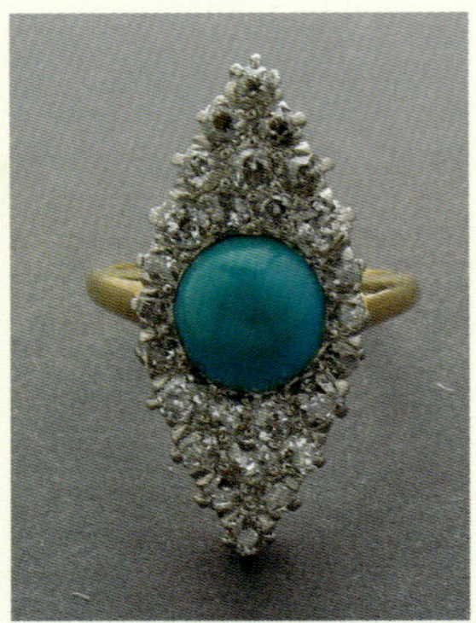

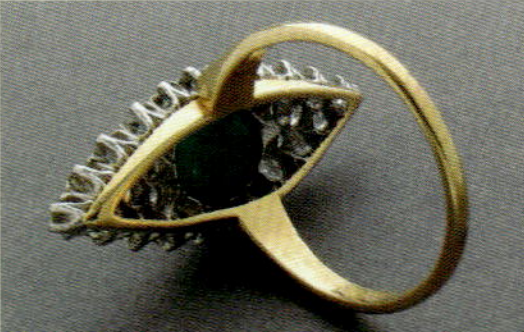

Fig. 137 a, b. Marquise bezel set with old mine-cut diamonds and a large Persian turquoise in platinum. Plain belcher shoulders and shank of yellow gold. *Circa* 1895. *Keith Austin Collection*

Daytime fashions were becoming simpler, so ring designs such as the gypsy, knot, buckle and chased hoop rings had become widely accepted for daytime wear. (Fig. 136) There was a great contrast between these simple, sturdy rings and the lavish gem-set rings worn by the leisured classes in the evenings. (Fig. 137 a, b) Many rings of the period were heavier than rings made prior to the 1870s. Expensive gem-set rings, of necessity, were substantially made to ensure the safety of the stones.

Gentlemen continued to wear rings, but the variety of styles had diminished, just as their dress had become less varied and more subdued.

From the mid-1880s, pale colours were fashionable, particularly for ladies' evening wear. Colourless or pale gems were very much in vogue, especially pale amethyst (Fig. 138), aquamarine, diamond (Fig. 139), moonstone (Fig. 140), opal (Fig. 141), pearl (Fig. 142), peridot and tourmaline. Moonstone, for instance, was so sought after that in 1887 it was fetching greatly inflated prices. (Fig. 143) Occasionally, a moonstone was carved into the face of a cherub or the man in the moon. (Fig. 144) Silver and platinum were used to set diamonds in barely visible claw settings, enhancing the delicate effect. Emeralds, rubies, sapphires and turquoises were still in demand, even though fashion was dominated by paler gems. (Fig. 145, Fig. 146)

One of the most enduring half-hoop styles to evolve in this period was the deep, carved gallery. The flat-sided scrollwork was partially pierced, terminating in small claws which held five or seven gems. (Fig. 147) Small gems were often used in this half-hoop design, resulting in a tall, narrow bezel. In some of these rings the bezel was curved while in others it was straight, allowing for a more ostentatious display of fine gems. Other half-hoop rings were set with gems in a variety of claw settings. (Fig. 148) Some were embellished with tiny gems between the larger stones (Fig. 149), and others were boat-shaped in outline, the effect being produced by graduated gems (Fig. 150).

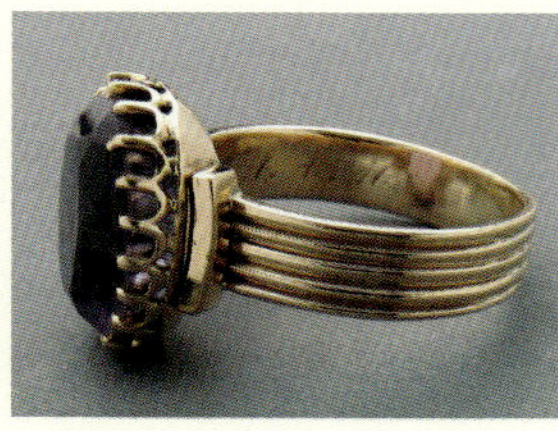

Fig. 138. Amethyst in a claw setting, with a curved section of plain gold at top of shoulder, wide reeded hoop. Rose gold. Faint initials engraved inside one shoulder: *A A M.* American, *circa* 1885-1900. Bezel 13x10mm, hoop diameter 16mm, width 4mm.

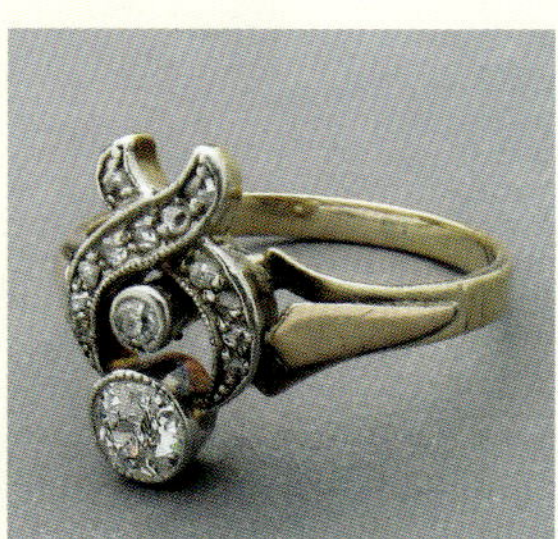

Fig. 139. Bezel comprises two old mine-cut diamonds in silver millegrained collets and a ribbon set with rose-cut diamonds in a millegrained silver thread setting all backed with gold. Bifurcated shoulders overlaid with a spear. Flat shank. Pale yellow gold, unmarked. American, *circa* 1890. Bezel 13x8mm, shank diameter 16mm.

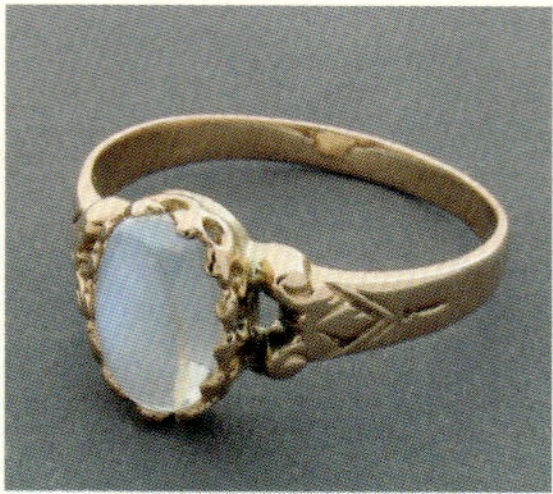

Fig. 140. Moonstone set in fleur-de-lis shaped claws on engraved shoulders and a plain, flat hoop of rose gold. American, *circa* 1885. Bezel 9x7mm, hoop diameter 18.5mm.

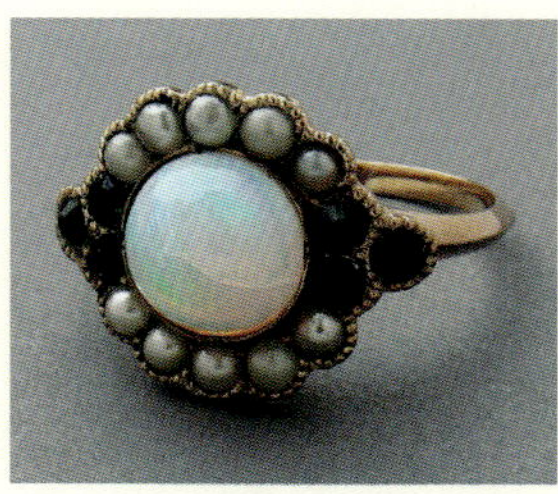

Fig. 141. Half pearls and green paste, in a millegrain setting, surround an opal; pearls are closed-set, opal and paste are open-set. Openwork gallery has a U-shaped design, plain shank is V-shaped in section. Rose gold. *Circa* 1890-1910. Bezel 17x13mm, shank diameter 17mm.

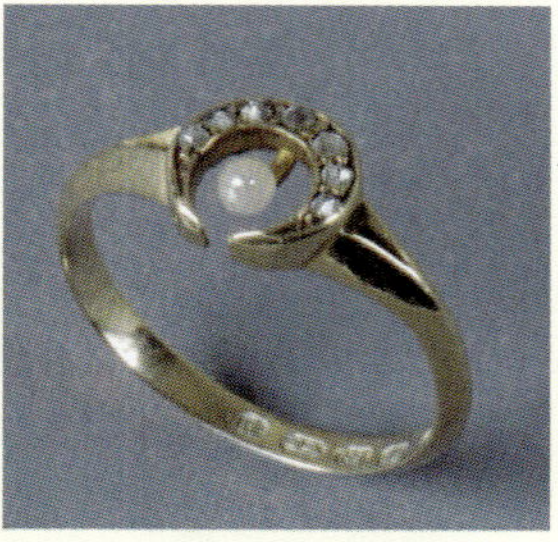

Fig. 142. Crescent set with diamond sparks around a tiny whole pearl that is attached to a short stem of hatched gold. The shank, triangular in section, separates to form the shoulders. Hallmarked: Birmingham, 18ct. pale yellow gold, maker's mark A & W, 1889. Bezel 7x7mm, shank diameter 17mm.

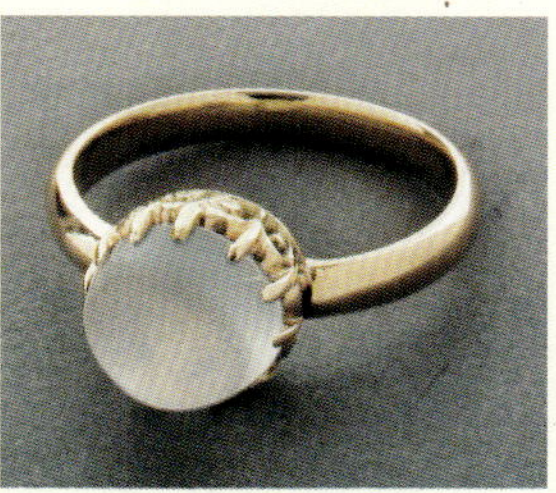

Fig. 143. Moonstone set in claws that emanate from a scrolled gallery. Plain rounded hoop. Rose gold. American, *circa* 1900. Bezel 8x8mm, gallery depth 2.5mm, hoop diameter 16mm.

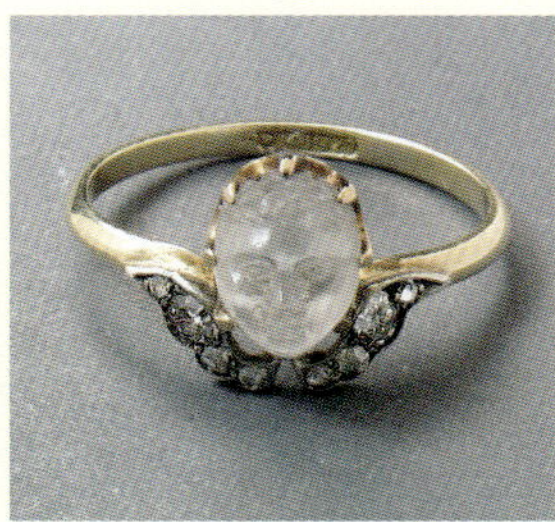

Fig. 144. Moonstone carved as a cherub's head in a claw setting framed by wings studded with rose-cut diamonds, the whole set on a narrow plain shank. English Registry mark for 1884, number Rd 141927, stamped inside the hoop. Possible made by Carlo Giuliano.

FINE GEM RINGS.

ALL STONES SET "À JOUR."

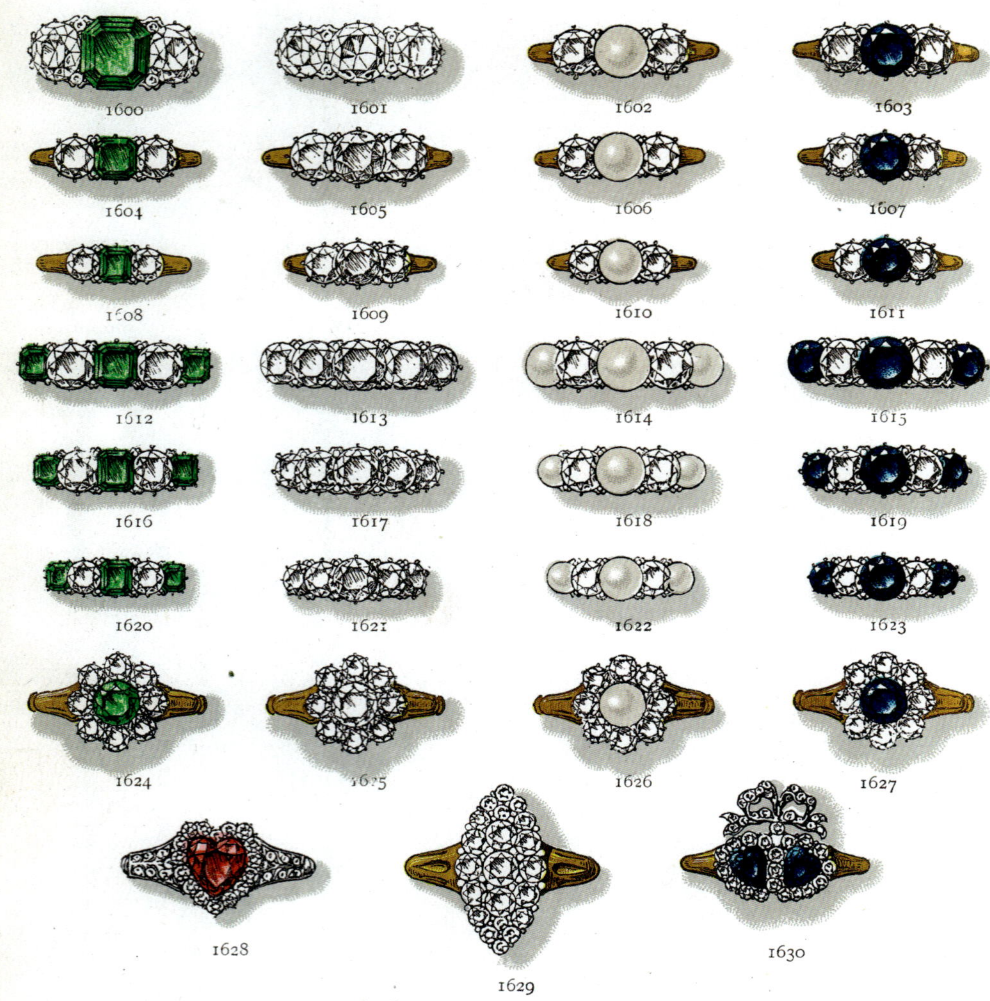

Emerald and Diamond Rings,   All Diamond Rings,   Pearl and Diamond Rings,   Sapphire and Diamond Rings,

from £40 to £200.   from £20 to £150.   from £12 to £200   from £15 to £150.

THESE DESIGNS ARE DRAWN TO ACTUAL SIZE, AND PRICES ARE QUOTED NET; SMALLER ORNAMENTS OF SAME
DESIGN CAN BE HAD, OR ANY GEM SUBSTITUTED FOR THOSE ABOVE AT PROPORTIONATE PRICES.

STREETER & CO., Ltd.

ALL STONES SET "à JOUR."

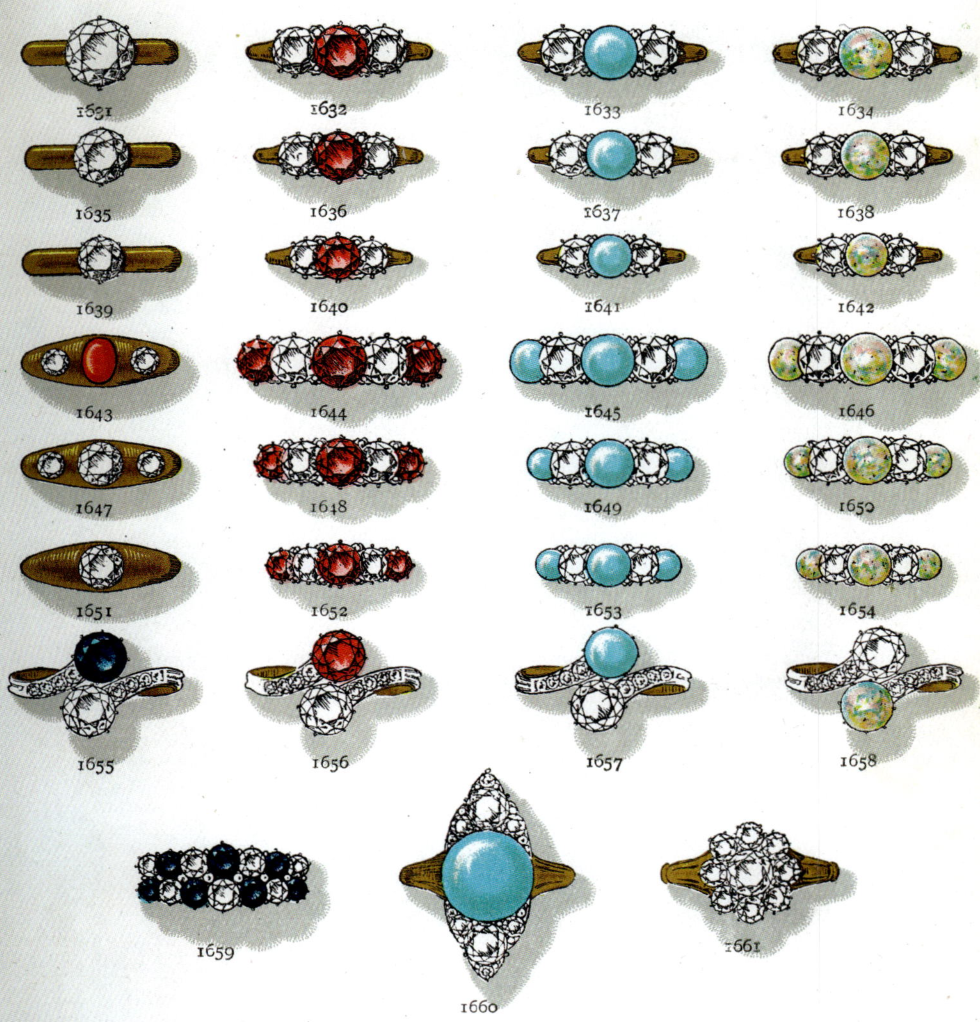

Single Stone Diamond Rings, Ruby and Diamond Rings, Turquoise & Diamond Rings, Opal and Diamond Rings,

from £10 to £135.   from £20 to £250.   from £12 to £80.   from £12 to £70.

THESE DESIGNS ARE DRAWN TO ACTUAL SIZE, AND PRICES ARE QUOTED NET ; SMALLER ORNAMENTS OF SAME
DESIGN CAN BE HAD, OR ANY GEM SUBSTITUTED FOR THOSE ABOVE AT PROPORTIONATE PRICES.

18, NEW BOND STREET, W.

Fig. 145. 'GEMS' by Streeter & Co. Ltd., 18 New Bond Street, London W., 101st Catalogue c. 1900.

[1885 - 1910]

ALL STONES SET "À JOUR."

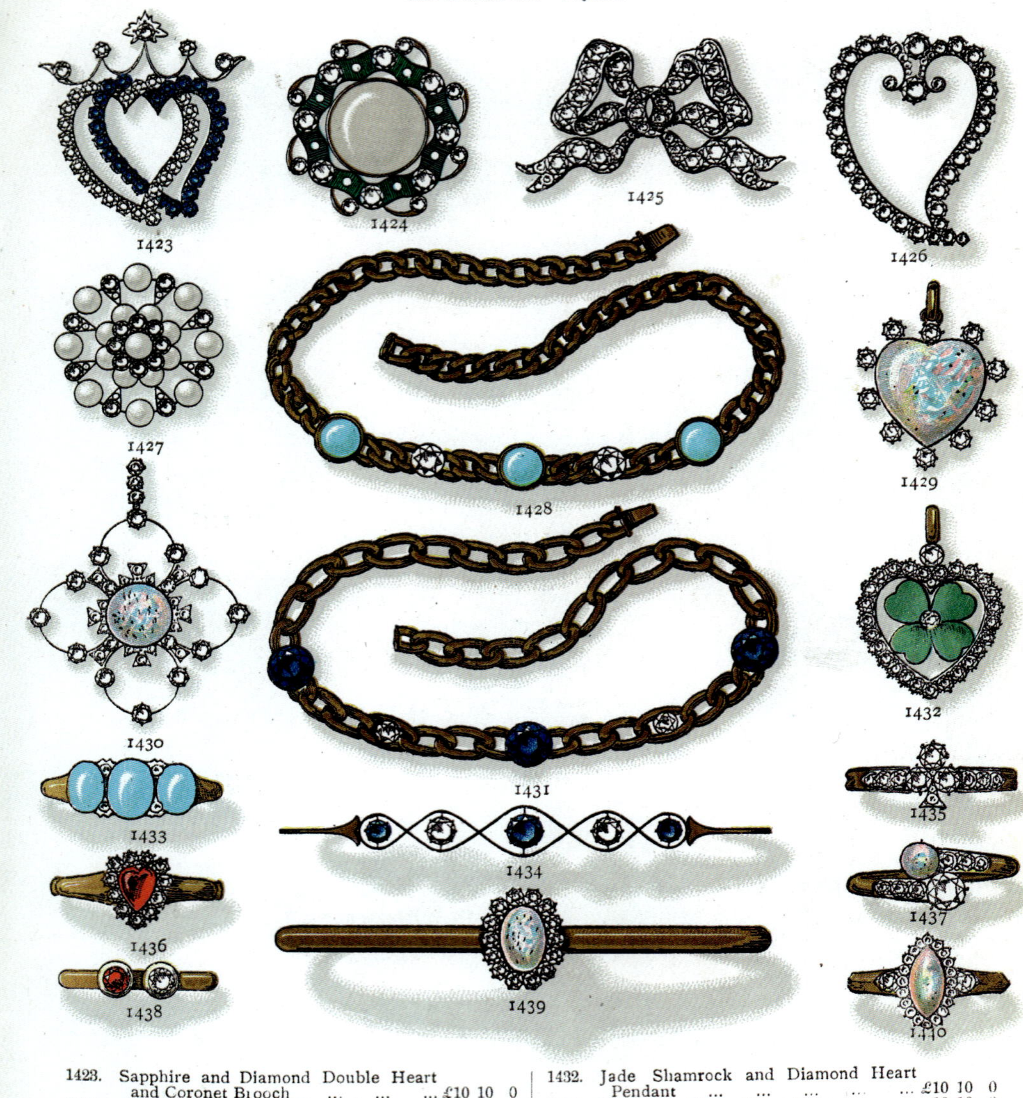

1423.	Sapphire and Diamond Double Heart and Coronet Brooch ... £10 10 0		1432.	Jade Shamrock and Diamond Heart Pendant £10 10 0	
1424.	Green Enamel and Diamond Brooch, Crystal Centre (any color enamel) ... 10 10 0		1433.	Turquoise Three-Stone Ring ... 10 10 0	
1425.	Diamond Tie Brooch 10 10 0		1434.	Sapphire and Diamond Fancy Half-Hoop Bracelet 10 10 0	
1426.	Diamond Fancy Heart Brooch ... 10 10 0		1435.	Diamond Trefoil Ring 10 10 0	
1427.	Pearl and Diamond Brooch ... 10 10 0		1436.	Cabochon Ruby and Diamond Heart Ring 10 10 0	
1428.	Turquoise and Diamond on Gold Curb Bracelet 10 10 0		1437.	Opal and Diamond Double-Part Ring 10 10 0	
1429.	Opal and Diamond Heart Pendant ... 10 10 0		1438.	Ruby and Diamond Bangle Ring ... 10 10 0	
1430.	Opal and Diamond Fancy Pendant ... 10 10 0		1439.	Opal and Diamond Cluster Bracelet ... 10 10 0	
1431.	Sapphires and Diamonds on Gold Curb Bracelet 10 10 0		1440.	Opal and Diamond Marquise Ring ... 10 10 0	

THESE DESIGNS ARE DRAWN TO ACTUAL SIZE, AND PRICES ARE QUOTED NET; SMALLER ORNAMENTS OF SAME DESIGN CAN BE HAD, OR ANY GEM SUBSTITUTED FOR THOSE ABOVE AT PROPORTIONATE PRICES.

18, NEW BOND STREET, W.

Fig. 146, 'GEMS' By Streeter & Co. Ltd.

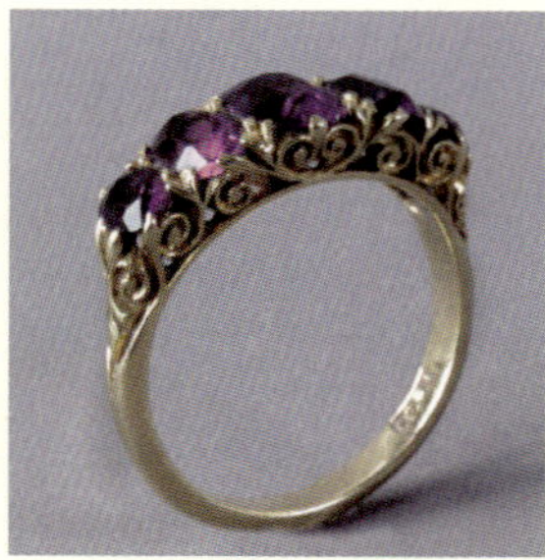

Fig. 147. Half-hoop ring set with amethysts in open-backed settings supported by a scrolled gallery that extends down the shoulders. Plain shank, D-shaped in section. 18ct. yellow gold. *Circa* 1895. Gallery depth 3mm, shank diameter 17mm.

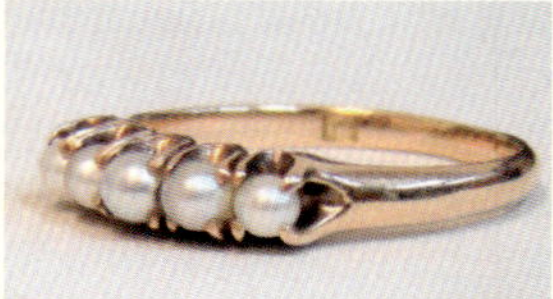

Fig. 148. Half hoop of five whole pearls in open claw settings on a plain shank, D-shape in section, rose gold. Stamped 14 and inscribed 'A B L...' (remaining inscription illegible). American, *circa* 1885-1900. Claws 3mm long, shank diameter 18mm.

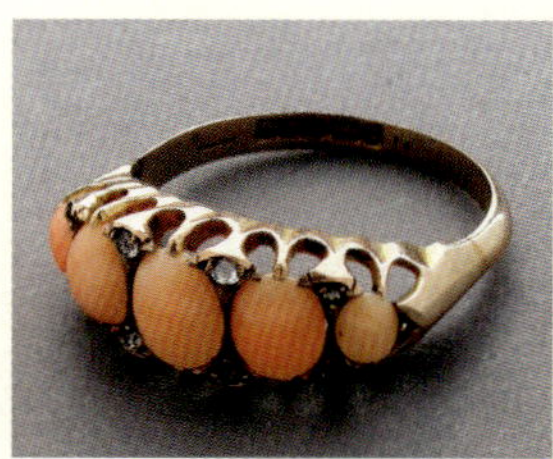

Fig. 149. Half-hoop comprising five corals interspersed with rose-cut diamonds in a crown claw setting. Plain shoulders and shank. Hallmarked: Birmingham, 9(.375) ct., 1900. *Keith Austin Collection.*

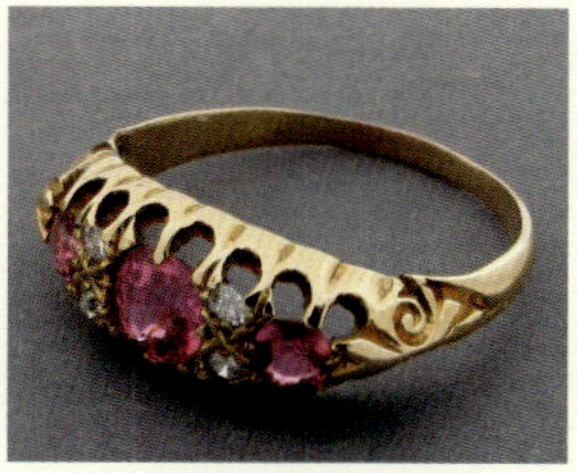

Fig. 150. Three claw-set spinel and four diamonds form the boat-shape bezel. The shoulders are carved with scrolls. Plain shank has been sized down so that the only remaining marks are a crown and 18. Rich yellow gold. *Circa* 1885–1910. Bezel 7x17mm.

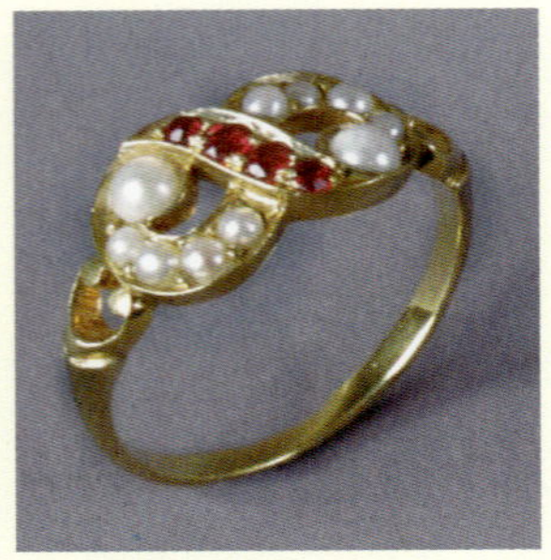

Fig. 151. Figure-of-eight bezel set with closed-back half pearls and faceted open-back rubies. Narrow scalloped shoulders, plain shank D-shaped in section. Yellow gold. *Circa* 1890-1900. Bezel 8x16mm, shank diameter 17mm.

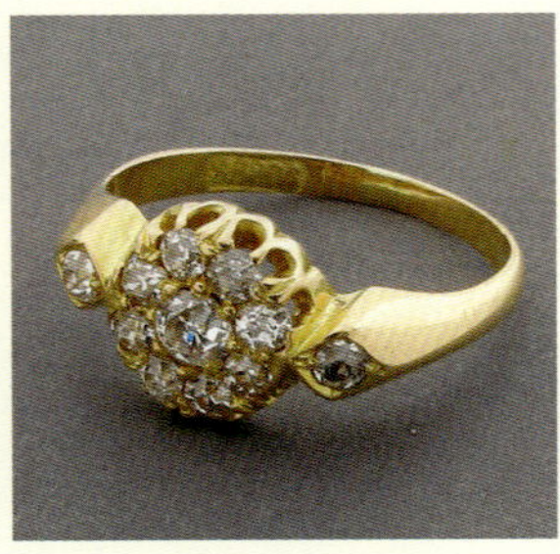

Fig. 152. Cluster of nine mine-cut diamonds in a claw setting. A diamond in a diamond-shaped setting decorates the top of each triangular-shaped shoulder. Yellow gold. Birmingham maker's mark S.BROS. *Circa* 1885-1900. Bezel 9x8mm, hoop diameter 17mm.

A number of new commercial designs evolved in this period. A large variety of flat rings that hugged the finger were fashionable: some had gems in square or thread settings, some bezels were given a slight twist and were decorated with small gems in gypsy or star settings. The borders of the bezel usually had some sort of moulded design - either a scalloped or segmented square edge or an asymmetrical outline. Some rings had leaves or flowers carved into the bezel. Most of these were set with small stones such as coral, diamond, emerald, pearl, sapphire or turquoise. The trefoil bezel made its appearance in England and America in rings and other forms of jewellery. (Fig. 151, Fig. 152, Fig. 153, Fig. 154, Fig. 155)

Sentimental and religious rings in gold or silver continued to be worn in this period, a fashion dating from about 1880, see Fig. 294 under DECADE RING in the Glossary. These rings were lightly or profusely chased, with or without gems. 'Mizpah' was one of the most popular sentiments. (Fig. 156) The motto 'I cling to thee' (Fig. 157) was often used in conjunction with ivy. A few rings were formed into clasped hands, sometimes with a hoop formed from several wires in a puzzle design (Fig. 158 a, b), and an occasional Irish claddagh ring made its appearance. (Fig. 159) The following excerpt shows that sentiment may have gone too far. *The Ladies' Treasury*, 1 December 1893, under the heading "Facts and Caprices of the Month", records the following:

> Another strange and gruesome fancy is that of setting a baby's tooth in diamonds, and wearing it in a ring. We must admit that the tooth was a small one - the first cut by the lady's first baby - but for all that it is scarcely a beautiful or romantic ornament, not one likely to come into general favour. (p.754)

It is interesting to note that baby teeth were also set in rings in the early part of the century, see Fig. 19.

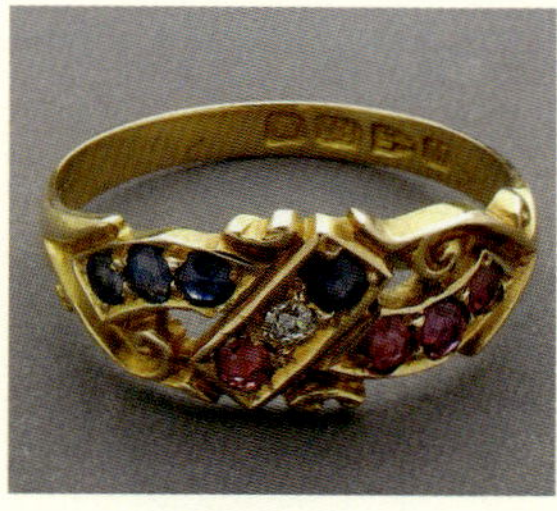

Fig. 153. Jubilee ring. Asymmetric, scrolled bezel set with spinels, sapphires and a single diamond. Plain hoop. Hallmarked: Chester 18ct. yellow gold, 1895. Bezel 8x21mm, hoop diameter 18mm.

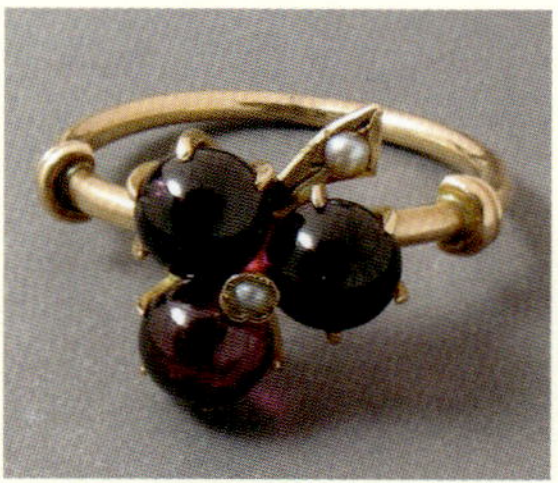

Fig. 154. Trefoil bezel comprising round amethysts, with a seed pearl in the centre and one in the stem. Thick round wire hoop, transverse ribs on shoulders. Rose gold. American, *circa* 1895. Bezel diameter 10mm, hoop diameter 16mm.

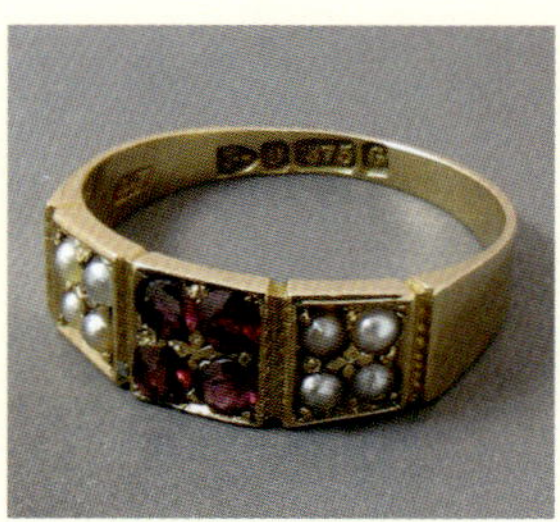

Fig. 155. Amethysts and pearls set in three sections on a plain tapering hoop. Hallmarked: Chester, 9(.375) ct., maker's mark B.K, 1890. Bezel 6x19mm, hoop diameter 18mm.

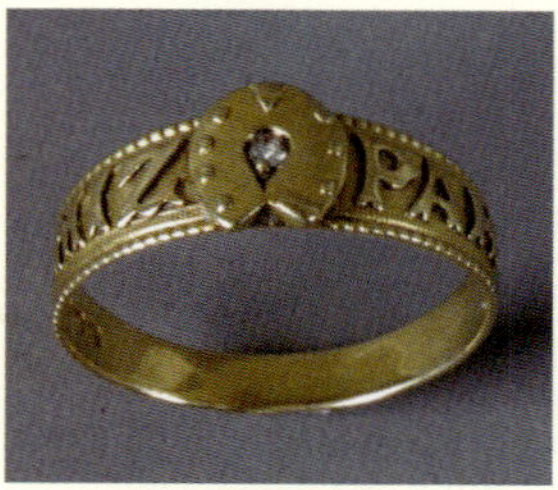

Fig. 156. 'Mizpah' set on a plain ground in raised letters around a horseshoe set with an open-back brilliant. Adjacent to the knurled edge of the hoop is a narrow band of vertical hatch marks. Hallmarked: Birmingham, 18ct. yellow gold, maker's mark H & S, 1897. Horseshoe 8x7mm, hoop diameter 19mm.

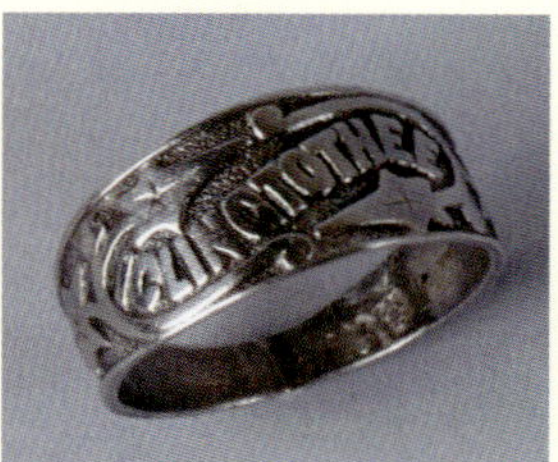

Fig. 157. Silver hoop ring conveying the message 'I Cling to Thee' surrounded by ivy. Hallmarked: Birmingham 1904. Middle of bezel 9mm deep, hoop diameter 18mm.

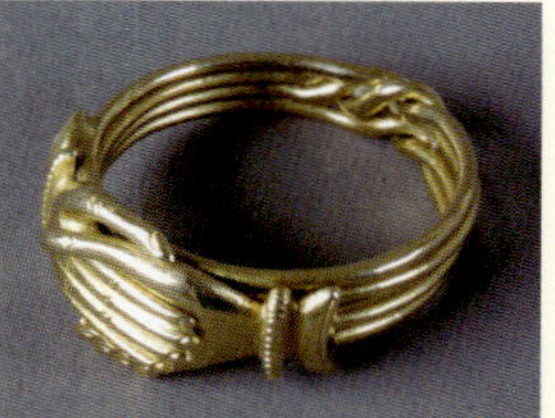

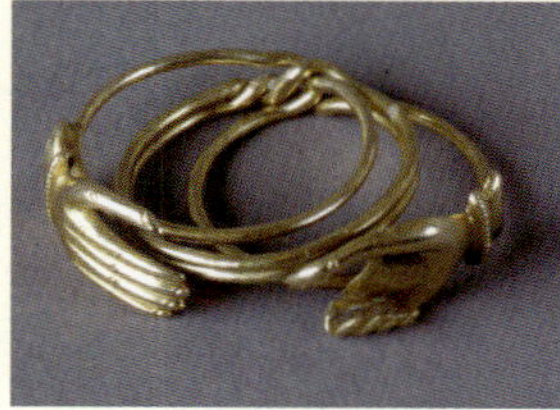

Fig. 158 a, b. Fede-puzzle ring comprising four round wires that intertwine at the back of the hoops, and cuffed hands attached to two hoops. Rich yellow gold. *Circa* 1880s. Cuffed hands 9x12mm, diameter of hoops 16mm.

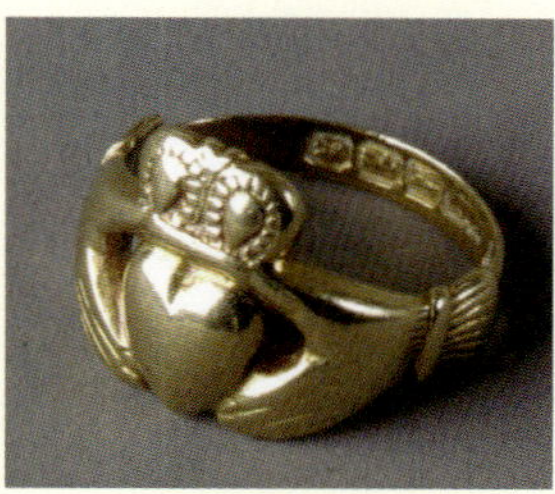

Fig. 159. Gentleman's claddagh ring inscribed inside bezel: 'from Clare 1897' above an arrow. Hallmarked: Dublin, maker's mark TD, 18ct. yellow gold, 1896. Bezel depth 13.5mm, hoop diameter 17mm.

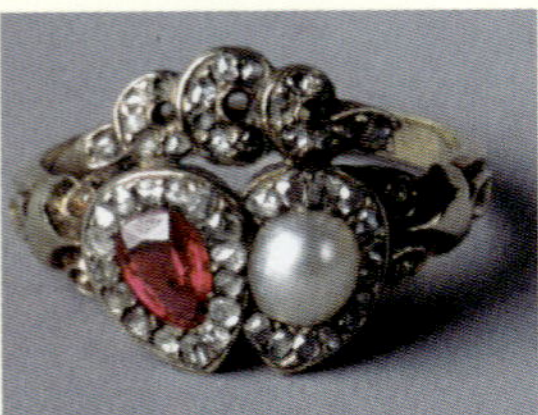

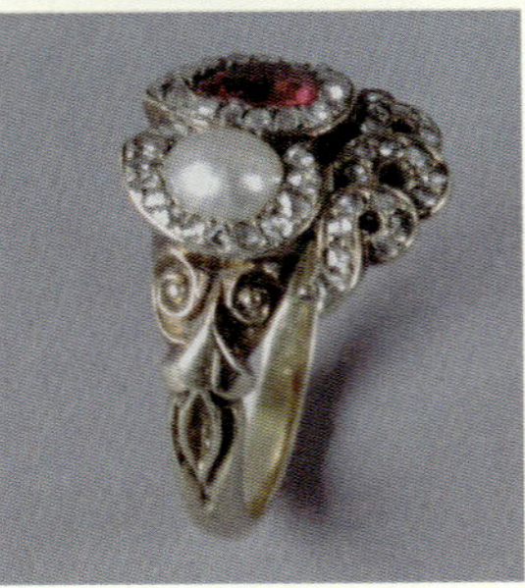

Fig. 160 a, b. Double heart ring with a ruby and a half pearl in open-back settings, surrounded by rose-cut diamonds in a closed setting, the hearts are embellished with a rose-cut diamond ribbon motif. Shoulders are deeply carved with symmetrical scrolls, plain D-shaped hoop, yellow gold. *Circa* 1885-1900. Bezel 13x13mm, hoop diameter 18mm.

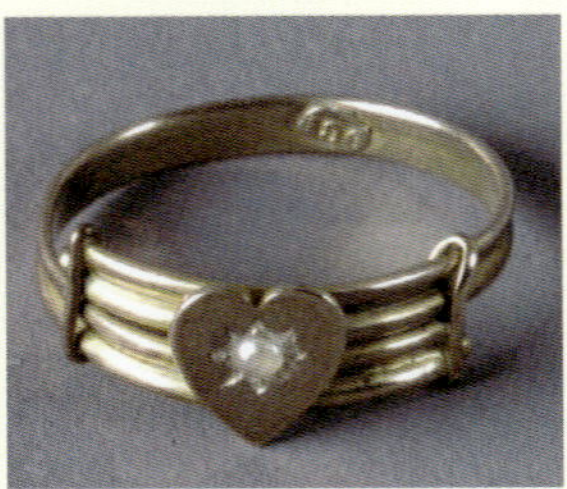

Fig. 161. Heart, with star-set pearl, is applied to one end of expandable, fused, double wire shank. A 9ct. stamp is applied to the inside of the hoop, yellow gold. *Circa* 1895. Heart 8x6.5mm, shank diameter 17mm.

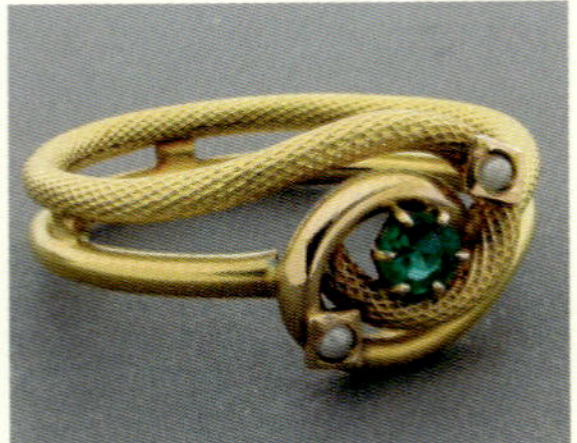

Fig. 162. Knot ring comprising two hollow hoops, one plain, the other engraved to resemble the scales of a serpent, joined together with three tiny beads of gold. The knot is set with two seed pearls in square settings and a green stone in claws. Rich yellow gold. American, *circa* 1890-1900. Bezel 10x10mm, hoop diameter 18mm, width 4mm.

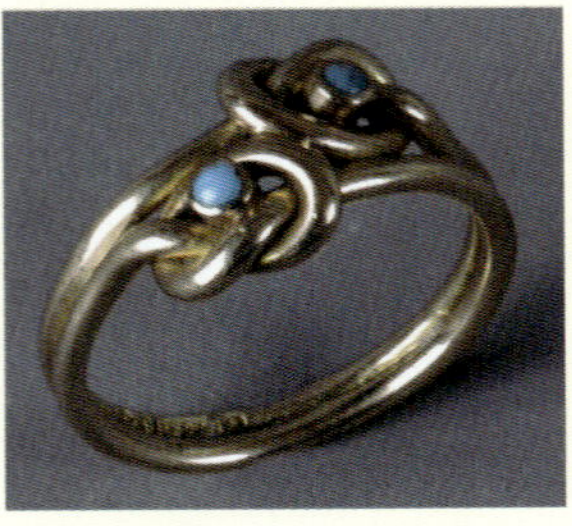

Fig. 163. Double knot ring decorated with two open-back, collet-set, turquoises. The substantial, round, double wire shank is an extension of the bezel. Hallmarked: Chester, 9(.375) ct. rose gold, maker's mark S.B. & S LD, 1903. Knots 9x15mm, shank diameter 18mm, width 2.5mm.

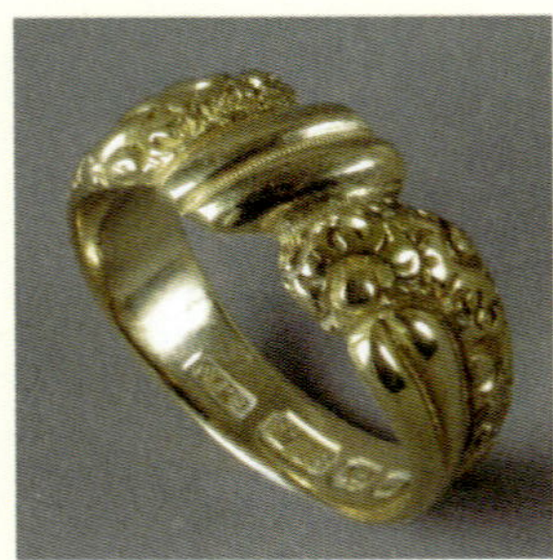

Fig. 164. Ring fashioned from chased and plain gold. Hallmarked: Birmingham, 18ct. deep yellow gold, maker's mark CYBS, 1896. Front of hoop 8mm, hoop diameter 17mm.

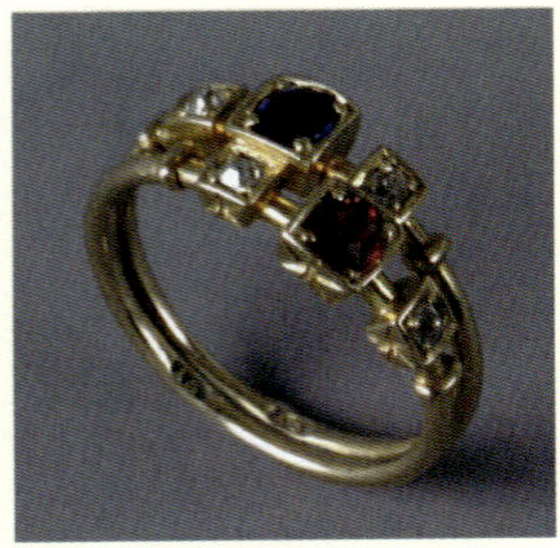

Fig. 165. Two-part ring of solid round wire decorated with two brilliants and a ruby on one hoop, two brilliants and a sapphire on the second hoop, all in open-back square settings, carved on each side with a six-pointed star. A transverse rib is set below each diamond. Both hoops are stamped 18. Yellow gold. *Circa* 1887-1900.

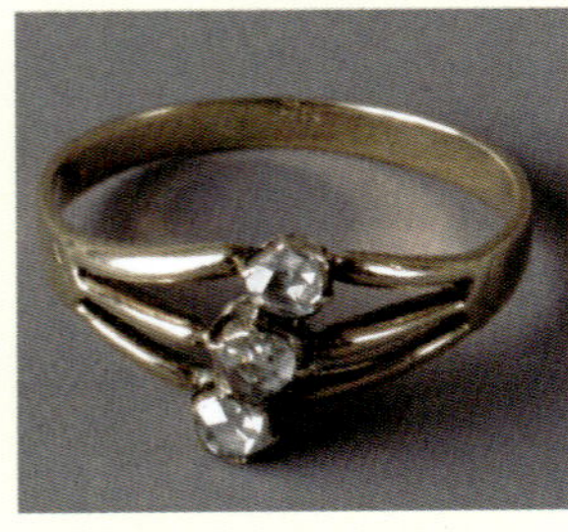

Fig. 166. Three-part bezel comprising three open-set rose-cut diamonds encased in a narrow band of gold supported in claw settings, narrow flat hoop, 14K rose gold. American, *circa* 1900. Similar designs were made in England at this time. Bezel depth 10mm, hoop diameter 19mm, width 2.5mm.

Double or single jewelled hearts topped with a ribbon motif, often a bow, were very much in evidence. The centre of the heart was set with one of following stones: rose or brilliant-cut diamond, ruby, pearl, moonstone, opal, sapphire, coral, turquoise or emerald. Double heart rings were set with identical or contrasting gems. (Fig. 160 a, b) The ribbon and the edge of the heart were usually set with tiny rose-cut diamonds, giving the rings a delicate quality, though small brilliant-cut diamonds were used occasionally. Modest versions of this design were made with one or two plump gold hearts decorated with a tiny star-set gem. (Fig. 161)

A popular ring in the 1890s was made from substantial round gold wire. Some were designed with one or two knots (Fig. 162) (Fig. 163), others were made into a plaited pattern with or without beading, still others parted at the shoulders to accommodate one or more gems in the bezel.

The curb-chain hoop ring was decorated with a heart or a plain gold shield that could be inscribed and worn as a signet ring. In 1895 it was fashionable for a lady to wear a signet ring. Gold rings decorated with carving were very popular in the 1890s. (Fig. 164)

Two-part or three-part rings, made to simulate two or three rings worn together, became fashionable during the last decade of the century. (Fig. 165, Fig. 166) These rings were usually set with diamonds, pearls, rubies or sapphires. At the same time, crossover rings set with a gem at the end of each terminal became very popular (Fig. 167, Fig. 168), and they usually contained diamonds, opals, pearls, rubies, sapphires, turquoises or emeralds. The shoulders might be set with small brilliants.

Jubilee rings appeared in 1887 and 1897 to commemorate the golden and diamond jubilees of Queen Victoria's accession to the throne in 1837. The rings were set with sapphire, ruby and diamond in a variety of the designs produced in this period, see Fig. 153 and Fig. 165. For more details and illustrations see the Commemorative and Historical ring section.

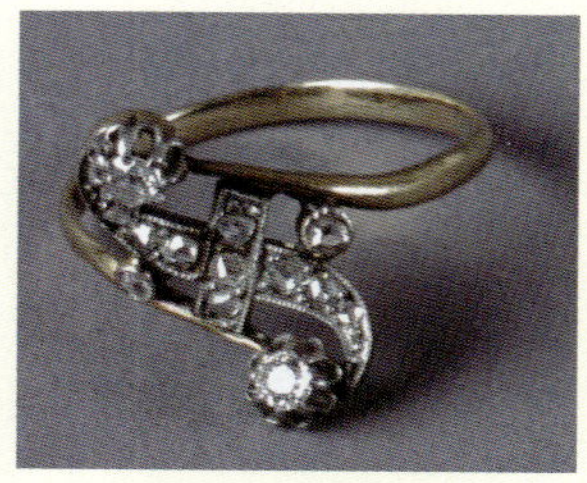

Fig. 167. Crossover ring set with rose-cut diamonds in millegrained silver, brilliant-cut diamonds in silver claws decorate each terminal. The bezel is backed with gold and all the settings are open at the back. Narrow, plain shank marked with an eagle's head (Paris 1838 onwards). Yellow gold. French, *circa* 1890. Bezel 15x10mm, shank diameter 17mm. *Reginald Davis (Oxford) Ltd.*

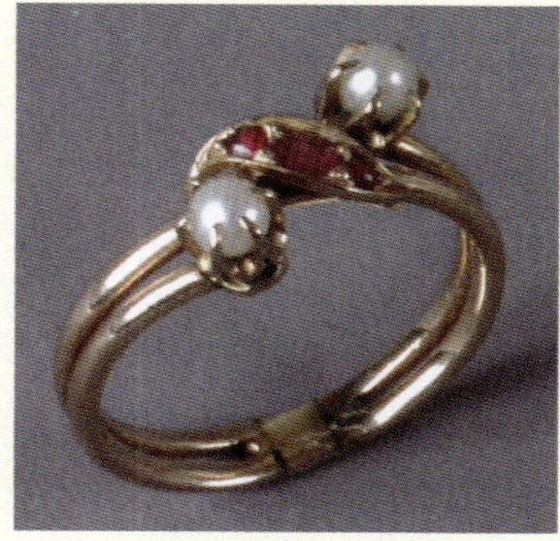

Fig. 168. Three-part crossover ring. The terminals of the D-shaped hoops are decorated with a single whole pearl in a six-prong claw setting with a ruby-set foliate motif placed diagonally between the pearls. Rose gold. *Circa* 1895. Hoop diameter 17mm, width 2.5mm. *Reginald Davis (Oxford) Ltd.*

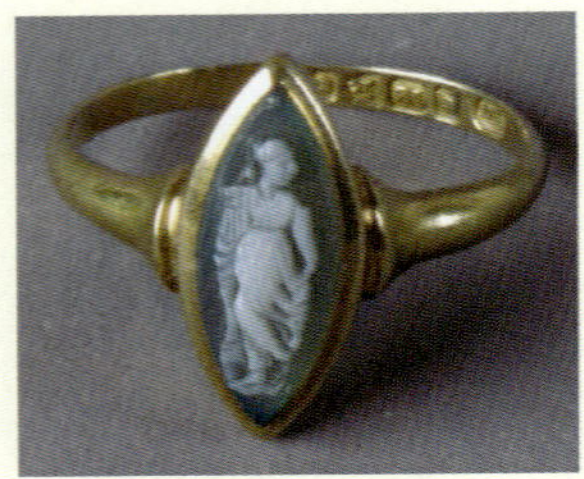

Fig. 169. Marquise-shaped translucent mint green stone with a white female figure in cameo held in a flush setting. Plain shank expands to form a small convex shoulder. Hallmarked: Chester, 18ct. yellow gold, maker's mark S.U, 1903. Bezel 17x7mm, shank diameter 19mm.

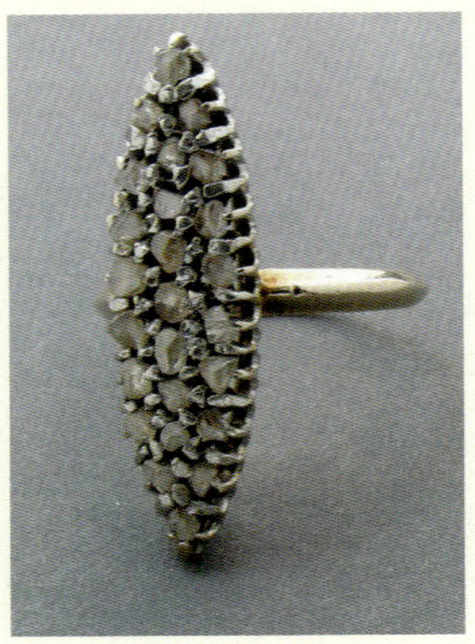

Fig. 170. Marquise bezel set with rose-cut diamonds in long, narrow platinum claws on a yellow gold triangular-shaped hoop. American, *circa* 1890-1910.
Keith Austin Collection

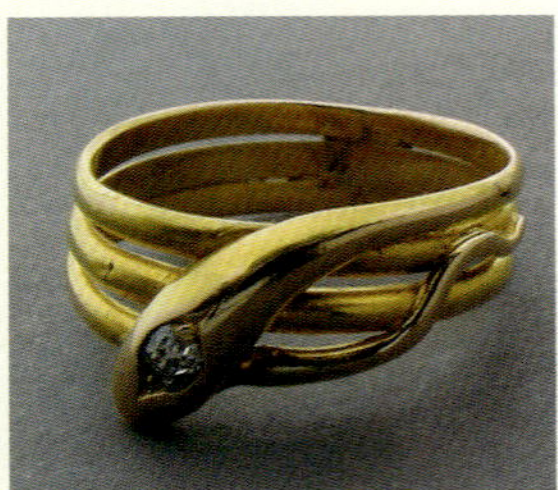

Fig. 171. Ladies' serpent ring set with a cushion-cut diamond in the head. Rich yellow gold. American, *circa* 1870.
Keith Austin Collection

The marquise ring was very fashionable during this period. (Fig. 169) In shape, it could be short and plump or long and narrow, pavé-set with rose or brilliant-cut diamonds (Fig. 170), pearls or turquoises. Coloured gems such as emerald, ruby and sapphire might be set in the centre of the bezel, sometimes in the form of a cross. A few marquise rings held a single moonstone or cameo surrounded by pearls or diamonds. Less costly examples were made in plain gold decorated with one or more star-set diamonds, rubies or sapphires. The galleries of many marquise rings were fashioned from tiny claws or from machine-made openwork designs.

Serpents still coiled around numerous fingers, but in a less artistic manner than formerly. Characteristic designs of the period had two or more flat coils ending with one or two heads set either with a single jewel and small stones in the eyes, or with gems in the eyes only. (Fig. 171) Other serpent rings were decorated with graduated gems set along the length of the head. The emphasis tended to be on the gems and the amount of gold rather than on the realistic form of the creature itself. There were a few flimsy, single coil snakes, equally uninteresting in variety of form, but these were less common than multi-coil serpent rings. An ornate style with elaborately engraved coils, appeared at the end of the century, but few examples are found today. (Fig. 172)

Cluster rings were as fashionable as ever, set with emerald, opal, pearl, ruby, sapphire or turquoise, bordered with pearls or diamonds. (Fig. 173) (Fig. 174 a, b, c) Large pearls surrounded by brilliants were a good example of the 'colourless' look. The traditional diamond cluster was still a favourite and double or triple clusters were widely produced. See Fig. 290. A variation of this design was an elliptical bezel holding three or five coloured stones surrounded by a border of brilliants. By 1900 the shanks of most cluster rings were narrow and plain.

Certain ring styles from earlier periods, including buckles, single or double horseshoes, gypsy rings (Fig. 175), and boat-shaped bezels (Fig. 176), were made in large numbers during this period. The simple boat-shaped style had become more elaborate, with a carved or moulded design around the stones, the gems themselves being separated by gold threadwork.

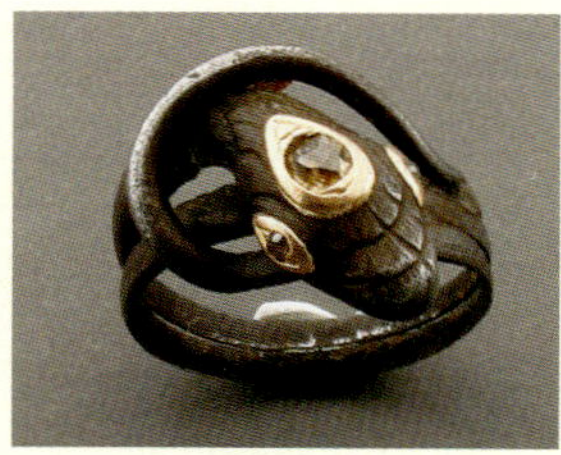

Fig. 172. Serpent ring fashioned from iron. The head is set with old mine-cut diamonds in gold. American, *circa* 1905.
Keith Austin Collection

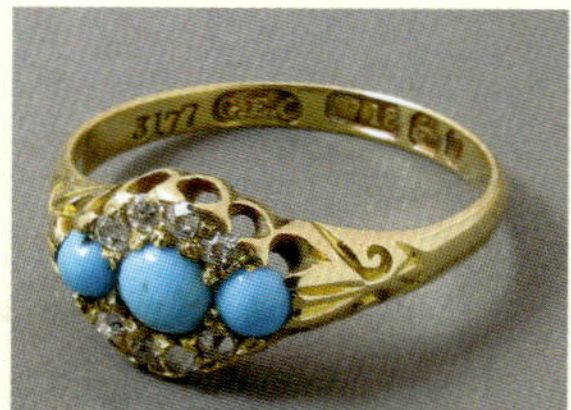

Fig. 173. Cluster of a Persian turquoise and brilliant-cut diamonds in claw settings, carved shoulders on a plain hoop. Hallmarked: Birmingham, 18ct. yellow gold, maker's mark G.E.C, additional mark 3117, 1898. Bezel 8x10mm, hoop diameter 17.5mm.

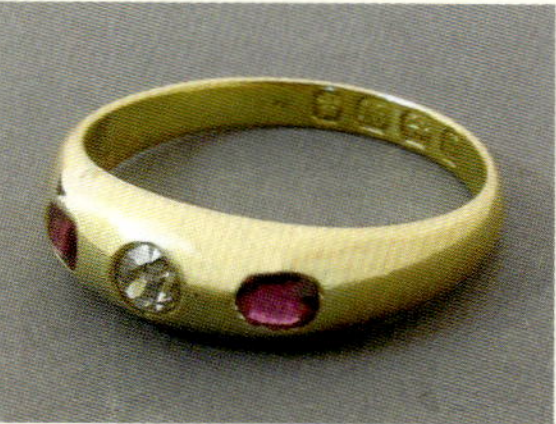

Fig. 175. Gypsy ring set with two rubies and a diamond. Hallmarked: Birmingham, 18ct. yellow gold, 1889. Bezel depth 5mm, hoop diameter 17mm.

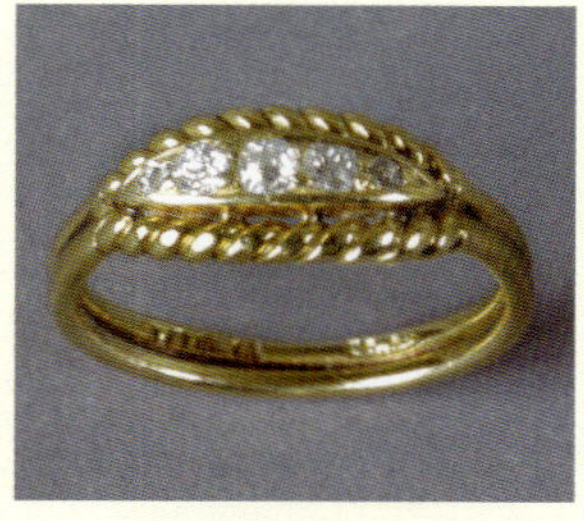

Fig. 176. A boat-shaped bezel set with five brilliant-cut diamonds, surrounded by a purled border. Plain double wire shank. Hallmarked: 1901, London, 18ct. yellow gold, maker's mark J.W.B., (J.W. Benson Ltd., 62 & 64 Ludgate Hill, London E.C., and 25 Old Bond Street, W., and 28 Royal Exchange E.C.). Originally the ring sold for £7.10s. Bezel 7x17mm, shank diameter 18mm, width 3mm.

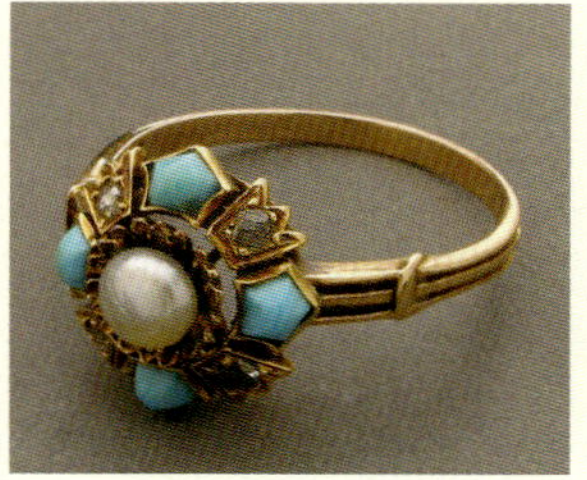

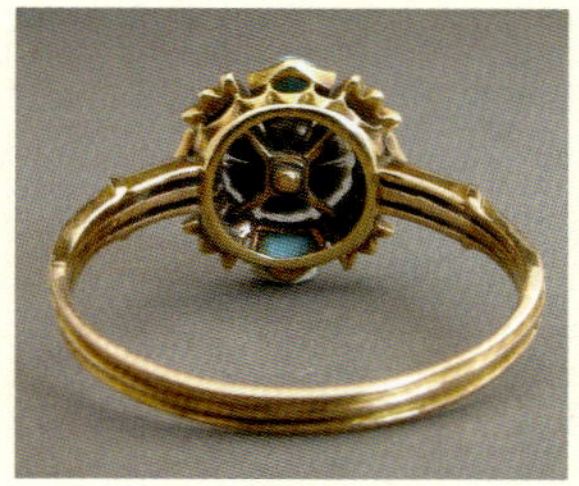

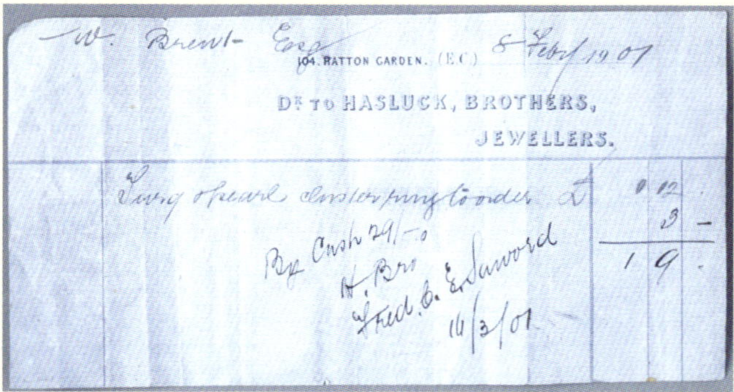

Fig. 174 a, b, c. Six triple petals, set with a tiny rose diamond in the middle petal, surround the central pearl, outer turquoises and diamonds are set at a forty-five degree angle to the central motif, the whole bezel being set on a gallery comprising a series of joined Ys. The shoulders are formed from three sections of gold that continue into the shank. A single rib embellishes each shoulder. Original sales receipt dated 1901. Bezel 12x12mm, gallery depth 2mm, shank diameter 19mm.

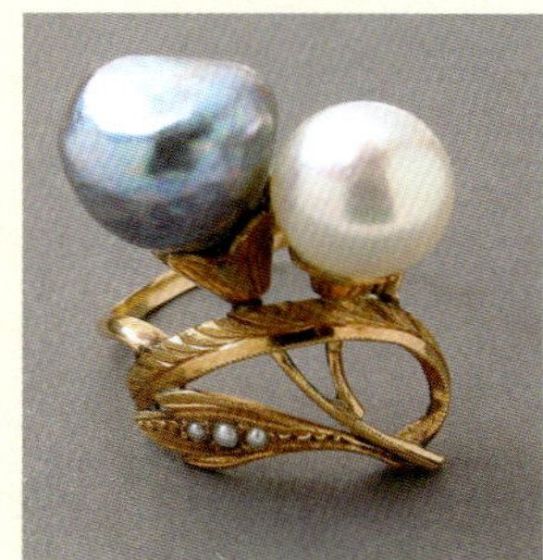

Fig. 177. Blue baroque pearl and a white pearl set in rose gold Art Nouveau setting, seed pearls decorate the milled and engraved foliate design. Marked K14 inside the narrow hoop. European, *Circa* 1900-1910. Bezel 23mm in length, hoop diameter 17mm.

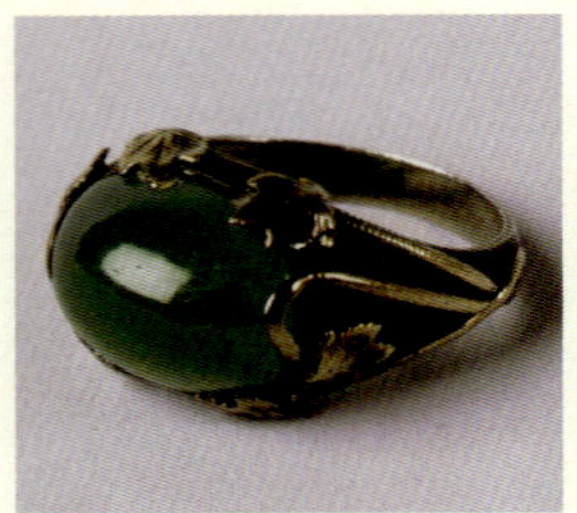

Fig. 178. Cabochon chryoprase is secured by gold vine leaves applied to an oxidized silver mounting. *Circa* 1890-1910. Gem 9x13mm, shank diameter 17mm.

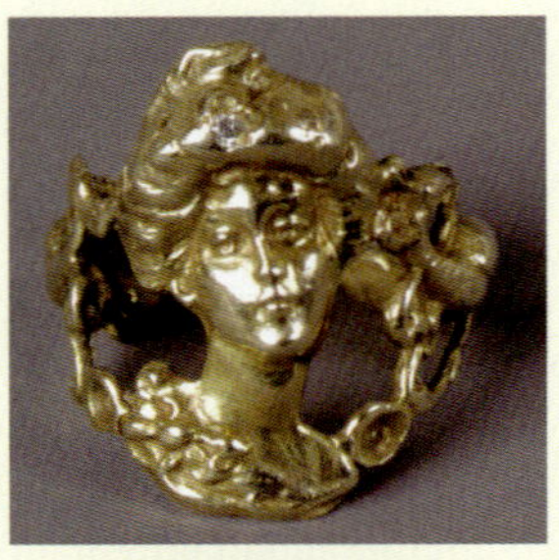

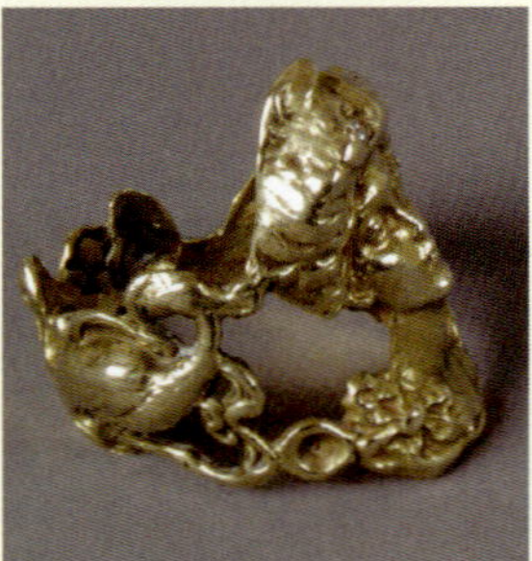

Fig. 179 a, b. Gibson Girl, full face with a tiny diamond set in the hair, a peacock on each shoulder and tail feathers forming the shank. Yellow gold. American Art Nouveau, *circa* 1900-1910. Depth of bezel 23mm.

In complete contrast to commercial designs, jewellers of the Art Nouveau school from Britain, the Continent and America frequently made rings from gold or silver, often enamelled and set with stones of appropriate colour or character to enhance the design. Moonstones, opals and pearls (Fig. 177) were used frequently along with other gems, usually cut as cabochons. Rings were decorated with applied flowers or foliage (Fig. 178), a female head or other human form (Fig 179 a, b), in swirling, asymmetrical designs. (Fig. 180) A number of mass-produced rings reflected the Art Nouveau influence, but these were more subdued in character. (Fig. 181)

A fashion for infants' rings is evident in this period; they are miniature examples of adult rings. These tiny rings were popular both in England and America. (Fig. 182) (Fig. 183)

As travel became more common, rings from abroad were found increasingly in England and America. Rings had certain features in common but each country had specific elements that indicated the country of origin. The accompanying illustrations show American rings made in this period. (Fig. 184) (Fig. 185) (Fig. 186) (Fig. 187) (Fig. 188) (Fig. 189) (Fig. 190) (Fig. 191 a, b, c) (Fig. 192)

Shoulder designs were varied at this time. They were gem-set, carved, forked (often from substantial wirework), formed from radiating panels, reeded, ribbed, openwork, occasionally engraved, or plain and narrow. Galleries were designed in a variety of openwork patterns or were deeply scrolled. Plain shanks were D-shaped, triangular or round in section, and flat. Occasionally a shank was engraved, reeded, channelled or made from openwork - a lingering reminder of earlier periods.

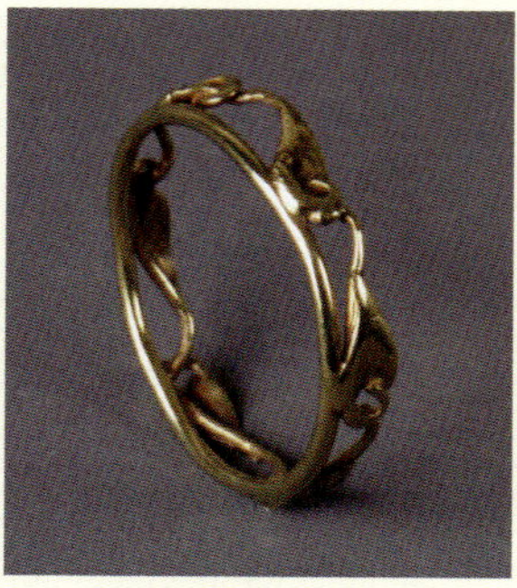

Fig. 180. An abstract Art Nouveau design applied to a narrow wire hoop, rich yellow gold. *Circa* 1900. Hoop diameter 16mm, width 3.5mm.

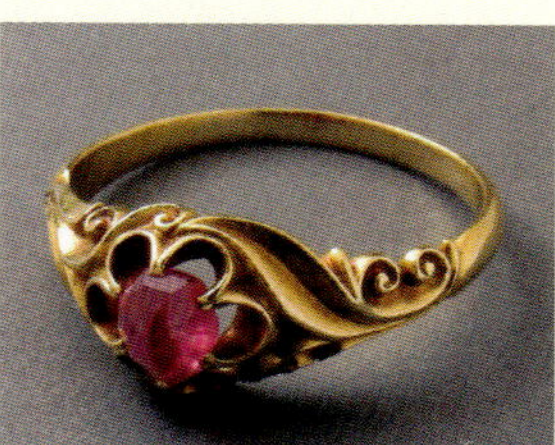

Fig. 181. Open claw setting holds a pale ruby, crudely faceted into a pyramid. Asymmetric carving decorates the bezel and shoulders, plain shank D-shaped in section. Yellow gold. *Circa* 1895. Bezel depth 8mm, shank diameter 17mm.

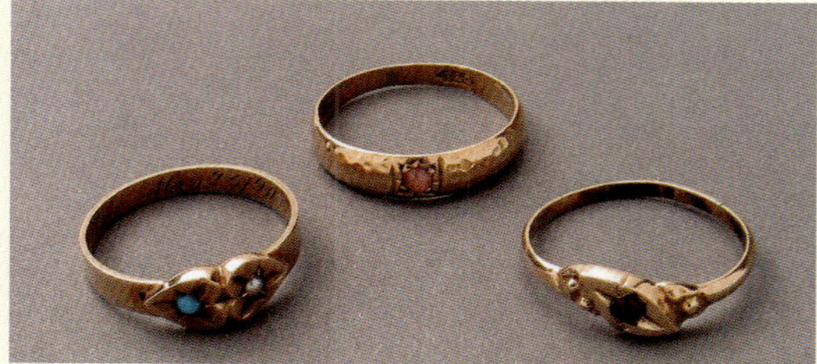

Fig. 182 shows the following three rings:

1)Infant's ring comprising two hearts set with a pearl and a turquoise in a flat shank, engraved inside: 'Willie May 25/90'. Rose gold. English. Bezel 4.5x4mm, shank diameter 12mm.

2)Hammered gold hoop ring set with a tiny amethyst. Hallmarked: Chester 9(.375) ct. rose gold, maker's mark T&G, 1914. Hoop diameter 13mm.

3) Infant's ring comprising diagonal diamond-shape bezel set with rose-cut garnet in a star setting, chased shoulders, plain shank. Rose gold. English, *circa* 1890-1900. Shank diameter 13mm.

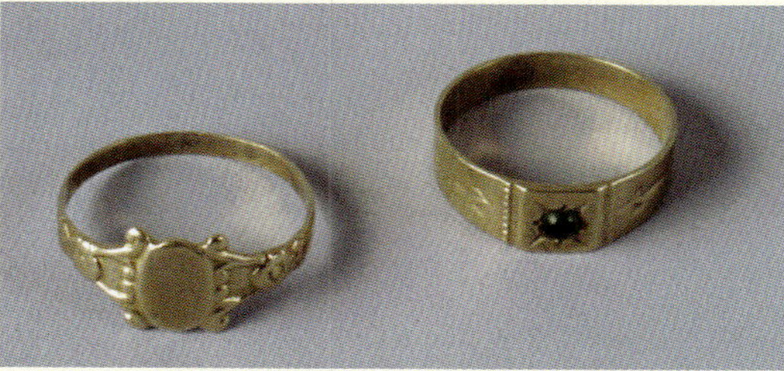

Fig. 183 shows the following two rings:

1) Infant's signet ring decorated with a flower and two leaves on each shoulder, 10k. pale yellow gold. American, *circa* 1895-1910. Bezel depth 5mm, shank diameter 12mm.

2) Infant's ring with a star-set cabochon green stone, shoulders decorated with modified fleur-de-lis; flat, wide shank. 10k. yellow gold, marked OB (for outer band). American, *circa* 1895-1910. Bezel diameter 4.5mm, shank diameter 12mm.

[1885 - 1910]

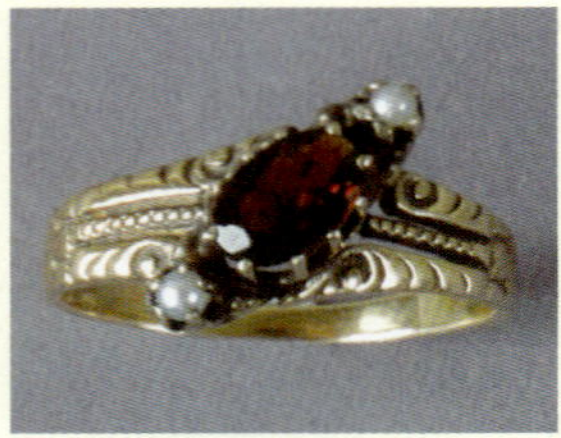

Fig. 184. Diagonal bezel set with a garnet and two pearls secured by claws, carved and beaded shoulders taper to a plain flat shank. Rose gold. American, *circa* 1895-1910. Bezel length 13mm, shank diameter 16mm.

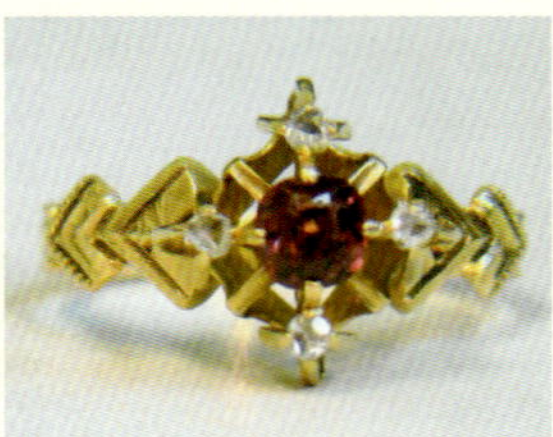

Fig. 185. Bezel comprises a cushion-cut almandine garnet and four rose-cut diamonds all in claw settings which are faceted to catch the light. Two carved and beaded V-shaped motifs decorate each shoulder, flat reeded shank. 18ct. yellow gold. American, *circa* 1885-1900. Bezel 11x10mm, shank diameter 16mm, width 2.5mm.

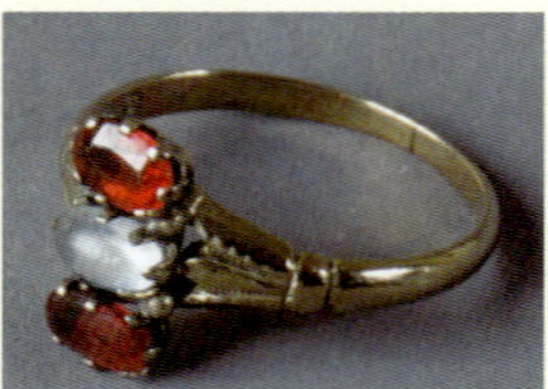

Fig. 186. Vertical bezel set with two garnets and a moonstone in claw settings, divided shoulders flank a faceted leaf motif above a wide transverse rib, plain D-shaped shank. Rose gold. American, *circa* 1895-1910. Bezel 11x5mm, shank diameter 16mm.

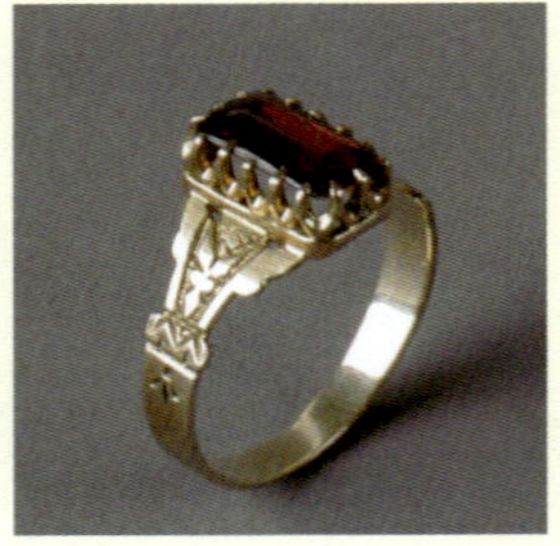

Fig. 187. Pyrope garnet set in 16 claws, engraved shoulders, flat hoop, maker's mark: a diagonal anchor and K, yellow gold. American, *circa* 1885. Bezel 10x6mm, hoop diameter 16.5mm, width 2.5mm.

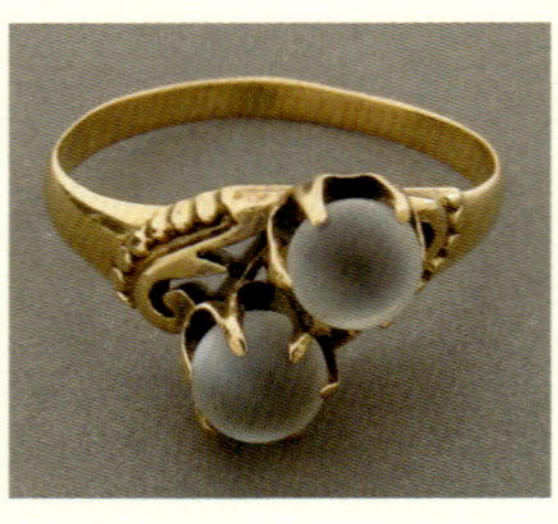

Fig. 188. Diagonal bezel holding 2 round claw-set moonstones, with beading around the bezel. Rose gold. American, *circa* 1895-1910. Bezel 12x5mm, hoop diameter 18mm.

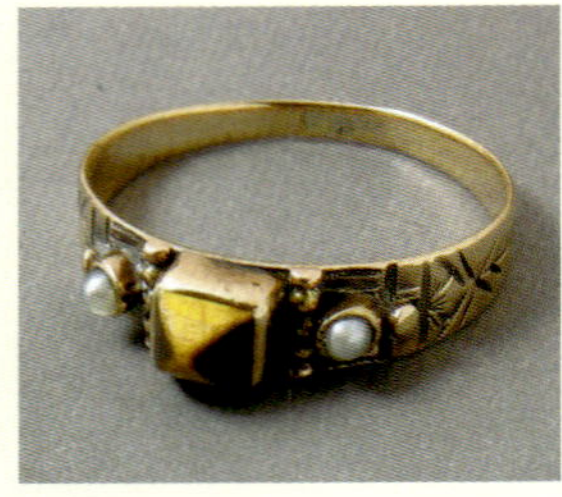

Fig. 189. Tiger's eye cut as a pyramid and two pearls in millegrained collet settings on a rose gold hoop, engraved on the shoulders. American, *circa* 1880-1900. Hoop diameter 17mm.

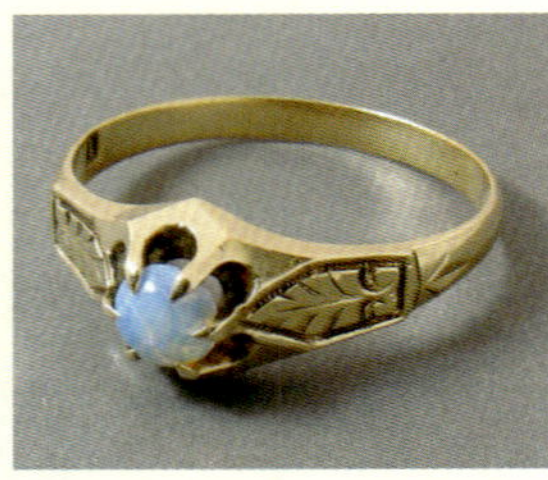

Fig. 190. Australian opal in a claw setting with engraved foliate design on each shoulder, plain shank. Yellow gold. American, *circa* 1890. Shank diameter 18mm.

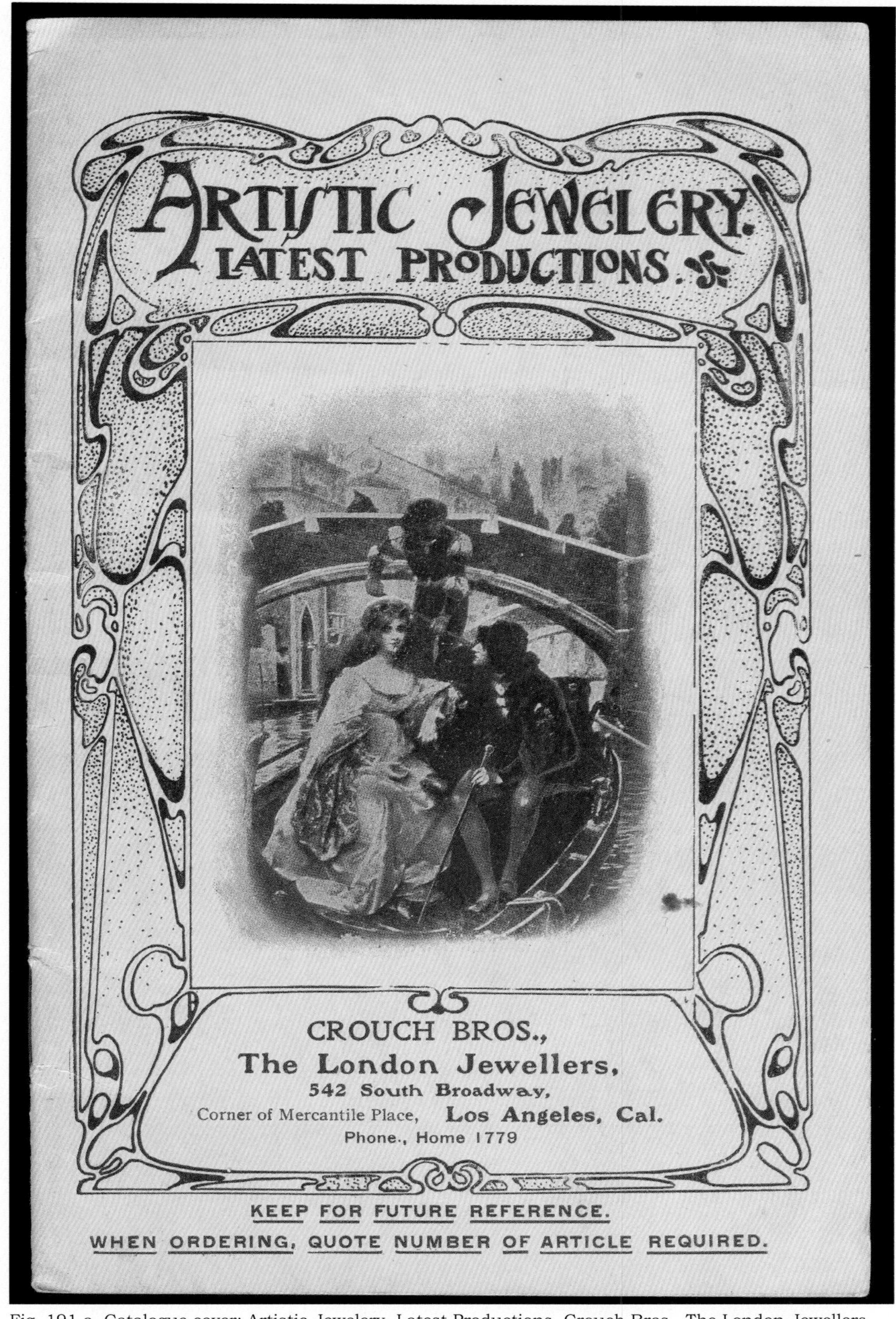

Fig. 191 a. Catalogue cover: Artistic Jewelery. Latest Productions. Crouch Bros., The London Jewellers, 542 South Broadway, Los Angeles, Cal.

[1885 - 1910]

The Object

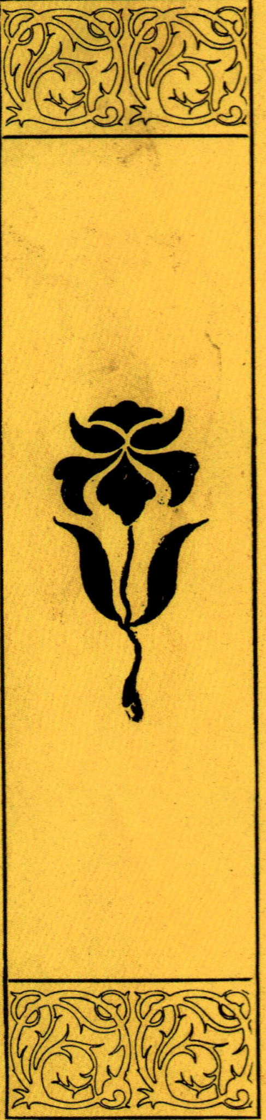

OF this booklet is to present, for your favorable consideration, a few illustrations (actual photographs) of the many beautiful and useful articles in Finger Rings and Jewelry, Watches and Cut Glass.

Such gifts are always acceptable on account of the lasting sentiment conveyed.

We request you to make a careful study of this booklet.

We extend a cordial invitation to our friends and patrons to visit our store.

Fig. 191 b. Inside cover from Artistic Jewelery.

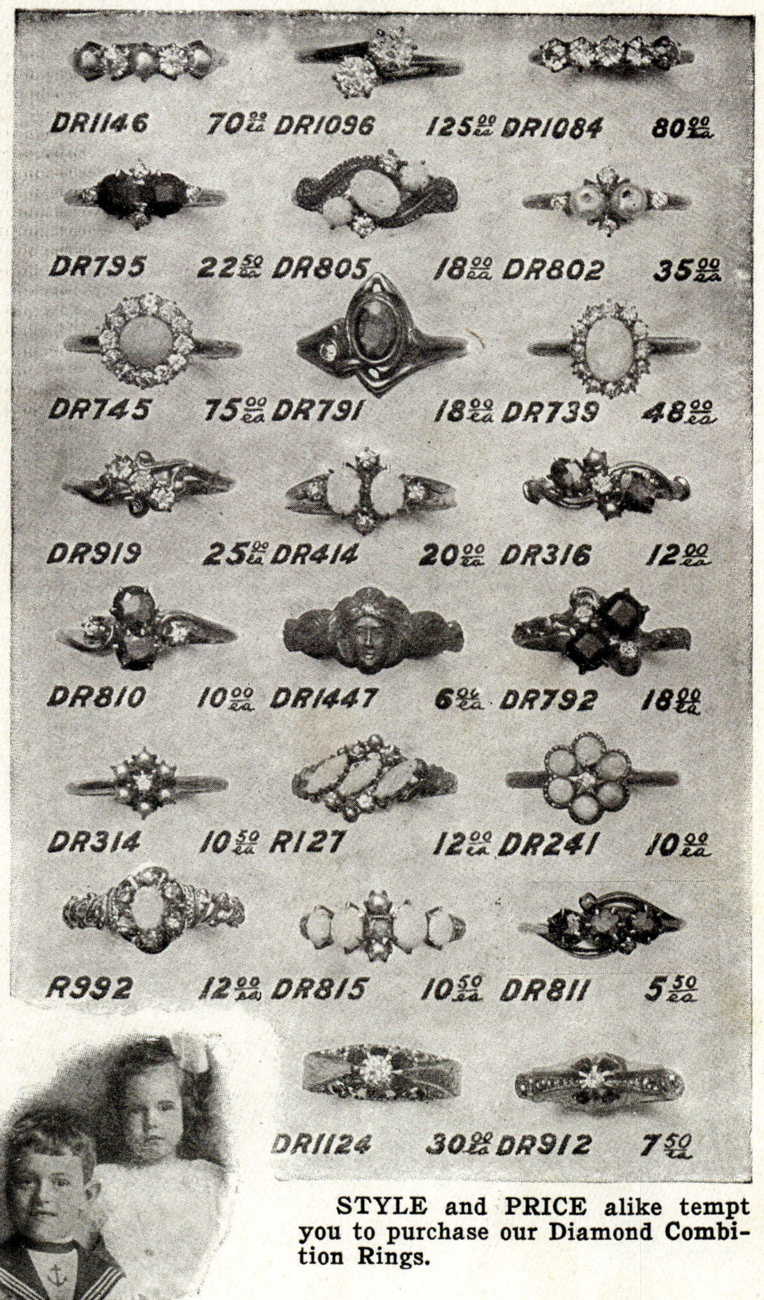

STYLE and PRICE alike tempt you to purchase our Diamond Combition Rings.

Fig. 191 c. Plate 1 from Artistic Jewelery.

[1885 - 1910]

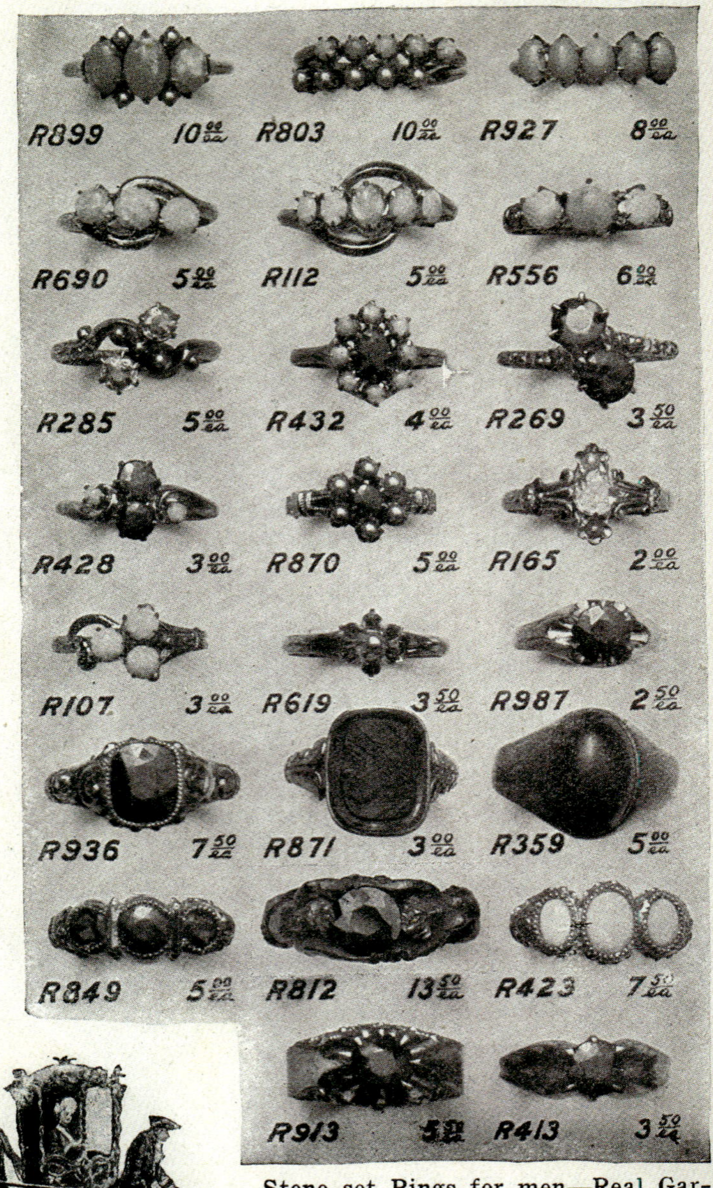

Fig. 192. Plate 4 from Artistic Jewelery.

A wide range of gem setting methods were employed: all types of claw setting (Fig. 193), pavé, square (Fig. 194), plain or star-set gypsy (Fig. 195), thread, see Fig. 151, and millegrain, see Fig. 139. Cramp and cut-down collet settings had all but disappeared.

Gold 'colouring' was used chiefly on 15ct. and 12ct. gold rings set with small gems. The fine gem-set clusters or half-hoops, usually made from 18ct. gold, were not 'coloured'. Red or a warm yellow shade of gold was preferred for 22ct. and 18ct., whereas 9ct. gold was often rose gold, reminiscent of the gold used between 1800 and 1815. A few hand-made hoop rings in this period were decorated with different shades of gold. (Fig. 196)

It should be mentioned that many rings of this era carried the Chester hallmark, regardless of where they were made; in earlier periods the Chester hallmark was not as prevalent.

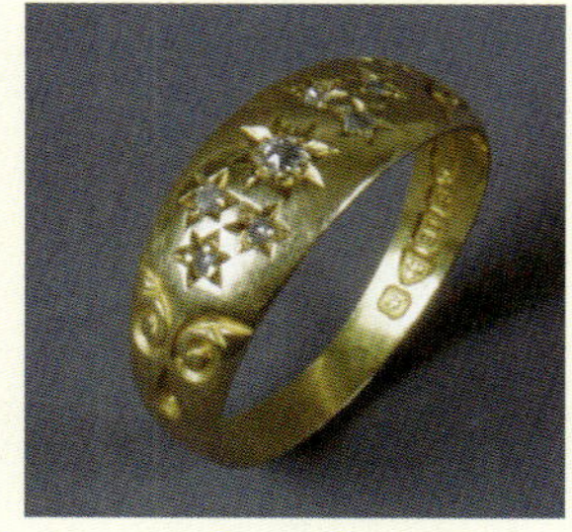

Fig. 195. Gypsy ring holding seven brilliant-cut diamonds in star settings. Carved scrolls on the shoulders. Hallmarked: Chester 18ct. yellow gold, 1906. Front of hoop 7mm deep, hoop diameter 18mm.

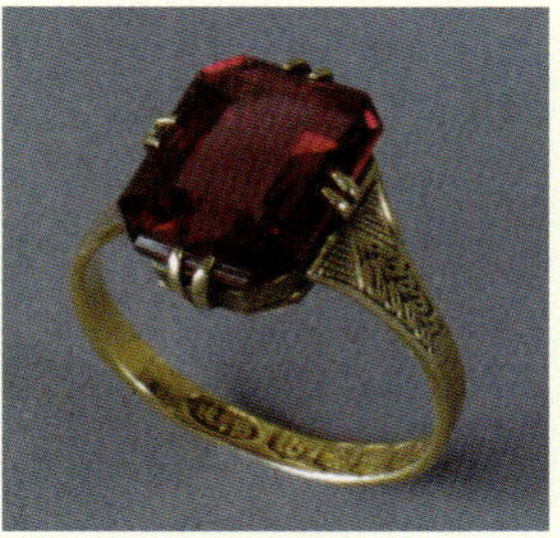

Fig. 193. Four double pronged claws extend the entire depth of the gallery securing an early example of a synthetic ruby, the gallery has a narrow slit around its circumference. Engraved spatula-shaped shoulders, flat, plain shank. Hallmarked: Glasgow, 18ct. pale yellow gold, maker's mark R.S, 1887. Bezel 11x8mm, shank diameter 16mm.

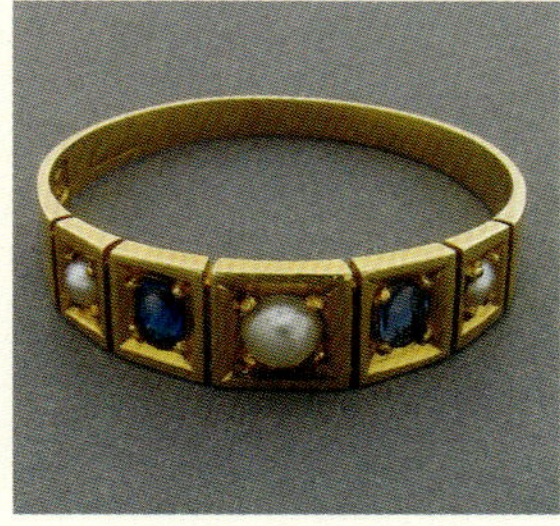

Fig. 194. Half-hoop comprising two sapphires and three pearls in square settings. Flat, tapering hoop. Hallmarked: Birmingham 18ct. yellow gold, 1901. This design was fashionable between 1885 and 1910. Hoop diameter 18mm.

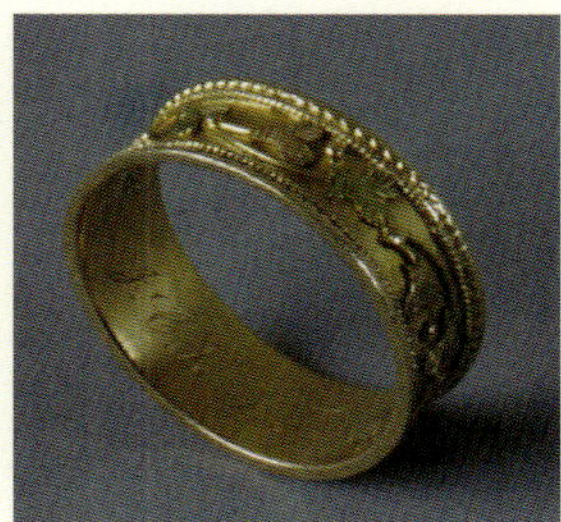

Fig. 196. Hoop ring made with a minutely scalloped flanged edge, a strip of applied purled gold inside the flanged edge, and beads and stylized leaves in red and green gold. Inscribed inside hoop: 'J.C. to I.F. 25/1/91'. Hallmarked: Birmingham, 18ct. 'coloured' gold, 1890. Hoop diameter 16mm, width 6mm.

BETROTHAL RINGS

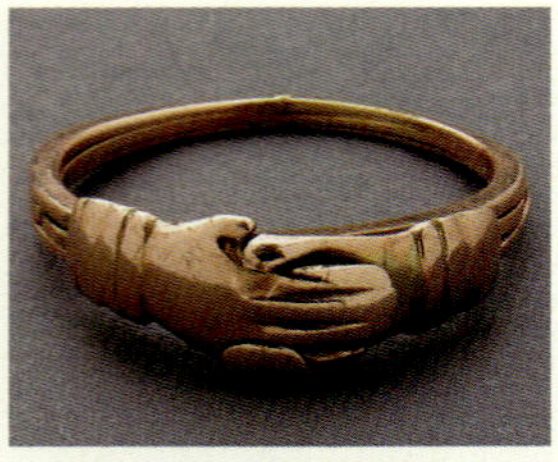

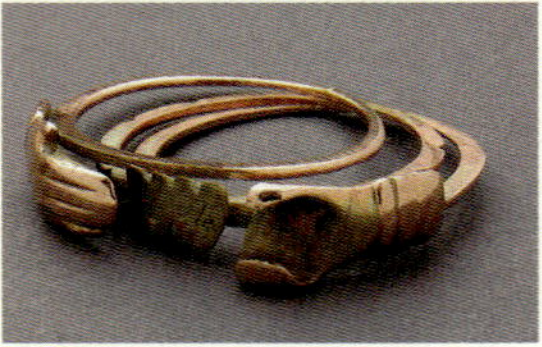

Fig. 197 a, b. Fede-gimmel ring (showing considerable wear) comprising three hoops secured by a single pivot. The outer hoops, when closed, form clasped hands, concealing double hearts (inscribed L04) attached to the middle, scalloped hoop, rose gold. *Circa* 1800-1810. Hands and cuffs 6x19mm, hoop diameter 16mm.

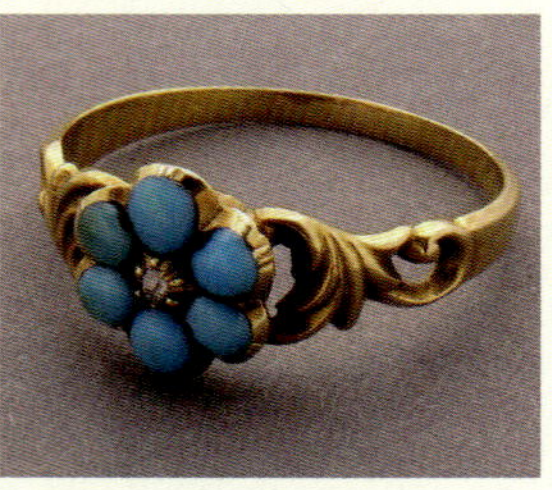

Fig. 198. Persian turquoise cluster with central diamond spark. Asymmetrical openwork shoulders. Yellow gold. *Circa* 1855. Bezel 8.5x8mm, hoop diameter 18mm.

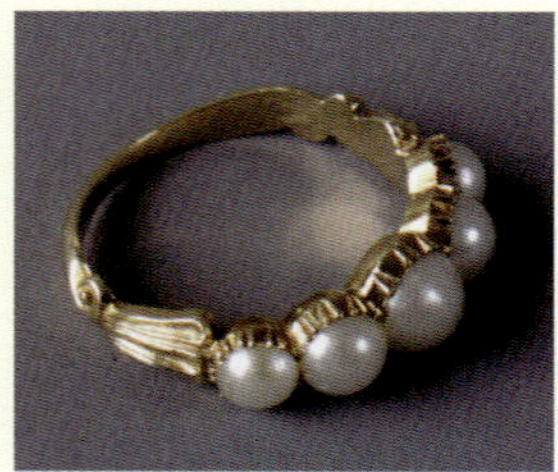

Fig. 199. Five half pearls in cut-down collets. Carved asymmetric shoulders and asymmetric hoop ending in a scroll at shoulders. Yellow gold. *Circa* 1840-1850. Centre pearl 6x6mm, gallery depth 3mm, hoop diameter 18mm.

Betrothal rings from the Middle Ages frequently used the 'fede' motif, and some 'fede' rings were made in the nineteenth-century.

A fede-gimmel ring, which originated on the Continent, comprised two or three rings with a tiny dowel at the back of the hoops allowing the rings to swivel apart. Each of the two rings was embellished with a hand; when they were closed each clasped the other. If there was a third hoop, it was usually decorated with a single or double heart that was hidden from view when the ring was closed. (Fig. 197 a, b) This type of ring was used in the first decade of the century as a betrothal ring.

Prince Albert gave Queen Victoria a betrothal ring in the form of a serpent studded with emeralds. Until about 1875 betrothal rings were chosen from any type of gem ring except diamonds or opals; diamonds were considered the prerogative of married women, and opals had gained a reputation for bad luck, though this superstition was beginning to fade by the 1880s (see OPALS in the Glossary).

Charles Dickens in *David Copperfield*, 1849-50, has a delightful description of the purchasing of a betrothal ring:

> When I measured Dora's finger for a ring that was to be made of forget-me-nots; and when the jeweller, to whom I took the measure, found me out, and laughed over his order book, and charged me anything he liked for the pretty little toy with its blue stones - so associated in my remembrance with Dora's hand, that yesterday, when I saw such another, by chance, on the finger of my own daughter, there was a momentary stirring in my heart, like pain. (Ch.33, p.417 The Reader's Digest Association Inc, N.Y., 1986.) (Fig. 198)

Pearls were considered eminently suitable for unmarried women and it is likely that pearl half-hoops were chosen as betrothal rings throughout the century. (Fig. 199) The following passage from Charlotte Yonge's 1856 novel *The Daisy Chain* (New York, Macmillan & Co. 1888 edition) gives an example:

Margaret lay...gazing on the hoop of pearls which Alan had chosen as the ring of betrothal. "The pearl of great price," murmured she to herself.... (Pt.1, Ch.28, p.279).

By about 1875 diamonds were finally considered appropriate for use in a betrothal ring (Fig. 200) (Fig. 201), and in the 1890s the diamond solitaire made its debut (Fig 202), though any type of gem ring was still considered a suitable token of betrothal. In 1895 Harrod's Stores, Limited, published a catalogue in which two pages were entitled 'Fine Gem Engagement and other Rings'. The rings displayed include a half-hoop set with precious gems, cluster, marquise, crossover, gypsy, twist and boat-shaped bezels, as well as the diamond solitaire. Which rings were engagement rings and which were considered 'other' rings is debatable. For much of the nineteenth century the term 'betrothal' was used, then towards the end of the century 'engagement' came into common usage.

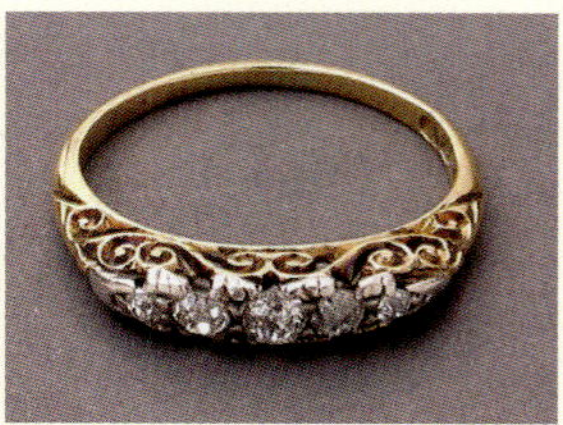

Fig. 200. Half-hoop set with small, graduated brilliant-cut diamonds set in platinum on deeply scrolled gallery. Narrow hoop, yellow gold. The engagement ring of the author's grandmother who was married 6th September 1910. Gallery depth 3.5mm, hoop diameter 16mm.

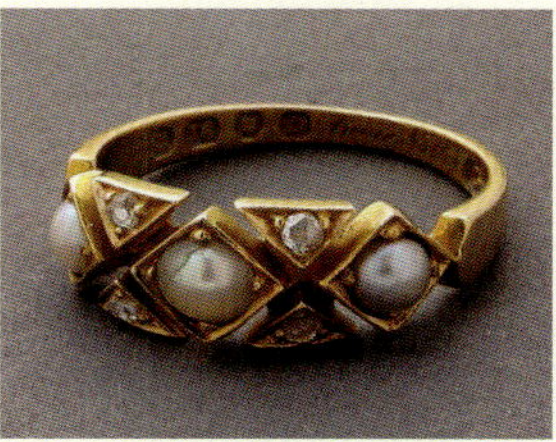

Fig. 201. Half-hoop comprising half pearls in square settings and rose-cut diamonds in triangular settings. Plain shank – rectangular in section – terminates in a point at the shoulders. Inscribed inside shank: 'Annie Nutter Oct. 8. '91'. Hallmarked: London, 18ct. yellow gold, maker's mark, CS FS, 1879. Unfortunately the gold 'colouring' was removed when a diamond was replaced and the gold was polished. Bezel 6.5x22mm, shank diameter 17mm.

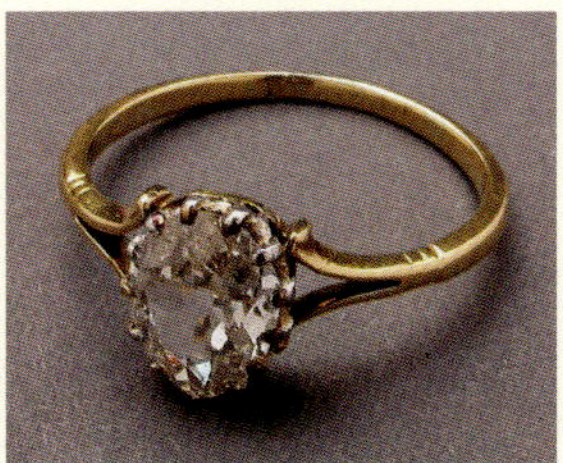

Fig. 202. Early nineteenth century pear-shaped brilliant-cut diamond secured with thirteen platinum claws that are attached to a pear-shaped gold frame, bifurcated shoulders, plain narrow shank, stamped 18ct Pl. Setting, *circa* 1900. Yellow gold. Bezel 9x6mm, shank diameter 17mm.

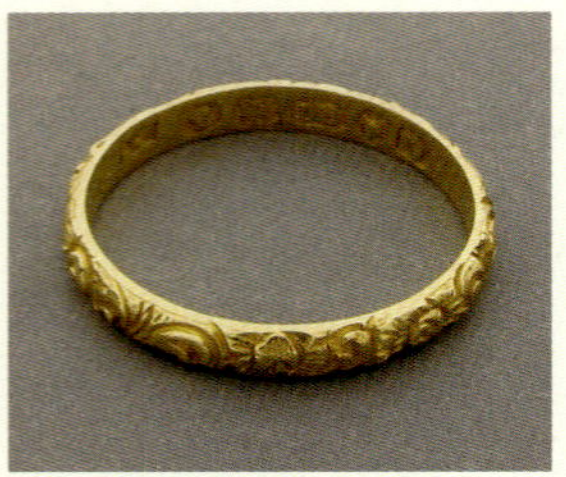

Fig. 203. Crisply chased, narrow hoop ring. Hallmarked: London, 18ct. yellow gold, maker's mark RC, 1839. The hallmark indicates it is a wedding ring, because many early decorative rings were not hallmarked. Hoop diameter 16mm, width 2.5mm.

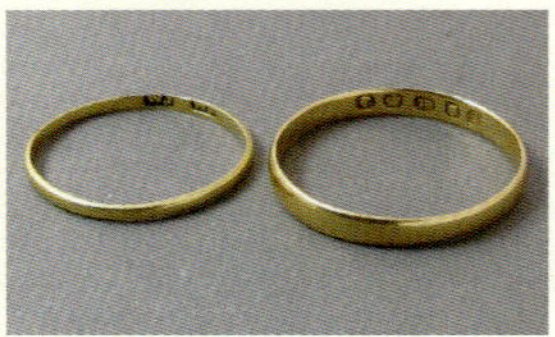

Fig. 204. Left: Scottish wedding ring, maker's mark WJ (stamped twice), the mark of William Jamieson, an Aberdeen goldsmith. No date mark. Hoop diameter 17mm, width 1.5mm. Right: wedding ring hallmarked London, 18ct., 1870. Hoop diameter 18mm, width 2.5mm.

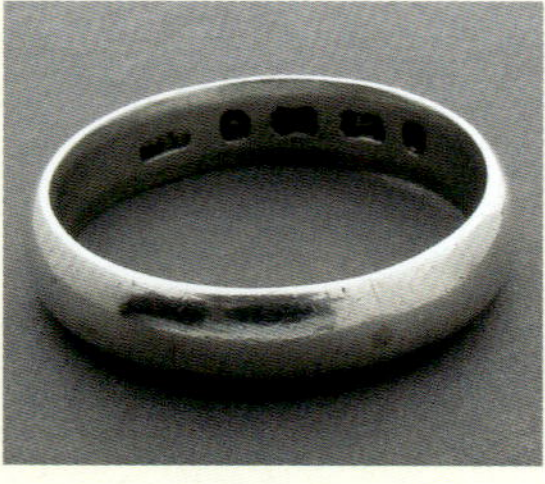

Fig. 205. Silver wedding ring, possibly a man's ring. Hallmarked: Birmingham 1867. Hoop diameter 20mm, width 5mm.

WEDDING RINGS

It was not until the nineteenth century that wedding rings were worn continuously by women, and then it was only the bride who received a ring during the marriage ceremony. The width and decoration of wedding rings varied throughout the century as the following illustrations show. (Fig. 203) (Fig. 204) (Fig. 205) (Fig. 206) (Fig. 207) (Fig. 208) (Fig. 209) In Britain the wedding ring was worn on the annular finger of the left hand. The groom might receive a ring from his wife later. Queen Victoria recorded in her diary that she gave Prince Albert his ring after the ceremony. A portrait of Prince Albert in the National Portrait Gallery, London, shows him with a plain gold band on the little finger of his left hand— perhaps he outgrown the ring! A portrait of the Prince of Wales, (later Edward VII) by von Angeli, 1876, on display at Sandringham, shows the Prince wearing a gypsy ring set with two diamonds and a sapphire, flanked by plain gold rings on the 'wedding ring' finger.

For centuries there have been many superstitions and customs surrounding wedding rings, a number of which have been recorded in *Finger-Ring Lore* by William Jones, F.S.A. The following quotation is to be found on p.173 of the first edition:

"The following notice of an advertisement is extracted from an Oxford paper of 1860, ... "IMPORTANT NOTICE!-The largest cake ever made in Oxford, weighing upward of 1,000 pounds, and containing 30 gold wedding and other rings, in value from 7s.6d. to Two Guineas each! To be seen for sale at No.1 Queen Street, Oxford, from Thursday, December 27th, until Saturday, January 5th, 1861, when it will be cut out at the low price of 1s.2d. per pound (this quality frequently sold for wedding-cake). Persons at a distance desirous of purchasing may rely upon prompt attention being given to their favours.

"N.B.–J.Boffin will feel obliged if persons obtaining the gold rings will favour him with their names."

Charles Dickens has a comment about wedding rings in *Christmas Stories II*, "Doctor Marigold", 1865, (Heron Books, Centennial Edition, p.88):

'Now what is it? Why, I'll tell you what it is. It's made of fine gold, and it's not broke, though there's a hole in the middle of it, and it's stronger than any fetter that ever was forged, though it's smaller than any finger in my set of ten';

'Now what else is it? It's a man-trap and a handcuff, the parish stocks and a leg-lock, all in gold and all in one.'

'Now what else is it? It's a wedding-ring.'

Some wedding rings were of the gimmel variety, comprised of two individual linked rings kept closed with a tiny dowel to form a single ring. (Fig. 210 a, b) The inside portion of each hoop was inscribed with the name of the bride and groom and the date of the ceremony. In 1785, the heir to the throne (to become George IV in 1820), gave a similar ring to Mrs. Fitzherbert, when, it is said, he married her. Early wedding rings, either the single hoop or the gimmel variety, might be engraved with a message. The custom ceased after 1855, when compulsory hallmarking of wedding rings was introduced in Britain. The gimmel wedding ring was still used until the 1890s on the Continent.

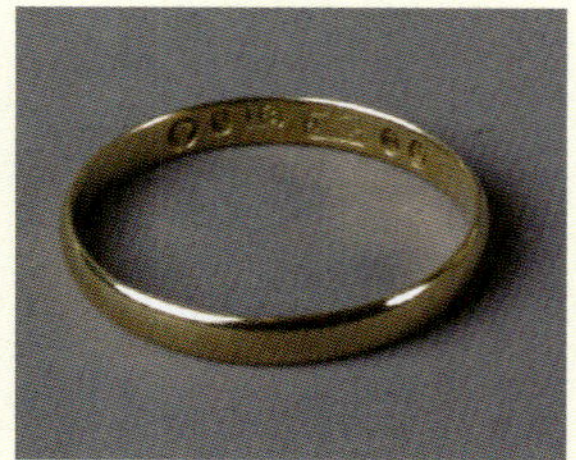

Fig. 206. Wedding ring. Hallmarked: Glasgow, 18ct. yellow gold, maker's mark J C, 1869. Hoop diameter 18.5mm, width 2mm.

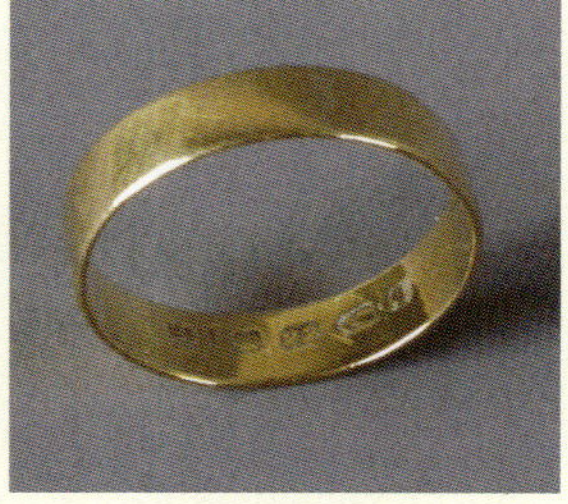

Fig. 207. Wedding ring. Birmingham 22ct. red gold, maker's mark SH, 1890. Hoop diameter 17.5mm, width 4mm.

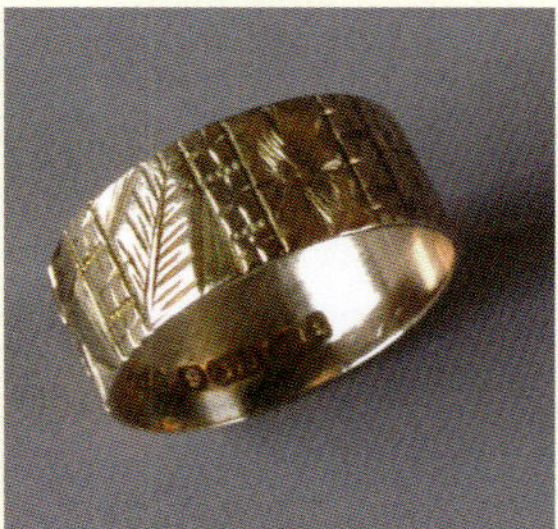

Fig. 208. Engraved hoop ring. Hallmarked: Birmingham, 9(.375) ct. rose gold, maker's mark J.A, 1893. Hoop diameter 19mm, width 8mm.

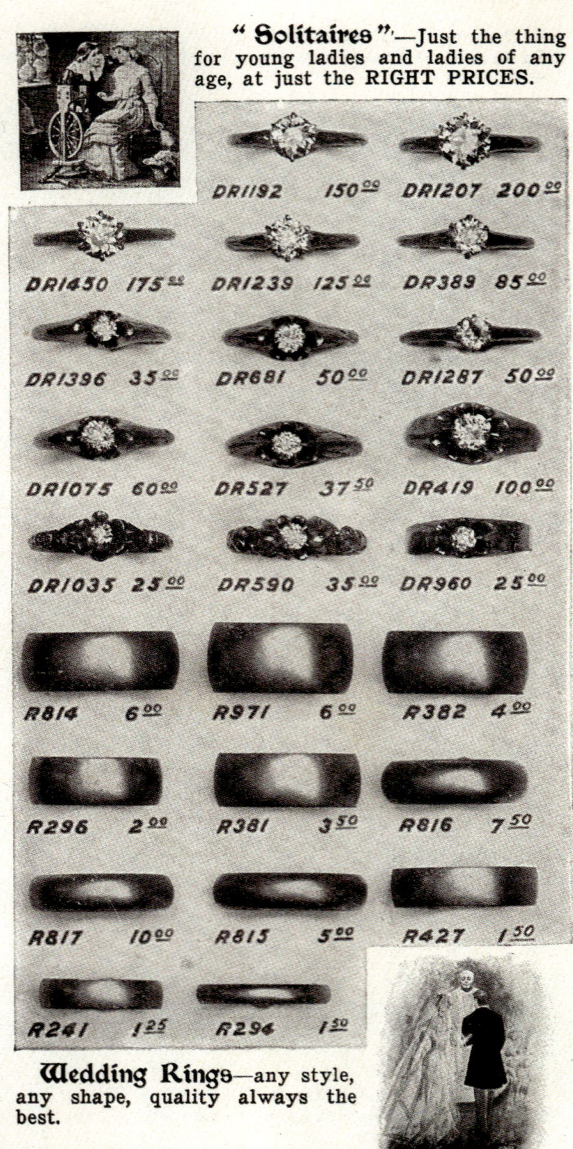

Fig. 209. Plate 3 from Artistic Jewelery. Latest Productions. Crouch Bros., The London Jewellers, 542 South Broadway, Los Angeles, Cal.

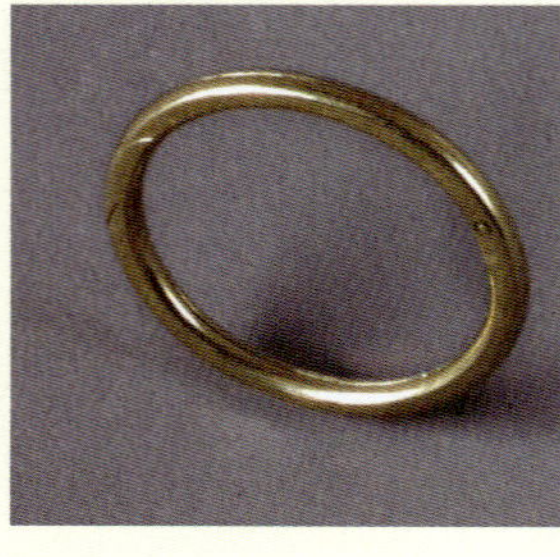

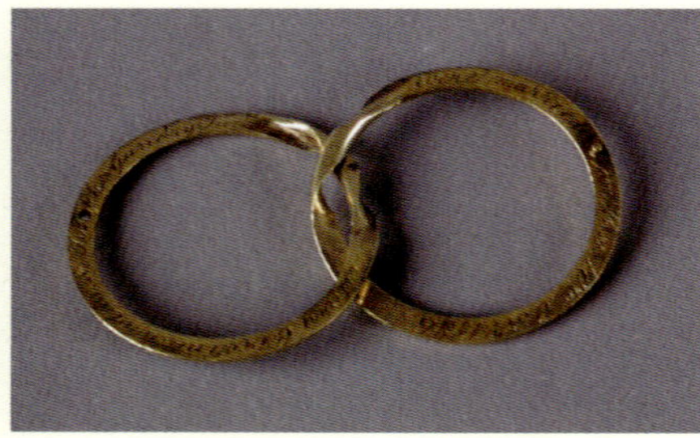

Fig. 210 a, b. Gimmel wedding ring formed from two inseparable rings kept closed by a tiny dowel. Inscribed inside the hoops: 'Mary Caroline Fowlds & Joseph Gundry Junr. (on one hoop) were married on the 10th October 1836' (on second hoop). Yellow gold. Hoop diameter 15.5mm, width 1mm.

KEEPER RINGS

The keeper or guard ring was worn next to the wedding ring to prevent its loss. Wedding rings were prized for their meaning rather than their monetary value. Many women never considered removing the wedding ring, and its accidental loss would have been considered tragic.

In *La Belle Assemblée*, July 1806, mention is made of a guard ring in the article 'A Letter On Dress, From a Young Lady resident in London, to her Friend in the Country':

> Lord George ... presented her with a gourd [sic] ring of the finest brilliants... (p.335)

In November 1807 another description of a guard ring is given in the article entitled 'Letter on dress, Introductory and descriptive, from Eliza to Julia', also from *La Belle Assemblée*:

> The rainbow hoop-ring, ... takes the place of the diamond, by way of guard to the wedding ring... But you and I, Julia, have as yet, nothing to do with this last mentioned article; and when we have, I trust that our guard will boast a more auspicious emblem than that of variety... (p.284) (Fig. 211)

In *Finger-Ring Lore*, William Jones states that, 'the Prince of Wales, on his marriage to the Princess Alexandra, (1863) gave her as a keeper one with the stones set with his familiar name Bertie - beryl, emerald, ruby, turquoise, jacinth, emerald'. (p.416)

Etiquette journals of the 1870s stressed that the engagement ring should not be worn as a keeper to the wedding ring. Many gold rings, such as the plait ring, serpent ring, stiff curb-chain or the engraved hoop ring, were worn as keeper rings in the 1890s. (Fig. 212)

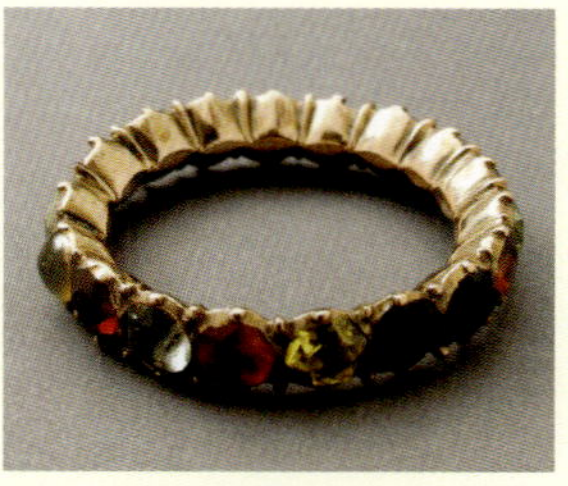

Fig. 211. 'Harlequin' or 'rainbow' hoop ring set in its entirety with fifteen star-cut gems, one brilliant-cut gem (a replacement), one cabochon and one rose-cut stone in cut-down collets the backs of which are triangular. The following stones are set in the ring: onyx, green tourmaline, citrine, fire opal, garnet, cat's eye, haematite, rose-cut diamond, amethyst, chrysoberyl. Pale rose gold. *Circa* 1800-1810. Hoop diameter 16mm, width 4mm.

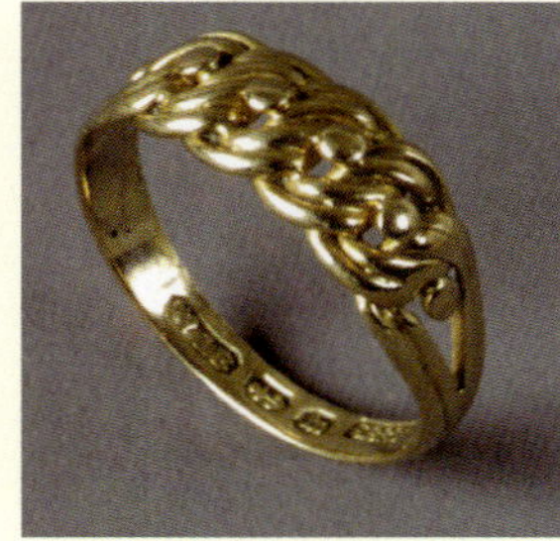

Fig. 212. Keeper ring. Double curb-chain bezel embellished with six gold beads on a plain shank. Hallmarked: Birmingham, 18ct. rich yellow gold, maker's mark S.BROS, 1896. Bezel 5.5x17.5mm, shank diameter 17.5mm.

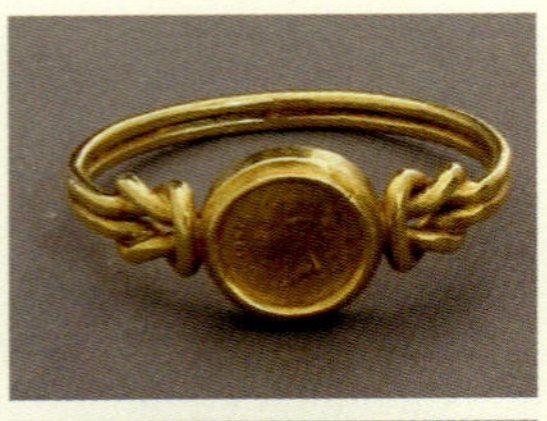

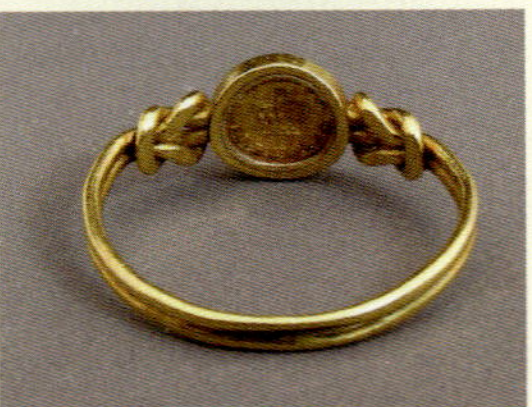

Fig. 213 a, b. The bezel contains a tiny medallion depicting Queen Victoria, with 'Victoria Regina' on either side of the head, the reverse shows a crown with the legend 'married 10 Feb 1840'. The double wire shank extends into a lovers' knot on each shoulder. Rich yellow gold. Bezel diameter 5.5mm, shank diameter 15mm.

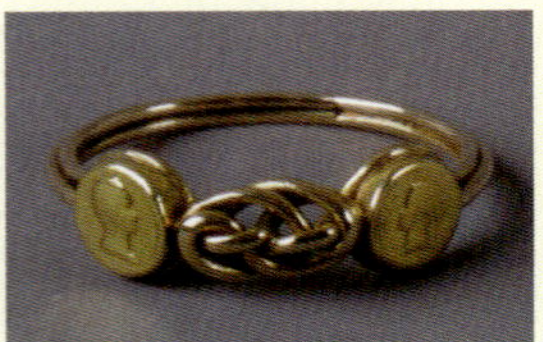

Fig. 214. Commemorative ring made for the wedding of Queen Victoria and Prince Albert (10 February 1840) set with medallions flanking a knot, set on a triple wire hoop, yellow gold. The face of each medallion is very worn. Knot 5x18.5mm, shank diameter 18.4mm.

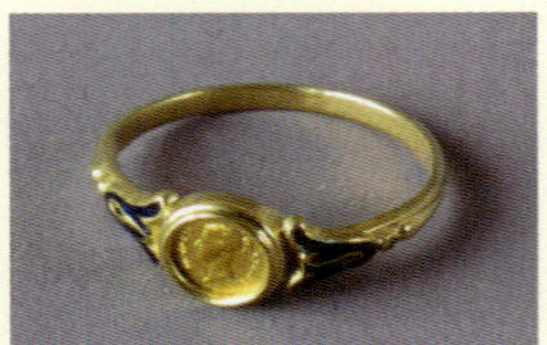

Fig. 215. Commemorative ring set with a tiny medallion depicting the head of the Queen and 'Victoria Regina' on either side of the head, shoulders enamelled in royal blue, narrow shank. Yellow gold. *Circa* 1840. Bezel diameter 5.5mm, shank diameter 16.5mm.

COMMEMORATIVE AND HISTORICAL RINGS

This section has examples of rings commemorating an historic event or personal events from 1800 to 1910.

In Britain, Queen Victoria came to the throne in 1837 and was married to Prince Albert on February 10th, 1840. Rings with tiny medallions bearing the head of Queen Victoria and Prince Albert were made to commemorate the accession to the throne and the marriage. According to William Jones in *Finger-Ring Lore*, 1877:

> At the marriage of Queen Victoria, Rings were distributed having the royal likeness in profile in gold: the legend being "Victoria Regina". The whole was less than a quarter of an inch in diameter, but with the aid of a powerful magnifying-glass the features were disclosed, beautifully delineated. The Queen was so pleased with this microscopic work of art that she ordered six dozen impressions to be struck and set by the court jewellers, Rundle and Bridges (sic), in gold rings for distribution among distinguished personages. (p.296)

One design had a plain double wire shank, with a lover's knot at each shoulder that widened to hold the single medallion of the Queen. (Fig. 213 a, b) A similar ring contained two medallions, one of the Queen and the second of Prince Albert, (Fig. 214) while a more elaborate design, holding medallions of both the Queen and her consort, was decorated with turquoises and diamonds. A fine example of the latter is in the Museum of London. Another ring with a medallion of Queen Victoria had blue enamel on the shoulders. (Fig. 215)

Rings were also made to celebrate the fiftieth (1887) and sixtieth (1897) Jubilees of Queen Victoria's accession to the throne. A registered design, for the 1887 Jubilee, was made in Birmingham. This ring had the letters V R (Victoria Regina) set with diamonds and engraved decoration of a sceptre, crozier and 'JUBILEE'. (Fig. 216 a, b, c, d) Many rings for both Jubilees were set with red,

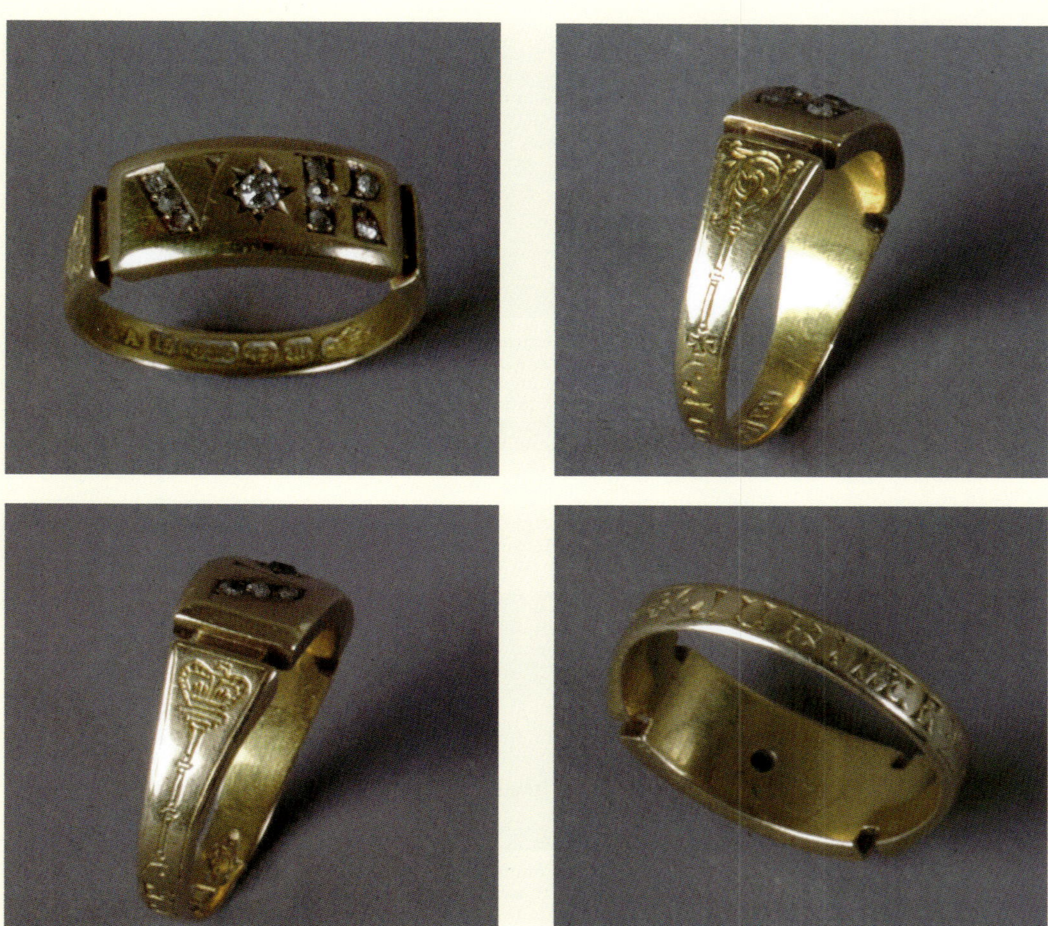

Fig. 216 a, b, c, d. Oblong bezel displaying V R (Victoria Regina) in diamonds and a star-set brilliant-cut diamond. Spatula-shaped shoulders, joined to the bezel by a short neck, are engraved, one with a sceptre, the other with a crozier; JUBILEE is engraved on the outside of the shank. Hallmarked: Birmingham, 15 (.675) ct. yellow gold, maker's mark A.A., damaged registration mark, 1886. Bezel 7x16mm, shank diameter 16.5mm.

Commemorative and Historical

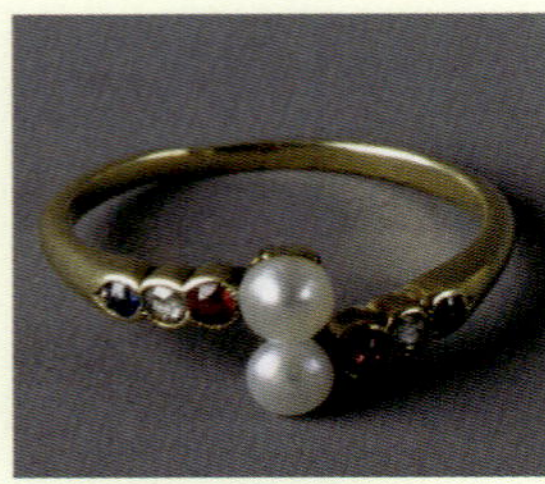

Fig. 217. 'Jubilee' crossover ring set with ruby, rose-cut diamond and sapphire on each shoulder in open-back millegrained collets and two pearls in the centre. Plain shank. Yellow gold. *Circa* 1897. Depth of pearl centre 7mm, shank diameter 17mm.

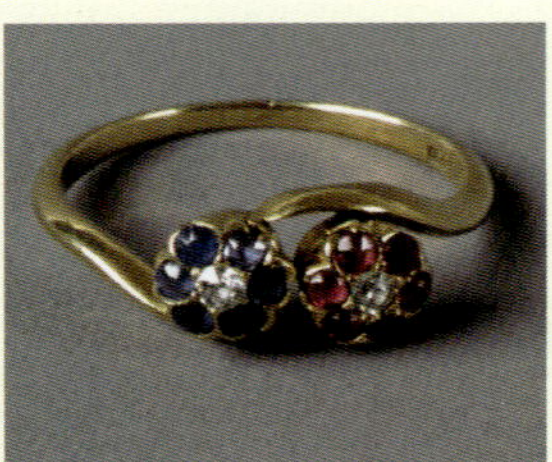

Fig. 218. 'Jubilee' cross-over ring. One cluster has rubies and a diamond, the other has sapphires and a diamond in claw settings. Narrow hoop stamped 18ct. Pale yellow gold. *Circa* 1897. Each cluster is 5mm in diameter, hoop diameter 17mm.

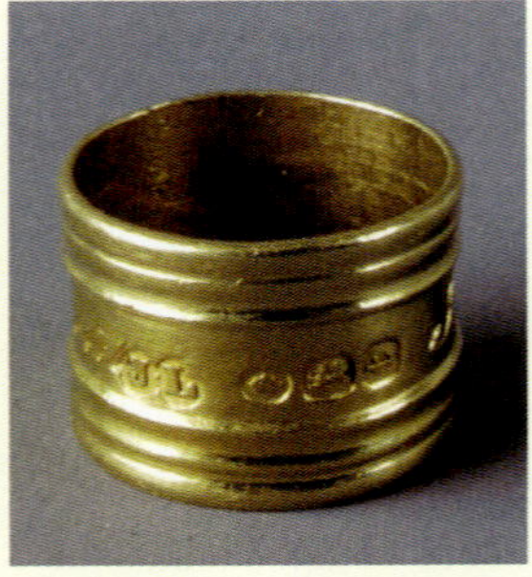

Fig. 219. Serjeant's ring. The circumference of the hoop is inscribed: 'Ingenuous per artes'. Hallmarked: London, 22ct. rich yellow gold, maker's mark J.L, 1834. It is a tiny ring, probably a gift to a minor official. Hoop diameter 15mm, width 12mm.

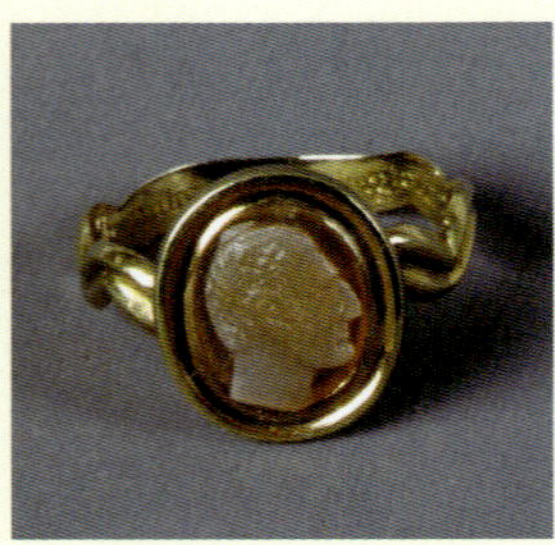

Fig. 220. Commemorative ring set with a hardstone cameo of the Duke of Wellington and a lock of his white hair in a compartment at the back of the bezel. The asymmetric, channelled hoop is inscribed inside: 'Hair of the Duke of Wellington 20 May 1840'. Pale yellow gold. Bezel 13x11mm, hoop diameter 18mm, width 3mm.

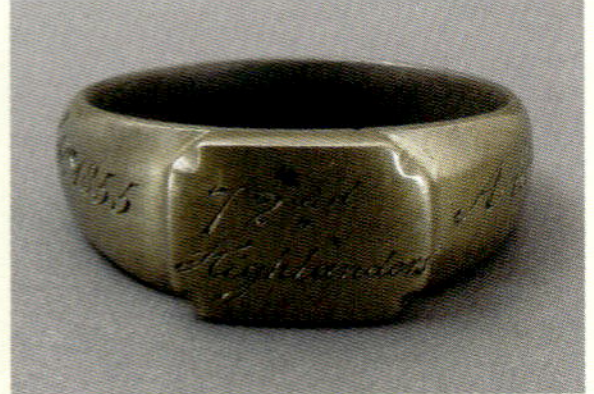

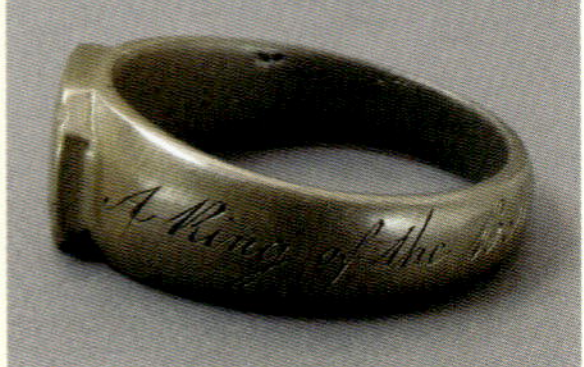

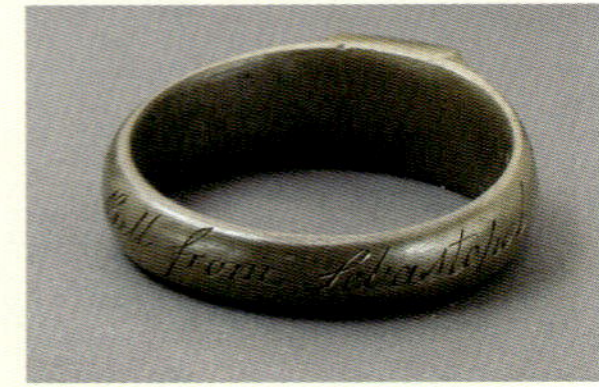

Fig. 221 a, b, c. 'A Ring of the Bell from Sebastapol Sepr 1855' is engraved around the outside of the hoop, bezel is engraved with '72nd Highlanders'. Bezel 8x11mm, hoop diameter 19mm.

white and blue gems in the prevailing designs of those years. (Fig. 217) (Fig. 218)

In Britain numerous rings were made for Serjeant-at-Law ceremonies. A Serjeant-at-Law was a member of a superior order of barristers from which Common Law judges were chosen. Upon being admitted to the Order, the candidates gave gold rings to those involved in the ceremony, such as the reigning Sovereign, Bishops, fellow Serjeants, judges and friends. (p.79}

Some rings were made as tokens because they were too small to be worn. The rings were inscribed on the outside with a motto and a full hallmark. The same motto was generally used on these rings by all the barristers who were admitted the Order at the same ceremony; however, in the nineteenth century a number of candidates chose personal mottos. The motto was generally in Latin, though French and German was known to have been used. The last 'call' to this Order was in 1875. Considering the large number of rings that were produced for this ceremony, comparatively few rings are available today. (Fig. 219)

A fine example of a commemorative ring is one made with a cameo of the Duke of Wellington in the bezel, with a lock of his white hair under rock crystal. The inscription engraved inside the hoop reads: 'Hair of the Duke of Wellington 20 May 1840'. (Fig. 220) It is not a mourning ring; the Duke died in 1852.

A survival of the Crimean War is a ring engraved on the bezel with '72ⁿᵈ Highlanders' and around the hoop with 'A Ring of the Bell from Sebastapol Sepr 1855'. (Fig. 221 a, b, c)

It was not only events and people of national significance that were commemorated. On a personal level, scholastic achievements and family events such as the birth of a child were sometimes recognised with the giving of a ring. (Fig. 222, Fig. 223)

The American Civil War period (1861-1865) produced a number of commemorative, political and mourning rings. The latter were made in the same manner as British mourning rings of the 1860s. Hoop rings were filled with woven hair between knurled or milled edges, with an engraved lozenge affixed to the hoop as a bezel. (Fig. 224)

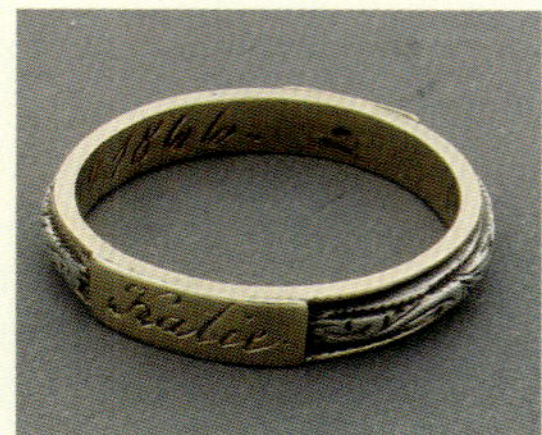

Fig. 222. Hoop ring of very pale yellow gold inset with chased silver. A lozenge of gold is inscribed: *Katie.* Inside the hoop the inscription reads: *Born 18 April 1866.* English. Hoop diameter 15.5mm, width 3mm.

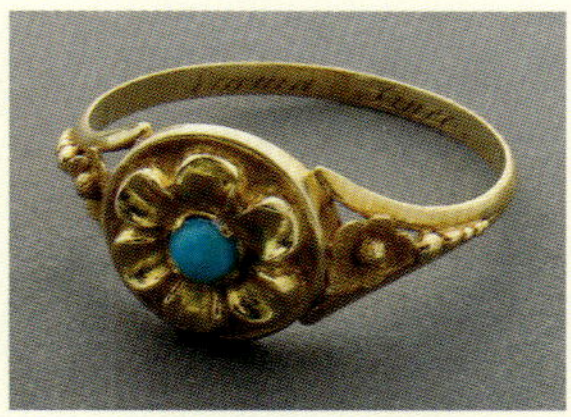

Fig. 223. Gold bezel decorated with petals in relief around a turquoise. Bifurcated shoulders decorated with tooled flower and graduated beads. Inscribed on back of bezel: 'First class Manor Park Midsummer 1836'. 'Emma Smee' is engraved inside the hoop. Rich yellow gold. Bezel 10mm in diameter, hoop diameter 19mm.

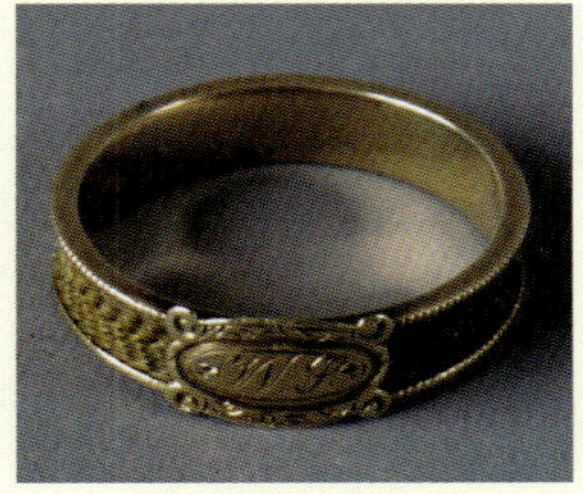

Fig. 224. Memorial hoop ring. The hollowed hoop with a milled edge is lined with mid-brown plaited hair, the oblong bezel is edged with engraving and inscribed with WP in the centre. Yellow gold. American, *circa* 1865. Bezel 6x10mm, hoop diameter 19mm, width 4mm.

Commemorative and Historical

Hoops made from hair secured by a small bezel were also made at this time. (Fig. 225, Fig. 226) One political ring that has survived from the Civil War supported Jefferson Davis who became president of the Confederacy on February 18, 1861. (Fig. 227 a, b) Another Civil War survival was made for volunteers from Huntingdon, Pennsylvania. (Fig. 228)

A rare survival is the American metal slave ring. The ring rattles when the body is moving, hence silence would alert owners or overseers to the fact that the slave was not working. (Fig. 229)

The latter part of the nineteenth century and early twentieth century produced souvenir rings from various Expositions held in America. The following illustrations give examples of rings made for two expositions. The first is for the 1893 World's Columbian Exposition in Chicago that celebrated Columbus's discovery of America in 1492. There were three souvenir rings made for this exposition, two of which are shown in the illustration. (Fig. 230 a, b) The second is for the 1904 St. Louis Exposition that celebrated the 100th anniversary of the Louisiana Purchase in 1803 by Thomas Jefferson from France during Napoleon's reign. (Fig. 231 a, b, c, d, e, f)

An interesting find is a wide, flat hoop ring of American origin. The bezel is enamelled with green and white with a single mast galley set off in gold. The sail displays the initials TBH. One shoulder is engraved with a black enamelled 7-pointed star with a cross of red enamel in its centre, the other is engraved with a camel that shows traces of red enamel. (Fig. 232 a, b, c)

Another enamelled ring has the letter S in black enamel and decoration of turquoise enamel on the bezel. Rings with other letters can also be found. (Fig. 233)

Some rings were custom-made.(Fig. 234). The opal bezel could be screwed into the ring or into the brooch. The brooch was attached to a stick pin by a small chain.

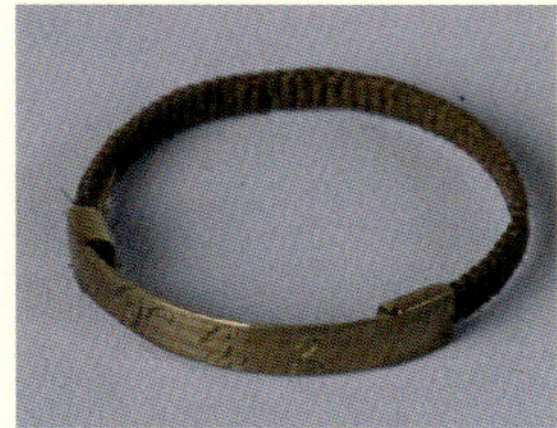

Fig. 225. Hair mourning ring, gold bezel engraved EGA. American, 1860s. Bezel 2.5x21mm, hoop width 2mm.

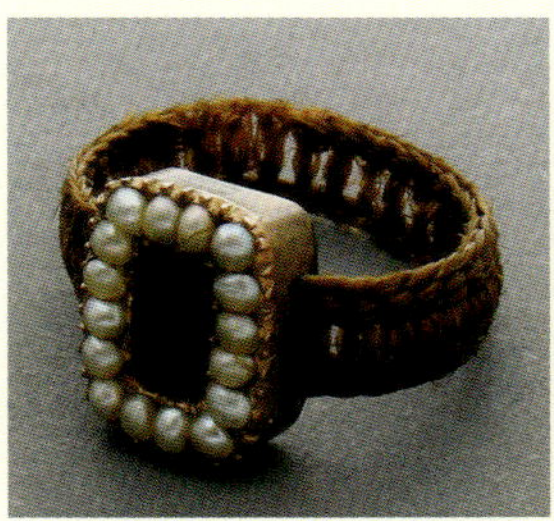

Fig. 226. Mourning ring. Half pearls border a rectangular onyx bezel that is engraved "Clara". Loosely woven golden brown hair forms the hoop. American, *circa* 1850. Very low carat gold.
Keith Austin Collection

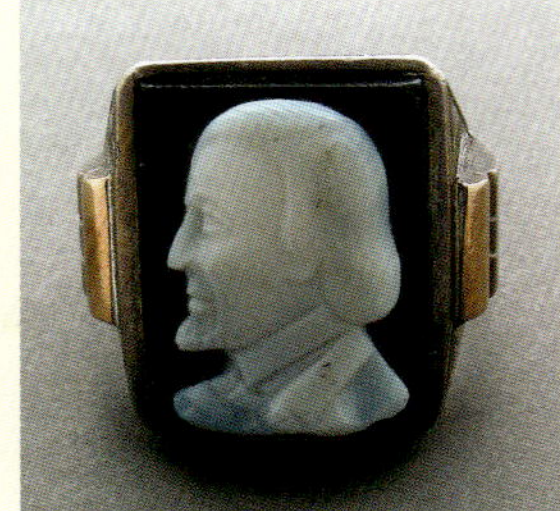

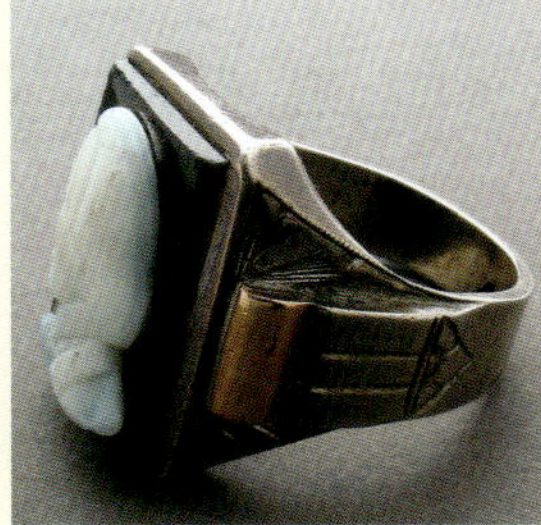

Fig. 227 a, b. Cameo of Jefferson Davis set in silver. Engraved shoulders embellished with gold. Marked sterling and 10K gold. Jefferson Davis became President of the Confederacy on February 18, 1861.
Keith Austin Collection

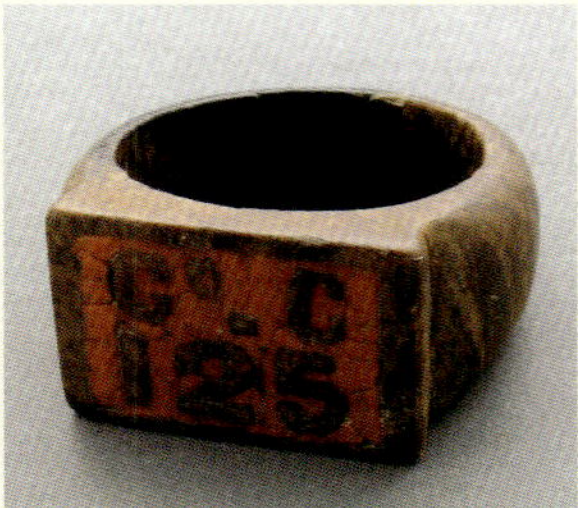

Fig. 228. Civil War ring. Co[mpany] C 125 painted in red on wood. A ring worn by volunteers from Huntingdon, Pennsylvania.
Keith Austin Collection

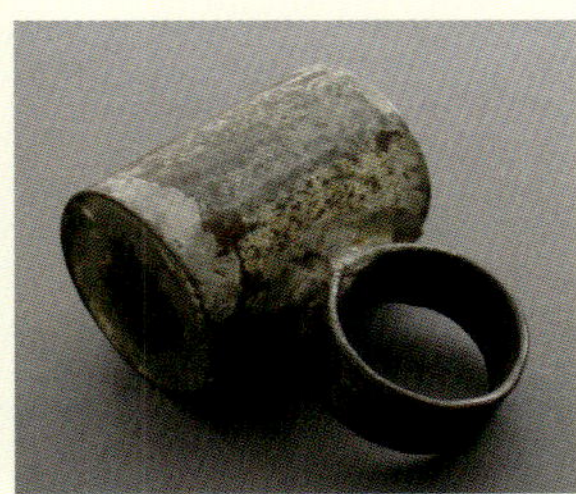

Fig. 229. American pre-Civil War slave ring comprising a cylindrical bezel containing a piece of metal that rattled when the body moved.
Keith Austin Collection

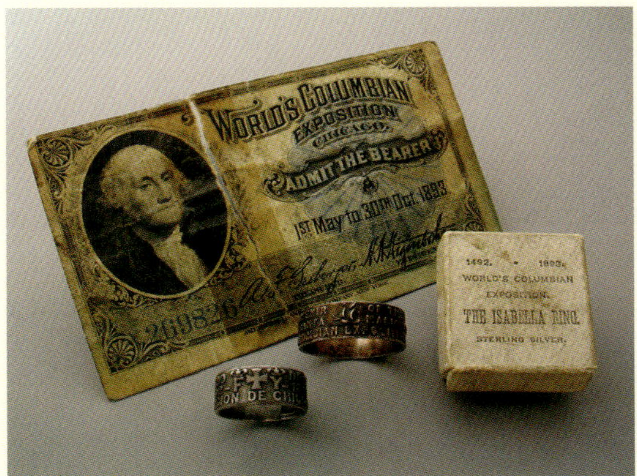

Fig. 230 a, b. Two rings from the 1492-1893 World's Columbian Exposition in Chicago. (a) Inscribed 'RECURED DE LA ESPOSICION DE CHICAGO ELANILLO YSABEL', inside the ring the marks are Gorham MFG CO. Sterling Registered 1892 and a right facing lion, anchor and Gothic G. (b) 'SOUVENIR OF THE 1492 – SANTA MARIA – 1893 COLUMBIAN EXPOSITION'.
Keith Austin Collection

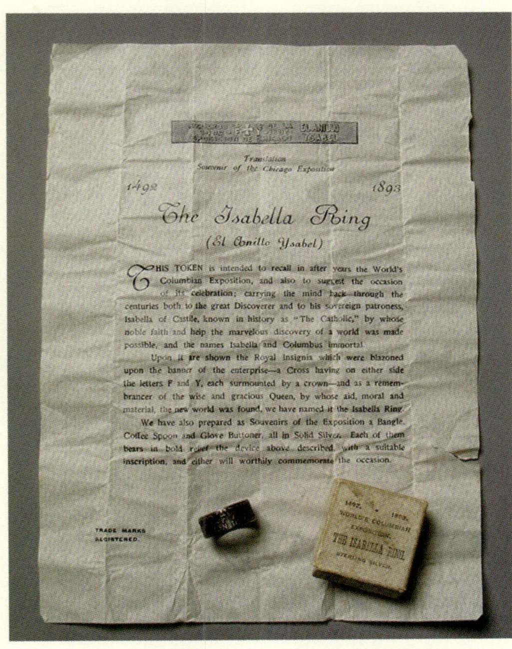

Commemorative and Historical

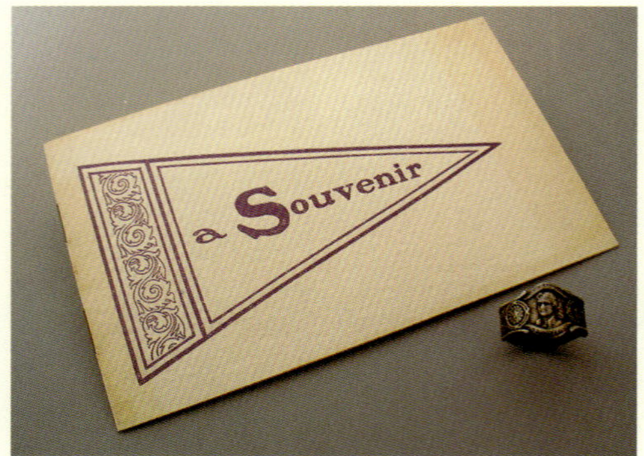

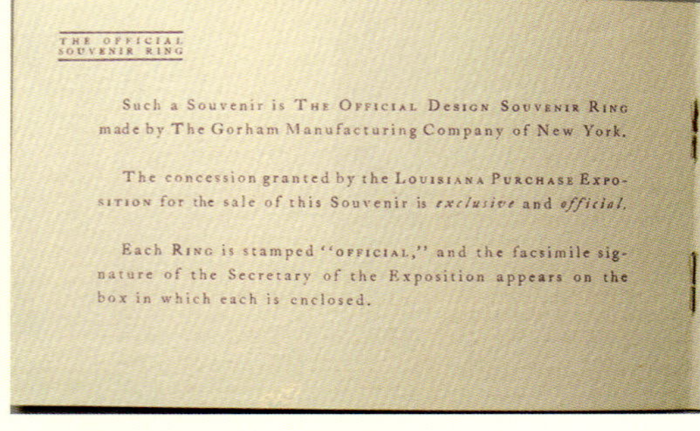

Such a Souvenir is THE OFFICIAL DESIGN SOUVENIR RING made by The Gorham Manufacturing Company of New York.

The concession granted by the LOUISIANA PURCHASE EXPOSITION for the sale of this Souvenir is *exclusive* and *official*.

Each Ring is stamped "OFFICIAL," and the facsimile signature of the Secretary of the Exposition appears on the box in which each is enclosed.

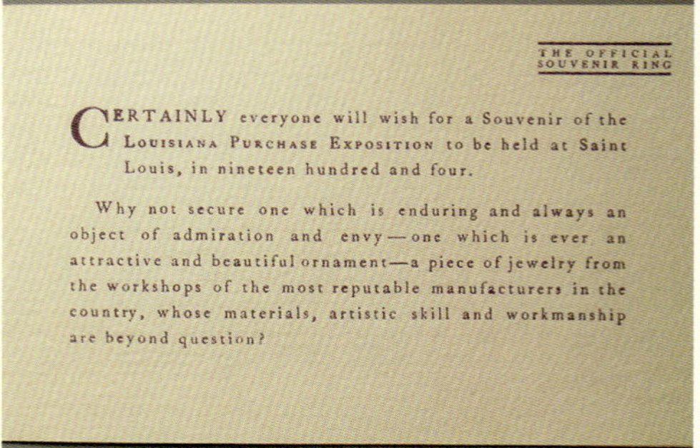

CERTAINLY everyone will wish for a Souvenir of the LOUISIANA PURCHASE EXPOSITION to be held at Saint Louis, in nineteen hundred and four.

Why not secure one which is enduring and always an object of admiration and envy—one which is ever an attractive and beautiful ornament—a piece of jewelry from the workshops of the most reputable manufacturers in the country, whose materials, artistic skill and workmanship are beyond question?

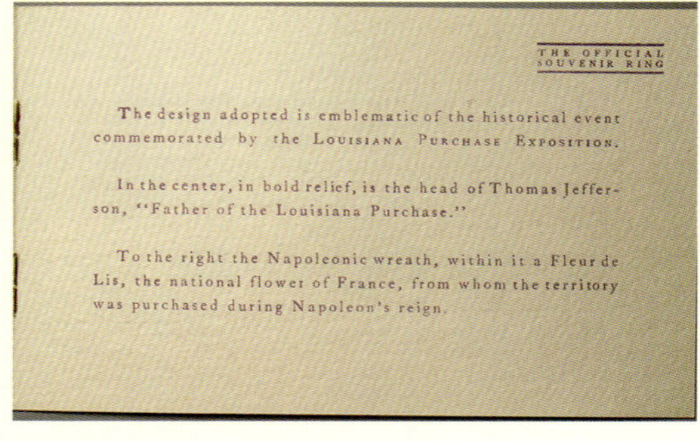

The design adopted is emblematic of the historical event commemorated by the LOUISIANA PURCHASE EXPOSITION.

In the center, in bold relief, is the head of Thomas Jefferson, "Father of the Louisiana Purchase."

To the right the Napoleonic wreath, within it a Fleur de Lis, the national flower of France, from whom the territory was purchased during Napoleon's reign.

Fig. 231 a, b, c, d, e. f. Souvenir items made for the St. Louis Exposition of 1904 that celebrated the 100th anniversary of the Louisiana Purchase in 1803 by Thomas Jefferson. Official description of the ring reads: In the center, in bold relief is the head of Thomas Jefferson, "Father of the Louisiana Purchase". To the right the Napoleonic wreath within it a Fleur de Lis, the national flower of France, from whom the territory was purchased during Napoleon's reign. To the left is a large star representing Louisiana, surrounded by thirteen smaller stars. Marked inside the ring: Official Souvenir Gorham Sterling with a lion facing right, upright anchor and a Gothic G.
Keith Austin Collection

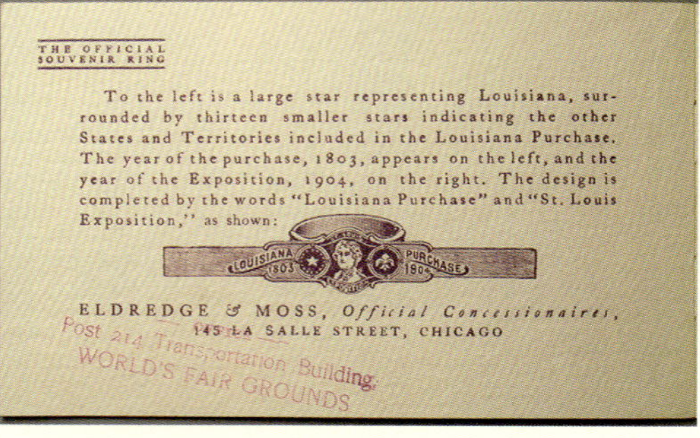

To the left is a large star representing Louisiana, surrounded by thirteen smaller stars indicating the other States and Territories included in the Louisiana Purchase. The year of the purchase, 1803, appears on the left, and the year of the Exposition, 1904, on the right. The design is completed by the words "Louisiana Purchase" and "St. Louis Exposition," as shown:

LOUISIANA 1803 PURCHASE 1904

ELDREDGE & MOSS, *Official Concessionaires,* 145 LA SALLE STREET, CHICAGO

Post 214 Transportation Building,
WORLD'S FAIR GROUNDS

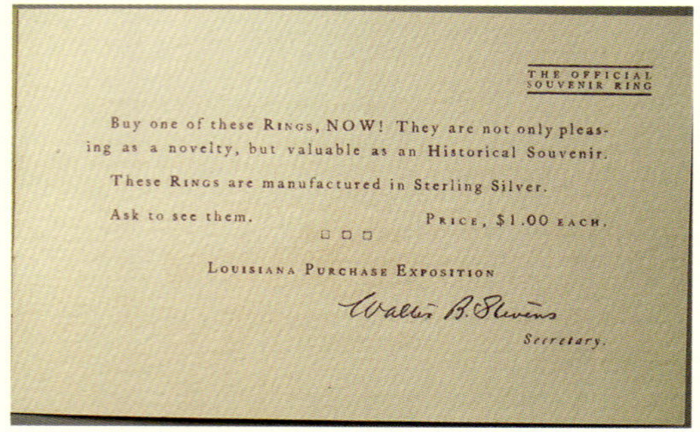

Buy one of these RINGS, NOW! They are not only pleasing as a novelty, but valuable as an Historical Souvenir.

These RINGS are manufactured in Sterling Silver.

Ask to see them.   PRICE, $1.00 EACH.

LOUISIANA PURCHASE EXPOSITION

Walter B. Stevens
Secretary.

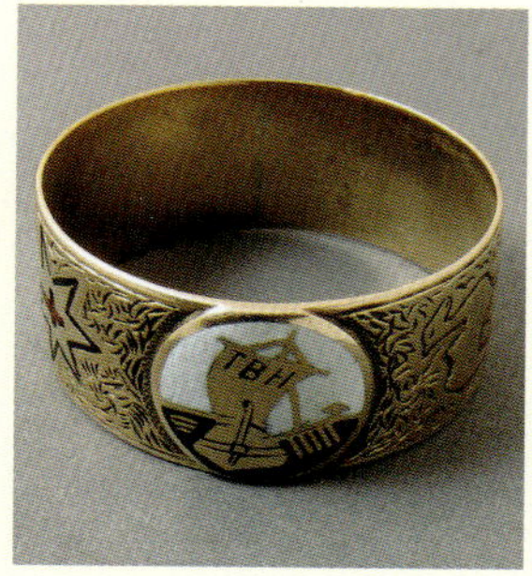 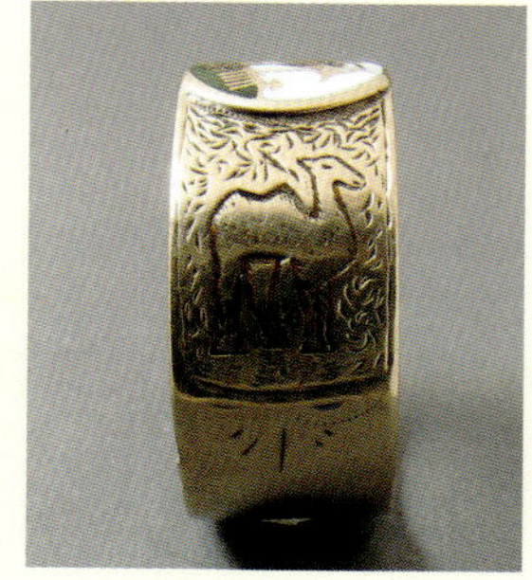 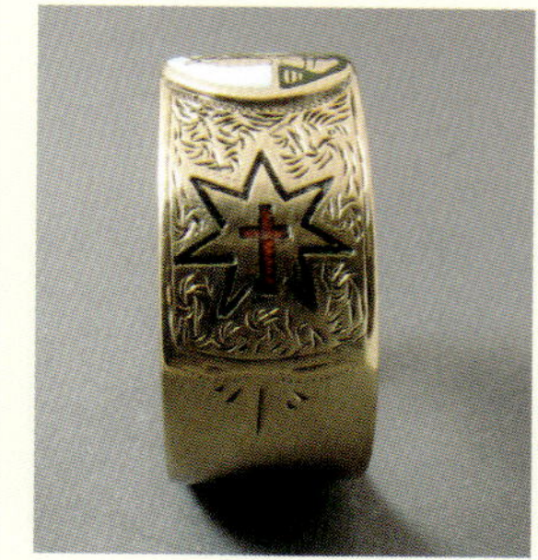

Fig. 232 a, b, c. Gentleman's hoop ring. Rose gold. American, *circa* 1880-1900. Enamelled panel 9mm in diameter, hoop diameter 19mm, width 9mm.

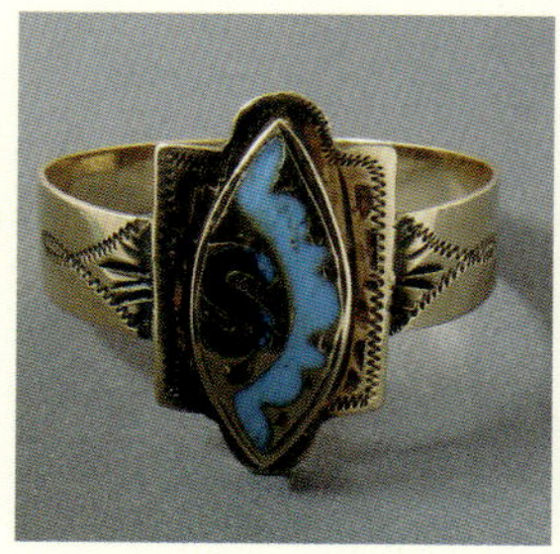 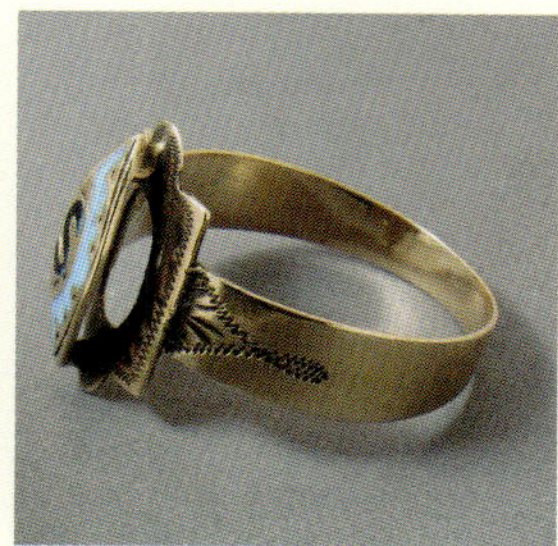

Fig. 233 a, b. Enamelled 'initial' ring, with engraved shoulders, flat hoop. Rose gold. American, *circa* 1890. Bezel 10x8.5mm, hoop diameter 19mm.

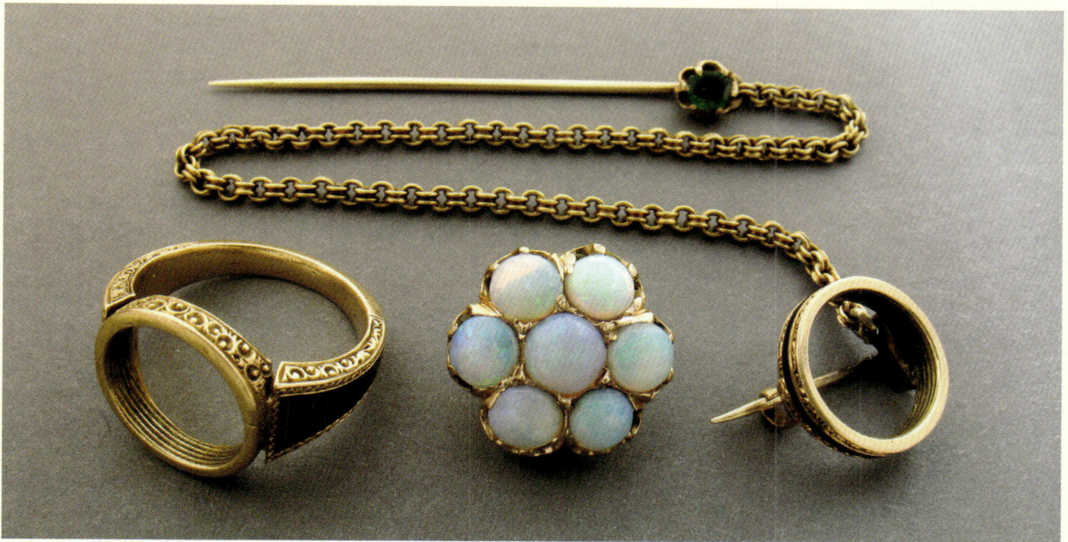

Fig. 234. Cluster bezel set with seven Australian opals in a crown claw setting. The bezel screws into either the chased and enamelled brooch that is attached by a chain to a stick pin set with a green stone, or into the ring that is chased and enamelled on the shoulders, and chased around the edge of the bezel. Yellow gold. American, *circa* 1890. Bezel diameter 15mm, hoop diameter 16mm.

                    Commemorative and Historical

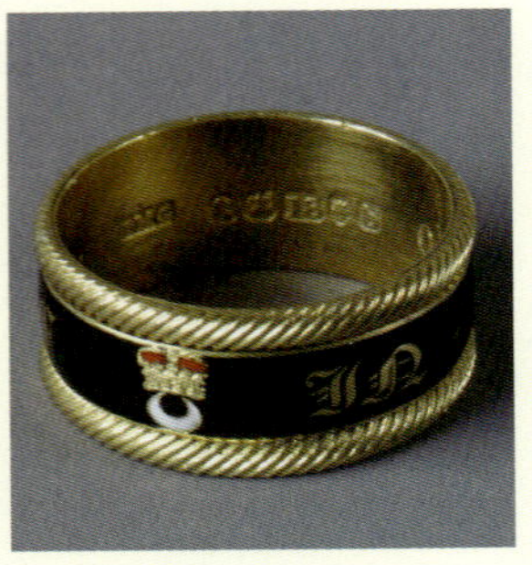

Fig. 235. Mourning ring. Borders of diagonal hatch marks protect a band of black enamel inset with 'IN MEMORY OF' in Black Letter capitals, and a ducal coronet above the device of the Duke of Northumberland. Inscribed inside hoop: 'Ob : 10 Julij 1817 AE : 74'. Hallmarked: London, 18ct. yellow gold, maker's mark I.M.G, 1817. Shank diameter 20mm, width 10mm.

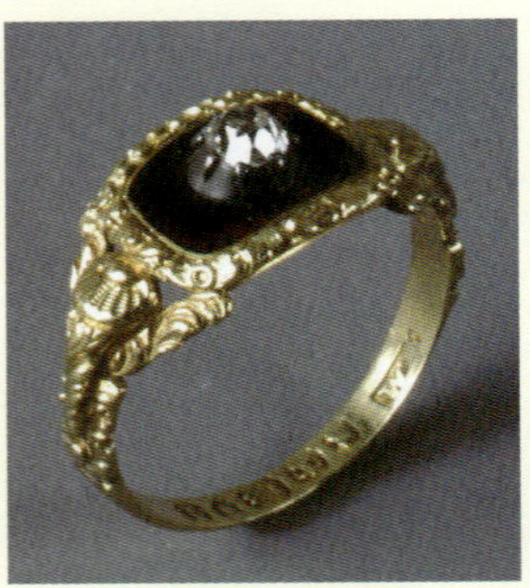

Fig. 236. Mourning ring. Chunky brilliant-cut diamond in a silver cut-down collet is applied to a bezel flooded with black enamel, bordered with chased gold, inscription on reverse is illegible as a result of wear or deliberate removal. Chased, bifurcated shoulders with embossed work set between the fork, grooved shank. Hallmarked: London, 18ct. yellow gold, maker's mark WE, 1826. Bezel 9x13mm, shank diameter 19mm.

MOURNING RINGS

Mourning rings were given and received by a broad spectrum of society: the Royal Family, the aristocracy, statesmen, clergy, lawyers, doctors and the ordinary man or woman. (Fig. 235)

Royal mourning rings, worn to commemorate the deaths of the sovereign and members of the Royal Family, were made from the time of Charles II's death in 1685 until the death of Prince Albert in 1861.

During the nineteenth century the usual period of mourning lasted up to two years. Deep or full mourning - during which time all clothing and much jewellery was black (Fig. 236) - was followed by the white, grey, lavender or purple of half-mourning dress. The length of mourning depended somewhat on a person's position in society. (Fig. 237 a, b) Many families suffered numerous bereavements caused by the ravages of war, complications in childbirth, illness and disease which struck down children and young people as well as adults; (Fig. 238) many relatives remained in mourning for years.

Contemporary fashion magazines illustrated mourning dress and jewellery, but rings were rarely shown. This does not mean rings were not made - they were, in great numbers, and were worn throughout the century. Once mass-production became widespread in the 1860s, and gold was produced in the lower standards of 15ct., 12ct. and 9ct., many mourning rings were produced at prices that were more affordable to the general public. (Fig. 239) Queen Victoria mourned Prince Albert, who died in 1861, until her own death in 1901 - a most unusual length of mourning. Her behaviour influenced her subjects' attitude towards death. The funeral, its trappings and the subsequent period of mourning were of the utmost importance for all, rich or poor. Towards the end of the century came a slight relaxation in the formerly strict codes of mourning.

At the beginning of the nineteenth century, it was customary to provide, in one's last will and testament, for mourning rings to be distributed to relatives, friends, and one's clergyman, doctor and lawyer. This expensive custom declined as the century progressed. The following is an excerpt from a will drawn up in 1829:

> The last Will and Testament of me Thomas Ansell of the Parish of Saint Nicholas in the Town of Abingdon in the County of Berks Watchmaker and Silversmith ... Also I give and bequeath unto my friends Mrs. Miller of Bampton Oxon Mr. and Mrs. Le Forrest of the same place Mr. and Mrs. James Weaving and their daughter Miss Marianne Weaving of Fyfield Mr. Charles Cox of the Kings Arms Inn in Oxford Mr. and Mrs Thomas Justice of Appleford Mrs. James Cole Mrs. Elizabeth Hawkes The Reverend Nathaniel Dodson The Reverend Mr. Kinsey Reverend Mr. Bishop The Reverend Mr. Dwyer Reverend Mr. Smith Thomas West Esquire my late Surgeon Miss Ann Spenlove Mr. Hester Surgeon Mr. Frankum Attorney Mrs. Hannah Hunsworth of Thames Street Abingdon my said Servant Hannah Berriman and my two executors a Mourning Ring each in token of the respect I bear them and do request my said executors will procure such Rings of my Goldsmith Mr. Pottinger No.6 Bells Buildings Salisbury Court Fleet Street London ... set my hand and seal this twenty first day of April in the year of our Lord one thousand eight hundred and twenty nine ...   (Fig. 240)

Charles Dickens wrote in *Great Expectations*, set in the 1860s:

> Casting my eyes on Mr. Wemmick [a lawyer's clerk] as we went along, to see what he was like in the light of day, ... I judged him to be a bachelor from the frayed condition of his linen, and he appeared to have sustained a good many bereavements; for he wore at least four mourning rings, besides a broach [sic] representing a lady and a weeping willow at a tomb with an urn on it.

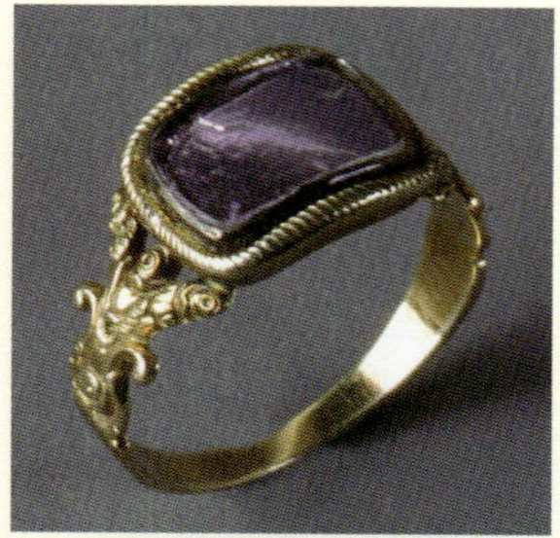

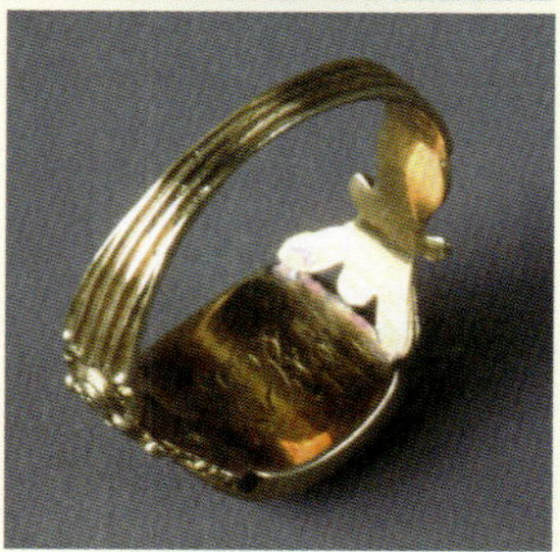

Fig. 237 a, b. Mourning ring. Rounded oblong bezel lined with lilac foil (a colour used for half-mourning dress) beneath glass bordered by a band of hatched gold, supported by chased three-part shoulders on a reeded shank. Inscribed 'ER' on back of bezel. Rich yellow gold. *Circa* 1820. Bezel 10x14mm, shank diameter 18mm.

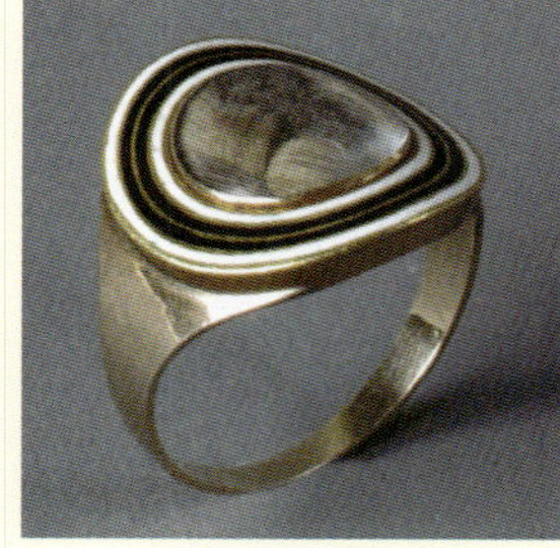

Fig. 238. Mourning ring. The circular bezel, curved to fit the finger, contains brown and blond plaited hair under glass surrounded by bands of black and white enamel on yellow gold. Plain wide and flat shoulders of rose gold taper to a narrow, flat shank. Inscribed on reverse of bezel: 'Revd. James Benamor Obt 2 Sepr. 1796 Aet 29; Joseph Benamor Obt 28 Augt. 1796 Aet 4 years'. This style of ring continued to be made during the first few years of the nineteenth century. Bezel 18x19mm, shank diameter 19.5mm.

Mourning

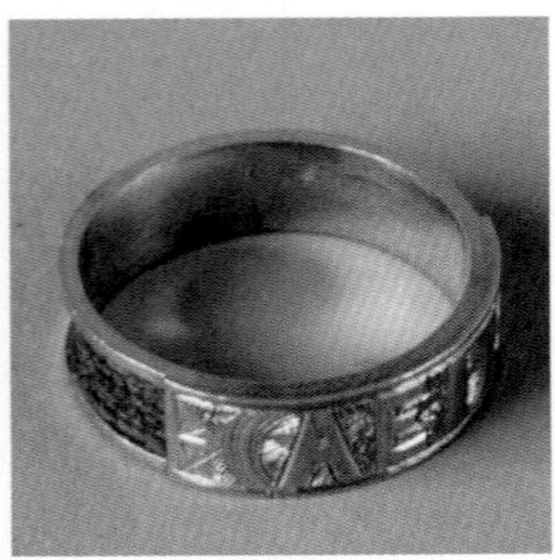

Fig. 239. Mourning ring. Bezel, engraved with A E I, (Greek for 'eternal'), and a geometric design, is applied to the flanged hoop that is lined with tightly plaited, brown hair. Hallmarked: Birmingham, 9(.375) ct. yellow gold, maker's mark T.W. & CO, 1878. Bezel 5.5x22mm, shank diameter 16mm, width 5mm.

I noticed, too, that several rings and seals hung at his watch-chain, as if he were quite laden with remembrances of departed friends ... He had had them, to the best of my belief, from forty to fifty years. (Chapman and Hall Ltd., 1880, p.152.)

On 27 February 1843, the Wardens of the Goldsmiths' Company, London, brought in stricter controls regarding the marking of mourning rings. An act passed in 1784 had required mourning rings to be hallmarked, but there were many permitted exceptions, such as a ring being too ornamental or fragile, with the result that individual jewellers often interpreted the law as they saw fit. Consequently an unscrupulous jeweller could skirt the law and make rings below the legal standards of 22ct. and 18ct. gold with little fear of discovery. The new controls stipulated that linings, properly sized and flat, and all parts relating to rings, plus the shoulders of all hallmarked rings must be marked. A mourning ring

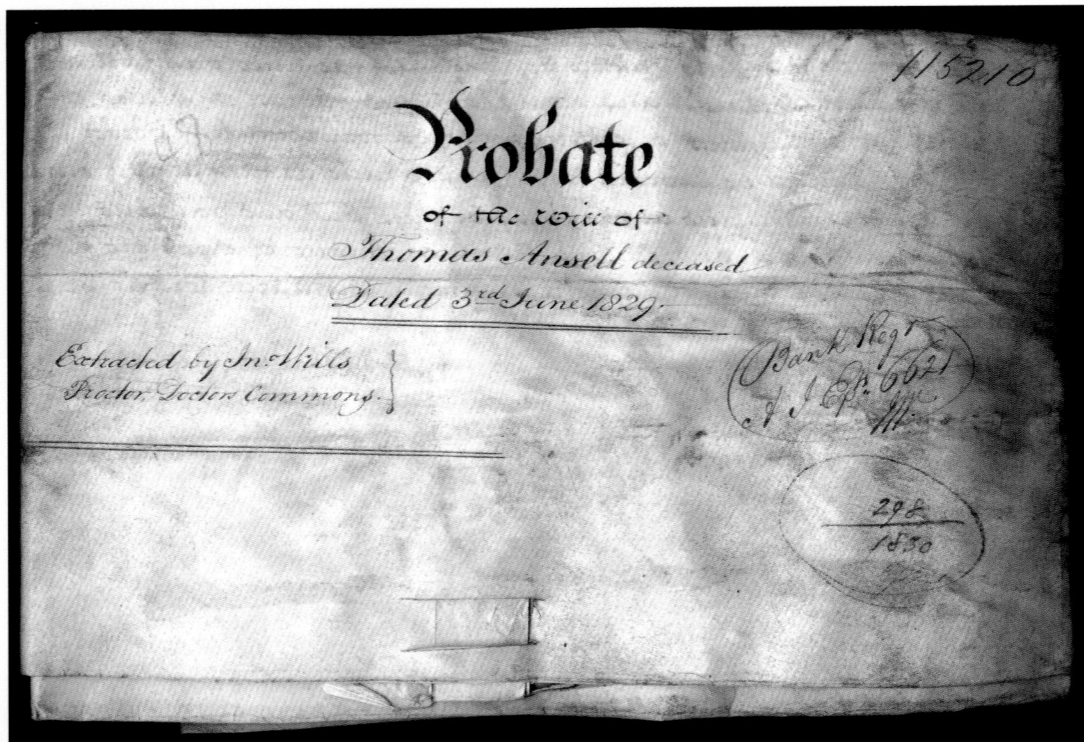

Fig. 240. Last Will & Testament of Thomas Ansell, 1829.

with a bezel had to be fully mounted but cut open at one shoulder for marking, and in addition there was to be a single mark stamped on one shoulder. As a general rule, no rings were to be marked unless all the component parts were complete and were sent in together for marking. If a mark was defaced, the ring had to be re-marked. These regulations were intended to prevent substandard gold from being used in any part of a ring. (Fig. 241 a, b)

Mourning rings, apart from hoop rings, followed the trends of decorative rings throughout the nineteenth century, and as they were hallmarked and often inscribed with the name of the deceased and the date of death, they provide a useful guide to the dating of unmarked decorative rings. Occasionally a mourning ring was re-used later in the century, it is, therefore, unwise to date rings solely from their inscriptions. (Fig. 242 a, b)

Mourning rings were usually set with onyx, jet, black glass, pearls, diamonds, crystal, cornelian or amethyst, and were decorated with black, pale or royal blue, white or red enamel. Hair was often used in addition to the above. Sometimes the bezel would swivel - a fashion that lasted until approximately 1830, although an occasional example turns up in the middle of the century. The obverse of the swivel bezel might be enamelled with the initials of the person being commemorated, inscribed in gold, and the reverse might have a compartment containing the hair of the deceased. (Fig. 243 a, b)

A distinctive bezel shape that was common from 1800 to 1845 was the rounded oblong, curved to hug the finger; it is found in a variety of styles from the very severe to the quite ornate. The name, date of death and age of the deceased was engraved on the reverse of the bezel. From about 1800 to 1815 this style was usually simple and rather austere, and was enamelled in black or white, occasionally with small amounts of red, with a legend or design in gold. The shoulders were often wide and flat, either plain or decorated with cross-hatching or enamelling, and tapering slightly to form the shank. Some of these rings had openwork wire shoulders. (Fig. 244) In a less severe design of the same period, 1800-1815, the bezel was comprised of a central hair compartment covered with glass, surrounded first by seed pearls, then by a row of gold decorated with tiny hatch marks and finally encircled with plain gold.

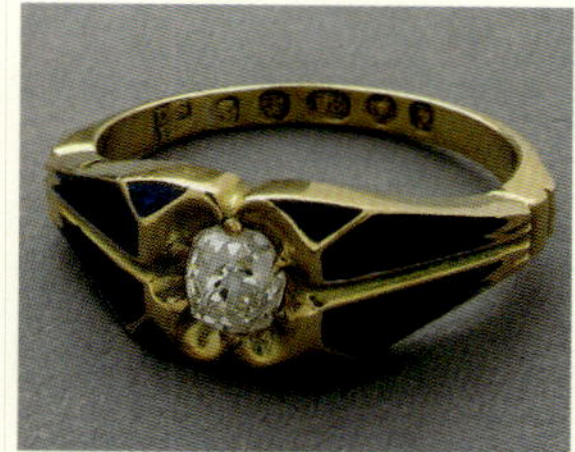

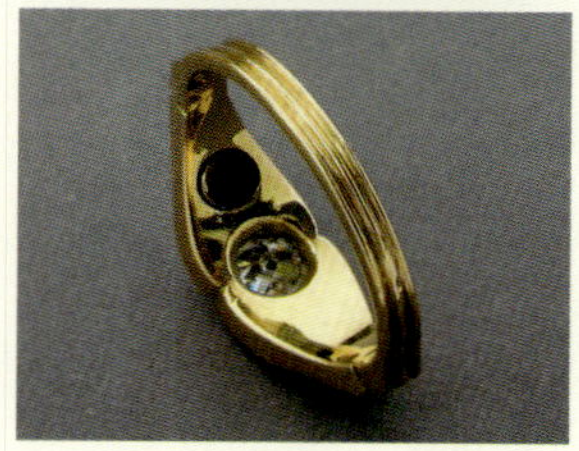

Fig. 241 a, b. Gothic-style memorial ring. A brilliant-cut diamond is open-set in a Tudor rose motif, royal blue enamel (re-enamelled) decorates spatula-shaped, sectioned shoulders, one of which has an empty hair compartment inside. Sturdy, reeded shank. Hallmarked: London, 18ct. yellow gold, maker's mark, DS ES, 1843. shank diameter 17.5mm.

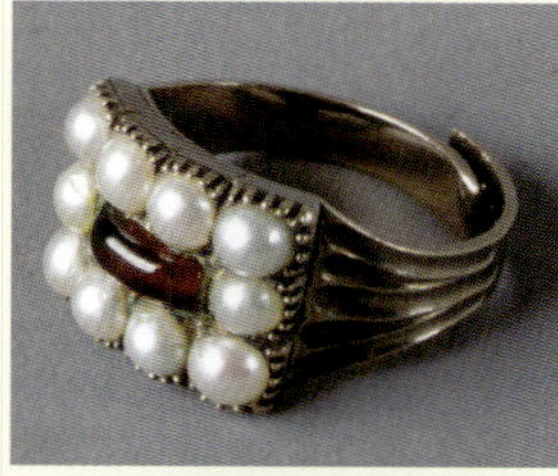

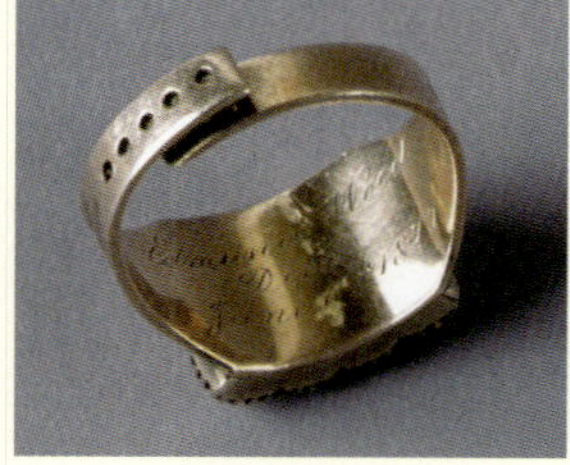

Fig. 242 a, b. Mourning ring. Oblong bezel set with ten half pearls and a cabochon garnet (replacing a hair compartment), inscribed on reverse of bezel: 'Edmund Wood Died June 6th 1877'. Wide flat shoulders taper to an adjustable shank. Rose gold. *Circa* 1800-1815. An example of an early ring used later in the century. Bezel 12.5x18mm.
Reginald Davis (Oxford) Ltd.

Mourning

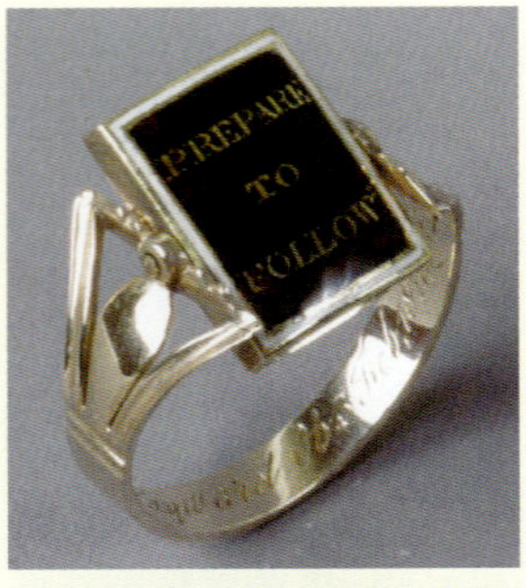

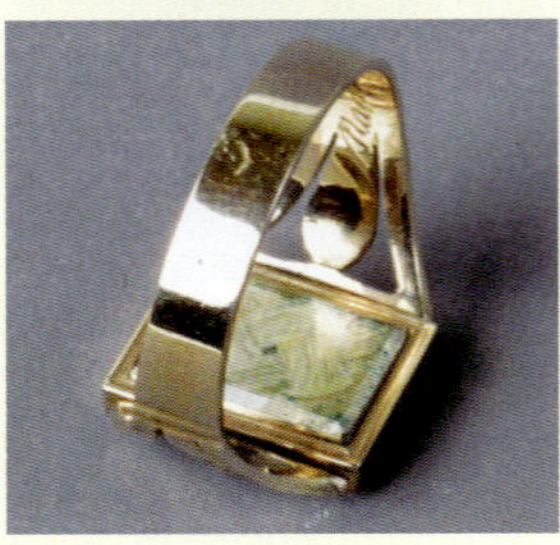

Fig. 243 a, b. Mourning ring. Swivel bezel decorated with black enamel, a border of white enamel and PREPARE TO FOLLOW set off in gold on one side, the other contains loosely plaited white hair. Shoulders comprise a leaf flanked by narrowly grooved sections of gold, supported by a transverse rib on a wide, flat shank. Rose gold. Inscribed inside hoop: 'Nathe. Hayward, ob 3 Feb. 1814 Aet 73'. Bezel 12x10mm, shank diameter 18.5mm, width 3.5mm.

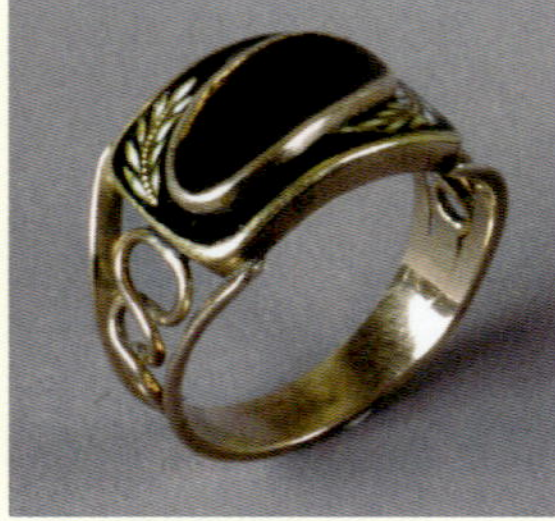

Fig. 244. Mourning ring. Black enamelled bezel is decorated with a white enamelled design in opposite corners. Canted edges of the channelled shank extend into the shoulders that are decorated with open wire-work. Rose gold. Inscribed on reverse of the bezel: 'Jerh. Grounds ob. 14 Feby. 1811 aet. 15 weeks'. Bezel 17x10.5mm, shank diameter 17mm, width 3.5mm.

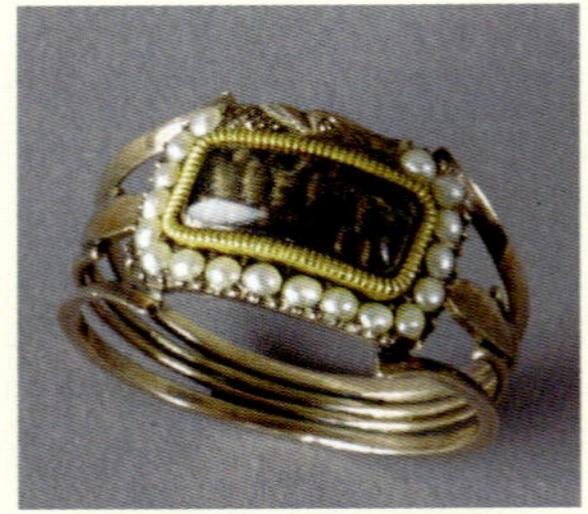

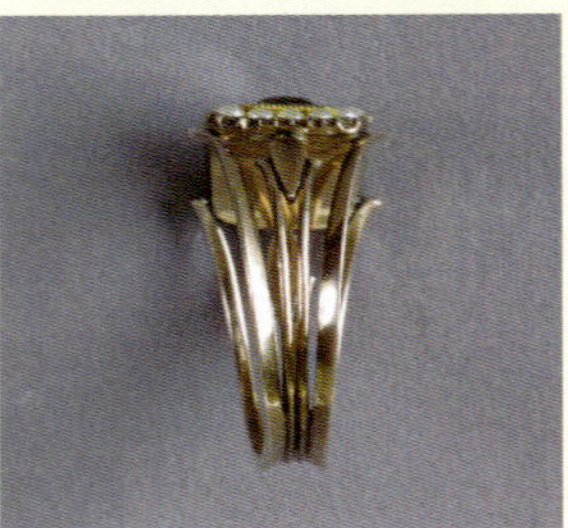

Fig. 245 a, b. Gentleman's mourning ring. Rounded oblong bezel comprising a compartment filled with woven chestnut hair under glass, surrounded by a strip of hatched yellow gold, bordered by a pearl-studded, rose gold serpent biting its tail. The outer sections of the shank are canted, and the inner gold wires terminate at the shoulders and are joined to the bezel by a convex leaf. *Circa* 1805-1815. Bezel 11x19mm, shank diameter 20.5mm, width 3.5mm.

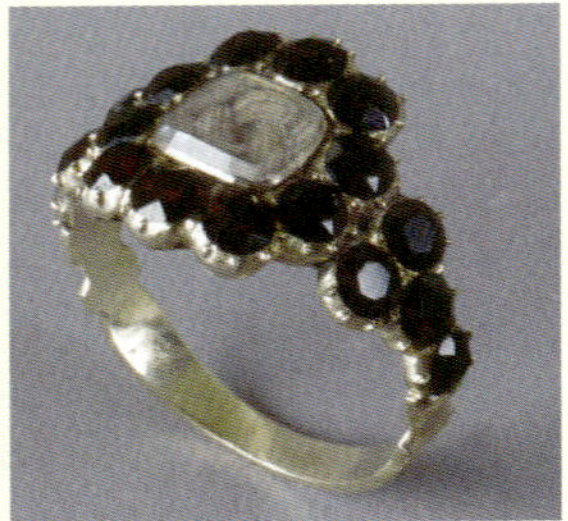

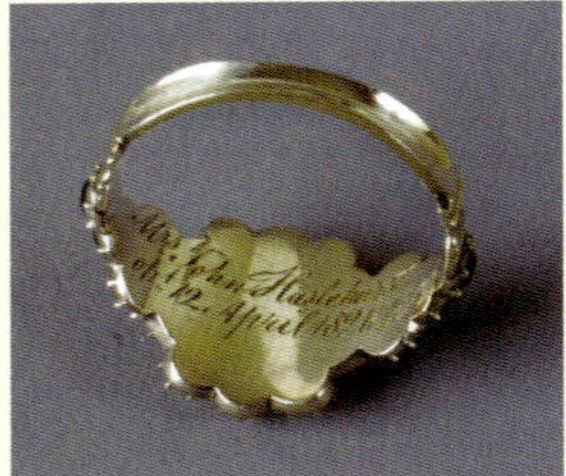

Fig. 246 a, b. Mourning ring. Hair compartment surrounded by onyx in cut-down collets, two sets of transverse ribs and onyx decorate the shoulders, single channelled shank ends in a leaf. Pale yellow gold. Inscribed on reverse of bezel: 'Mrs. John Haselhurst Obt. 12 April 1821 Aet 26'. Bezel 15x15mm, shank diameter 20mm.

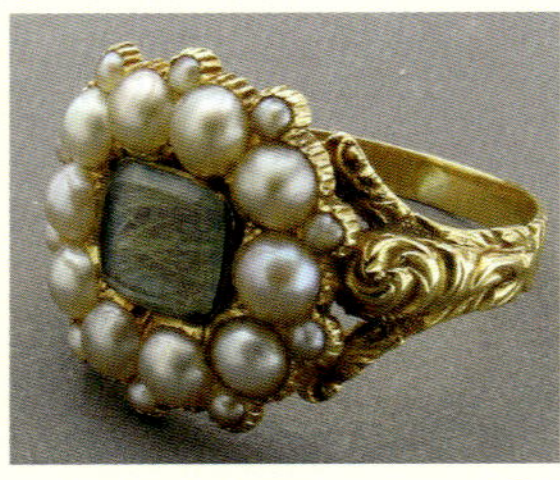

Fig. 247. Mourning ring. Pearls around a hair compartment (slight discolouration of the back of the glass). Chased shoulders on a channelled hoop. Yellow gold. Inscribed on back of bezel: 'Henry Selfe obt. 18 Aug. 1831 Aet. 71'. Bezel 15x15mm, hoop diameter 17.5mm.

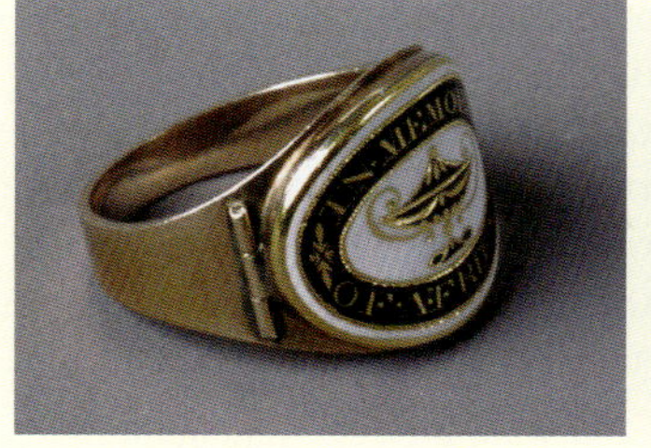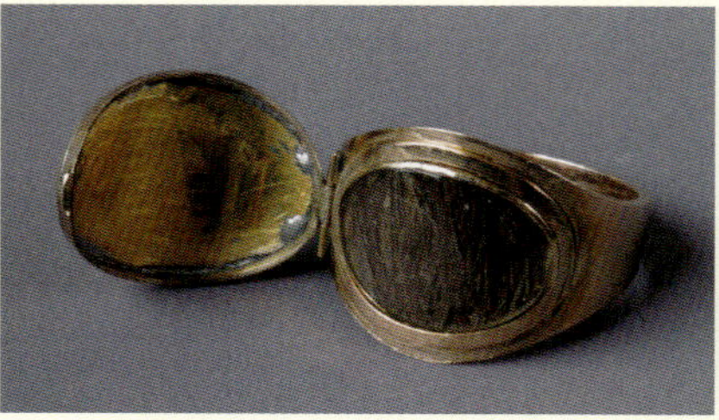

Fig. 248 a, b. Mourning ring. The bezel, decorated with a gold urn on a white enamel ground surrounded by a black enamel border, with 'IN MEMORY OF A FRIEND' in gold Roman capitals, is hinged at one side, opens to reveal a hair compartment. Rose gold. Inscribed on reverse of bezel: 'TES drowned July 24th, 1811. Aged 15'. Bezel 15x18mm, hoop diameter 17mm.

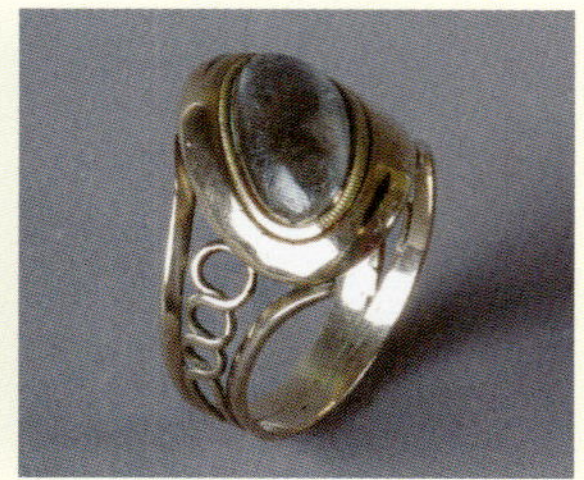

Fig. 249. Diagonal oval bezel, containing plaited hair beneath glass (slightly rubbed), surrounded by a strip of hatched wire and a border of plain gold, parts of which have been rubbed away indicating the bezel is gold-cased. Split, canted shoulders, inset with wirework. Rose gold. *Circa* 1805-1815. Bezel length 18mm, shoulder width 9mm, shank diameter 18mm, width 4mm.

A serpent might also surround the bezel. The snake biting its tail was a symbol of eternity. (Fig. 245 a, b) After 1815 a change appeared in this silhouette. Deeply chased gold surrounded the hair compartment, sometimes with the addition of black enamel; the shoulders were bifurcated and chased, and the shank was channelled. The hair compartment could also be surrounded by pearls, onyx, jet, or black glass; sometimes additional stones were set in the shoulders. (Fig. 246 a, b) (Fig. 247)

Other styles fashionable from 1800 to 1815 had oval (Fig. 248 a, b), oblique oval (Fig. 249) and rectangular bezels, which curved to fit the finger. Some bezels were enamelled, while others were set with pearls around a hair compartment. (Fig. 250) *Circa* 1815 some pearl-set rings had oval bezels on deeply chased hoops. One finds rings in which the original hair compartment has been replaced with a cabochon garnet, see Fig. 242. The urn motif was used until about 1815, often in conjunction with enamelling, and set with diamonds.

Simple hoop rings were enamelled in pale blue (Fig. 251), white or black, often edged with hatched gold. After about 1820 black enamel predominated; colours and white were used less frequently. Occasionally one finds a boxed set of two simple hoops, enamelled and inscribed to commemorate the deaths of a husband and wife. About 1815, hoop rings began to be decorated with heavy chasing in conjunction with enamel and continued in popularity until the 1850s. (Fig. 252)

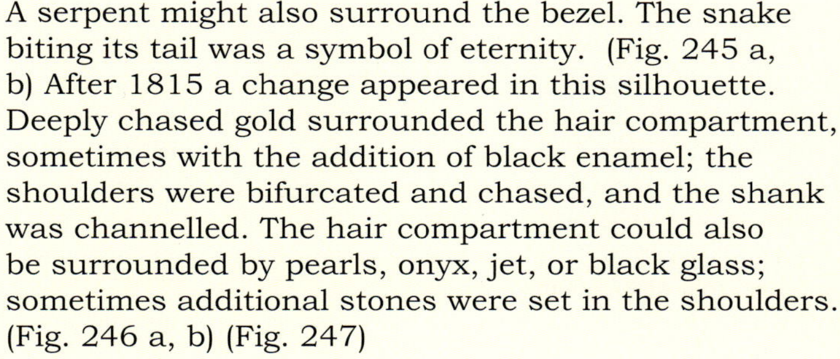

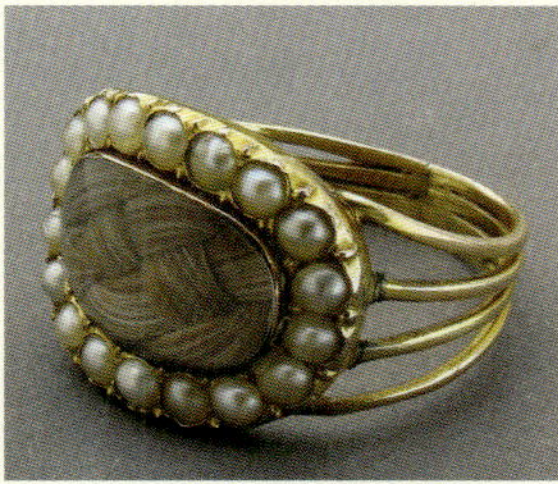

Fig. 250. Mourning ring. Bezel of loosely woven grey and light brown hair beneath glass surrounded by small pearls in a communal cut-down collect. Four wires form the shank and separate at the shoulders. Inscribed on back of bezel: 'Ann Uppill Ob: 31 Dec 1808 Ae. 69'. Bezel 13x15mm, shoulder width 18mm, shank diameter 17.5mm, width 3.5mm.

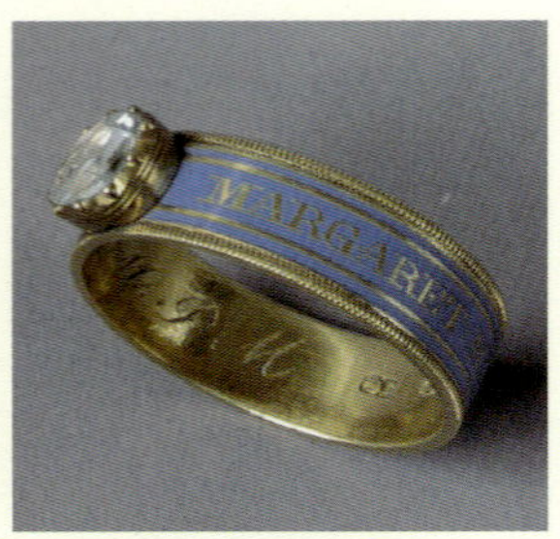

Fig. 251. Mourning ring. 'Margaret Millar. OB: 14. March 1819', is set into pale blue enamel, a white beryl in a closed, cut-down collet is applied to the hoop the edges of which are finely hatched. Yellow gold. The following initials are inscribed inside the hoop: 'BM.HM.PMM. IMM.MM.PM.', along with duplicate maker's marks 'IG'. Scottish. Bezel 6x7.5mm, shank diameter 19mm, width 6mm.

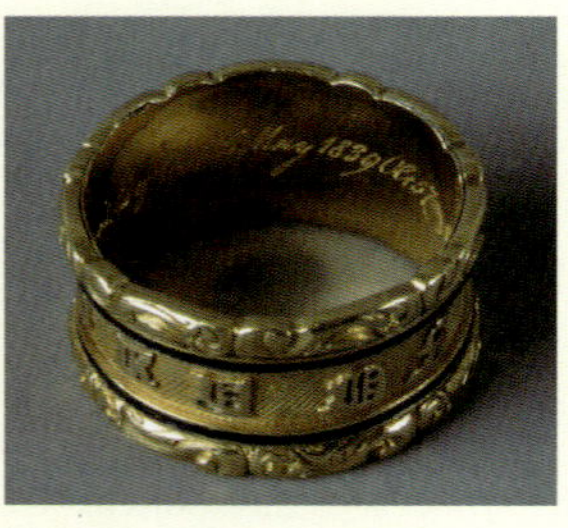

Fig. 252. Mourning ring. 'IN MEMORY OF', in Black Letter capitals, set in relief on a ground of diagonal hatch marks, bordered by a narrow band of black enamel and edged with chasing. Inscribed inside hoop: 'Willm. Davies Jervis, Esqr. obt. 15 May 1839 aet 57'. Hallmarked: London, 18ct. yellow gold, maker's mark L.V, 1839. shank diameter 19mm, width 11mm.

During the 1820s and 1830s, many mourning rings were made with chased or carved shoulders, which lent a more decorative appearance to the rings. (Fig. 253 a, b) Some had delicate hands supporting the bezel. (Fig. 254) The pansy motif set with dark amethysts was favoured at this time. Round cluster rings with openwork shoulders often set with onyx, jet or pearls became fashionable in the 1830s. By now the hair compartment was set in either the obverse or the reverse of the bezel. A bezel of onyx, carved with a forget-me-not, continued in popularity from about 1830 throughout several decades; (Fig. 255 a, b) some later rings had pearl borders. A few mourning rings were fashioned in the Gothic style, which continued to be used periodically throughout the century. (Fig. 256 a, b) Gentlemen wore many of the styles described above, except for the very dainty fashions obviously made for a woman's hand.

A mourning ring design that became fashionable in the 1840s had a shield-shaped bezel set with hair under glass, with an enamelled and sectioned shank (Fig. 257 a, b); or a shield-shaped bezel enamelled with a forget-me-not motif. (Fig. 258) By mid-century a shield-shaped hardstone, such as onyx, was commonly used. An interesting example has a hinged shank which closes at one side of the bezel; it was made especially for a person with arthritic joints. (Fig. 259)

Hoops of woven hair were made from about 1840 to 1865. The hair was secured inside a bezel, usually a small rectangular piece of gold (Fig. 260), but occasionally, the bezel is the fede motif, see Fig. 299, or a hair compartment surrounded by pearls, see Fig. 226.

Serpents were a common feature in mourning rings, prior to 1850. Sometimes the ring itself was formed as a serpent, or the snake decorated the bezel or the shoulders of a ring, see Fig. 25.

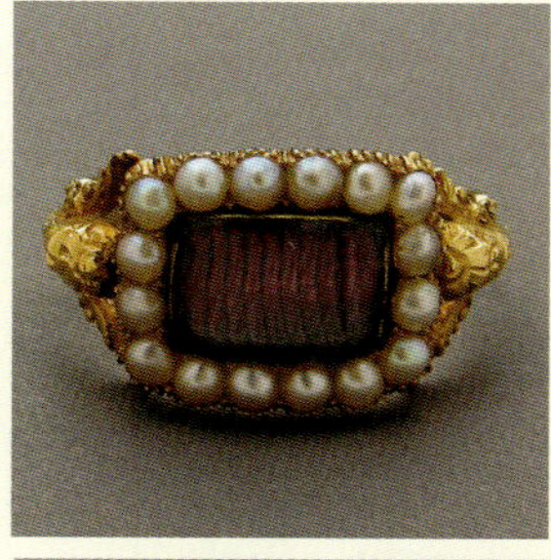

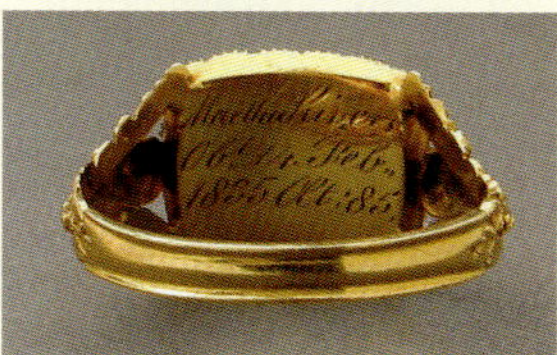

Fig. 253 a, b. Mourning ring. The bezel is decorated with a border of half pearls around woven pink and blue fabric, under glass. Chased, bifurcated shoulders inset with embossed work, channelled shank. Yellow gold. Inscribed on reverse of bezel: 'Martha Rivers obt. 14 Feb. 1835, Aet 85'. Bezel 11.5x14mm, shank diameter 18mm.

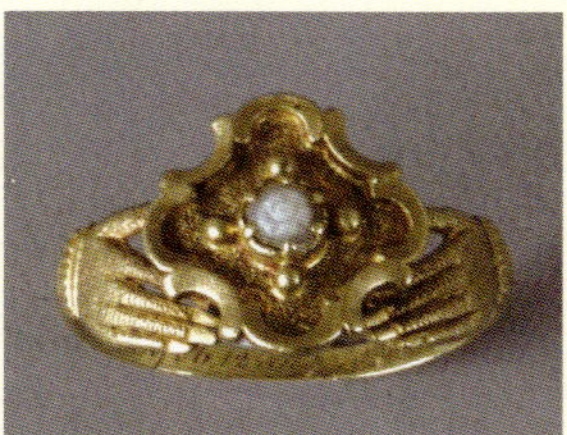

Fig. 254. Mourning ring. Quatrefoil bezel bordered with sections of curved gold, an onyx forget-me-not in a cramp setting centred on a matted ground, surrounded by four beads, cuffed hands are attached to a plain shank. Hair compartment set in the reverse of the bezel. Matt, pale yellow gold. Inscribed inside shank: 'John Morley Ob. 12 Aug 1830 aet 2 yr 3 mos'. Bezel 11x11mm, shank diameter 16.5mm.

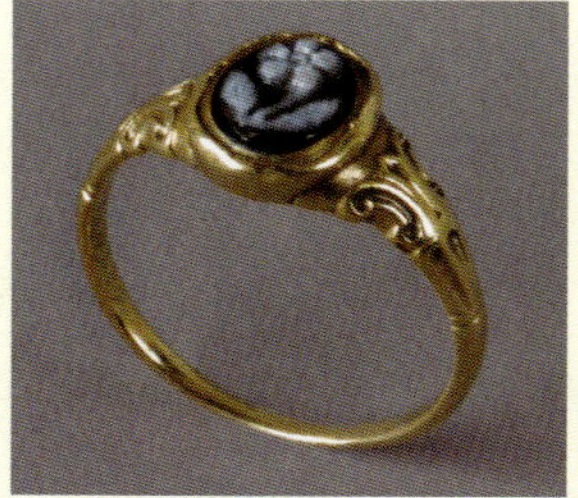

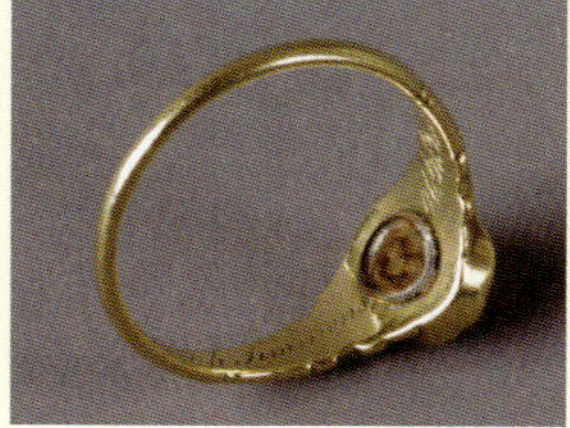

Fig. 255 a, b. Mourning ring set with an onyx forget-me-not and a compartment in the reverse of the bezel containing auburn hair. The lower shoulders are carved with three radiating panels, the upper shoulders with a scrolled design. Plain shank, D-shaped in section, inscribed inside: 'Sarah Simmons, obt. 11 July 1834 Aet 33'. Pale yellow gold. Bezel 9x7mm, hair compartment 5x5mm, shank diameter 18mm.

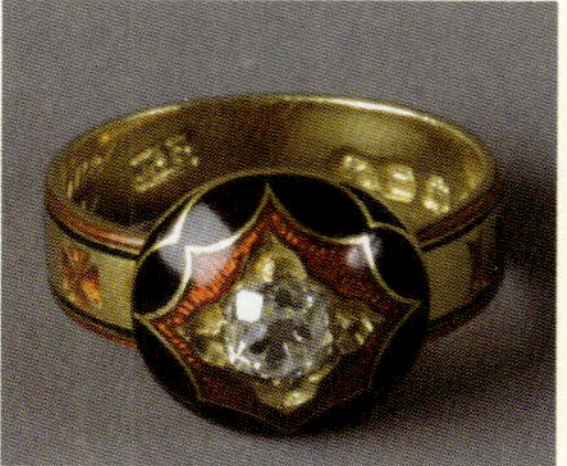

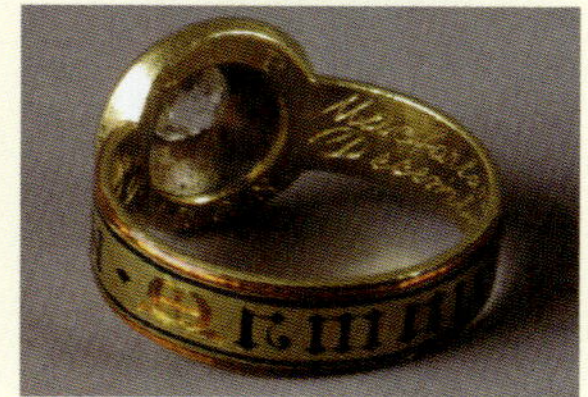

Fig. 256 a, b. Gothic-style mourning ring. The applied bezel is enamelled orange and black around a brilliant-cut diamond. The wide, flat hoop is edged with orange and black enamel with 'In Memory Of' enamelled in black with the initial letter of each word enamelled in orange. Inscribed inside hoop: 'William Macfarlane died 9 December 1868. R.I.P.' Hallmarked: London, 22ct. yellow gold, maker's mark T.E, 1866. Bezel 11x11mm, shank diameter 15.5mm, width 5mm.

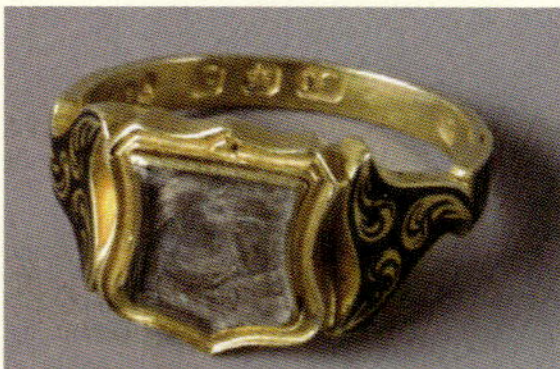

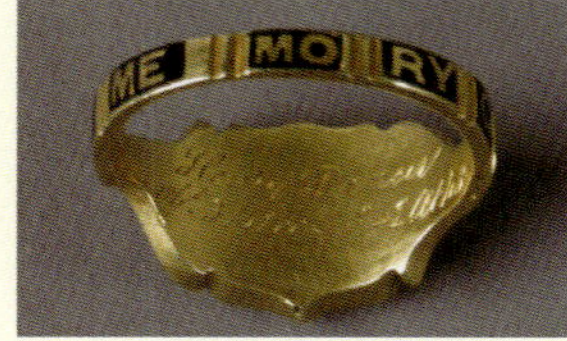

Fig. 257 a, b. Mourning ring. Shield-shaped bezel contains a hair compartment in a Roman setting. Wide, asymmetric black enamelled shoulders, a segmented, enamelled shank with two gold letters per section conveying the message IN-ME-MO-RY-OF. Inscribed on reverse of bezel: 'Henry Dancer, Obt. 31 Dec. 1842 Aet 48'. Hallmarked: London, 18ct. 'coloured' gold, maker's mark JL, 1842. Bezel 10.5x9mm, shoulder width 8mm, shank diameter 15.5mm.

Mourning

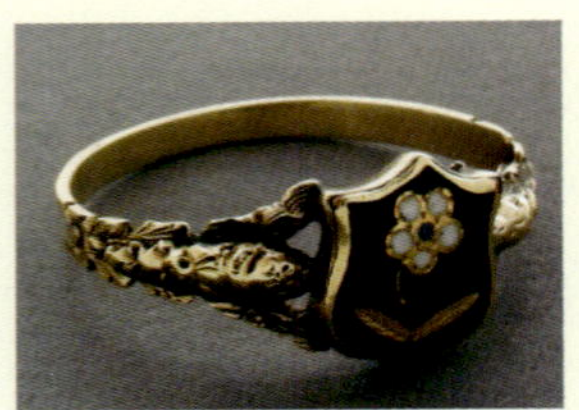

Fig. 258. Cartouche-shaped enamelled bezel. White flower, blue centre set in a black ground. Embossed chased shoulders on a channelled hoop. Pale yellow gold. *Circa* 1840. Bezel 8x7mm, shank diameter 16.5mm.

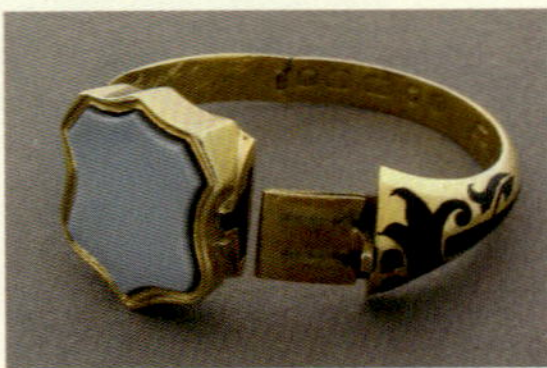

Fig. 259. Mourning ring. Shield-shaped bezel set with plain nicolo in a Roman setting, and an empty hair compartment in the reverse of the bezel. Belcher shoulders are decorated with a foliate design in black enamel, a narrow band of enamel runs the entire length of the hinged shank that opens by pressing the small dowel at one side of the bezel. Inscribed inside shank: 'John Paynter Esqr. obt. 11th Aug. 1858'. Hallmarked: London, 18ct. yellow gold, 1858. Bezel 13x11mm, shank diameter 19mm.

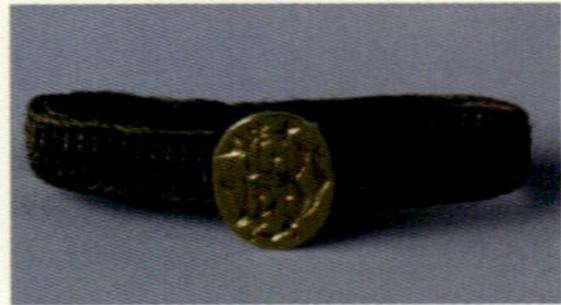

Fig. 260. Hair hoop secured within an oval engraved bezel of rich 'coloured' gold. American, *circa* 1865. Bezel 8.5x7mm, hoop width 4mm.

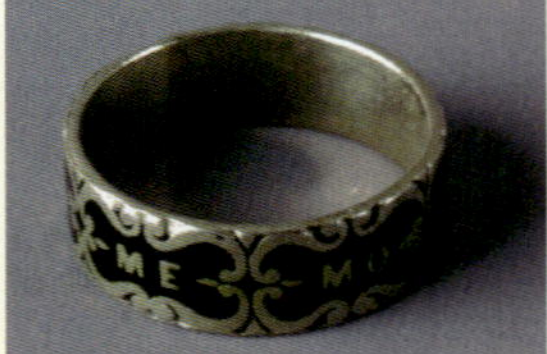

Fig. 261. Mourning ring of gilded brass inlaid with 'IN-ME-MO-RY-OF' in black enamel within a scrolled design. *Circa* 1880. Hoop diameter 18.5mm, width 7mm.

A.B. Savory & Sons, Watchmakers & Jewellers, 9, Cornhill, opposite the Bank produced a catalogue for 1851 (p.59) that described several mourning rings for ladies and gentlemen:

MOURNING JEWELLERY:

Ladies' Rings

	Neat	Elegant	Rich
Solid standard gold Hall-marked Rings, for hair.................each	21s	28s	42s
Ditto, set with fine Oriental pearls, and enamelled................	30s	45s	63s
Ditto, with fine single-stone brilliants ditto.............................	56s	105s	210s
Ditto, with diamonds, forming a beautiful Forget-me-not flower on black enamel...................	60s	84s	126s
Ditto, Widows' Hoops, with motto - In Memory of - on black enamel.........	18s	24s	30s

Gentlemen's Rings

	Neat	Elegant	Rich
Solid standard gold Hall-marked Mourning Rings, with chased borders, and enamelled motto. ....each	30s	45s	65s
Ditto, signet shape, and space for hair inside.....................	38s	52s	65s
Ditto, set with fine single-stone brilliants........................	50s	84s	210s

During the middle of the nineteenth century, several styles of hoop rings evolved that remained popular for the rest of the century. Some were enamelled in black with the words 'in memory of' set off in gold around the outside of the hoop, which was sometimes segmented into oblongs with the letters spaced evenly between the sections, perhaps with an additional hinged hair compartment. A few hoop rings were decorated with black enamel only. Hoop rings made with knurled edges and lined with plaited hair of the deceased could be decorated with one or more applied squares or rectangles of engraved gold; this style was also made as a buckle ring. (Fig. 261) (Fig. 262) (Fig. 263) (Fig. 264)

By the 1870s, instead of using the hair of the deceased, one could purchase braided hair from catalogues for use in mourning rings. This departure quite devalued the purpose of using hair in a ring.

In the 1860s and 1870s, a number of rings with a gypsy ring silhouette were embellished with pearls in a cluster design and black enamel, or fashioned with diagonal or vertical stripes with alternating enamel and gems, usually pearls or diamonds, see Fig. 105.

Occasionally rings contained a photograph of the deceased, a custom dating from the 1860s but not common until the late 1880s. (Fig. 265 a, b) Queen Victoria's mourning ring for her husband contained an oval photograph of Prince Albert in profile. The photograph was covered by rock crystal faceted around its edge then bordered by ropework. The shoulders of the ring were enamelled in black, with A and V intertwined and set off in gold with white enamel. Unfortunately photographs deteriorate when constantly exposed to light, and few of these rings have survived. At the Liverpool Museum, (England) an 1825 setting has been reused, with a photograph replacing the hair receptacle.

By 1880 mourning ring designs had become rather unimaginative, though they were still well made. (Fig. 266) Hoop rings set with plaited hair between chased, flanged edges, sometimes decorated with rectangular or oblique sections of engraved gold set at intervals across

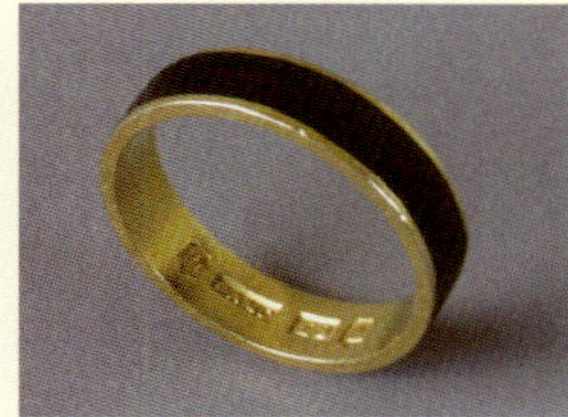

Fig. 262. Mourning ring decorated with plain, matt black enamel. Inscribed inside hoop: '2 Feb. 1868.'. Hallmarked: Edinburgh, 18ct. 'coloured' gold, maker's mark G & MC, no date mark. Hoop diameter 15.5mm, width 4.5mm.

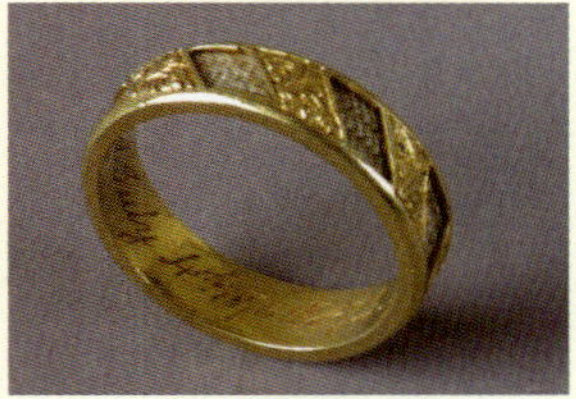

Fig. 263. Mourning ring. Hollow hoop lined with tightly braided white hair, with diamond-shaped sections of engraved gold set diagonally across the hoop. Inscribed inside the hoop: 'J.B. Died July 4th 1876. Aet 74'. Hallmarked: London, 18ct. 'coloured' gold, maker's mark J.W, 1876. Hoop diameter 16mm, width 4.5mm.

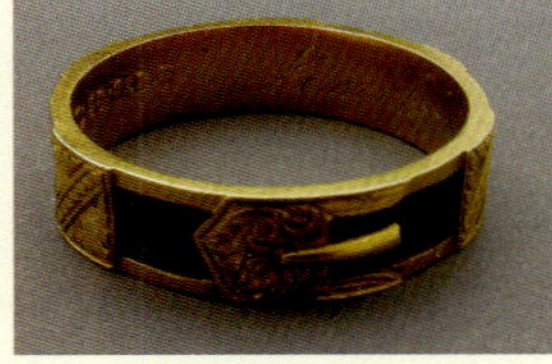

Fig. 264. Buckle mourning ring. Brown plaited hair lines the hollowed hoop that is decorated with engraved rectangles of gold. 'Emily' is inscribed inside the hoop. Hallmarked: Chester, 15 (.675) ct. 'coloured' gold, maker's mark, WGM, 1898. Hoop diameter 17mm, width 4.5mm.

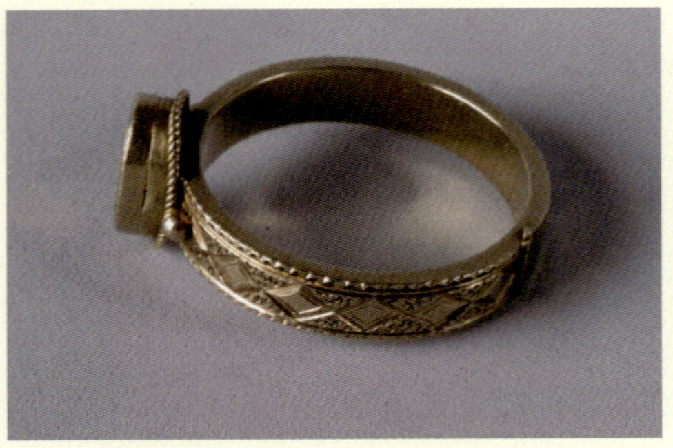
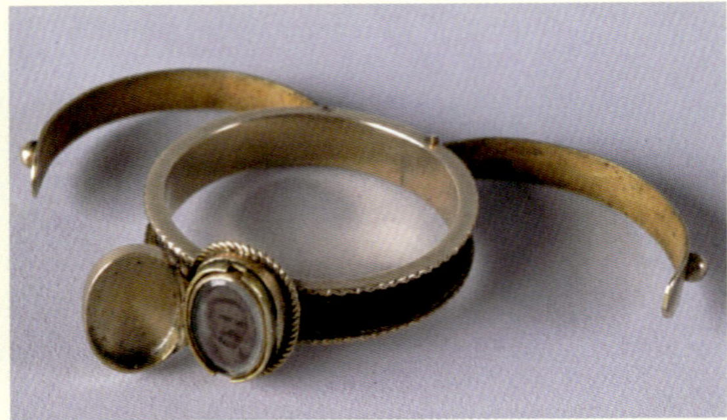

Fig. 265 a, b. Mourning ring. An engraved and hinged oval bezel, concealing a glass covered photograph of a gentleman, has purled work applied to the base of the bezel. A succession of bevelled diamond-shapes - the gold between is engraved - decorate the outer hoop which opens by pressing the large bead on either side of the bezel to reveal plaited hair. Rose gold. *Circa* 1885-1900. Bezel 11.5x7mm, hoop diameter 20.5mm, width 5mm.

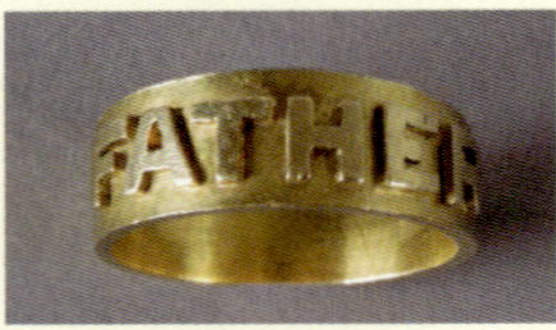

Fig. 266. Mourning ring with FATHER, in applied letters. Hallmarked: London, 18ct. 'coloured' gold, maker's mark M.M. in Gothic script, 1881. Hoop diameter 16mm, 7mm wide at front.

the hoop, were still being made. At this time the gold sections were often enamelled with the message 'In Memory of' or 'Mother' spelt out in gold. Sometimes a hoop ring was embellished with the symbols for Faith (a cross), Hope (an anchor) and Charity (a heart). (Fig. 267)

The gypsy form was still being used incorporating a pearl or diamond-set flower or a cross on a matt, black enamelled ground. A similar design had its bezel decorated with a boat-shaped application of enamel set with pearls or diamonds. The marquise and circular bezels were enamelled and decorated with pearls and diamonds. (Fig. 268 a, b) (Fig. 269 a, b) Personal inscriptions were still engraved inside the hoop.

Mourning rings were a staple of many a jeweller's trade; the availability of these rings today testifies to the vast numbers produced in the nineteenth and early twentieth centuries. (Fig. 270 a, b)

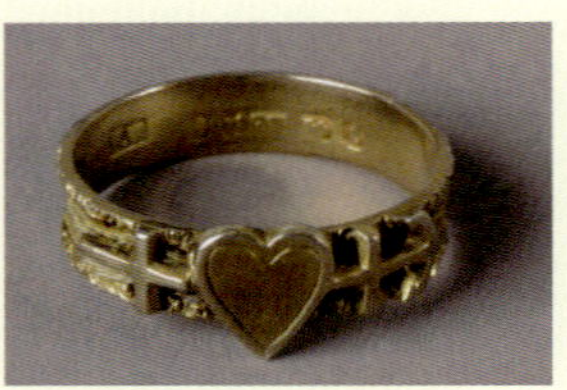

Fig. 267. Faith, hope and charity hoop ring lined with plaited hair. Hallmarked: Birmingham, 9(.375) ct. worn 'coloured' gold, 1891. Heart 7mm long, hoop diameter 17mm, width 4.5mm.

Mourning

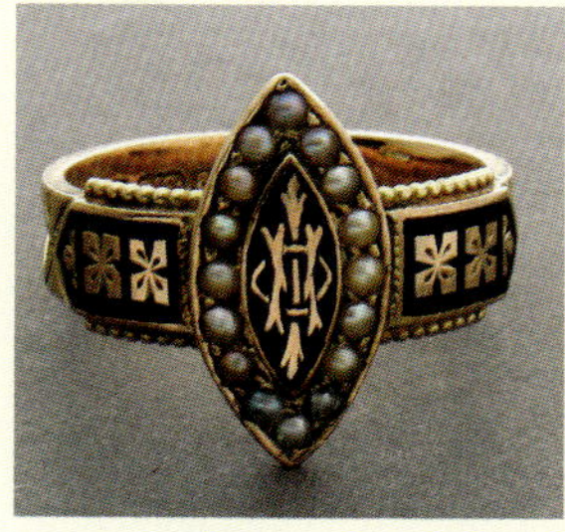

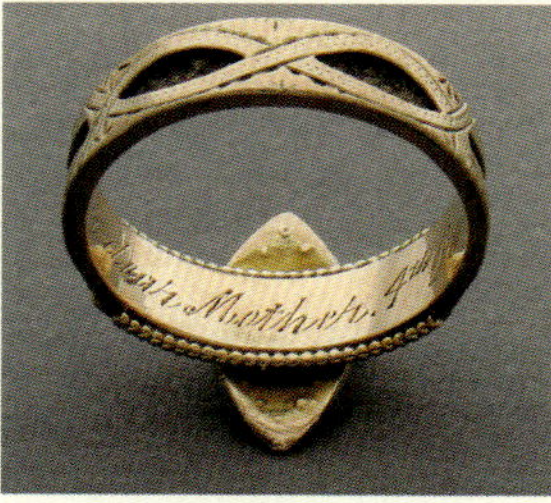

Fig. 268 a, b. Mourning ring.
Marquise bezel enamelled
in black with an intricate
design of gold: I M O (in
memory of) set in the
enamel. Half pearls border
the bezel. Black enamel,
beading decorate the
shoulders. The hoop is lined
with pale brown hair that is
visible through the engraved
gold. Inscribed inside the
hoop: My dear Mother 4th
December 1901. Hallmarked:
Chester, 9(.375) ct., 1901.
Keith Austin Collection

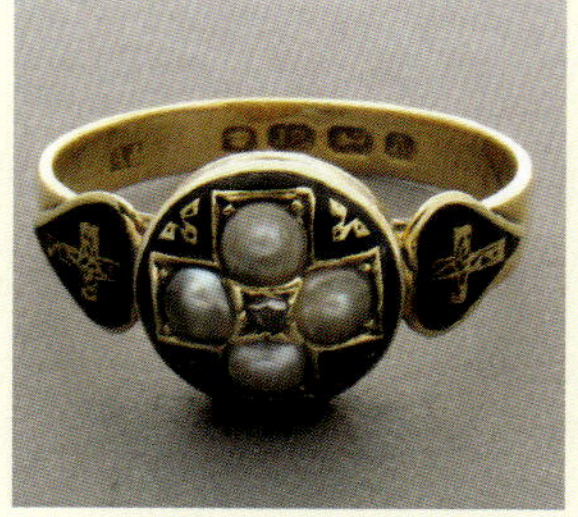

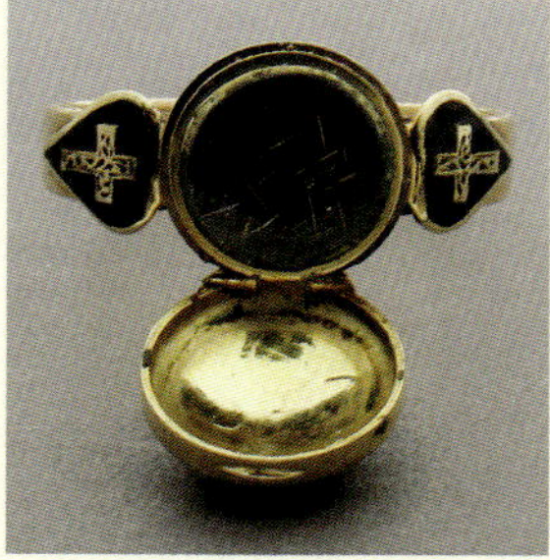

Fig. 269 a, b. Mourning
ring. Bezel comprises four
pearls around a rose-cut
diamond. The hinged bezel
covers hair beneath glass.
A gold cross decorated each
black enamelled shoulder.
Flat hoop. Hallmarked:
Birmingham 18ct. yellow
gold, 1900.
Keith Austin Collection

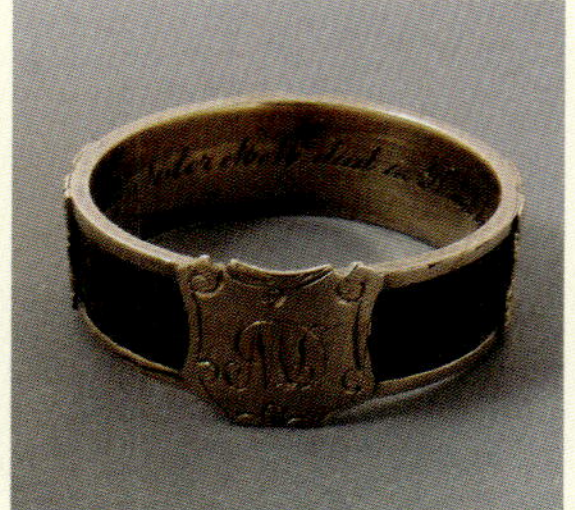

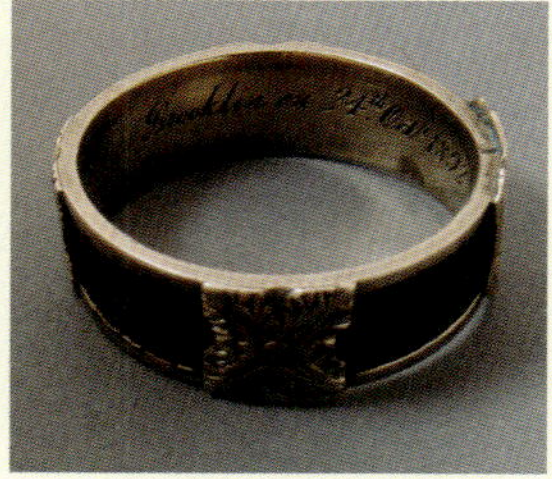

Fig. 270 a, b. Hoop ring
lined with brown hair, and
sections of engraved gold are
set at intervals across the
hair. Rose gold. Inscribed: 'In
memory of my sister M.Mc
died in Brooklin on 24th Oct
1892'. *Courtesy of Michael
O'Neill, photographer.*

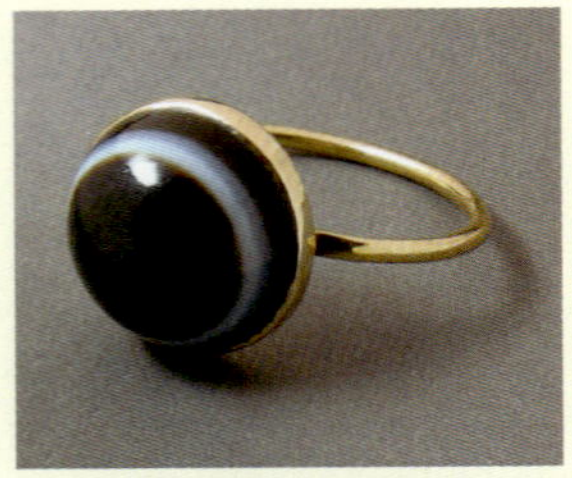

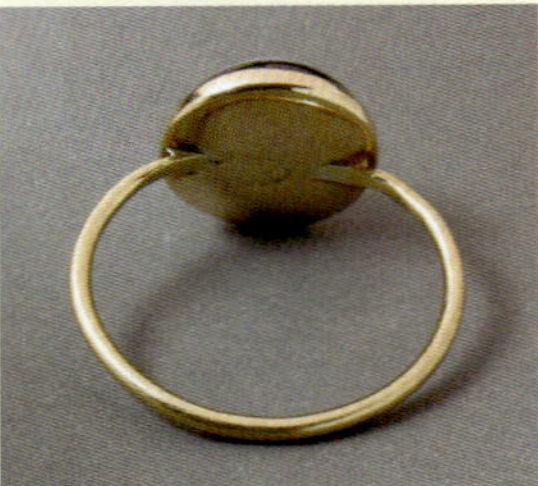

Fig. 271 a, b. Onyx in a rub-over setting on a wire hoop. The onyx was possibly a stick pin at one time and has been converted to a ring. Yellow gold. *Circa* 1890. Bezel 12x12mm, hoop diameter 18mm.

CARE, CAUTIONS AND REPAIRS

All rings should be removed by placing the fingers on either side of the bezel to avoid touching any stones; this prevents gems from becoming loose in their settings, and helps to prevent porous stones, such as opal, pearl and turquoise, from becoming discoloured. It is advisable to check the stones regularly to make sure they are not loose in their settings. The constant wearing of two rings on the same finger can quickly erode the shank and gallery of both rings.

Rings should be removed before putting the hands in water, otherwise, they may become clogged with soap, grease, and dust; eventually porous stones will be damaged, and closed-back settings ruined. Some late ninetheenth-century rings can be cleaned safely with commercial jewellery cleaner or a little household ammonia diluted with water. Exceptions are pearl, turquoise, opal, coral, any ring containing hair and all closed-back settings. The use of any sharp tool to remove grime should be avoided as damage may occur to the gems and settings. Closed settings can be cleaned with dry whiting powder brushed over the metal with a soft-bristled brush.

Few rings from the first half of the century can be safely cleaned with any liquid, and whiting powder should be used sparingly because it cleans by abrasion. It would be advisable to have early nineteenth-century rings cleaned by a professional.

It is advisable to store rings in the slots provided in jewellery boxes, or in special ring boxes. Failing that, individual re-sealable plastic bags will protect your rings.

A number of nineteenth- or twentieth-century shanks have been attached to nineteenth-century buttons, cuff-links, stick pins, parts of necklaces, earrings or brooches, and the resulting rings are sometimes sold as originals. Generally, it is fairly easy to recognize a ring of mixed ancestry. There are a number of features to look for: traces of grey lead soldering, untidy soldering, marks on the back of the bezel that indicate the removal of pins or loops, (Fig. 271 a, b) and file marks. Sometimes a portion of a shank, hallmarked to indicate high quality gold, has been cut out of a ring and illegally inserted into the shank of a ring of much lower quality. Wedding rings were sometimes converted into decorative rings. An entire hallmarked shank or part of a wedding ring of an earlier date is sometimes attached to a later bezel, making the ring appear older and consequently more desirable. Familiarity with the styles of the different periods will help one develop the ability to recognize that bezel and shank did not start life together. (Fig. 272 a, b) It is difficult to match the colour of gold exactly when creating one ring from pieces made at different times, so slight variations in the colour of the gold should be viewed with suspicion. Collectors should be particularly careful to examine gem settings; when they have been disturbed, it is difficult to disguise the alteration. It is not uncommon to find a basic half-hoop ring which has had its gems removed and replaced with the appropriate stones to turn it into a 'regard', 'dearest' or similar 'acrostic' ring, in an attempt to enhance its value. Sometimes a lost stone is replaced with a gem that is not contemporary with the setting. One good example would be an early nineteenth-century ring that has a late nineteenth-century Australian opal set in the ring. Often a replacement can be detected if glue has been used, and it can even be visible with the naked eye.

Reproductions of nineteenth-century rings are being manufactured in considerable numbers today; some are easy to spot as they lack the delicacy of the original, and the gems, particularly diamonds, are of a modern cut. Signs of wear may help to authenticate the age of a ring, though a few reproductions are set with chipped or discoloured gems and sold as original. Many are honestly described as copies, but others are sold to the unsuspecting as original, thereby perpetuating the fraud.

Nineteenth-century rings can be repaired, but it is essential to find a specialist in that field. Some rings should not be sized owing to their fragility, ornate decoration, position of the hallmark on the shank, if an inscription might be spoiled or if the gold has been 'coloured'. Sizing can be inadvisable if pearls, opals, turquoises, hair or enamel are present in the ring. Tinted gold must be treated by a specialist as the colours can be affected by any process involving heat.

On the whole, patient, close inspection of an antique ring will serve as a useful guide to its authenticity.

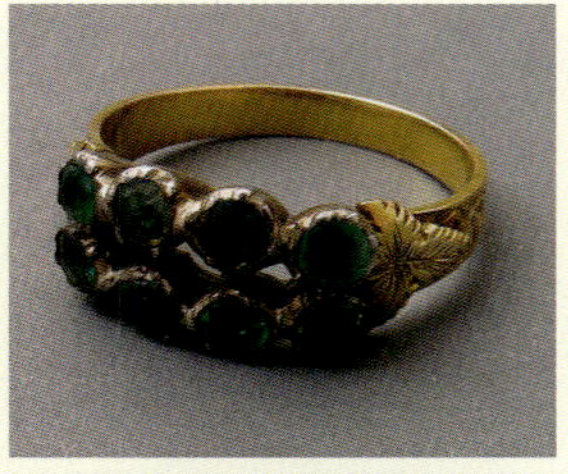

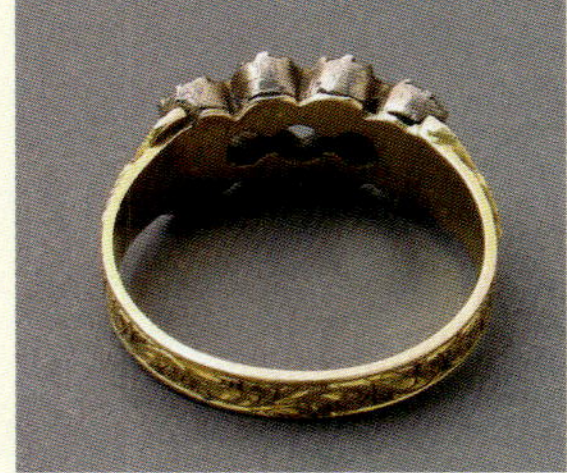

Fig. 272 a, b. Silver-gilt bezel comprising eight emeralds, set in closed collets, *circa* 1810; 1850s replacement shank of finely engraved yellow gold, applied vine leaf decorates each shoulder. Bezel 7x14mm, shank diameter 16.5mm, width 2.5mm.

          Care, Caution and Repairs

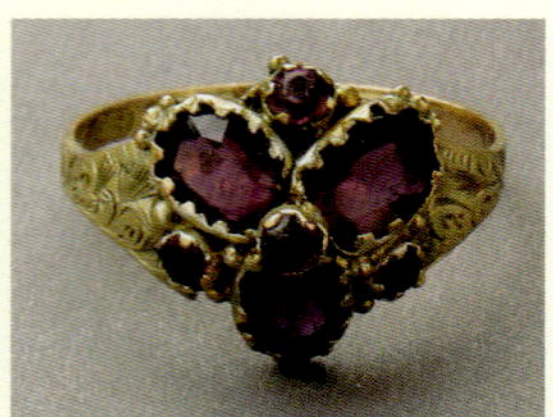

Fig. 273. Trefoil bezel of dark amethysts in open-back cramp settings, decorated with small amethysts and beads. Wide, flat shoulders taper to the shank, both are engraved. Hallmarked: Birmingham, 12(.5) ct. green gold, maker's mark JH, 1863. Bezel 12x10mm, shank diameter 15mm.

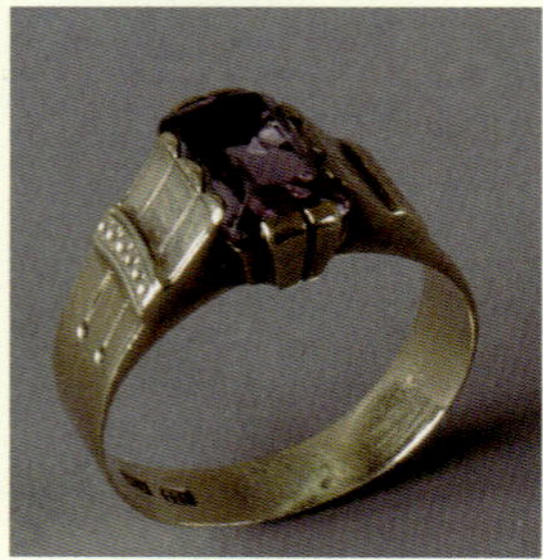

Fig. 274. Amethyst secured by eight scallops supported by wide, flat shoulders divided into three sections by milled-work above a curved, transverse section decorated with punched-work. Wide, flat shank, marked 14k., 333 and FW inside one shoulder. American, *circa* 1875-1900. Bezel 11x6mm, shoulder 6mm wide, shank diameter 19mm.

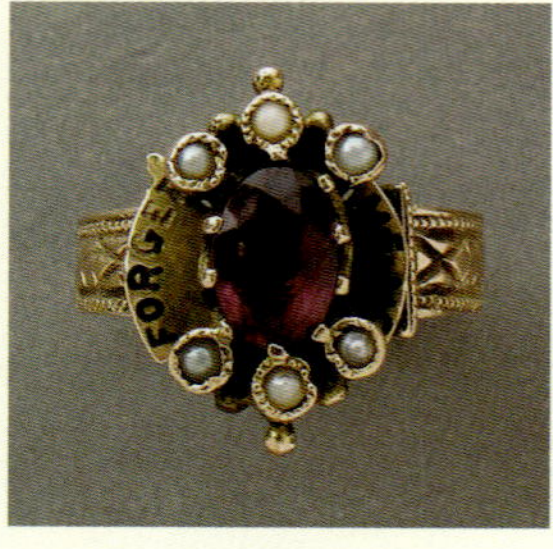

Fig. 275. Amethyst and pearl set bezel that has a rotating slide inside the bezel. The black enamelled message on the slide is FORGET ME NOT. Flat, engraved shoulders, flat hoop. American, *circa* 1870. Bezel 10x8mm, shank diameter 16.5mm, width 4mm.

GLOSSARY

ACROSTIC: Rings containing gems, the initial letter of which spelt out words such as DEAR(EST), REGARD, REPEAL or SEMAINE. These rings were fashionable from about 1810 to 1875. See Figs. 17, 49, and 57.

AMETHYST: Mauve or purple quartz. Early in the century pale amethysts, frequently foiled, were used but were not as prized as purple gems. *Circa* 1825-1835 a combination of amethyst and turquoise was often found in rings and other jewellery. When pale colours for costume and jewellery were fashionable in the 1880s and 1890s, pale amethysts were again in demand. As a result of Brazilian discoveries, by the 1890s, amethysts were plentiful and less prized than in previous decades. The stone was popular throughout the century partly because it could be worn with mourning dress. (Fig. 273) (Fig. 274) (Fig. 275)

AQUAMARINE: A member of the beryl family. According to John Mawe in *A Treatise on Diamonds and Precious Stones*, p.114, the aquamarine 'though one of the cheapest of the gems, and the most abundant, is in considerable demand, and is esteemed a fashionable stone'. He noted in his 1823 edition that the aquamarine was less valued at that time. According to Edwin Streeter in *Precious Stones and Gems*, Section IV, Chapter V, page 184, 'this gem is a great favourite with the English, chiefly because it possesses the advantage of retaining its lustre in artificial light'. Despite the stone's popularity one does not find many nineteenth century rings set with aquamarine. (Fig. 276)

ART NOUVEAU: Designs incorporated animal or female forms, often the female head with flowing hair, flowers, foliage and swirling tendrils. Rings, frequently asymmetric in outline, were made from silver or gold, set with colourful stones, often cut as a cabochon, or with baroque pearls, and decorated with enamel. Plique-à-jour enamel was a feature of Art Nouveau work. Interest in these designs, which were a complete departure from current styles, began in the 1870s and continued, in diluted form, until the early 1920s. The popularity of Art Nouveau jewellery was at its peak between 1895 and 1910. Today the term covers all work of this style and period regardless of the country of origin. (Fig. 277)

ARTS AND CRAFTS MOVEMENT: A number of guilds were established in Britain during the 1880s to encourage the production of original handmade crafts including jewellery. (Fig. 278)

ASYMMETRY: Asymmetric form and decoration was used between 1840 and 1875 and in Art Nouveau work.

BAROQUE: See PEARLS.

BEADING: Between 1825 and 1880 beading frequently decorated the bezel and shoulders of rings. It was also used on the shanks of filigree rings between 1820 and 1835, occasionally during the latter part of the century, and on Italian souvenir rings. Beading was executed both by hand and machine. (Fig. 279)

BELCHER: Various uses of the term are to be found in nineteenth century literature:

a) a term used in an 1830s design book from a Derby goldsmith to describe the convex shoulders of a ring.

b) a gentleman's ring formed 'of thick, solid half round wire; cast whole or manipulated from the flat metal and left hollow', T. B. Wigley 1898, *The Art of the Goldsmith & Jeweller*, p. 97.

BETROTHAL RINGS: See narrative section.

BEZEL: The term bezel is now commonly used to describe the head or the central ornament of a ring. An 'applied' bezel is soldered to the ring rather than being made in one piece with the shoulders and the shank. The term, bezel, is also used for the metal rim holding a gemstone.

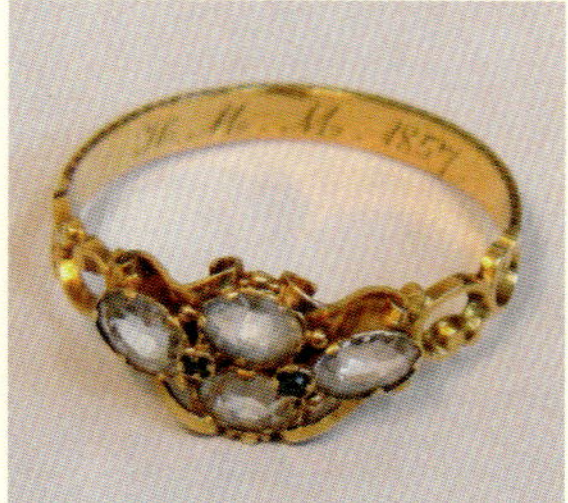

Fig. 276. Bezel comprising four open-set aquamarines and two closed-back emeralds, all in cramp settings, with scrolled wire-work decorating the gallery. Asymmetric openwork shoulders, shank engraved on all outer edges. Yellow gold. Inscribed inside hoop: 'H.M.M. 1857'. Bezel 8x12mm, shank diameter 19mm, width 2.5mm.

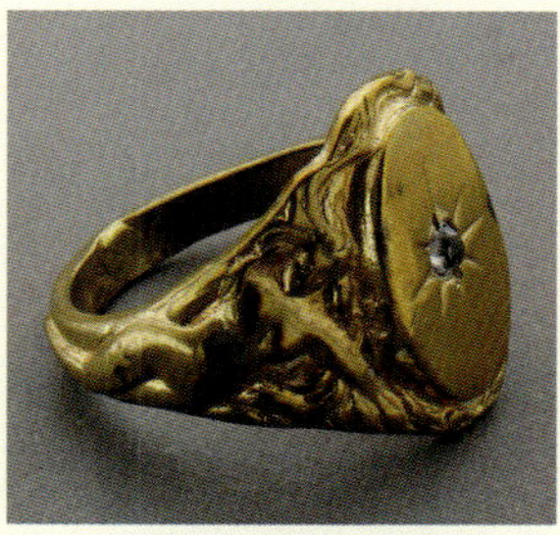

Fig. 277. Brass signet ring set with a rose-cut glass. Asymmetric design of a nude on each shoulder. American, 1900-1910. Bezel 17x9mm, shank diameter 18mm.

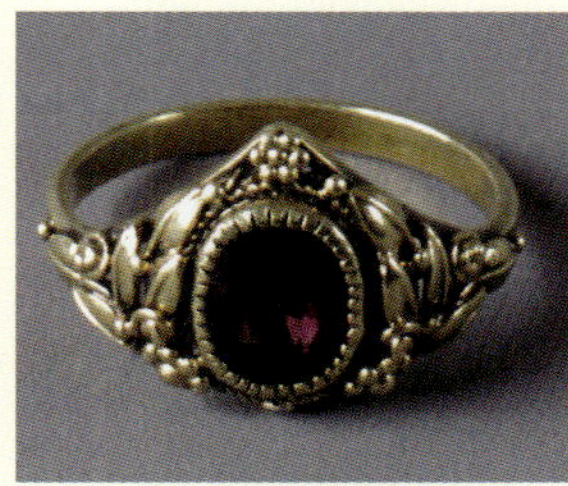

Fig. 278. Arts & Crafts ring. Heraldic-shaped bezel, decorated with a beaded flower at one end, is set with a faceted almandine garnet in a closed saw-tooth setting, shoulders are decorated with flowers and leaves supported by a substantial grooved shank. Yellow gold. *Circa* 1900-1910. Garnet 7.5x5.5mm, shank diameter 17mm.

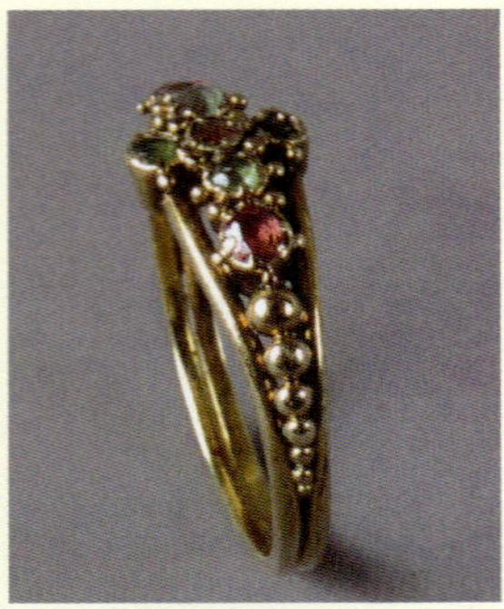

Fig. 279. Bezel comprising pale emeralds and rubies in closed cramp settings and individual beads decorating the settings. Double wire shank separates at shoulders to accommodate seven graduated gold beads. Yellow gold. *Circa* 1840-1850. Bezel 7.5x15mm, shank diameter 17mm.

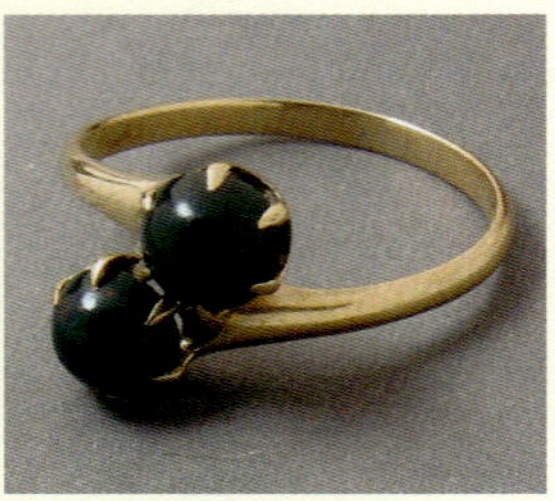

Fig. 280. Cross-over ring set with bloodstones in claw settings, maker's mark M C. Yellow gold. American, *circa* 1890-1910. Bezel 11x5mm, hoop diameter 16.5mm.

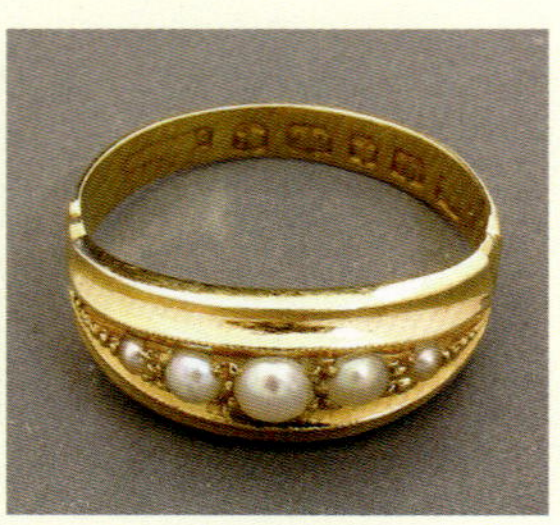

Fig. 281. Boat-shaped bezel set with seed pearls and tiny beads that are outlined with a concave section of gold. Plain hoop. Hallmarked: Exeter, 22ct., yellow gold, illegible maker's mark, 1877, with engraved initials M.A.L. Exeter hallmarks are rare. Bezel depth 7mm, hoop diameter 17mm.

BIRTHSTONES: The following excerpt from 'Rambles of an Archeologist among old Books and in old Places', by F.W. Fairholt, p.195, reflects the moral tone of the Victorian mind:

> January. - Garnet: Constancy and Fidelity.
> February. - Amethyst: Sincerity.
> March. - Bloodstone: Courage and Presence of Mind.
> April. - Diamond: Innocence.
> May. - Emerald: Success in love.
> June. - Agate: Health and long life.
> July. - Cornelian: Contented mind.
> August. - Sardonyx: Conjugal felicity.
> September. - Chrysolite: Antidote against madness.
> October. - Opal: Hope.
> November. - Topaz: Fidelity.
> December. - Turquoise: Prosperity.

As might be expected in so fanciful a matter, the moral qualities attributed to the stones vary greatly according to different authorities, and moreover, other gems than those mentioned above have been set apart as emblems of the different months.

It is interesting to compare this list with modern ones and to note the high proportion of modest stones in the Victorian list.

BLOODSTONE: A member of the chalcedony family also known as heliotrope. Colour: dark opaque green flecked with red. It was used in signet rings throughout the century. (Fig. 280)

BLOOM: See GOLD ('colouring').

BOAT-SHAPE: A bezel style which was popular from about 1870 onward. Some hoop rings had a boat-shape cut into the gold and set with fine gems secured with gold grains. Other designs had the boat-shape formed solely by graduated gems, occasionally bordered by a narrow strip of gold. Many boat-shaped bezels in the 1890s were surrounded by moulded patterns, with the gems held in thread settings. (Fig. 281)

BOSS: A domed form, often pavé-set with turquoises or pearls *Circa* 1860 onward. (Fig. 282 a, b)

BRILLIANT CUT: 'According to the number of the facets, the Brilliant is said to be single, double, or, Old English, cut. The Brilliant depends greatly upon the facetting (sic) for its exceeding beauty', wrote Edwin W. Streeter in *Precious Stones and Gems* 1877, Section I, Chapter IV, page 32. A round, single-cut gem had 9 facets above the girdle, 9 below. Double cut is an older style of cutting, with 17 facets above the girdle, including a square table, and 17 duplicate facets below the girdle, except that the culet was smaller than the table. Old mine or cushion cut had 33 facets above the girdle and 25 below. The brilliant cut went through several stages of improvement. Early in the century, gems were cut to preserve as much weight as possible, consequently they were chunkier than late nineteenth-century examples. The modern brilliant cut (33 facets above the girdle, 25 below) has a larger table and tiny culet and has less depth than nineteenth-century gems, thus enhancing the brilliance of the diamond. The term 'brilliant' is used when referring to any of the above styles of cutting. See DIAMONDS.

BUCKLE: Buckle rings became fashionable about 1850 and are still being produced today. The style was used primarily for decorative rings and occasionally for mourning rings (Fig. 283) (Fig. 284). Buckle rings, in a variety of widths, were decorated in a number of ways: set with one or two gems, or entirely covered with gems; carved or chased (1890s). Occasionally, double buckle rings were made; a few rings were designed with a hinged bezel concealing hair, a name or message, see Fig. 123, and others were hinged in several sections so that the ring could be unbuckled to remove it, see Fig.75. The buckle design was also used to decorate the shoulders of signet rings.

BURNISHING: Bringing a bright polish to metal by rubbing the surface with a hard, smooth tool. Many rings were burnished by machine, but fine pieces were still finished by hand.

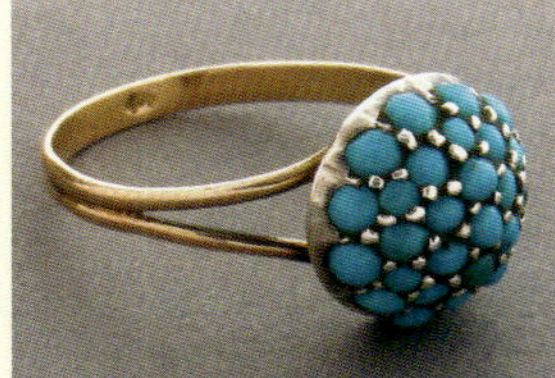

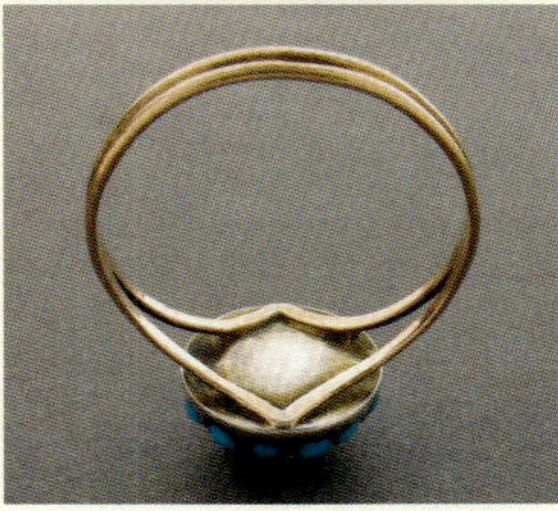

Fig. 282 a, b. Boss-shaped bezel, pavé-set with turquoise in silver. Rose gold shank separates at the shoulders and is attached beneath the bezel in a curved diamond shape. *Circa* 1870. The ring belonged to the author's great-grandmother. Bezel diameter 10mm, shank diameter 17.5mm.

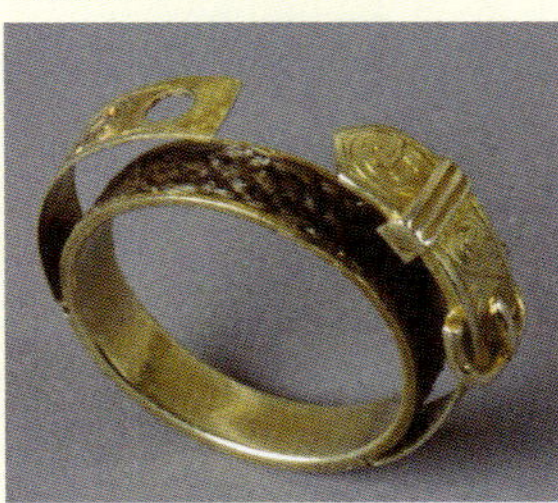

Fig. 283. Buckle ring used as a mourning ring. The engraved hoop is filled with hair that is visible upon raising the buckle. 'Coloured' gold. American, *circa* 1885. Hoop diameter 17mm, width 4mm.

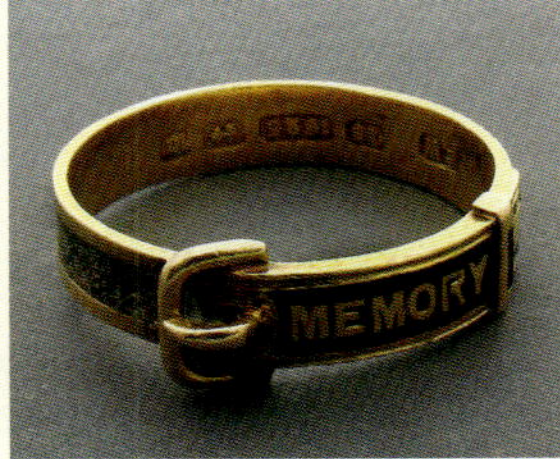

Fig. 284. Mourning ring in the buckle design. Memory in black enamel, and hoop filled with light 'coloured' hair. Hallmarked: Birmingham, 15(.625)ct., 'Coloured' gold, maker's mark FW, 1878. *Keith Austin Collection*

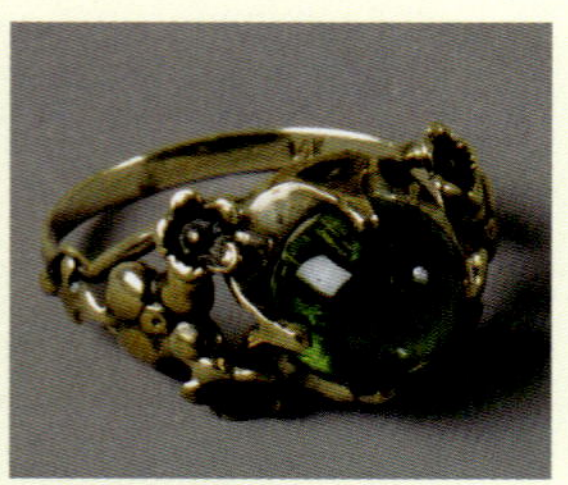

Fig. 285. Yellow-green cabochon tourmaline secured in an open-claw setting, openwork floral and foliate shoulders, narrow, flat shank. 14k. yellow gold. American, *circa* 1900-1910. The design reflects the influence of Arts & Crafts work. Shank diameter 18mm.

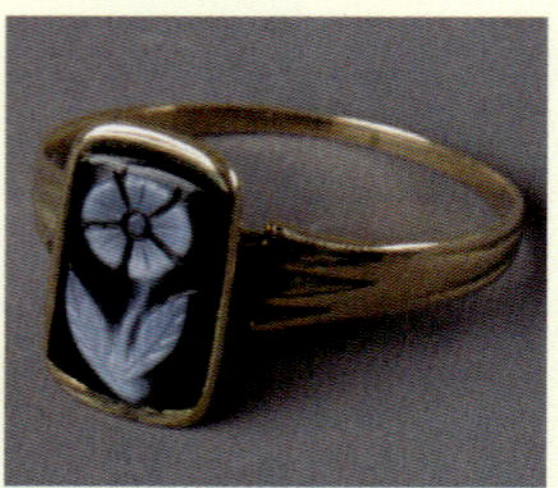

Fig. 286. Onyx forget-me-not cameo in a flush setting set on moulded shoulders and a channelled hoop. Rose gold. American, *circa* 1870. Bezel 11.5x7.5mm, hoop diameter 17mm.

CABOCHON: A convex polished cut, without facets, used for some transparent gems such as almandine garnet (carbuncle), dark amethyst, cat's eye, moonstone and opal. The cabochon cut is also used for opaque stones such as coral and turquoise. (Fig. 285)

CALIBRÉ CUT: A cut used on small stones, usually in a rectangular step cut, and often set in circular designs. See Fig. 98.

CAMEO: A stone carved in relief, usually from agate, coral, onyx, sardonyx, shell or lava. Opal and moonstone were used occasionally towards the end of the century. Among the rings produced in the neo-classical period was the striking blood-red coral cameo, using the Roman or rub-over setting with a plain shank. Onyx cameos depicting a white forget-me-not on a black ground were used in mourning rings from the early 1830s to the late 1870s. (Fig. 286) Stone cameos regained favour during the 1860s. During the 1880s and 1890s, numerous inexpensive stone or paste cameos were made displaying the figure of a woman set in a marquise, oval or rectangular frame, sometimes surrounded with pearls. A few nineteenth-century rings were set with valuable antique cameos.

CANNETILLE: A form of filigree in imitation of gold thread embroidery. According to Henri Vever in *La Bijouterie Francaise au XIXe Siècle* Vol. I, (see p.72), in France the fashion for cannetille lasted well beyond the first Empire (1804-1815), into the Restoration period (1815-1830) and the reign of Louis-Philippe (1830-1848). Vever describes cannetille as a tight spiral of fine wire, which is either soldered to gold or silver or is freestanding. It was usually intermingled with gold grains, often in a peascod motif, tiny leaves or small stamped roses, and was set around less costly gems. In England cannetille work became popular about 1820 and remained in fashion until about 1835. It was usually set with amethyst, aquamarine, chrysoberyl, pearl, or pink or gold topaz. Cannetille was generally made in gold, though cheap imitations, in gilded brass, stamped to resemble cannetille, do exist. See Fig. 48.

CARAT: 1) A term used to denote the quality or purity of gold. Pure gold is 24 carats. The gold standards of 22, 18, 15(.625), 12(.5) and 9(.375) carat indicate the proportion of pure gold in the alloy, the balance being other metals such as copper, silver or zinc.

2) Carat also refers to the measure of weight used for diamonds and other gemstones. A carat is equal to one fifth of a gramme.

CARBUNCLE: A cabochon-cut almandine garnet. To relieve the density of colour, the stone was hollowed out at the back and placed on foil in a closed rub-over setting. It was fashionable from about 1850 to 1880 in gentlemen's rings. See Fig. 107.

CARVING: The cutting of a design into metal. This method of decoration was used periodically throughout the century, particularly on ring shoulders.

CAT'S EYE: The cymophane variety of chrysoberyl produces the finest cat's eyes. Quartz and tourmaline also produce cat's eyes which were used in rings. Colour: honey-yellow to greenish or brownish yellow, and grey-green, displaying a floating line of reflected light from within the stone when cut as a cabochon. The cat's eye was popular from 1813-1823 and again in the late 1870s. According to E.W. Streeter, *Precious Stones and Gems*, 1877, Chapter VII, page 168:

> On the whole, perhaps, the most popular colours are the clear apple-green and dark olive: both of these form a splendid back ground, and contrast well with the line....A ring-stone may be worth from £10 to £100, or even more; and there are large specimens at present in the market which are worth upwards of £1000.

In the 1880s and 1890s the honey-coloured or brown shades were much in demand as ring stones.

CHALCEDONY: Crypto-crystalline quartz. Varieties of chalcedony include agate, onyx, cornelian, sard, chrysoprase, bloodstone, sardonyx. The common use of the word 'chalcedony' normally indicates the white or greyish-blue variety of the stone.

CHASING: The art of executing a clearly defined, raised decoration on metal, modelled from the solid metal with a hammer and other tools. Some rings had bold chasing, others had chasing more delicate and matt in appearance. Chasing was popular from about 1815 to 1850 and again in the 1890s. (Fig. 287)

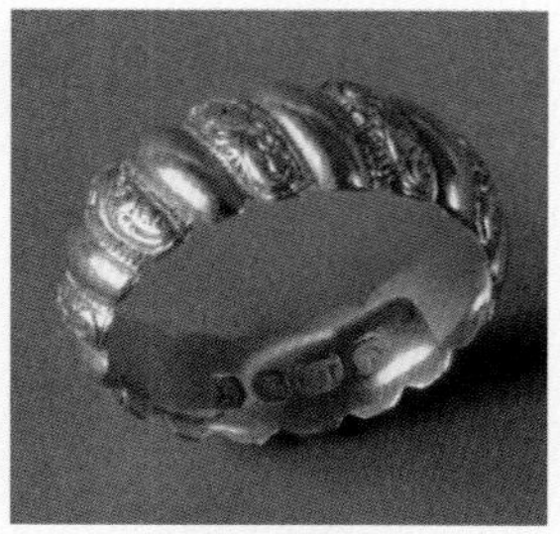

Fig. 287. Hoop ring decorated with alternating bands of plain or chased gold. Hallmark: London, 18ct. yellow gold, 1894. Hoop diameter 16mm, width 6mm.

Glossary

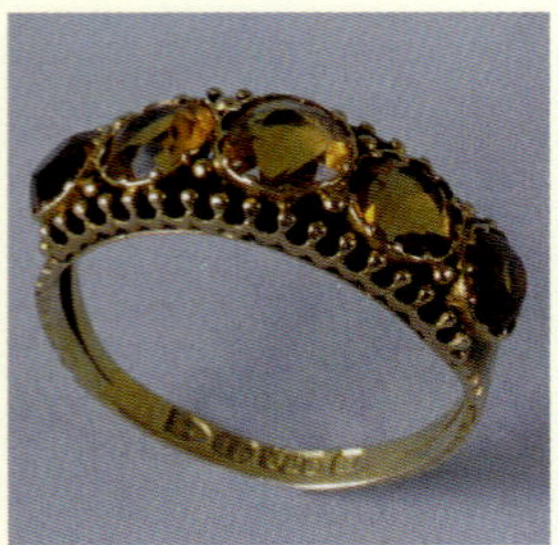

Fig. 288. Half-hoop comprising five citrines in open-back cramp settings, decorated with a strip of beading on either side of the bezel, engraved shoulders and shank. Hallmarked: Chester, 15(.625) ct. yellow gold, 1891. A late example of a style usually associated with earlier decades. Bezel depth 7mm, shank diameter 17mm.

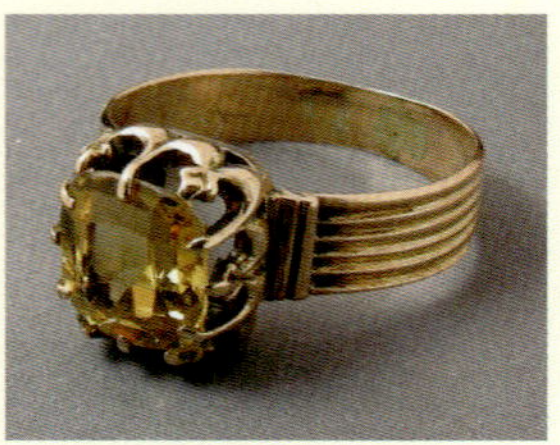

Fig. 289. Yellow citrine in an ornate claw setting, wide reeded hoop. American, *circa* 1885-1900. Gem 7x6.5mm, bezel rises 5mm from finger, hoop diameter 15mm.

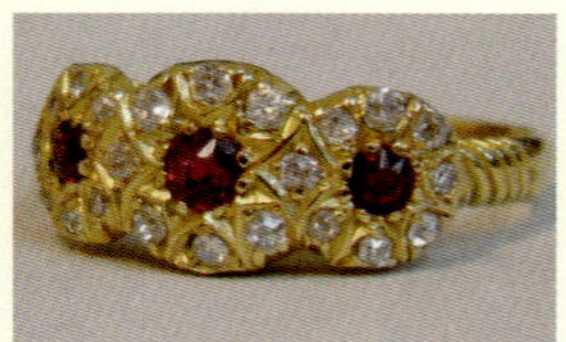

Fig. 290. Triple cluster ring set with rubies surrounded by brilliant-cut diamonds in thread settings. Openwork y-shaped gallery, diagonal carving on shoulders. Hallmarked: Birmingham 1899, 18ct. yellow gold.

CHRYSOBERYL: Occasionally referred to as chrysolite. Yellow chrysoberyl was used intermittently throughout the century. It is often found in cannetille work and in early Victorian rings. See CAT'S EYES.

CHRYSOPRASE: A translucent apple-green chalcedony. Chrysoprase was set in filigree work of the 1820s and 1830s, in delicate half-hoop rings during the 1840s, in signet rings of the 1870s, in Art Nouveau and Arts and Crafts work.

CITRINE: Pale yellow or golden-brown quartz. Citrine was used periodically throughout the century. In Scotland it was called cairngorm and was used in Scottish pebble jewellery, popular from about 1850 to 1880. (Fig. 288) (Fig. 289)

CLADDAGH: A plain or jewelled design of a crowned heart held between two hands. The design dates back to late seventeenth century Ireland. Claddagh rings were worn during the eighteenth century, very early in the nineteenth, and again towards the end of the century, but they were not common. Claddagh rings became popular again in the twentieth century and are being manufactured in large quantities today. See Fig. 159.

CLUSTER: Variations of the cluster design were extremely popular throughout the century. From about 1830 until about 1875 many cluster rings contained a sealed compartment for hair set in the reverse of the bezel. (Fig. 290)

CORAL: Skeletal deposit of the small coral polyp. The neo-classical years (1800-1815) produced the largest number of coral-set rings, some of which were carved as cameos. At certain times a particular shade of coral was in favour: early nineteenth century — blood red and a medium shade; mid-century — pink and red; late nineteenth century — pale pink. Coral from the Mediterranean was carved in Italy and France. (Fig. 291)

CORNELIAN: (Alternative spelling CARNELIAN) A chalcedony of blood-red or brownish-red hue. Widely used as a signet ring stone throughout the century, cornelian was especially fashionable from 1800-1820, particularly in swivel bezels. See SARD.

CROSSOVER BEZEL: A design which first appeared about 1890. The hoop was not formed in the usual circle; instead the ends of the hoop curve, back to back, across the finger to form the bezel. The curves and terminals are gem-set. See Fig. 280.

CULET: The tiny basal facet of a brilliant-cut gem. In 1823 and again in 1831, contemporary writers mention that the culet should equal 1/5th the diameter of the table facet; however, the culet became progressively smaller as cutting techniques improved later in the century.

CUT-STEEL: Woodstock in Oxfordshire and Birmingham were centres for the production of cut-steel jewellery and fashionable accessories, which were popular in the late eighteenth and early nineteenth centuries. Tiny multi-faceted studs of steel were riveted to a plate of steel or other metal, which was then fashioned into a particular article. Towards the end of the popularity of cut-steel jewellery, studs were being stamped out in strips rather than being cut individually. Cut-steel rings are comparatively rare. (Fig. 292)

DEAR OR DEAREST RING: The first letter of each gem spells 'dear' or 'dearest'. Diamond, Emerald, Amethyst, Ruby, Emerald, Sapphire, Topaz. Gem-set rings, usually in half-hoop form, were popular between 1810 and 1875. *Circa* 1885, hoop rings with the word 'dearest' in letters around the hoop were made. See REGARD, REPEAL. (Fig. 293)

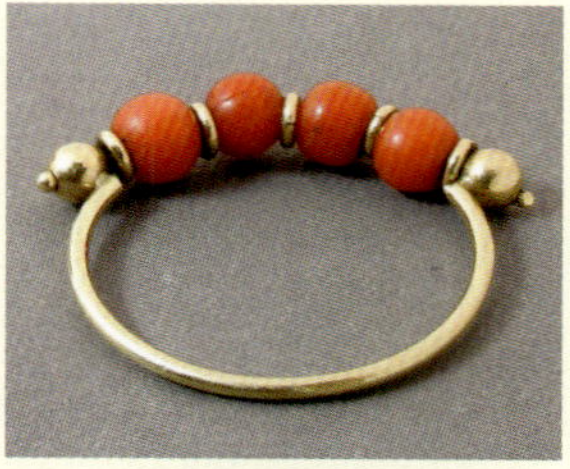

Fig. 291. Neo-classical ring set with four corals interspersed with gold rings set on a wire hoop. Pale yellow gold. *Circa* 1800-1815. Bezel width 18mm, hoop diameter 15.5mm.

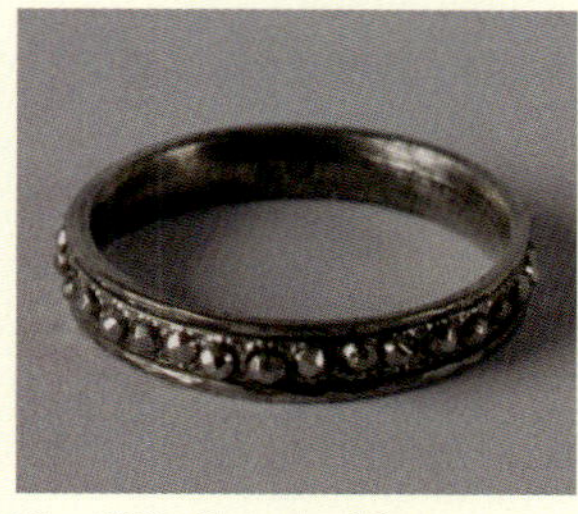

Fig. 292. Cut-steel hoop ring. Rose-cut steels, each surrounded by beading, are attached to a strip of steel which in turn is attached to the outside of a hoop. The edges of the hoop are decorated with narrow diamond-shaped facets which catch the light, the inside of the hoop is convex. *Circa* 1800-1810. Hoop diameter 19mm, width 4mm.

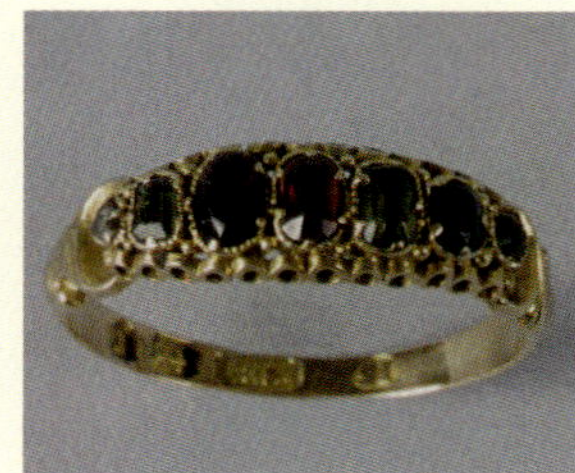

Fig. 293. 'Dearest' ring set with a (d)iamond, (e)merald, (a)methyst, (r)uby, (e)merald, (s)apphire, (t)opaz in closed-back cramp settings, figure-of-eight wirework gallery, carved asymmetric design on the shoulders, plain, narrow shank. Hallmarked: Birmingham, 15(.625)ct. yellow gold, 1868. Bezel 6x19mm, shank diameter 16mm.

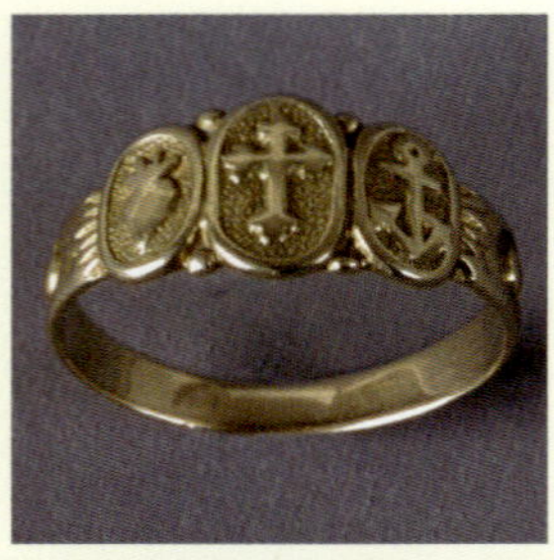

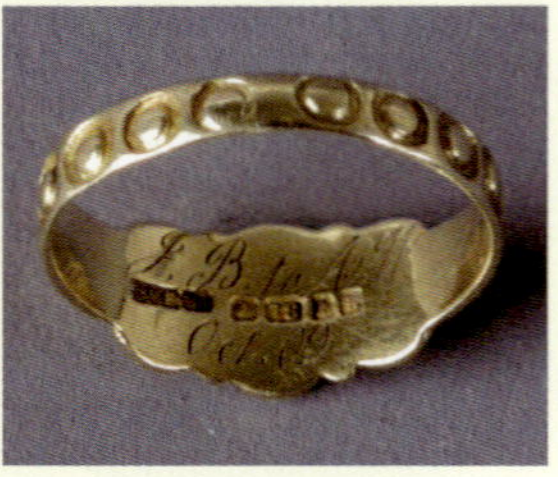

Fig. 294 a, b. Decade ring. The bezel decorated with the symbols for faith (cross), hope (anchor), charity (heart), and the shank with ten shallow knobs. Inscribed inside hoop: 'J.B. to A.W. Oct. 09. C.V.E. BS'. Hallmarked: London, 18ct. yellow gold, 1905. Bezel 9x16mm, shank diameter 17mm.

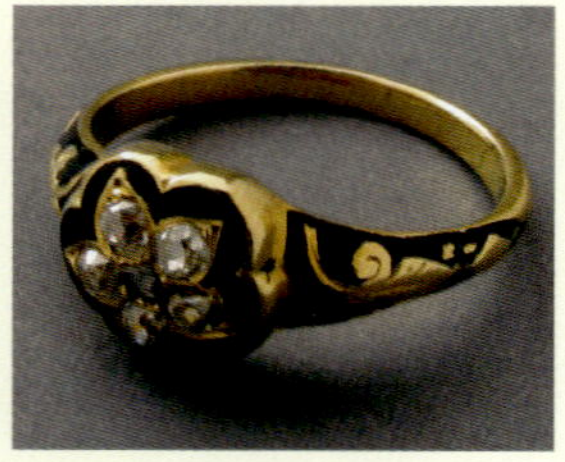

Fig. 295. Gothic-style cinquefoil bezel set with open-backed, brilliant-cut diamonds around a tiny rose-cut diamond in a ground of black enamel, enamelled shoulders, plain D-shaped shank. Yellow gold. *Circa* 1850-1860. Bezel 8x9mm, shank diameter 15mm.

DECADE RING: Decorated with ten stones or knobs around the circumference of the shank, the decade ring was used in the same manner as a rosary. These rings often had a bezel with a cross (faith), an anchor (hope), and a heart (charity); some were enamelled. Decade rings are comparatively rare. (Fig. 294 a, b)

DIAMONDS: Early in the century, diamonds came from Brazil and, to a lesser extent, from India. They were used lavishly in England from 1800-1815 but were less in evidence by the end of the Napoleonic wars, owing to widespread financial hardship; by 1831 diamonds were once more on display. From about 1850-1865 the use of diamonds increased ten-fold (Fig. 295); then in 1867, with the discovery of diamonds in South Africa, supply and demand multiplied.

The rose cut was frequently used until about 1840, by which time the brilliant cut had become more common, although small rose diamonds continued to be used for the remainder of the century, see Fig. 160. In the 1870s and 1880s the occasional large rose-cut diamond was set in a ring. Many fine old rose-cut diamonds were re-cut into brilliants with a great reduction in the weight of the gem.

Until about 1840, brilliant-cut diamonds were usually displayed in closed-back settings, with the exception of really fine diamonds, which were set open at the back. Until about 1870 diamonds were usually cushion-shaped, see Fig. 122, and occasionally pear-shaped; from the 1870s round brilliants were being fashioned, and by 1900 this shape had superseded the cushion-shape.

John Murray in *Memoir on the Diamond*, London 1831, p.34, records the following prices:

1 ct. Brilliant cut	£8
2 ct. Brilliant cut	£32
3 ct. Brilliant cut	£72
4 ct. Brilliant cut	£128

Rose cut £4 per carat-value can never approach half that of a brilliant.

Account books of Payne and Son, Oxford, contain the following entries regarding diamonds:

1879 Sept 9 SS. Dia Ring 80/- [80 shillings]

1897 Feb 16 Fine 3 stone (1st Water) Diamond
ring £66
1898 Dec 24 Very finest 3 stone claw set
Diamond Ring. Perfect stones all matching in fine
brilliancy and purity £125/-/-.

DOUBLET: A composite stone consisting of a thin layer of
gemstone overlaid on crystal or glass. As early as 1823,
doublets were being produced, and by the last quarter
of the century they were widely used. Doublets can be
detected by careful examination of the girdle area.

EGYPTIAN STYLE: Archaeological discoveries and
Admiral Nelson's victory in the Battle of the Nile in 1799
promoted interest in Egyptian designs, but it was not
until later discoveries and the opening of the Suez Canal
in 1869 that the Egyptian style widely influenced ring
design. A preponderance of this style was shown at the
South Kensington International Exhibitions in 1871,
1872, 1873, and 1874. The scarab or dung beetle - a
symbol of rebirth to the Egyptians - the lotus flower
and hieroglyph motifs were used, often with mosaic and
enamel. See Figs. 98, 99 and 100.

EMBOSSING: Decoration formed by the shaping of metal
from the reverse.

EMERALD: The emerald belongs to the beryl family.
Many nineteenth-century rings were set with pale
emeralds, often foiled, because fine coloured stones
were scarce and costly; the best emeralds are invariably
found in the finest settings. Green paste was often used
in early nineteenth-century rings as a substitute for
emeralds, see Fig. 11. During the first half of the century
emeralds and rubies were a popular combination in rings
and other jewellery. According to nineteenth-century
author John Mawe, in 1813 and 1823 the emerald was
more popular than the ruby. Edwin Streeter writes that
by 1877 its desirability had been supplanted by the
sapphire.

ENAMEL: Black, pale and royal blue, red and white
enamels were used until about 1820 on mourning rings,
after which black enamel was predominant. (Fig. 296)
Enamel was also used on rings made in the Gothic,
Renaissance and Egyptian styles, and other rings of
the 1860s and 1870s in a wide range of colours: black,
green, orange, red, royal blue, turquoise and white. (Fig.
297, Fig. 298)   Rings produced by the Arts and Crafts

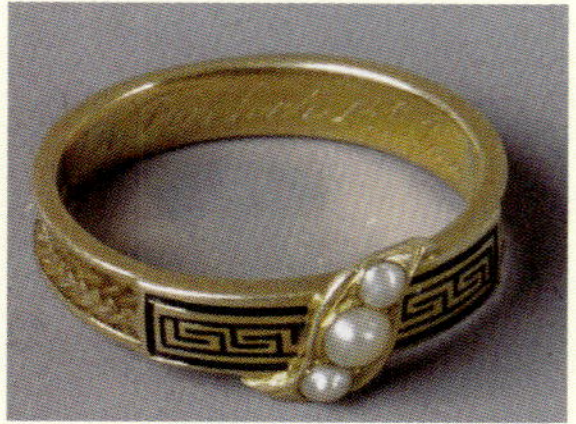

Fig. 296. Mourning ring.
Bezel decorated with the
Greek key pattern enamelled
in black and an applied
serpentine section set with
three pearls, golden-brown
plaited hair lines the hoop.
Inscribed inside hoop: 'A.M.
from her Father 1st Jan
1867'. Yellow gold. Bezel
7x18mm, hoop diameter
17mm, width 3mm.

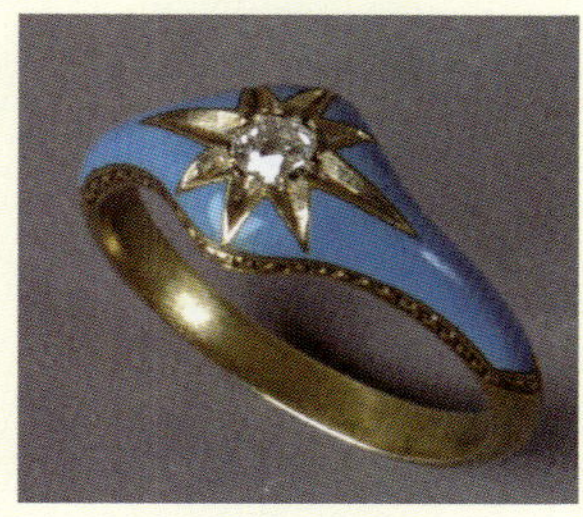

Fig. 297. Brilliant-cut
diamond in a closed-back
star motif, surrounded with
turquoise-blue enamel, edged
with a border of engraving.
Yellow gold. *Circa* 1865-1875.
Star motif 8x14mm, shank
diameter 17mm.

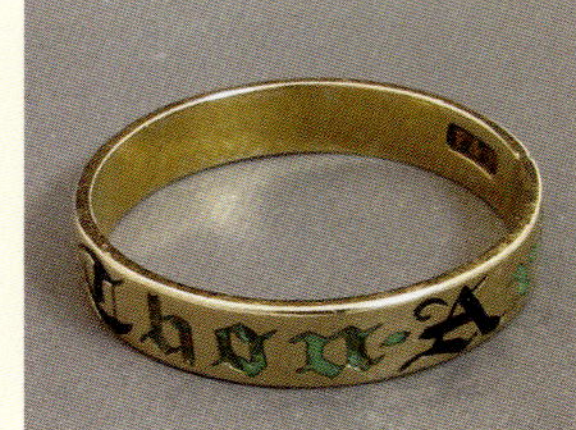

Fig. 298. Hoop ring
enamelled in black and green
in Black Letter script – Thou
Art Only Mine. Hallmarked:
Birmingham 15(.625) ct.
yellow gold, 1867. Maker's
mark F & P. Hoop diameter
16mm, width 3mm.

113

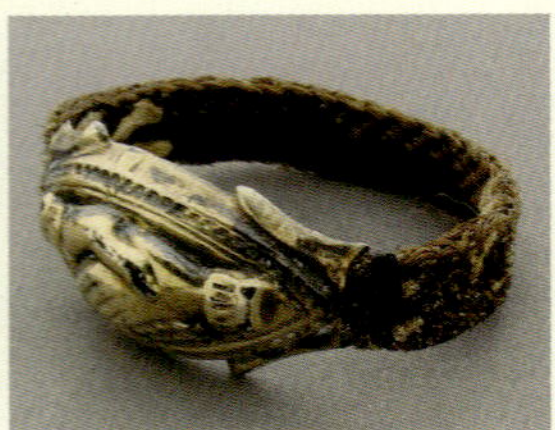

Fig. 299. Woven hair hoop secured by a brass plated bezel showing the fede motif of clasped hands. This ring was much loved; it is almost worn out. American, *circa* 1865. Bezel 10x20mm, hoop width 4.5mm.

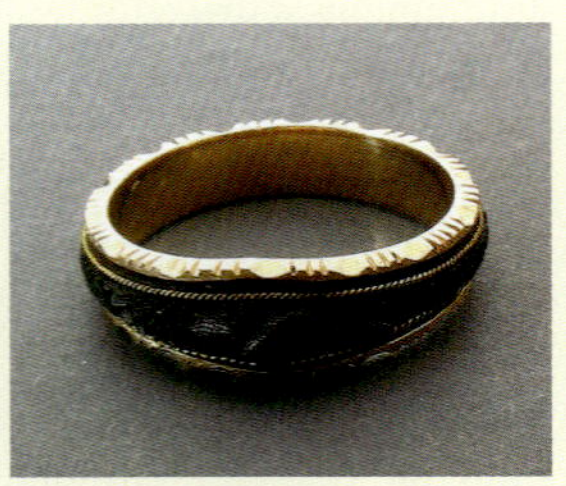

Fig. 300. Hoop ring of gutta percha set in gold. A fede motif is carved into the gutta percha at the front of the hoop, flanked by a row of purled gold. The edge of the hoop is crisply carved. Rich yellow gold. *Circa* 1860-1870. Country of origin unknown, but possibly American.
Keith Austin Collection

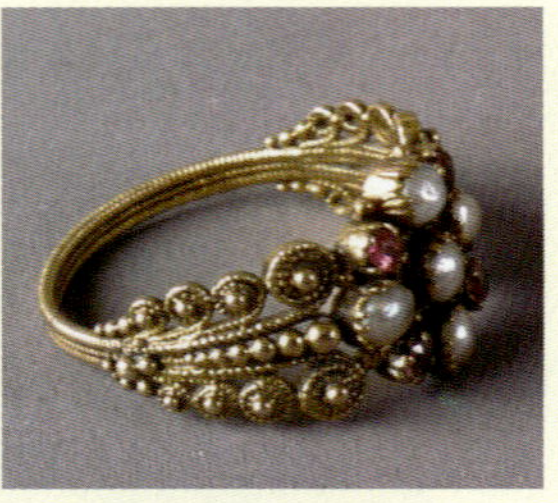

Fig. 301. Filigree ring decorated with pale rubies and half pearls in closed cramp settings, shoulders formed from graduated gold beads flanked by milled-edged wirework; hatched, triple wire shank. Matt yellow gold. *Circa* 1825.

and Art Nouveau movements were frequently decorated with highly sophisticated forms of enamelling.

ENGRAVING: The incising of letters or designs into metal, used on shanks, shoulders and hoop rings.

ETRUSCAN: Copies of the archaeological finds of Etruscan jewellery excavated beween 1836 and 1850 were made in England from about 1860 to about 1885. Characteristics of this work were granulation, gold beading and applied filigree. If gems were used they were often cabochon stones such as onyx, cornelian, pearl or even glass. Some of the finest Etruscan work was produced by the Castellani family.

EYE: A single eye and brow, painted on ivory or porcelain, was set into an oval or oblong bezel until about 1830. See Fig. 40.

FACET: A flat, polished surface of a cut gemstone; occasionally metalwork is faceted.

FEDE RING: The name derives from the Italian phrase Mani in Fede (hands in faith), and is represented by two clasped hands. Used as a betrothal ring on the Continent in the early part of the nineteenth century, there are four variations; a simple hoop ring with two hands that clasp each other; a hoop which opens into two sections on a pivot, with a hand on each hoop that clasp each other when the ring is closed; a similar ring divided into three sections, the third hoop with a single or double heart that is concealed when the ring is closed; a puzzle ring with the bezel formed of clasped hands. These rings were made throughout the century. (Fig. 299, Fig. 300) See GIMMEL.

FILIGREE: The use of fine wires, plain or milled, to produce lacy, openwork styles for entire rings. Filigree was made from the beginning of the nineteenth century. It was popular from about 1820 to about 1835. More subdued filigree decoration was applied to rings occasionally from the 1840s to the mid-1870s. (Fig. 301) See CANNETILLE.

FINDINGS: Towards the end of the nineteenth century jewellers were able to purchase ready-made component parts for rings such as galleries, shanks and claws.

FLOWER MOTIF: Flower bezels were fashionable from about 1810 onwards, and flowers decorated shoulders and shanks from about 1825 to 1870. From about 1820 to 1840 the pansy was popular for both mourning and decorative rings. The snowdrop (representing 'hope' in flower language) and forget-me-not carved in onyx were used in mourning rings. Forget-me-nots set with turquoises were a popular sentimental design in the middle decades of the century. Flowers were used in Italian and English pietra dura work and in Italian Roman mosaic work.

FOIL: Plain or coloured foil was used to line a closed setting; it reflected light out of the stone and gave uniformity of hue to weak or irregularly-coloured gems. Foil was used widely in ring settings until about 1860, after which its use declined. See Fig.5.

GALLERY: Simple or ornate metalwork supporting the setting of the gems, generally employed in half-hoop or marquise rings. See Fig. 325.

GARNET: Between 1800 and 1885 garnets were widely used, then suffered a temporary eclipse during the fashion for pale or colourless gems at the end of the century. There are several varieties of garnet mostly used between 1800 and 1910:

ALMANDINE: A purplish-red gem, cut in a variety of ways: faceted with a large table (1800-1820), see Fig. 7; multi-faceted (1820 onwards) (Fig. 302) or cabochon cut (1850-1880), see Fig. 107. Large cabochons were used in gentlemen's rings and were called carbuncles.

DEMANTOID: A bright green gem of great brilliance, first discovered in Siberia in 1868. Usually found only in very small sizes, demantoids were rare and greatly prized towards the end of the nineteenth century.

HESSONITE: A brownish-orange colour. This stone was referred to as Hyacinth during the nineteenth century. Hessonite was used during the first half of the century rather than in later years. It is sometimes confused with citrine. See Fig. 67.

PYROPE: Deep blood red in colour. (Fig. 303 a, b.) Bohemian garnets that were so popular from the 1870s onward were usually rose-cut. Large quantities of these garnets came from an area near Trebnitz in the old kingdom of Bohemia; they had a

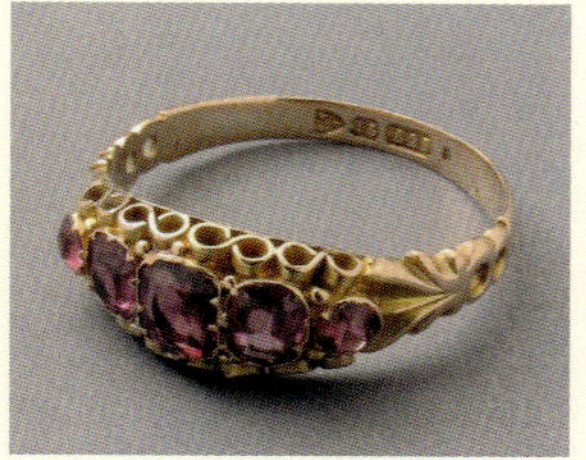

Fig. 302. Half-hoop ring of five graduated almandine garnets in open-back cramp settings, figure-of-eight wirework gallery, carved foliate design and circles decorate the shoulders, plain, flat shank. Hallmarked: Chester, 15(.625) ct. yellow gold, no date mark. *Circa* 1870-80. Bezel 8x18mm, shank diameter 18mm.

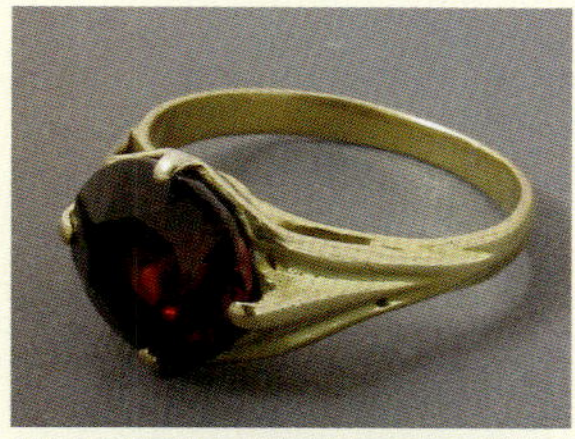

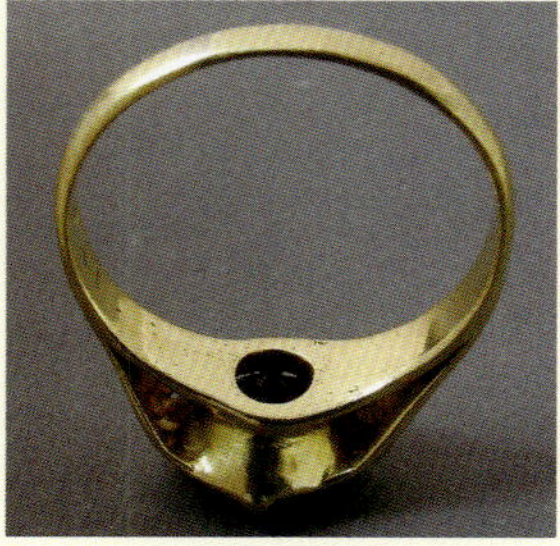

Fig. 303 a, b. Pyrope garnet set in four claws, moulded shoulders, plain shank. Yellow gold. *Circa* 1900. Garnet 9mm in diameter, shank diameter 17mm.

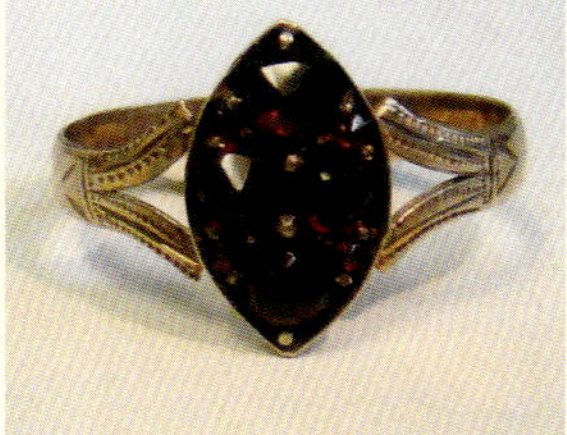

Fig. 304. Marquise ring set with Bohemian garnets (rose-cut pyrope garnets) in very low grade rose gold. *Circa* 1885. Bezel 12x7mm, hoop diameter 15mm.

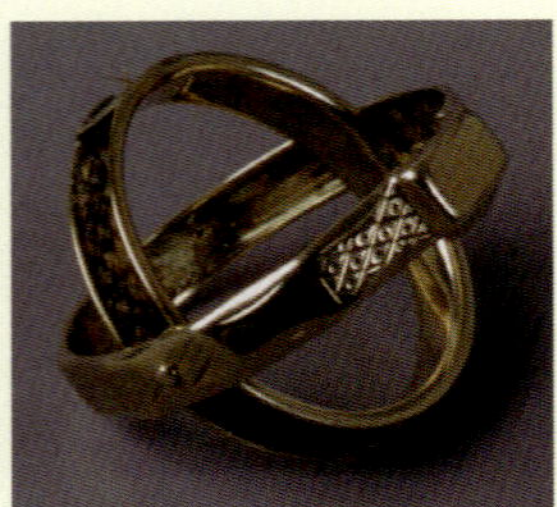

Fig. 305. Mourning ring fashioned from two hoops which pivot at the sides. The outer hoop has twelve lozenges alternating between plain and engraved gold (there are three different patterns), the inner hoop contains plaited hair and is stamped 14P. Pale yellow gold. *Circa* 1880. Hoop diameter 16mm, width 4mm.

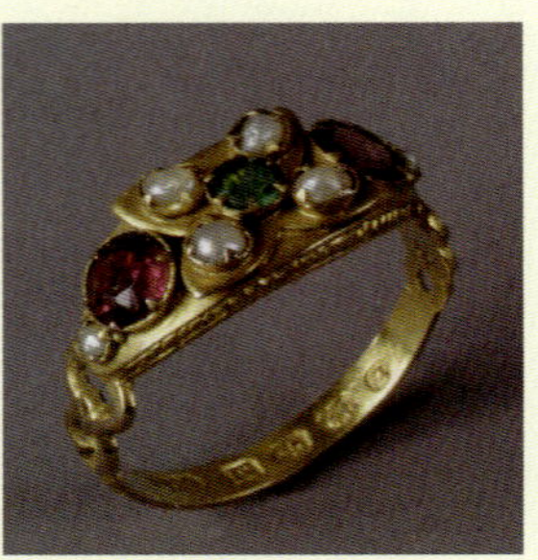

Fig. 306. Gothic-style ring. Boat-shaped bezel has an applied quatrefoil design decorated with a green stone in an open-back cramp setting, and four half pearls, almandine garnets and pearls flank the quatrefoil motif. Openwork shoulders, engraved shank. Hallmarked: Birmingham, 12(.5) ct. 'coloured' gold, maker's mark L.H.J, 1874.

yellowish tinge and were not of the best quality. (Fig. 304)

GEORGE IV: 1762-1830, Prince Regent 1811-1820, succeeded George III as King in 1820. At the beginning of the century, his flamboyance made him the natural leader of fashionable society. A number of cameo and intaglio rings of his portrait were produced.

GIMMEL RING: A ring that separates into two parts and is held together by pivots, or two rings that can be parted but not separated. (Fig. 305) Gimmel rings were used as wedding or betrothal rings and occasionally as mourning rings. Sometimes the name of the bridal couple was engraved inside the hoops. A number of gimmel rings were decorated with clasped hands. See FEDE.

GIRDLE: The widest part of a cut gemstone, the girdle separates the crown and pavilion facets.

GOLD: The world's average annual production from 1801 to 1810 was just 590,750 ounces. Between 1851 and 1860, it rose to 6,350,000 ounces owing to the opening of new gold fields. In 1798 an Act of Parliament, which remained in effect until 22 December 1854, allowed the manufacture of 18ct. gold in addition to 22ct. gold. The Act of 1854 permitted the use of 15ct., 12ct. and 9 ct. gold, after which time large quantities of 15ct. and 12ct. gold rings were produced. Towards the end of the century, 9ct. gold rings were manufactured in large numbers. The quality of gold cannot reliably be judged by its colour.

Examples of colours produced by certain alloys as used in the nineteenth century: red gold — gold with copper; green gold — gold with silver; pure gold colour — gold with silver and copper; pale yellow — gold with silver or zinc; blue gold — gold with iron; white gold — gold with silver. The various shades depend on the proportion of base metal mixed with the gold; e.g. both green and pale yellow gold are created by a mix of gold and silver, but in different proportions.

A technique called gold 'colouring' was achieved by dipping an article made from alloyed gold into an acid bath, which removed the base metal from the surface, leaving a layer of pure gold that was often left in its frosted state. Prior to 1854, 18ct. and 22ct. gold had been 'coloured' but to a limited extent; after 1854 15ct. and 12ct. gold were frequently 'coloured', see Fig. 134.

The use of 'colouring' declined during the 1880s, dying out by the First World War. Wear, sizing and repair of these treated rings removes the layer of pure gold. A ring can be re-'coloured' but this usually necessitates the removal of the gems, with the risk of damaging the setting. An example of re-'colouring' comes from an entry in an account book of Payne & Son, Oxford:

1879, April 24   New stone, enlarging ... colouring ring 9/6d.

It is quite common to see Victorian rings which have lost some or most of their 'colouring'. Traces of old 'colouring' may help to date a ring; a nineteenth-century snake ring may appear very modern until an area of 'colouring' on the back of the head is discovered indicating its nineteenth-century origin.

A few rings were made from 'cased gold', which consists of a base metal core covered with gold. See Fig. 249.

GOTHIC: Especially popular from about 1830, Gothic-style rings were made in limited numbers throughout the nineteenth century. Characteristic features include pointed arches, rounded or pointed quatrefoils, fluting, moulding, cusps, the Tudor rose, fleur-de-lis, stiff leaf, trefoil leaf, and the vine scroll. (Fig. 306) (Fig. 307)

GRANULATION: Minute beads of gold applied as a decoration to the surface of gold jewellery. It is an ancient and extremely difficult process which nineteenth-century jewellers rarely perfected.

GYPSY RING: A broad, tapering ring with gems deeply set into the ring, so that the surface of the stones was almost flush with the metal. A 'star' effect was often cut around the setting of the gems to enhance them, and a number of rings had carved or enamelled decoration. The gypsy ring, worn as a decorative or mourning ring, by men and women alike, became popular in the mid-1860s and remained fashionable well into the twentieth century. Men's rings were plainer and more robust compared with those worn by women. (Fig. 308)

HÆMATITE: Colour: blue-black with an iridescent surface. When reduced to powdered form it is red and is used as a polishing agent called jewellers' rouge. Hæmatite is usually faceted in a rose cut.

HAIR: The hair of a loved one was used in mourning or decorative rings, occasionally horsehair was substituted

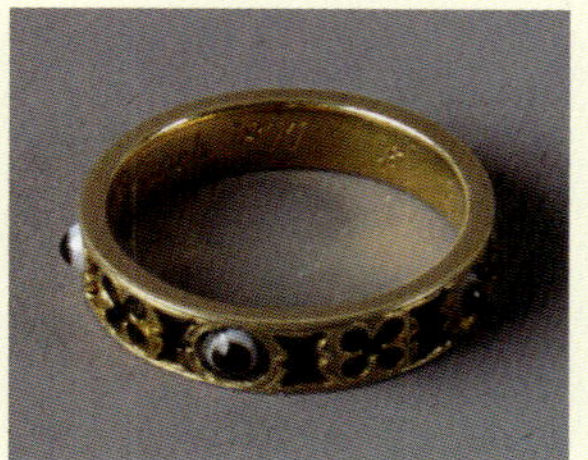

Fig. 307. Gothic-style mourning ring. The hoop, lined with plaited hair, is decorated with alternating engraved quatrefoils and onyx beads, inscribed inside: 'Frances Margaret Denne Obt 11th Mar 1877'. Yellow gold. Hoop diameter 17mm, width 4mm.

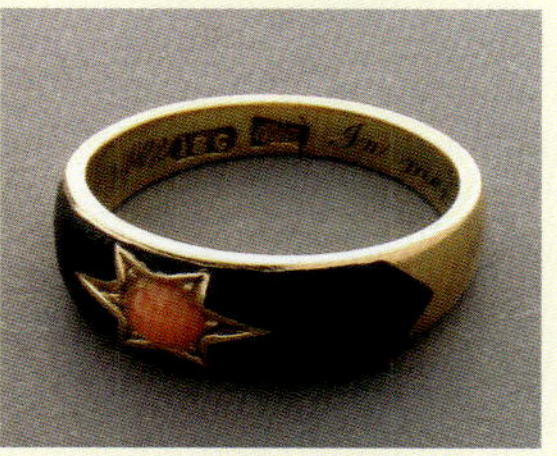

Fig. 308. Gypsy ring flooded with black enamel, set with a coral in a star setting. Inscribed: In memory of M.C. Cox died 9 June 1892. Marked 18C.
Keith Austin Collection

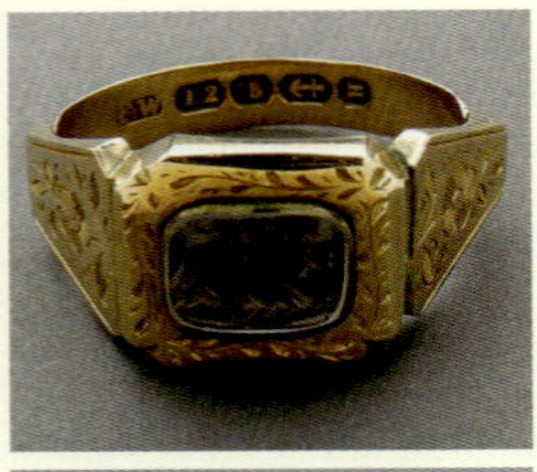

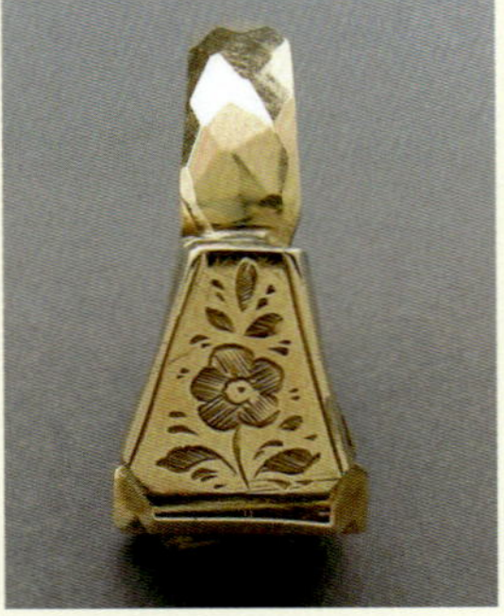

Fig. 309 a, b. Mourning ring. Oblong bezel with an engraved foliate design around a hair compartment, engraved spatula-shaped shoulders, faceted diamond-shaped pattern decorates entire shank. No inscription. Hallmarked: Birmingham, 12(.5) ct. pale yellow gold, maker's mark, FW, 1856. Bezel 9x10mm, shoulder 10mm long, shank diameter 17mm, width 4mm.

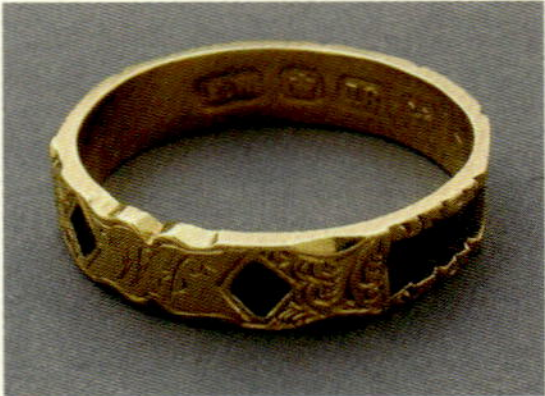

Fig. 310. A hollowed hoop, lightly chased on the edges at intervals, is lined with medium brown plaited hair, the applied bezel is decorated with chasing and diamond-shaped openings, I M (In Memoriam) is engraved in the centre. Inscribed inside hoop: '1st March 1868'. Hallmarked: Birmingham, 18ct. yellow gold, maker's mark, F.W, 1863. Hoop diameter 15.5mm, width 4mm.

for human hair. Until about 1860 mourning rings displayed a hair compartment in the face of the bezel (Fig. 309 a, b); otherwise it was hidden in the reverse of the bezel in both mourning and decorative rings though its use declined towards the end of the 1870s in decorative rings but continued to be used in mourning rings until about 1910. The hair compartment is often missing, either through accidental loss or deliberate removal.

Hair was also used to line hoop mourning rings. The edges were often flanged, with one or more lozenges of engraved openwork gold set at intervals across the hoop. (Fig. 310) From about 1840 to 1870, a few rings were made with a shank of woven hair, the ends of which were secured in a small gold engraved bezel. (Fig. 311)

HALF-HOOP: Strictly speaking half the ring should be set with stones; however, if just a third is gem-set it is still referred to as a half-hoop. This style was worn throughout the century owing to the feasibility of wearing several rings on one finger. (Fig. 312)

HALLMARKING: In 1784 an Act of Parliament required the hallmarking of mourning rings. See Fig. 309a. Exempt from hallmarking were gem, signet and other fancy rings, though any ring could be marked voluntarily, as indeed many were in the second half of the nineteenth century. From 1855 hallmarking of wedding rings was obligatory; this finally curtailed the use of lengthy inscriptions inside wedding rings, although the custom was already on the decline.

The Birmingham assay office marked the greatest number of rings on a voluntary basis, partly because the jewellery manufacturing community there wanted to prove its gold wares were up to legal standard. This has left the jewellery historian with an excellent legacy of marked rings, along with the fewer numbers marked in London and Chester. Rings with a York, Edinburgh, Dublin, Exeter, Glasgow or Newcastle mark are not common.

The following punches make up a full hallmark:

STANDARD MARK: guaranteed that the quality of the gold was 18ct. or 22ct., hence the phrase 'up to standard'.

QUALITY MARK: denoted by 22, 18, 15(.625), 12(.5), or 9(.375) which guaranteed the proportion of gold in the alloy. (24ct. being 100% gold).

HALLMARK or MARK OF ORIGIN: the town mark used by the assay office where the marking took place. Each assay office chose its own mark.

DATE MARK: a variable letter of the alphabet which was changed each year. Each assay office decided which letters of the alphabet would be used in the cycle; some letters were omitted. The hallmark year did not coincide with the calendar year. For example, London began its year on 30 May while Birmingham started its year at the beginning of July, but it should also be noted that this was not strictly adhered to.

DUTY MARK: represented by the sovereign's head, indicating duty had been paid. An Act of Parliament effective 1 December 1784 imposed duty on all gold items, including mourning rings and, after 1855, wedding rings, that were subject to compulsory hallmarking. Duty was introduced in Dublin in 1807 and in Glasgow in 1819. The law was repealed on 30 April 1890.

MAKER'S MARK: denoted by the initial letters of the first and last names of the maker or the mark of the merchant or wholesale dealer. The maker's mark punch used at the factory had to correspond exactly with the punch registered at the assay office. If the maker's mark was changed, a new punch with the manufacturer's name, address and place of business had to be re-entered in the register book. Towards the end of the century, rings were marked with the maker's mark and the quality mark only. This is not a hallmark and is not a guarantee of the quality of gold used.

FOREIGN MARK: To comply with an 1842 customs act, any foreign ring entering Britain had to be assayed and marked before it was put on sale. Items for private use were not subject to this law. From 1883 to 1904 the letter F in an oval punch mark was added to the standard mark.

HAMILTON & CO., CALCUTTA: Silversmiths and jewellers established in 1808 in Calcutta, India, by Robert Hamilton under licence from the East India Company. With branches

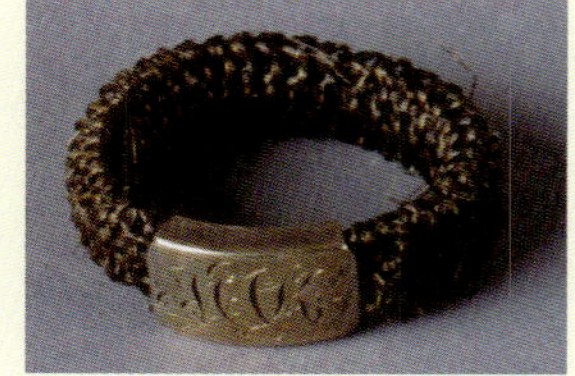

Fig. 311. Hoop ring fashioned from loosely woven brown hair, the ends are secured with a hollow oblong of rose gold inscribed M A K on the obverse and H A on the reverse. *Circa* 1840. Bezel 5.5x9mm, hoop width 5mm.

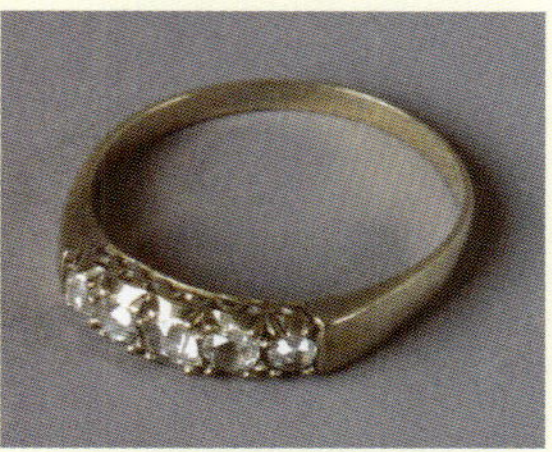

Fig. 312. Half-hoop with 5 rose-cut diamonds in cut-down collets set on a narrow openwork gallery. The diamonds are backed with gold. Dutch mark on hoop, used 1853-1906. 14K yellow gold. *Circa* 1880. Bezel 4x15mm, gallery 2mm, hoop diameter 19mm.

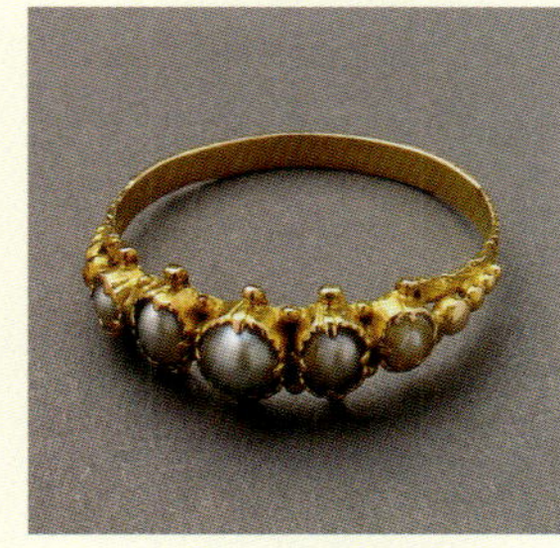

Fig. 313. Five pearls in closed-back cramp settings, beads decorate the settings and shoulders, light chasing on the flat shank resembles engraving, rich yellow gold. *Circa* 1845. Possibly Indian, made for English expatriates. Bezel depth 6mm, shank diameter 18mm.
Reginald Davis (Oxford) Ltd..

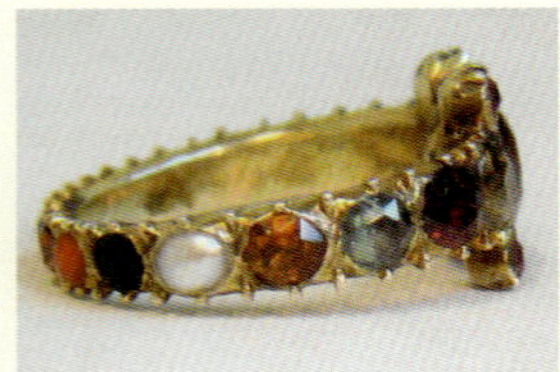

Fig. 314. Harlequin ring with a garnet bezel and variety of graduated gems in cut-down collects that form the hoop. Pale yellow gold. *Circa* 1800-1810. Bezel 9x10mm, hoop diameter 19mm, width 5mm.

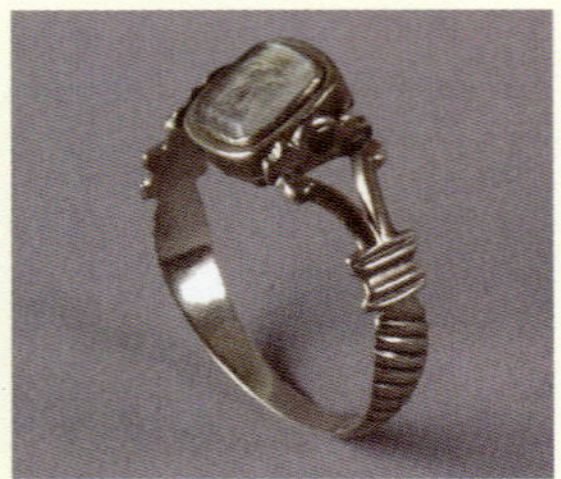

Fig. 315. Swivel bezel set with plain coral in a cut-down collet on one side, and hair on the other. The shank is partially decorated with diagonal hatch marks above which two transverse ribs support formed shoulders. Pale rose gold. *Circa* 1805-15. Bezel 7x6mm, shank diameter 16.5mm.

in Delhi and Simla, the firm made copies of English work for expatriates throughout the century. (Fig. 313)

HANDS: This motif appeared as the clasped hands of the fede design throughout the nineteenth century, or decorating the shoulders of rings, usually between 1800 and 1850.

HARLEQUIN: A fashion of the first decade of the nineteenth century, the 'harlequin' ring consisted of a hoop set all the way around with different coloured gems in cut-down collets. *La Belle Assemblée* in November 1807 has a reference to a 'rainbow hoop-ring'. (Fig. 314)

HATCH MARKS: Engraving of parallel lines on shank, shoulders, or narrow decorative strips of wire in the bezel. Cross hatching was also used, usually on ring shoulders. (Fig. 315) (Fig. 316)

HEART: A motif that appeared at intervals throughout the century but was especially fashionable during the 1840s and 1850s and from about 1870 onwards. (Fig. 317 a, b)

HELIOTROPE: See BLOODSTONE.

HINGE: Decorative, mourning and signet rings were sometimes made with a hinged shank or bezel.

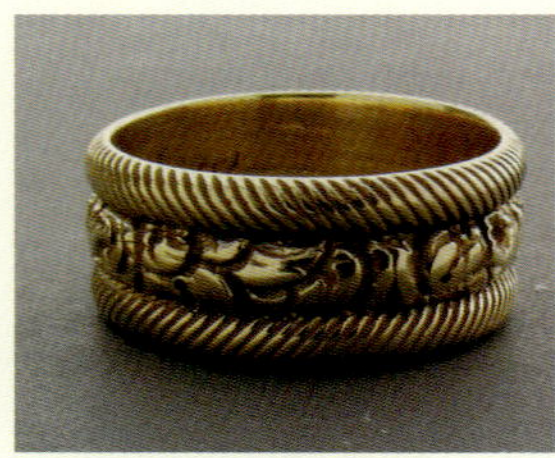

Fig. 316. Hoop ring decorated with deep chasing and diagonal hatch marks. The direction of the hatch marks gives the illusion that the ring is narrower at one side than the other. The photograph does not capture the illusion to the fullest extent. Engraved with the initials CJH in an ornate script (worn). Pale yellow gold. *Circa* 1880–1900.

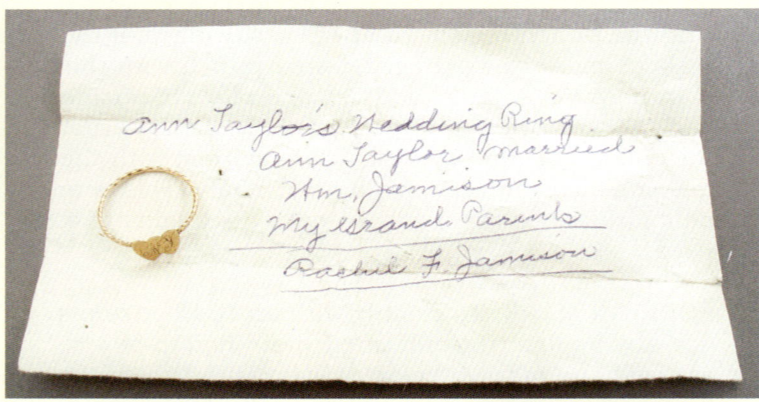

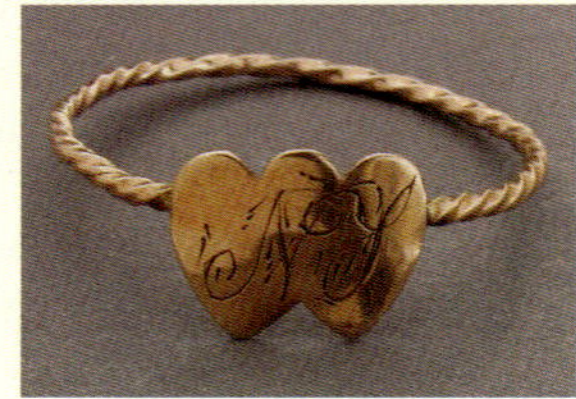

Fig. 317 a, b. Double heart engraved NJ. Twisted wire hoop. Rose gold. American, *circa* 1890. Hearts 7x9mm, hoop diameter 18.5mm.

Occasionally a hoop ring was designed with a hinged compartment concealed on the inside. The hinged bezel usually concealed a hair compartment (Fig. 318 a, b) (Fig. 319) or sometimes a vinaigrette; see VINAIGRETTE RING.

HOOP RING: A ring without a bezel. Hoop rings, made throughout the century, were used as wedding, keeper, decorative or mourning rings. They could be gem-set in their entirety, engraved, chased or left plain. (Fig. 320)

HORSESHOE: The interest shown by women in sporting activities resulted in the production of items of jewellery relating to particular sports. One of these was the horseshoe ring, popular in the 1880s and 1890s. See Fig. 110 and Fig. 111.

HYACINTH: See JACINTH and ZIRCON.

INSCRIPTIONS: Mourning ring inscriptions, usually engraved inside the ring, gave personal details of the deceased, often in English and abbreviated Latin: aet or at.-aged; obit or obt.-died. Wedding rings of the gimmel variety were sometimes engraved inside each half of the ring with the name of the bride and groom and the date of the ceremony. (Fig. 321) (Fig. 322)

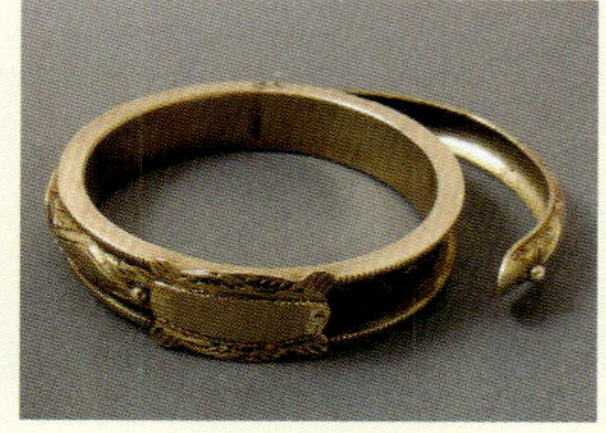

Fig. 319. Mourning ring of engraved gold. Small gold bead on either side of the bezel is pressed to open the hoop that covers woven hair. Yellow gold. American, *circa* 1890. Hoop diameter 20mm, width 4.5mm.

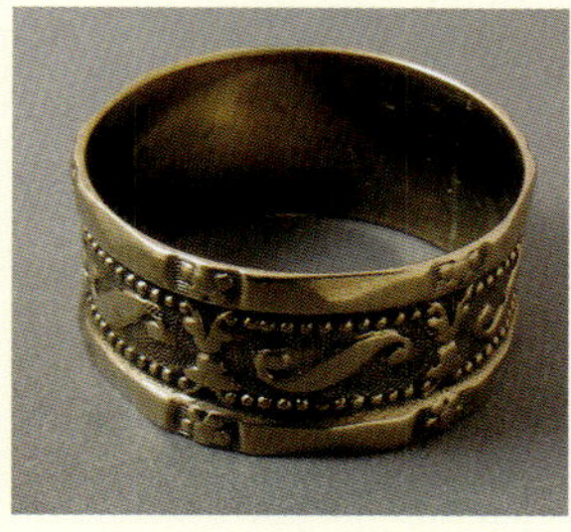

Fig. 320. Wide, embossed hoop ring. No marks. American, *circa* 1890. Hoop diameter 17mm, width 9mm.

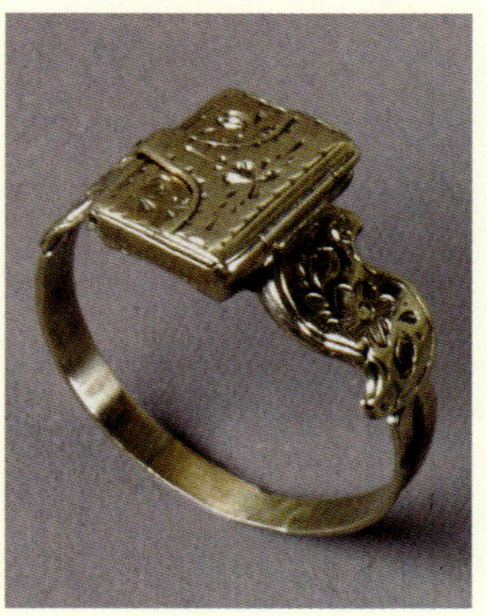

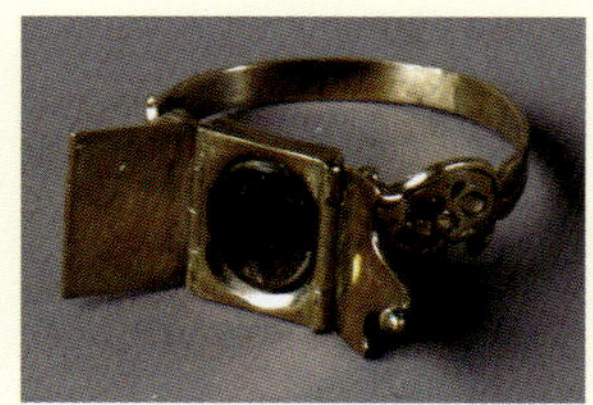

Fig. 318 a, b. Envelope–style memorial ring. The engraved envelope conceals an oval hair compartment, asymmetric shoulders are engraved with a floral and foliate design (one shoulder has been restored), channelled shank. Yellow gold. *Circa* 1855. Bezel 9x7mm, hair compartment 7x5.5mm, shank diameter 18mm.

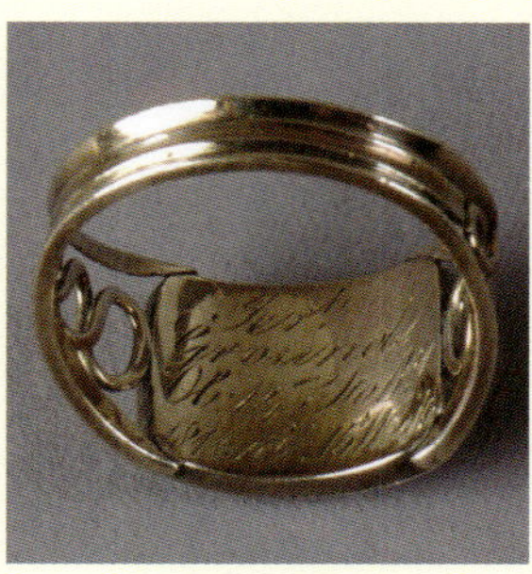

Fig. 321. Mourning ring inscribed on reverse of bezel: 'Jerh. Grounds ob. 14 Feby. 1811 aet. 15 weeks'. See Fig. 244 for a different view of the ring.

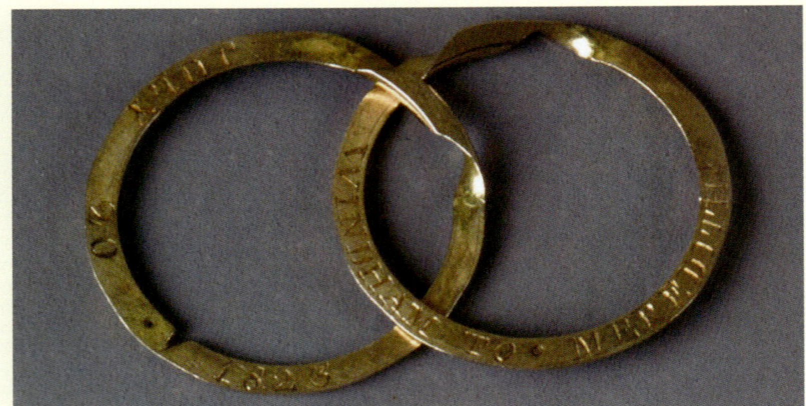

Fig. 322. Split wedding ring inscribed on the inside of one hoop: WINDHAM TO MEREDITH, on the second hoop JULY 20, 1823. The dowel that holds the two hoops together is missing. Yellow gold. Hoop diameter 15mm.

INTAGLIO: A design cut into the stone for making impressions in sealing wax.   Intaglio rings were in demand from 1800 to 1820 and continued to be produced in modest numbers during the remainder of the century; they were worn principally by men. Antique as well as contemporary intaglios, some of which were being passed off as antique, were set in nineteenth-century rings. The stones were generally secured in flush or Roman settings. (Fig. 323)

JACINTH OR HYACINTH: Names used to describe both the orange-red variety of zircon and hessonite garnet in the nineteenth century.

JARGOON: See Zircons.

JET: Fossil driftwood, subjected to chemical action, flattened by great pressure, formed over the centuries while lying in stagnant water.

The town of Whitby, Yorkshire, produced the best jet and its industry flourished during the nineteenth century. It was at its height in 1870, after which time it declined, dying out by the beginning of the twentieth century owing to a change in mourning customs and the introduction of glass imitations from France and Spain.

Because of its softness, jet was used less often in rings than in other forms of jewellery. Hoop and half-hoop rings set with carved jet were made early in the century, see Fig. 21. Mourning rings, set with faceted jet surrounding a hair compartment and on the shoulders, were made from about 1815 to 1840. One rarely finds jet rings from later in the century.

JUBILEE: See detail under Commemorative and Historical ring section.

KEEPER RING: A hoop ring (also known as a guard ring), decorated with chasing, engraving or stones or formed from woven gold, was worn to prevent the loss of the wedding ring, see Fig. 212. In 1875, according to the etiquette of the day, young women were advised not to wear the engagement ring as a keeper ring. Thomas B. Wigley in *The Art of the Goldsmith and Jeweller*, 1898, page 97, mentions that keeper rings were given as keepsakes or as tokens of friendship. Most were worn by women.

KNOT: A design popular during the 1840s and 1850s, when the knot sometimes had an additional pendant heart. Large numbers of knot rings were produced from 1885 onward and were worn by both men and women. (Fig. 324 a, b)

LAPIS LAZULI: Cut as a cabochon or flat for intaglios and signet rings, lapis lazuli was used occasionally throughout the century; its use was limited owing to its cost and its softness as a ring stone.

LAVA: Jewellery made from lava was popular in the 1850s. Many Victorian travellers to Italy brought home souvenirs, usually bracelets, brooches and earrings. Lava is found in shades of pale to dark grey, brown, pale yellow to pale pink. It is usually cut as a cameo in a classical head, but one finds other designs as well. Few original rings appear to have been made from lava. See Fig. 80.

MARQUISE: The pointed oval shape of the marquise bezel excluded the wearing of several rings on one finger, which may have contributed to its decline at the end of the eighteenth century; as a ring design it had periods of great popularity followed by total eclipse. The revival of marquise rings began about 1870, and they remained fashionable into the Edwardian era. The bezel was frequently pavé-set with diamonds, pearls or turquoises; sometimes a number of contrasting gems were set in the middle of the bezel. Other marquise rings were set with a cameo depicting the figure of a woman or with an onyx forget-me-not, either in a plain border or surrounded by diamonds or pearls. Modest examples were popular in the 1890s: a small gold marquise bezel set with one or three gems along its length. The marquise bezel varied

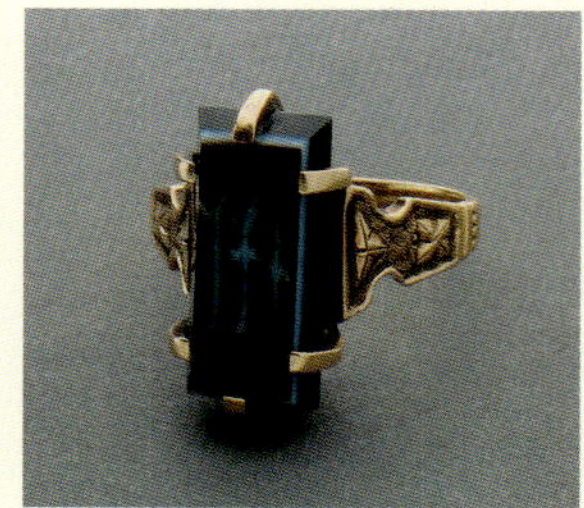

Fig. 323. Onyx intaglio secured with six claws. Decorated shoulders, flat hoop. American, *circa* 1880. *Keith Austin Collection*

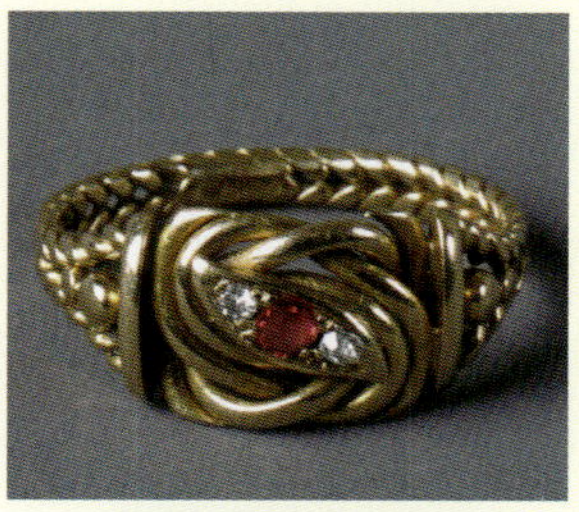

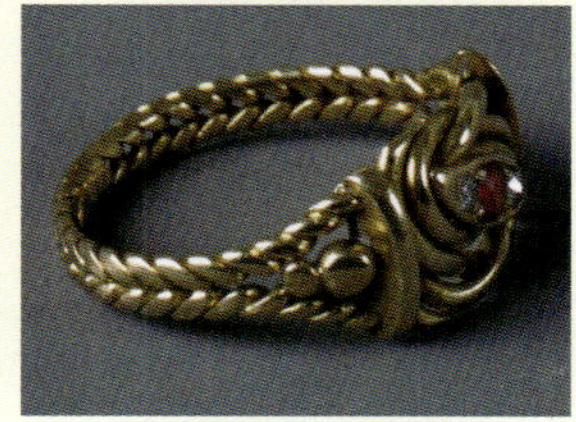

Fig. 324 a, b. Knot ring set with a ruby and two diamonds on a plaited hoop. Yellow gold. *Circa* 1890. Bezel 8x11mm, hoop diameter 17mm.

Glossary

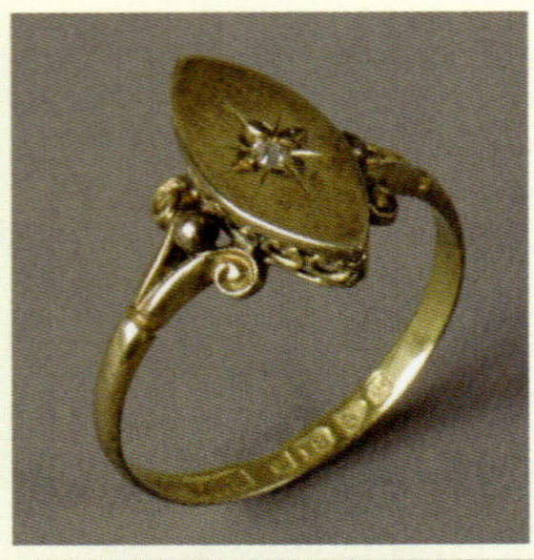

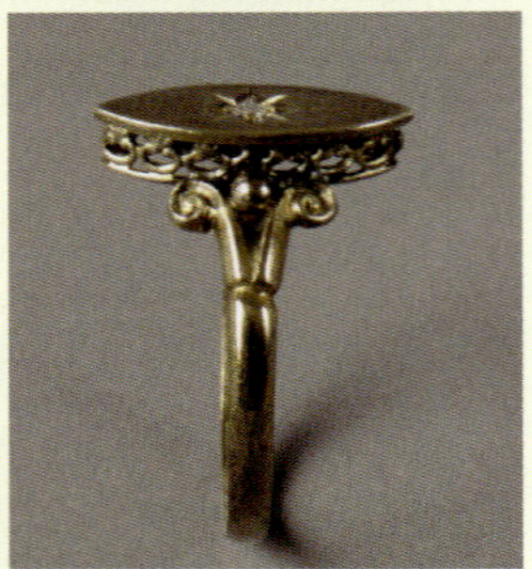

Fig. 325 a, b. Marquise bezel decorated with an open-back brilliant in a scalloped setting on a gallery of scalloped openwork. Forked, scrolled shoulders with single bead are attached to a plain D-shaped shank. Hallmarked: Chester, 18ct. yellow gold, maker's mark T & S, 1898. Bezel 14x6mm, gallery depth 2.5mm, shank diameter 17mm.

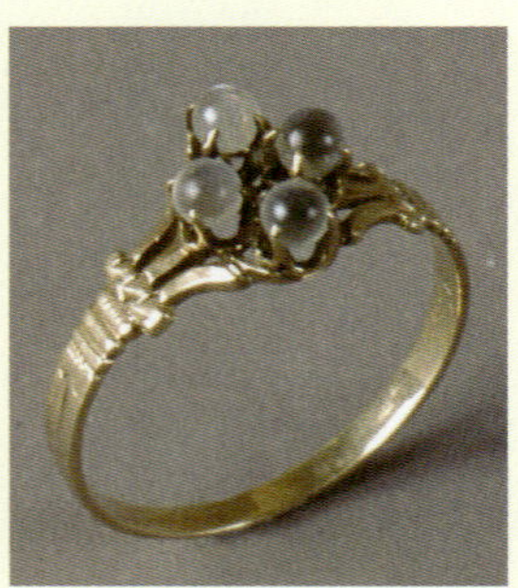

Fig. 326. Four round moonstones each secured in a four-claw setting, three radiating panels above four transverse ribs form the shoulders. Plain, flat shank, marked I.S. in a diamond-shaped stamp. Rose gold. American, *circa* 1895-1910. Bezel 8x7mm, shank diameter 16mm.

in dimension from long and narrow to short and plump. (Fig. 325 a, b)

MATT: Gold or silver with a dull finish, often produced by tooling or 'colouring'. See Fig. 81.

MIZPAH: The word Mizpah comes from Genesis 31:48-53, 'Laban said, "This heap is a witness between you and me today." Therefore he named it Galeed, and the pillar Mizpah, for he said, "The Lord watch between you and me, when we are absent one from the other. If you ill-treat my daughters, or if you take wives besides my daughters, although no man is with us, remember, God is witness between you and me."' These rings were popular from about 1880 onwards. Many Mizpah rings were ornamented with chasing; some were set with a single small gem, others were decorated with horseshoe or a sentimental motif of hearts, birds and flowers. See Fig. 156.

MOONSTONE: A member of the feldspar group. It is sometimes carved, but usually cut as a cabochon, which displays the gem to advantage. Used occasionally throughout the century, it was particularly fashionable from about 1885 onward, especially in Arts and Crafts and Art Nouveau designs. (Fig. 326)

MOSAIC: Roman mosaic was made from tesserae — tiny pieces of glass or stone of uniform length — which were assembled to form designs ranging from temples, fountains and other classical architecture to religious symbols, insects, birds and portraits. As the century progressed the quality of tesserae and workmanship became much coarser. See Fig. 78.

Florentine mosaic, also known as pietra dura, is made of shaped pieces of marble, coral, malachite, opal, lapis lazuli and turquoise inlaid into a black marble ground. The designs were usually of flowers and insects. Pietra dura work was also made in England, but the designs and colours were not as subtle as those in Italian work. Travellers to the Continent brought home numerous pieces of mosaic souvenir jewellery. See Fig. 79.

According to *The Resources, Products, and Industrial History of Birmingham* - A Series of Reports, collected…, in 1865: '….formerly mosaics produced in Rome were largely used but are now out of fashion'. (p.458).

Original rings made from Roman or Florentine mosaic are scarce; it is likely that many were damaged or destroyed by wear. Many mosaic rings today have been made up from other forms of mosaic jewellery.

MOSS AGATE: A variety of agate prized for its fine inclusions, usually dark in colour. These stones were particularly popular at the beginning of the nineteenth century and again in the last quarter of the century. (Fig. 327 a, b)

MOURNING RINGS: See narrative section.

NATURALISTIC: A term given to jewellery incorporating life-like botanical and animal forms dating from the 1840s onwards. Designs such as vine or ivy leaves, tendrils, flowers and insects were popular. This fashion was more evident in other forms of jewellery, but a small number of rings incorporating elements of the naturalistic style were made.

NEO-CLASSICAL: The simple lines of neo-classical taste were evident in jewellery made between 1800 and 1815. Rings embraced the general characteristics of simplicity and pleasing proportions.

NICOLO: Black or dark brown onyx with bluish-white banding, usually cut and polished so that a thin white surface appears to overlay the dark colour beneath. Nicolo was used in signet and intaglio rings.

ONYX: A blackish-brown chalcedony, often banded with white. In the Victorian period, stones cut to display a greater number of concentric circles were the most prized. See Fig. 308 under GOTHIC. Onyx was used throughout the century in mourning and signet rings, and during the latter part of the century in decorative rings. In the late 1870s onyx was combined with diamonds, a fashion which recurred in Art Deco work in the twentieth century.

OPAL: Until the opal mines in Australia were in operation in the 1890s, Czechoslovakia supplied most opals for jewellery. These opals, with a milk-white background and flashes of red, blue and green, were referred to as 'harlequin' opals at the time.

Australia produced opals with an intense play of colour, easily distinguishable from European opals. (Fig. 328)

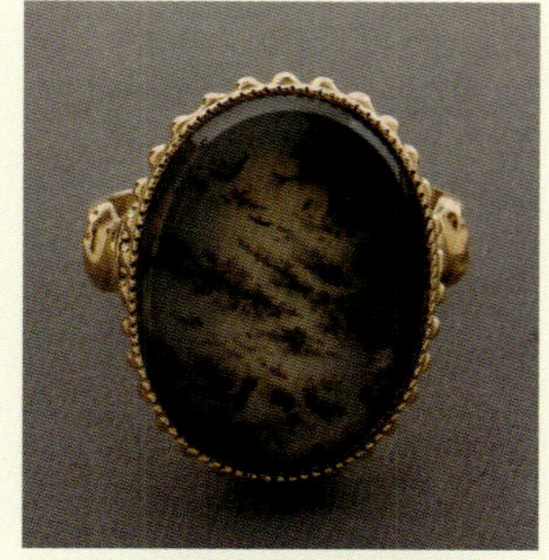

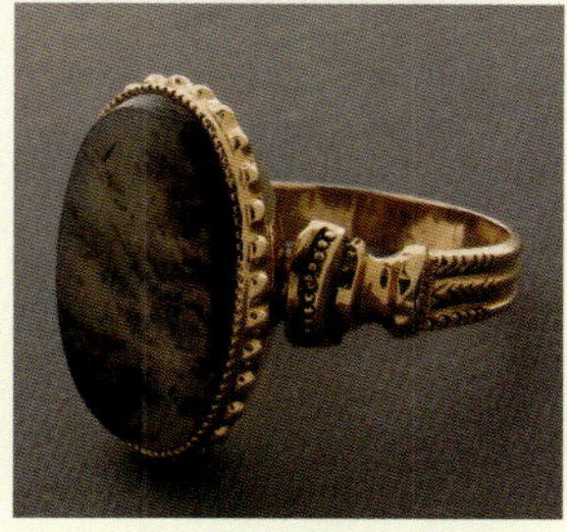

Fig. 327 a, b. A fine example of moss agate in a flush setting that is purled on the edge with an additional border of beading. The shoulder and top of the reeded shank is also beaded. Yellow gold. Scottish or English, *circa* 1880. Note the similarity to American rings of the same period.

Glossary

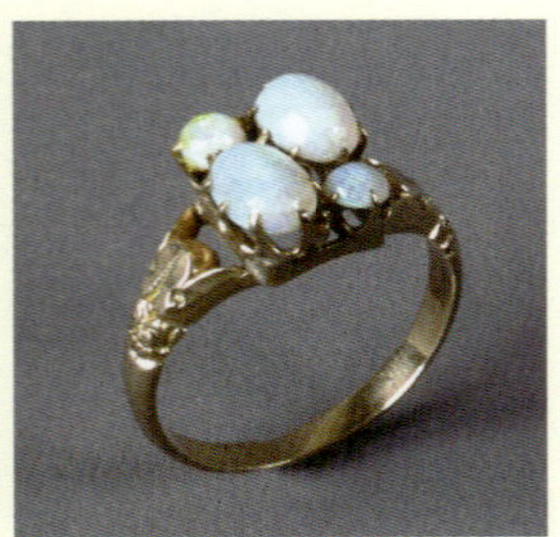

Fig. 328. Rectangular bezel of four opals in claw settings, a stamped design on the shoulders, plain shank. Rose gold. American, *circa* 1900. Bezel 10x8mm, shank diameter 16.5mm.

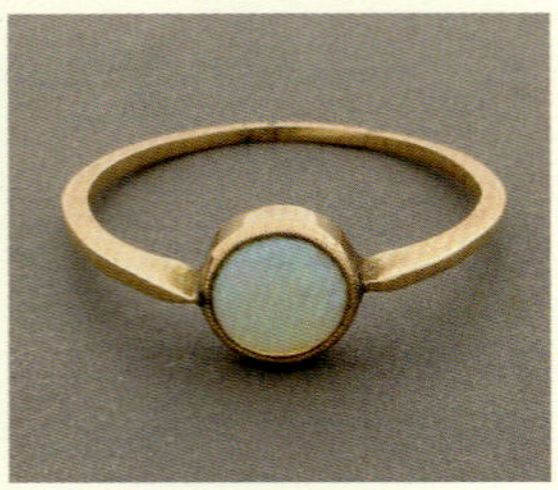

Fig. 329. Australian opal in millegrained open-back collet setting. Knife edged hoop. Rose gold. *Circa* 1905.

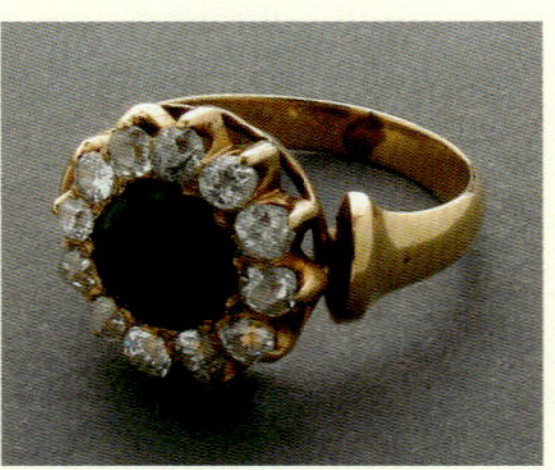

Fig. 330. Black opal bordered with old mine-cut diamonds in a crown claw setting. American, *circa* 1905. *Keith Austin Collection*

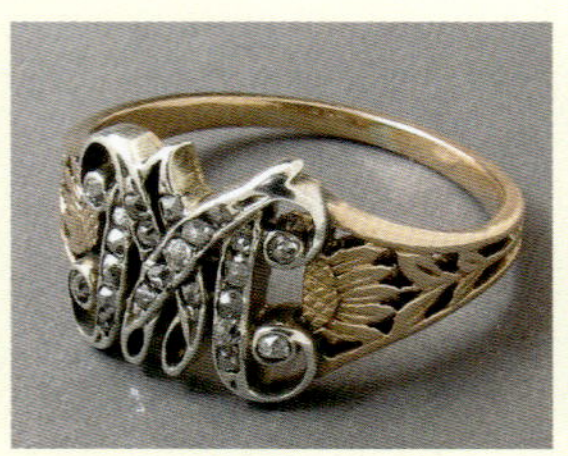

Fig. 331 a, b. Letter M decorated with brilliant-cut diamonds set in silver on gold, openwork shoulders are decorated with an engraved sunflower (meaning 'adoration' in flower language), a row of rectangular beading decorates the shank. Rose gold. *Circa* 1870-1880.

(Fig. 329) The prized Australian black opal was first discovered in 1903. (Fig. 330) The transparent to translucent Mexican fire opal, with or without a play of colour, occurs in shades of yellow to deep red. Water opal is a transparent variety with a subtle play of colour. Opals were usually cut as cabochons for ring stones. Some Mexican opals were faceted.

The opal has had a temperamental career. Superstitions existed in the eighteenth and nineteenth centuries that caused individuals to think that opals brought bad luck to the wearer with the result that opals were not considered suitable for engagement rings during the the nineteenth century. Prince Albert, however, liked opal and influenced the Queen, who in turn was reputed to have encouraged its use. Small opals are to be found in rings dating from 1840 to 1880, set alone or with rubies, diamonds or pearls. Larger stones were used more frequently in rings in the last quarter of the century.

OPENWORK: The term is used whenever parts of a ring were fashioned so that light could pass through the design. (Fig. 331 a, b)

PANSY: This flower formed the bezel of mourning and decorative rings from the 1820s to the 1840s. The most common gems used in the design were dark amethyst, chrysoberyl, pearl and turquoise. In other examples the pansy was engraved or enamelled. The word originates from the French 'pensées' (thoughts). See Fig. 15 and Fig. 46.

PASTE: Glass manufactured to resemble gemstones. (Fig. 332) Paste of excellent quality and colour was made in Birmingham about 1820 but under great difficulties owing to the excise laws relating to the glass trade. By 1876 the paste used in jewellery was made chiefly in France. Paste was frequently set in gold, and the settings are of comparable quality to those of gem rings, see Fig. 22 and 29; a combination of paste and real gems was not uncommon, see Fig. 20. Paste rings of the first three or four decades of the century are easily identified; the colours are very bright. John Mawe, in *A Treatise on Diamonds and Precious Stones*, 1823 edition, commented that 'paste imitating the diamond appeared too white'.

PATTERN BOOKS: A working jeweller would keep a book in which he would record his ring designs to be submitted to customers, sold to a middleman, or (in the second half of the century) sent out on approval to retail jewellers.

PEARLS: They were used extensively throughout the nineteenth century in both decorative and mourning rings. (Fig. 333) Pearls were considered suitable adornment for single and young married women, and pearl half-hoops were often chosen as betrothal rings. Many pearls were imported drilled and strung, so that when whole pearls were used in rings the drill hole was quite noticeable; however, half pearls were preferred for rings. Blister pearls, which come from the pearly deposit cut away from the oyster shell, were used in jewellery in the 1890s. Baroque pearls were much loved by Art Nouveau jewellers for their irregular shape, see Fig. 177. Freshwater pearls can be distinguished from the sea-water variety by their whiteness.

PERIDOT: A yellowish-green gem, in great demand for all forms of jewellery in the 1890s. Peridot is rather soft and few stones have survived in good condition in rings.

PIETRA DURA: See MOSAIC.

PIQUÉ: The inlay of gold and silver into tortoiseshell or ivory. During the early part of the century, this was carried out by hand, often in scroll patterns. During the 1870s piqué work was executed by machine, and geometric designs became common. (Fig. 334)

PINCHBECK: An alloy of five parts copper and one part zinc used as a substitute for gold. Its inventor, Christopher Pinchbeck, was a watchmaker who died in 1732. Genuine pinchbeck is valuable but, today, many nineteenth century items of jewellery made of yellow metal or gilt metal are frequently, but incorrectly, described as pinchbeck.

PLAIT RING: The entire hoop or the bezel was formed as a plait or braid. Sometimes small gold beads were set into the design. Plait rings were worn by men and women from the 1890s onwards, sometimes as a keeper ring. See Fig. 324.

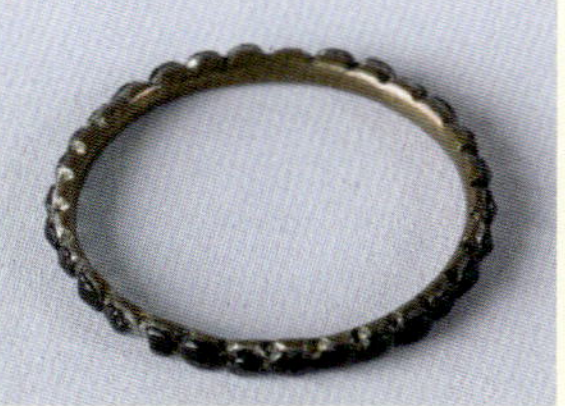

Fig. 332. Vauxhall glass hoop ring of base metal set with faceted purplish-red glass, convex on the inside. *Circa* 1800.

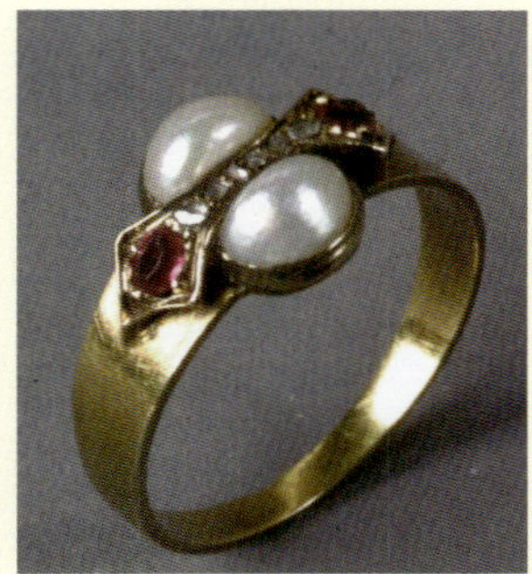

Fig. 333. Two pearls flank an applied section of gold set with two rubies and five rose-cut diamonds on a flat, tapering hoop. Yellow gold. *Circa* 1870.

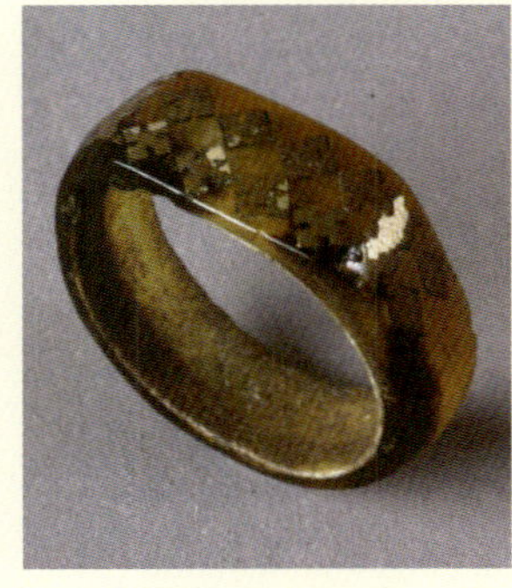

Fig. 334. Ring set with gold plated piqué work in a geometric design. Very crude finish inside ring. *Circa* 1875.

Glossary

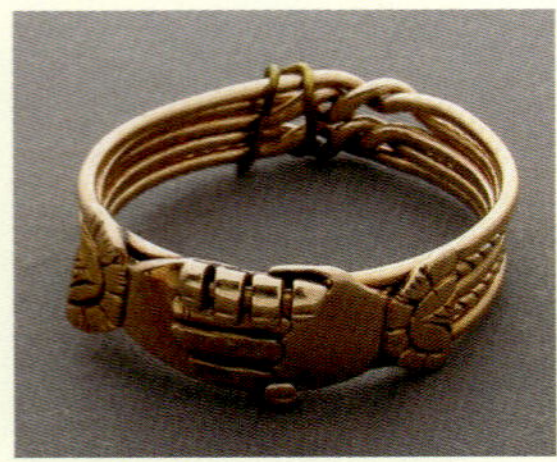

Fig. 335. Fede puzzle ring comprised of five hoops, two purled and three plain gold. *Circa* 1880.
Keith Austin Collection

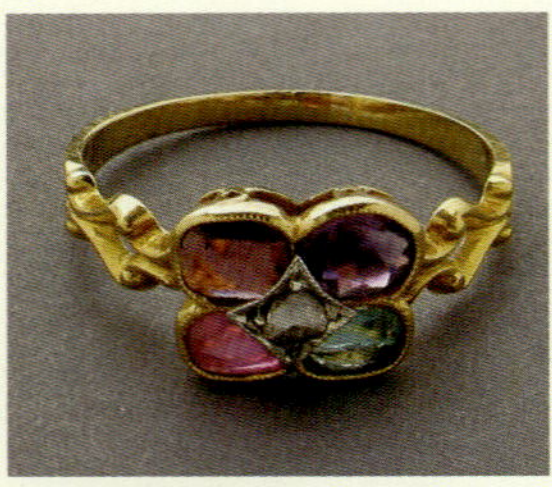

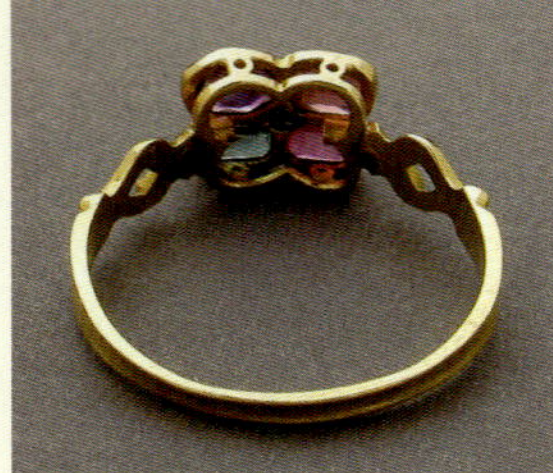

Fig. 336 a, b. Bezel comprises a ruby, emerald, garnet, amethyst in open-back millegrained collets, and a diamond spark set in an applied millegrained silver setting. Using the ruby twice, the gems spell 'regard'. Upper and lower sections of the gallery are held together with six tiny gold rings. Yellow gold. *Circa* 1825. Replacement shank, 1840 period.

PLATINUM: A precious metal not generally used in England until the end of the nineteenth century. According to Henri Vever in *La Bijouterie Française*, Vol. I, p.119, in 1828, platinum mourning rings were advertised for sale in France. Occasionally, platinum was used in three or four colour gold work although white gold was more common. It is an exceptionally strong metal, and because it does not tarnish it was eminently suitable for the fragile gem settings in vogue at the end of the century. See Fig. 202.

PURL: A cord of twisted gold or silver used to decorate the bezel or shoulders of a ring or to form the shank. See Fig. 176.

PUZZLE RING: This type of ring comprises several hoops intertwined at the back of the shank and forming a design in the bezel. Small numbers of puzzle rings were made throughout the century. (Fig. 335)

REEDING: Deep, narrow grooves cut close together leaving fine, raised, reed-like lines.

REGARD RING: The bezel is set with gems such as Ruby, Emerald, Garnet, Amethyst, Ruby, Diamond, the initial letters of which spell R-E-G-A-R-D. Gem-set rings appeared about 1810 and were very popular until 1875. They were generally formed into a cluster or a half-hoop ring. During the 1880s gold or silver rings with REGARD in raised letters on the hoop were fashionable. A number of mourning rings also carried the 'regard' message. See DEAR, REPEAL. (Fig. 336 a, b.)

REGISTRY OF DESIGN MARKS: Once a design had been registered at the British Patent office, a Registry mark was stamped on British manufactured goods between 1842 and 1883. From 1884 onward a serial number was used. These marks are occasionally found on rings. Registry mark and hallmark dates do not necessarily coincide; the registry mark shows the date of the design, which might subsequently be manufactured for many years. See Fig. 144.

RENAISSANCE: Nineteenth-century jewellers revived the style, incorporating enamelling, engraved decoration, scroll work, strapwork and the shape of the ring, in which the ornate shoulders often merge with the bezel. Carlo Giuliano (1831-1895) was an important protagonist of this style, adapting it to suit the taste of his Victorian clients. Neo-Renaissance rings were in fashion during the second half of the century.

REPEAL RINGS: Rings worn as a sign of support for the political agitation for the repeal of the English Corn Laws in Ireland, c.1838 to 1846. An interesting quotation is used by William Jones, F.S.A., in *Finger-Ring Lore*, 1877, p. 414 (first edition):

'So,' as the late Mr. Crofton Croker observed, 'when the Repeal question was agitated in Ireland, rings and brooches, set in precious stones, made to represent the word "Repeal" were popular:

> **R**uby
> **E**merald
> **P**earl
> **E**merald
> **A**methyst
> **L**apis lazuli

One of these was given to a gentleman as a relic of this memorable agitation, but the bit of lapis lazuli had dropped out, and he took it to a working jeweller in Cork to have the defect supplied. When it was returned, he found that a topaz had been substituted for the missing bit of lapis lazuli. "How is this?" he inquired, "you have made a mistake." "No mistake, sir," said the witty workman, whom he afterwards discovered to be an ardent Repealer, "It is all right: it WAS repeaL, but let us repeaT that we may have it yet."'

RIBBING, TRANSVERSE: Rounded or flat sections of gold placed horizontally across the shank, usually on or below the shoulder.

RING BOXES: These were made throughout the period, usually leather covered with a velvet and silk interior. A strapwork design inside the top of the ring box indicates the box was made after 1860. (Fig. 337)

ROCK CRYSTAL: The colourless variety of quartz. Rock crystal was used occasionally throughout the nineteenth century for the hair compartments and sometimes as an imitation of diamond.

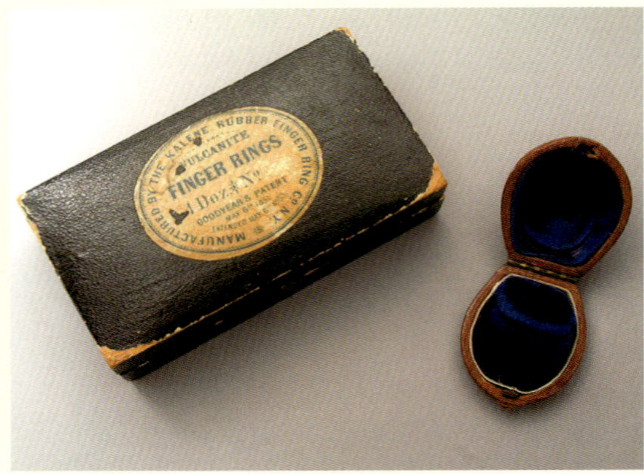

Fig. 337. Ring boxes, American.   *Keith Austin Collection*

ROSE CUT: A gem cut into a faceted dome, the base of which is flat, usually mounted in a closed setting. The cut was used primarily on diamonds during the early years of the century until it was superseded by the brilliant cut. A few large stones were used in the 1870s and 1880s, small stones continued to be used throughout the century. The rose cut was widely used for Bohemian garnets.

RUBY: A member of the corundum family. Rubies were often set in a colourful partnership with diamonds, emeralds, opals, pearls and sapphires. Between 1820 and 1835 it was fashionable to set rubies with turquoises. Later in the century rubies were often set without additional gems, particularly in half-hoop rings.

SAPPHIRE: A member of the corundum family. Sapphires were popular thoughout the century in fine quality rings, including gentlemen's gypsy rings. Towards the end of the century small stones were used in modest, mass-produced rings. Sapphires occur in many colours but cornflower blue is the most prized.

SARD: A chalcedony of yellowish or brownish-red hue. (Fig. 338 a, b.)

SARDONYX: A chalcedony banded with layers of deep red and white, used throughout the century in gentlemen's rings, for cameos, and as small beads that were occasionally set in rings.

SAW-PIERCING: Openwork design executed by piercing metal and cutting it away into the required pattern with a jeweller's saw. The design was smoothed down, and all excess metal removed, after which it was finished as required. Saw-piercing was used on the shoulders of rings between 1840 and 1875 and on the galleries of half-hoop rings made from the 1890s. See Fig. 61.

SCARAB: A conventionalized depiction of a dung beetle. The flat side of the scarab was incised with an inscription or symbol. The dung beetle was the god of the morning sun, and Egyptians regarded it as a symbol of resurrection. Scarabs were used in Egyptian-style rings in the nineteenth century. See Fig. 100.

SEMAINE: French acrostic ring, popular around 1820. The first letter of each day of the week is represented by a stone: Dimanche - Diamond, Lundi - Lapis lazuli, Mardi - Marcasite, Mercredi - Malachite, Jeudi - Jargoon or Jacinth, Vendredi - Verde Antique or Vermail, Samedi - Sardonyx.

SERJEANT-AT-LAW RINGS: Please see the information in Commemorative and Historical rings.

SERPENT (SNAKE) RINGS: The coiled serpent represented eternity. Georgian and early Victorian examples of the serpent ring were more imaginative than the heavier, plainer ones made from about 1875 onward. The early rings were made as mourning or decorative rings. One or more coils may be engraved, filled with hair, studded with gems, enamelled or even flexible (c.1850). From about 1860 to 1870 the hoop was generally round and undulating, the head might be set with a diamond, with small sparks representing the eyes. Later serpent rings were often modelled with as many as four flat coils; the head might have gem-set eyes only, or the whole of it might be ablaze with gems. A few examples were made without gems. Serpents also bordered hair compartments of mourning rings until about 1820 and decorated ring shoulders until about 1850. (Fig. 339)

SETTINGS:

CLAW: The claw setting raised the gem from the finger allowing light to enter the gem from the back. There was a wide variety of claw settings used in nineteenth-century rings starting in about 1860.

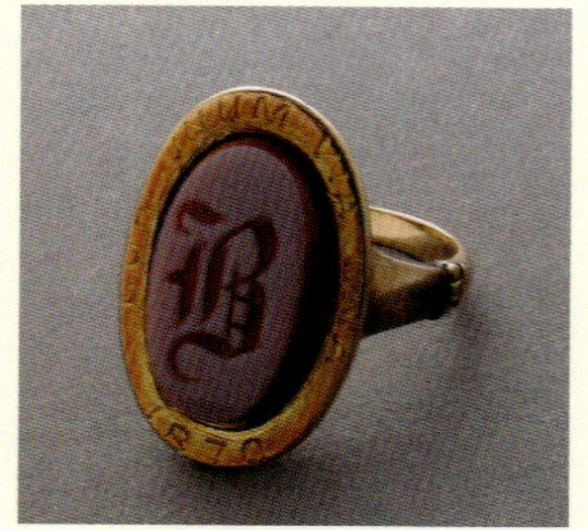

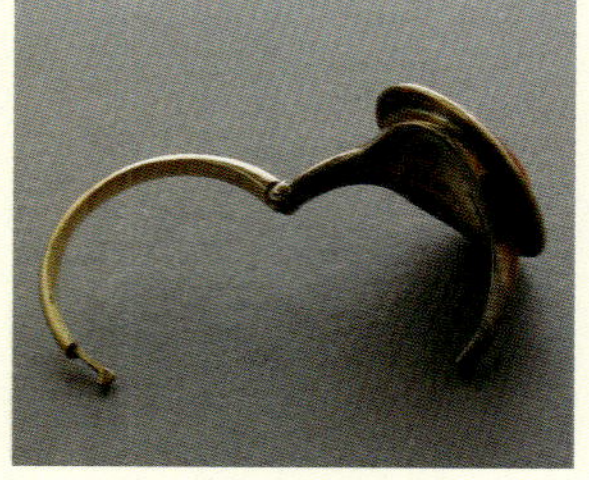

Fig. 338 a, b. Oval sard incised with B in a flush setting, engraved C—UNUM VIA UNA 1870. Plain belcher shoulders, hinged hoop. *Keith Austin Collection*

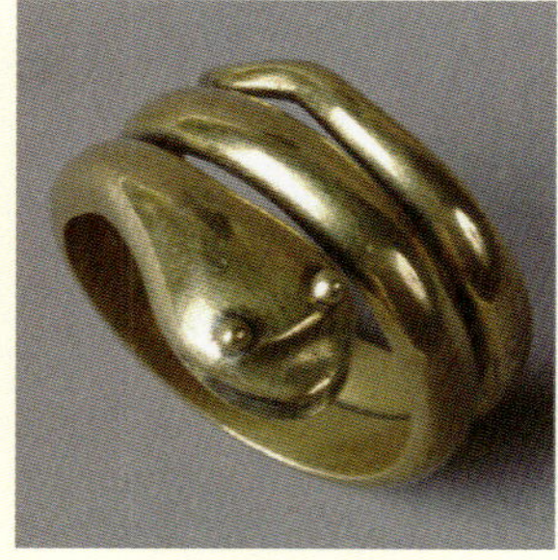

Fig. 339. Multi-coiled serpent, brass. *Circa* 1885-1900. Head of serpent 7mm wide, hoop diameter 18mm.

CLOSED-BACK: A 'cup' of metal forms the setting for the stone. As no light could enter the stone from the back, foil was placed beneath a transparent gem to give it more life and uniformity of colour. Most early rings had closed settings; later in the century closed settings were combined with open-back settings. See Fig. 29.

COLLET: A tube or cup of metal is formed to the depth of the stone, the edge of which is rubbed over the girdle of the stone to keep it secure. The collet setting was most prevalent in the early nineteenth century, when it was normally closed at the back. It was used occasionally later in the century, but open at the back. See Fig. 72.

COLLET, CUT-DOWN: The metal is pressed tightly against the gem to prevent dirt and moisture from penetrating the setting, then it is cut away at an angle from the top, leaving a buttress-like decoration set close together or widely spaced. In some designs the collet is distinctly conical in shape. This setting was popular from about 1800 to 1860, though it was sometimes used later in the century.
See Fig. 199.

COLLET, CRIMPED: The gem is set in a collet with its edges pressed at intervals against the stone, giving a petal-edged effect. It was used sporadically during the century.
See Fig. 86.

CRAMP: The edge of the setting is minutely serrated, with a number of triangular claws extending from the metal edge, which are then rubbed over the girdle of the gem. Cramp settings are either open or closed at the back. This setting was used from about 1820 to 1880, and occasionally during the remainder of the century. See Fig. 57.

FLUSH: The ring is made with a narrow support for the stone so that it rests just below the edge of the setting. The stone fits snugly in its setting, and the metal is flattened over the edge of the stone to secure it. This setting was used mainly for signet and intaglio rings.
See Fig. 169.

GYPSY: The girdle of the gem is flush with the surface of the metal, giving the impression that the stone is pressed in the metal. This method of setting became popular from about 1865. See Fig. 175.

MILLEGRAIN: Similar to the collet setting, but the edge gripping the stone is milled. From a distance the tiny cuts in the edge of the setting resemble beads. Millegrain was used occasionally early in the century, then reappears about 1890. See Fig. 139.

OPEN-BACK: The stone can be seen from the back of the setting. In 1800 few gems were set open or 'transparent'; however, by 1830 many more faceted transparent gems were set in this fashion, and by the 1860s it was the preferred method of setting. See Fig. 62.

PAVÉ: Small stones are arranged so that they touch each other, usually in a boss or marquise design. The stones are secured with raised grains of metal. Pavé settings were especially popular from about 1870 onward. Diamond, pearl and turquoise look particularly effective set in this manner. See Fig. 113.

ROMAN: Similar to the flush setting, with the addition of a groove in the gold around the stone. The Roman setting was used for signet and intaglio rings throughout the century. See Fig. 257.

RUB-OVER OR GLASS: The band of metal surrounding the gem is rubbed over the edge of the stone. It was used to set cabochon stones and cameos. See Fig. 13.

SAW-TOOTH: Similar to the cramp setting, but the triangular claws are set side by side, thereby resembling the teeth of a saw. It was found primarily on rings made between 1820 and 1870. See Fig. 48.

SQUARE: A single stone, set in a square frame, is secured by tiny grains of metal in each corner of the setting. This style of setting appeared in the early 1860s. Other geometric settings are the triangular, diamond-shaped and shield-shaped frame. See Fig. 194.

STAR: The setting is similar to the gypsy; however, grains of metal secure the stone, and the 'rays' carved into the metal appear to emanate from the stone. See Fig. 135.

THREAD: From about 1870 onwards, individual or groups of stones were outlined by a thin, bright, thread of metal. Grains of metal secured the stones. See Fig. 113.

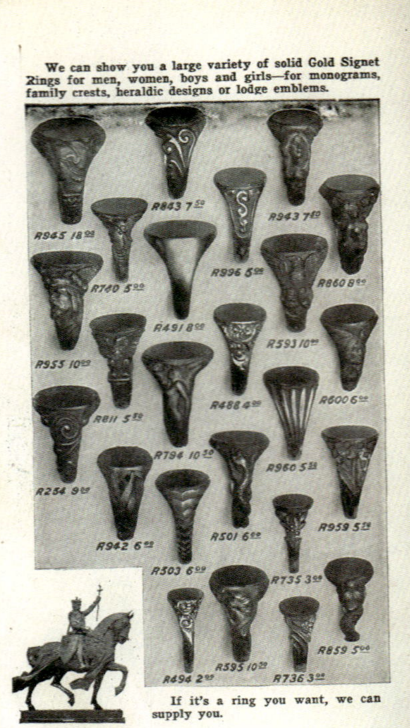

Fig. 340. Plate 2 from Artistic Jewelery. Latest Productions. Crouch Bros., The London Jewellers, 542 South Broadway, Los Angeles, Cal.

SHANK (HOOP): The section of the ring which encircles the back of the finger. Early designs were much more varied and decorative than those made late in the century. At the end of each dated narrative section there is a description of the styles used in that period.

SHOULDERS: The section of the ring between the bezel and the shank. Designs were varied and decorative for the entire period covered by this book. During some periods more emphasis was placed on the shoulder design than in other periods. Each dated narrative section has details of the styles used in that period.

SIGNET RING: In the eighteenth century the signet ring was overshadowed by the fob-seal, but it returned to favour in about 1830 and has remained in use ever since. Signet rings were either made entirely of gold or the bezel was set with bloodstone, red or white cornelian, onyx, nicolo, sard, sardonyx or occasionally, lapis lazuli. The bezel was engraved with a coat-of-arms, crest, monogram or other device, such as the emblem of a particular society. The shoulders were plain belcher, fluted or carved in various designs. (Fig. 340)

SILVER: Diamonds were frequently set in silver to enhance the brilliance of the stone; the setting was then backed with gold to prevent discolouration of the skin. Silver was often used in pavé-set turquoise rings. Inexpensive hoop rings, decorated with various mottos, were fashionable from the early 1880s onward. Silver was used frequently by Art Nouveau and Arts and Crafts jewellers in preference to gold.

SPARK: A tiny pointed gem, resembling a rose-cut stone but with irregular facets, often set in the centre of a cluster ring.

SOUVENIR RINGS: Another acrostic ring, made in France, was fashionable between 1815 and 1840. According to William Jones in *Finger-Ring Lore*, 1877, page 415, the following gems were used in French souvenir rings: Saphir or Sardoine, Onyx or Opale, Uraine, Vermeille, Emeraude, Natralithe, Iris, Rubis or Rose diamante. See Fig. 50.

SPINEL: This gem occurs in many colours, red being the most sought after, and it was used throughout the century. In 1813 contemporary sources record its use in rings surrounded by diamonds. Fine red spinels were often confused with rubies; even John Mawe erroneously describes spinel as a variety of ruby. The value of this gem was entirely dependent upon the caprice of fashion. See Fig. 150.

STAR: This motif was usually found in the centre of a cluster of stones, around a single gem as in the gypsy setting, or set into a cabochon gem from about 1860 1885. Between 1870 and 1890 rings were occasionally decorated with small stars carved into the gallery or the shoulders. See Fig. 87.

STRAPWORK: A decoration used on rings from about 1840 to 1875, sometimes in Renaissance revival work. (Fig. 341)

SWIVEL: A double-sided bezel that revolves on tiny pivots and is decorated on each side. It was used primarily in mourning rings, 1800 to 1835. Occasionally swivel rings were made later in the century. See Fig. 27.

TESSERAE: See MOSAIC.

THREE-PART RING: A single ring with a three-part bezel giving the appearance of three individual rings. It was popular from about 1890 onwards. See Fig. 166.

TIGER'S EYE: A member of the quartz family, tiger's eye is a striped golden brown stone displaying a floating line of reflected light. It was used primarily from about 1890 onwards, usually cut as a cameo. It was very popular in America. See Fig. 118.

TOPAZ: Gold and pink topaz became popular at the beginning of the nineteenth century and were used in filigree and cannetille work. Pink topaz was used until the 1850s but subsequently lost its popularity; gold topaz was popular from 1800 to about 1860 and again from about 1885. Early rings were generally made with foil-lined, closed settings surrounded by pearls or occasionally by white topaz.

TORTOISESHELL: A few rings were fashioned from this material in the first half of the nineteenth century, and again from 1870. See Fig. 1.

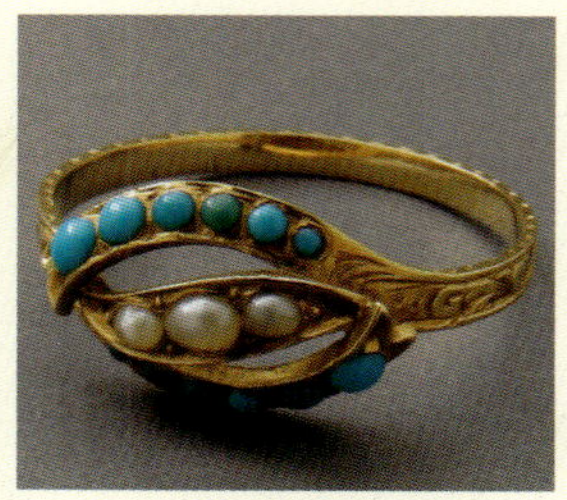

Fig. 341. Asymmetric openwork bezel set with turquoises and half pearls in a strapwork design. Shank engraved on the outer surfaces. Yellow gold. *Circa* 1860. Bezel 8x13mm, shank diameter 17.5mm.

Glossary

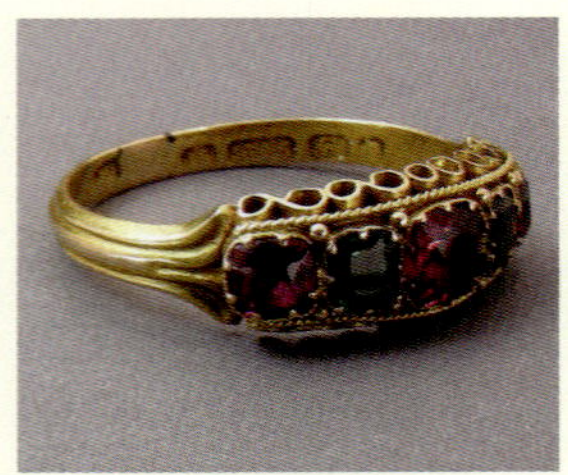

Fig. 342. Half-hoop set with tourmalines in closed-back cramp settings. Figure-of-eight wirework and rope work decorate the gallery. Grooved shank. Hallmarked: Birmingham 15(.625) ct. yellow gold, 1876. Bezel 7x19mm, shank diameter 17.5mm.

TOURMALINE: This gem occurs in a wide range of colours: grey, yellow, blue, brown, olive, dark green, red, pink and black. It was especially popular from about 1880 onward, and was often used in Renaissance-style and Art Nouveau work. (Fig. 342)

TURQUOISE: According to John Mawe in *A Treatise on Diamonds and Precious Stones*, 1813, p. 145, turquoise was very popular but the demand exceeded the supply, resulting in the use of imitation turquoise; the colour was accurate but the lustre was too glassy. Turquoise deposits in Cornwall were poor in colour; the best coloured stones came mostly from Persia. By 1823 more turquoise was available owing to increased imports. In the 1830s and 1840s it was frequently used in fashionable contrast with rubies or garnets, or with chrysoberyl and pearls. Turquoise was worn throughout the century.

TWO-PART RING: A design that became fashionable in the 1890s along with the three-part ring. The bezel is designed to resemble two rings when worn. See Fig. 165.

URN: A motif often used in mourning rings until about 1815. The entire bezel may be urn-shaped, or the design could be incorporated into an enamelled and jewelled bezel. (Fig. 343)

VERD ANTIQUE: A green stone that could be mistaken for jade.

VERMEIL (VERMEILLE): Orange-red stones - garnet, spinel or zircon.

VICTORIA, QUEEN: Born 24 May 1819; ascended the throne 1837; crowned 28 June 1838; married 10 February 1840; widowed 14 December 1861; died 22 January 1901. The Queen had a tremendous influence on her subjects and this extended into the areas of dress, jewellery and mourning. The Queen had a great love of jewellery and her husband, Prince Albert, designed pieces for her. Her long mourning for Prince Albert influenced her people's attitude to death and mourning, and one of her legacies is the large amount of mourning jewellery that was manufactured in the second half of the nineteenth century.

VINAIGRETTE RING: Two styles of vinaigrette ring were made: in one, a chain was attached by a small hoop at the back of a finger ring from which the vinaigrette hung so that it could be carried easily in the hand; alternatively, the vinaigrette formed the bezel of ring. See Fig. 56.

VULCANITE: A rubber product that was used as a substitute for jet. Unfortunately this substance turned brown with prolonged exposure to light. Found in the second half of the nineteenth century.

WEDDING RINGS: For full details, see the narrative section.

WIREWORK: Used in the first half of the nineteenth century for shoulders and shanks and in cannetille and filigree rings, on the gallery of the very ornate rings produced in Birmingham between 1860 and 1885, and on Italian imports.

ZIRCON: This gem occurs in a variety of colours: red, orange, brown and colourless. These varieties were commonly known as jacinth or hyacinth in the nineteenth century. The white variety was used as a substitute for diamonds and was called jargoon. Contemporary literature referred to the smoky quality of the jargoon. The blue zircon was not used until the twentieth century; its colour was created by heating brown zircon. Zircons were not in great demand as ring stones until the last quarter of the century, and they are not entirely suitable because their softness makes them prone to damage.

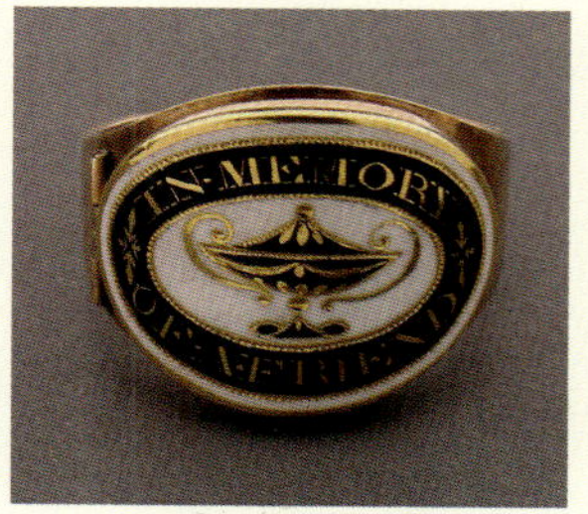

Fig. 343. Mourning ring. The bezel is decorated with a gold urn on a white enamel ground surrounded by a black enamel border, with 'IN MEMORY OF A FRIEND' set off in gold Roman capitals. For other views of this ring see figure 248.

SELECT BIBLIOGRAPHY

Armstrong, Nancy, *Jewellery - An historical survey of British styles and jewels* (Guildford & London, Lutterworth Press, 1973).

Armstrong, Nancy, *Victorian Jewelery* (London, Studio Vista, 1976).

Baker, Lillian, *Art Nouveau & Art Deco Jewelry*, (Paducah, Kentucky, Collector Books, 1981).

Becken, A.C., *13th Annual Illustrated Catalogue and Price List of A.C. Becken, The Chicago Wholesale Jeweler* (Powers Building, 156 Wabash Avenue - Chicago, Illinois, 1904).

Becker, Vivienne, *Antique and 20th Century Jewellery* (London, N.A.G. Press, Ltd., 1980)

Becker, Vivienne, *Art Nouveau Jewelry* (London, Thames and Hudson Ltd., 1985).

Bell, Jeanenne, *Answers to Questions about Old Jewelery "1840 to 1950"*, (Krause Publications, Iola, WI, USA, 1999).

Bell, C. Jeanenne, *Collector's Encyclopedia of Hairwork Jewelery*, (Collector Books, Paducah, Ky., 1998).

J.W. Benson Ltd. (London, c.1901). *Catalogue*.

Boardman, John and Scarisbrick, Diana, *The Ralph Harari Collection of Finger rings* (London, Thames and Hudson, Ltd., 1977).

Boutell, The Rev. Charles, M.A., *'Goldworking', British Manufacturing Industries*, p.51, (London 1876).

Bradford, Ernle, *English Victorian Jewellery* (Spring Books, London 1959, Feltham, Middlesex 1967).

Bruton, Eric, F.G.A., *Diamonds* (London, N.A.G. Press Ltd., 1978, 2nd Ed.).

Burgess, Fred W., *Antique Jewellery and Trinkets* (G.P. Putnam, London, 1919).

Bury, Shirley, *Jewellery Gallery Summary Catalogue*, Victoria and Albert Museum (London, Victoria and Albert Museum, 1982).

Bury, Shirley, *An Introduction to Rings*, (London: Her Majesty's Stationery Office, 1984).

Chadour, Anna Beatriz & Joppien, Rüdiger, *Fingerringe*, (Köln 1985: Kunstgewerbemuseum Der Stadt Köln).

Christie's, *Rings from Antiquity to the Present Day*, (London, Oct. 1988, 1989, Catalogue).

Clifford, Anne, *Cut-Steel & Berlin Iron Jewellery* (Adams and Dart, Bath, 1971).

Cooper, Diana and Battershill, Norman, *Victorian Sentimental Jewellery*, (Newton Abbot, David & Charles, Publishers, Limited, 1972).

Cornish's Stranger's guide through Birmingham (Cornish, London, 1853).

Curran, Mona, *Collecting Jewellery* (ARCO Publications, London 1963).

Davenport, Cyril J.H., *Jewellery* (Methuen & Co. Ltd., London, 1905).

Edwards, Charles, *The History & Poetry of Finger-Rings*, (Redfield, 110 and 112 Nassau Street, New-York, 1855).

Evans, Joan, *English Jewellery* (Methuen & Co. Ltd., London 1921).

Evans, Joan, *A History of Jewellery 1100-1870* (Boston, MA., Boston Book and Art, 1970, 2nd Ed.).

Fairholt, F.W., F.S.A., *Rambles of an Archeologist among old Books and in old Places* (London, 1871).

Fales, Martha Gandy, *Jewelry in America 1600-1900*, (Antique Collectors' Club Ltd, Woodbridge, Suffolk, 1995).

Falkiner, Richard, *Investing in Antique Jewellery* (Cresset Press, London, 1968).

Flower, Margaret, *Victorian Jewellery* (London, Cassell & Company Ltd., July 1973 2nd Ed.).

Gee, George E., *The Hall-Marking of Jewellery* (Crosby Lockwood, London, 1882).

Gee, George E., *The Jewellers' Assistant in the Art of Working in Gold* (Crosby Lockwood & Son, London, 1892).

Gee, George E., *The Practical Gold-Worker [or the Goldsmith's and Jeweller's Instruction]* (Crosby Lockwood & Co., London, 1877).

Gere, Charlotte, *European and American Jewellery 1830-1914* (Heineman, London, 1975).

Gere, Charlotte, *Victorian Jewelery Design* (Chicago, Henry Regnery Company, 1973).

The Goldsmith & Editor, (Magazine, Nos. 1-27, London, 1869).

Gregorietti, Guido, *Jewellery Through the Ages* (Hamlyn, London, 1970).

Hinks, Peter, *Jewellery* (London, Hamlyn, 1973 reprinted).

Hinks, Peter, *Nineteenth Century Jewellery* (London, Faber and Faber, 1975).

Jarvis, Charles A., F.C.A., *Jewellery Manufacture and Repair* (London, N.A.G. Press Limited, 1978).

The Jewellers' Chronicle and Horological Gazette, Vol.5, March 1, 1892 - Sept 1, 1893, (London, 1892-93).

The Jewellers' and Watchmakers' Trade Advertizer, (Birmingham, 1892-93).

Jones, William, *Finger Ring Lore*, (London, Chatto and Windus, Piccadilly, 1877).

Kunz, George Frederick, *Rings for the Finger* (New York, Dover Publications, Inc., [1973]).

La Belle Assemblée [or Bell's Court and Fashionable Magazine addressed particularly to the Ladies] (John Bell, London, 1806 - 1828).

Luthi, Ann Louise, *Sentimental Jewellery*, (Shire Publications Ltd, Princes Risborough, Bucks, 2001).

Marquardt, Brigitte, *Schmuck - Klassizismus und Biedermeier 1780 - 1850* (Munchen, Kunst & Antiquitäten, 1983).

Mason, Anita, *An Illustrated Dictionary of Jewellery* (Reading, Berkshire, Osprey Publishing Ltd., 1973).

Mason, Shena, *Jewellery Making in Birmingham 1750-1995*, (Phillimore & Co. Ltd., Chichester, West Sussex, 1998).

Mawe, J., *Treatise on Diamonds and Precious Stones* (London, 1813, 1st Ed., London, 1823, 2nd Ed., printed and sold by the author).

McCarthy, James Remington, *Rings Through The Ages* (New York, Harper & Brothers, 1945).

Muller, Helen, *Jet Jewellery and Ornaments*, (Shire Publications Ltd, Princes Risborough, Bucks., 2003).

Munn, Geoffrey, *'The Giuliano Family'*, The Connoisseur (Nov. 1975).

Murray, J., *A Memoir on the Diamond* (London, 1831).

Newman, Harold, *An Illustrated Dictionary of Jewelery*, (London, Thames and Hudson Ltd., 1987, 1st. paperback edition).

Oman, Charles, *British Rings 800 - 1914* (London, B.T. Batsford Ltd., 1974).

Percival, Maciver, *Chats on Old Jewellery and Trinkets* (T. Fisher Unwin, London, 1912).

Peter, Mary E.B., *Collecting Victorian Jewellery* (MacGibbons & Kee, London, 1970).

Poynder, Michael, *The Price Guide to Jewellery 3000 B.C. - 1950 A.D.* (Woodbridge, Suffolk, Bacon Publishing [The Antique Collectors' Club], 2000).

Reade, Brian, *Regency Antiques* (London, B.T. Batsford Ltd., 1953).

Roche, J.C., *The History, Development and Organisation of the Birmingham Jewellery and Allied Trades, published as a Supplement to the Dial* (Birmingham, 1927).

Schroeder, Joseph J. Jr., Ed., *Montgomery Ward & Co. 1894-95 #56* (Northfield, Ill., DBI Books Inc., [1977]).

Schroeder, Joseph J. Jr., Ed., *Sears, Roebuck and Co. [Fall 1900] #110* (Northfield, Illinois, DBI Books Inc. [1970]).

Smith, Harold Clifford, *Jewellery* (Methuen & Co. Ltd., London 1908).

Stopford, Francis, *The Romance of the Jewel* (printed for private circulation by Mappin and Webb, London, 1920).

Streeter, Edwin W., *Precious Stones and Gems [their History and distinguishing characteristics]* (Chapman and Hall, London, 1877).

Taylor, Gerald and Scarisbrick, Diana, *Finger Rings from Ancient Egypt to the Present Day* (London, Lund Humphries, 1978).

Vever, Henri, *La Bijouterie Francaise au XIXe Siecle* (H. Floury, Paris, 1906).

Wallis, George, *'Jewellery'*, British Manufacturing Industries (London, 1876).

Ward, A., Cherry, J., Gere, C., Cartlidge, B., *Rings Through the Ages* (New York, Rizzoli, International Publications, Inc., 1981).

Webster, Robert, F.G.A., *Gems - Their Sources Descriptions and Identification* (London, Butterworths, 1975, 3rd. Ed.).

Webster, Robert, F.G.A., *Gemmologists' Compendium* (London, N.A.G. Press Limited, 1947).

Wigley, Thomas B., *The Art of the Goldsmith and Jeweller* (Charles Griffin and Company Limited, London, 1898).

Wilkinson, Wynard R.T., *A History of Hallmarks* (London, Queen Anne Press, 1975).

Wilson, Henry, *Silverwork and Jewllery* (London, Pitman,[1978]).

Wolstenholme, Suzanne, *'Sentimental Jewelery'*, The Franklin Mint Almanac July/Aug 1985, Vol 16, No. 4 (Franklin Center, PA, The Franklin Mint, 1985).

Woodhouse, Charles Platten, F.R.S.A., *The Victoriana Collector's Handbook* (Geo. Bell & Sons, London, 1970).

Wright, J.S., *'The Jewellery and Gilt Toy Trades'*, The Resources, Products and Industrial History of Birmingham and the Midland Hardware District : A Series of Reports, collected by the local Industries Committee of the British Association at Birmingham in 1865 (Robert Hardwicke, 192 Piccadilly, London, 1866).

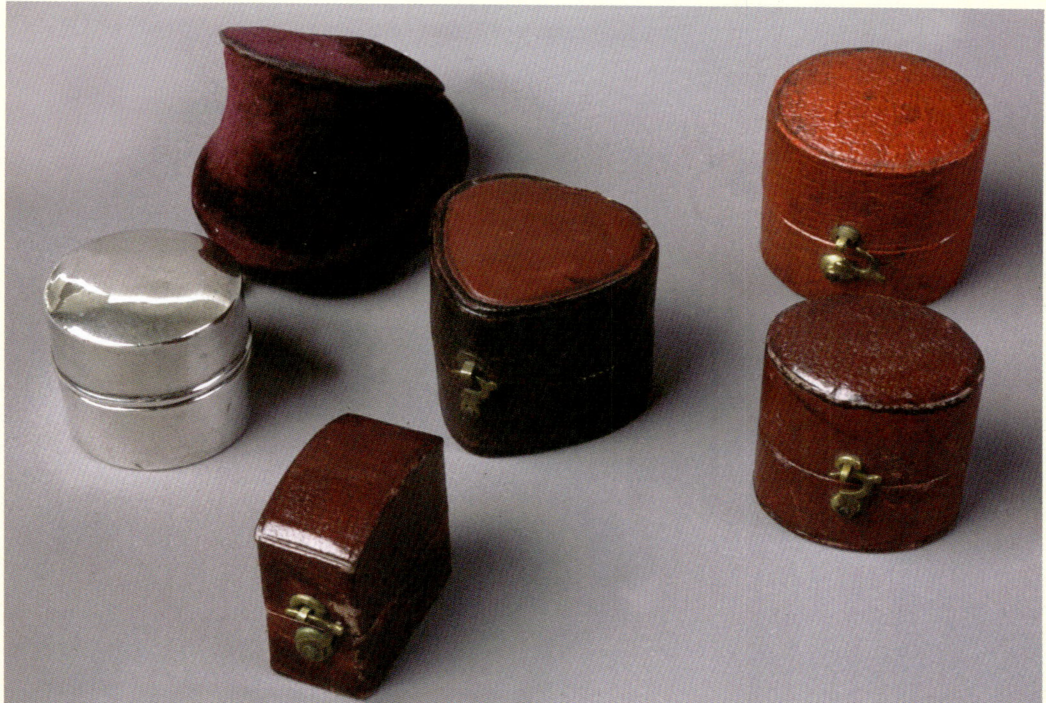

English ring boxes.

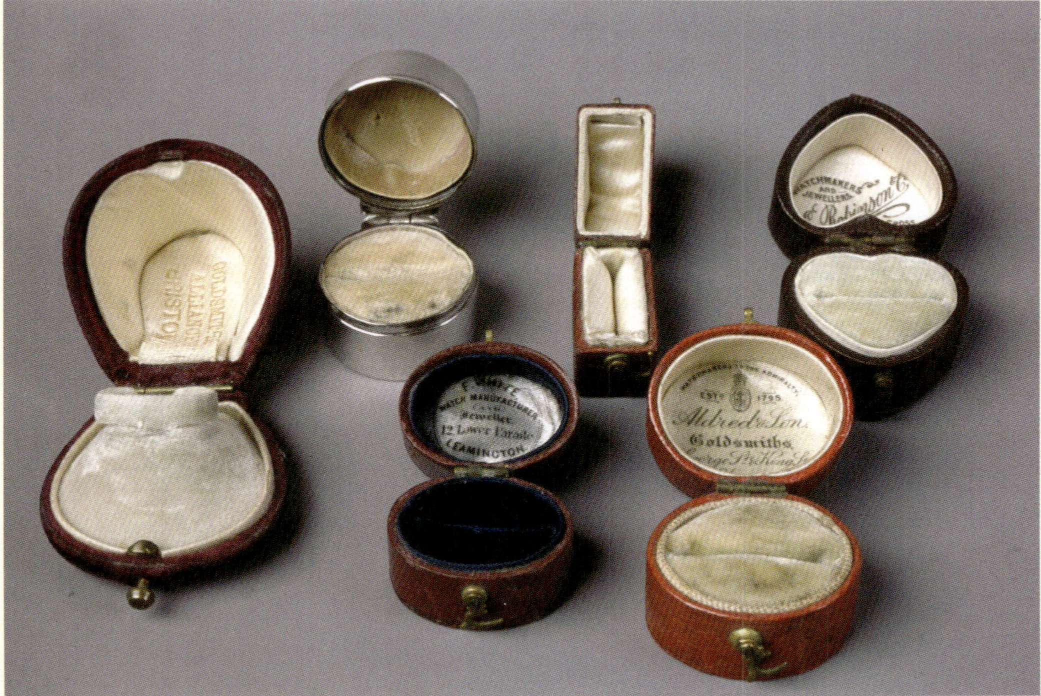

The English ring boxes opened.